THE CRIME FILMS OF ANTHONY MANN

Anthony Mann, 1964 (Photofest).

THE CRIME FILMS OF ANTHONY MANN

MAX ALVAREZ

UNIVERSITY PRESS OF MISSISSIPPI / JACKSON

In memory of Peter Bogdanovich

www.upress.state.ms.us

Designed by Peter D. Halverson

The University Press of Mississippi is a member of the Association of American University Presses.

Copyright © 2014 by University Press of Mississippi
All rights reserved

First printing 2014

∞

Library of Congress Cataloging-in-Publication Data

Alvarez, Max Joseph, 1960–
The crime films of Anthony Mann / Max Alvarez.
pages cm
Includes bibliographical references and index.
ISBN 978-1-61703-924-9 (hardback) — ISBN 978-1-61703-925-6 (ebook) 1. Mann, Anthony, 1906–1967—Criticism and interpretation. 2. Crime films—United States—History and criticism. I. Title.
PN1998.3.M36A58 2013
791.4302'33092—dc23   2013023369

British Library Cataloging-in-Publication Data available

CONTENTS

Introduction 3

1. From Lomaland to Broadway 9
2. From Broadway to Hollywood 19
3. *Dr. Broadway* (1942) 35
4. *Strangers in the Night* (1944) 45
5. *Two O'Clock Courage* (1945) 51
6. *The Great Flamarion* (1945) 60
7. *Strange Impersonation* (1946) 70
8. *Desperate* (1947) 76
9. *Railroaded!* (1947) 89
10. *T-Men* (1947) 101
11. *Raw Deal* (1948) 117
12. *He Walked By Night* (1948) 135
13. *Follow Me Quietly* (1949) 155
14. *Border Incident* (1949) 170
15. *Side Street* (1950) 191
16. *The Tall Target* (1951) 210
17. The Lost *Noir* of Anthony Mann 226

Postscript 241
Acknowledgments 248
Anthony Mann Crime Filmography 251
Notes 263
Archival Sources 302
Bibliography 304
Index 308

THE CRIME FILMS OF ANTHONY MANN

INTRODUCTION

In the world of cinema history studies, Anthony Mann is an enigma: a celebrated twentieth century Hollywood filmmaker whose life and career is shrouded in haziness and mystery. Compounding this is the fact that what little has been written about Mann in his native country is erroneous and apocryphal. While never reluctant to talk about his work when journalists interviewed him on infrequent occasions, Mann did not leave behind a detailed account of his private and professional existence. Some have used his erratically documented background as an excuse not to investigate further or, even worse, to consult well-worn and dubious sources, thus guaranteeing the preservation of myths and distortions.

Although this book was initially conceived to focus exclusively on one genre in the diverse Mann filmography (the crime thrillers), it became apparent that the existing record of his early life was going to have to be corrected in order to adequately comprehend the films under examination. Few are aware that Mann came late to filmmaking and had careers as stage actor, theatrical director, and even television producer/director before Hollywood engaged him to stage stories with 35 mm Mitchell cameras. Upon inspection of these heretofore unknown aspects of his career, we find that his theatrical, television, and film work are not mutually exclusive. We see links between dark crime melodramas of the 1940s and his earlier Broadway and television plays. Our understanding of Anthony Mann's working methods and philosophies becomes clearer the further we delve into his pre-Hollywood existence.

Mann's international reputation is based on the pensive and intense westerns he made from 1949 to 1960, the most acclaimed of which starred James Stewart (*Winchester '73*, *The Man from Laramie*). Most are expensive Technicolor productions serving as forerunners of the director's widescreen 70 mm spectaculars (*El Cid*, *The Fall of the Roman Empire*), which he made after his break with Stewart in the late 1950s. Less known and studied are Mann's black-and-white crime thrillers made from 1942 to 1951, and the director would have liked it to remain that way.

"You make these things and hope nobody will ever remember them," Anthony Mann remarked in 1953, "and then they come back to haunt you on television. One of my two daughters is always rushing to me with a 'Hey, Daddy—one of your pictures!' And sure enough it is—*Railroaded, The Great Flamarion, Strangers in the Night* or what-not else."[1] Mann is referring to three of the films studied in this book, each made before he felt he hit his stride as a commercial Hollywood director.

In 1957, when interviewers Charles Bitsch and Claude Chabrol mentioned to him that the crime thriller *T-Men* (1947) was the first of his pictures to get released in France, Mann responded with relief that they had not seen the films preceding it. Not long before his death, the director lamented, "My first films were shot under conditions that I'd rather not talk about ... After all! What do you want, with a budget of 50 or 60,000 dollars, actors who can't be made to say lines, and non-existent sets?"[2]

"Tony did not think much of his earlier films," admitted Jean-Claude Missiaen, author of the first book ever written on Mann. "He thought his career took off with *Desperate*. Before that film, he did not have anything to do with the writing, choice of actors."[3]

"I think it's just lucky that they got made," said Mann in his last published interview. "They cost nothing so there were no losses. They were made as second features, but in terms of skill and ability I don't think they have much. In terms of experience, I learned a lot. People can't learn the easy way."[4]

Given these testimonies, we can safely assume that Anthony Mann would not have approved of this book. Many of the films studied here are pictures he would have likely preferred us to forget, bread-and-butter assignments for a young, charismatic freelance director new to a Hollywood unprepared to trust him with lavish budgets and top marquee stars. The discomfort Mann felt for his 1940s pictures is easier to comprehend when considering the low opinion polite society held of crime melodramas, which studios viewed as nothing more than inexpensive box office attractions—pseudo-exploitation products capitalizing on violence, lurid criminality, and sexual tension. Back in the day, movie critics dismissed the crime genre as banal, tasteless, and unoriginal—and featuring actors on their way up or down. The same opinion went for their directors. There was nothing remotely cool or hip about being assigned to direct a sixty-eight-minute black-and-white cops-and-crooks saga or what later came to be characterized as a *film noir*. For every *Double Indemnity* and *The Big Sleep*, there were dozens of smaller crime productions destined not for Radio City or Grauman's Chinese, but for the bottom half of a Forty-Second Street double feature. There were no elegant academic terms to describe such pictures in the United States of the 1940s. *Variety* labeled a film of this type a "murder meller" (Robert Wise's

Born to Kill), a "gangster meller" (Mann's *Desperate*, *Railroaded!*, and *Raw Deal*), or an "action meller" (Mann's *Border Incident*).[5] These projects held no prestige for their participants, many of who forgot making them as soon as production ended.

Those who hastily apply the term *film noir* to the Mann crime pictures, with their high contrast cinematography balancing hard lighting and deep shadows, risk arousing academic ire. Arguments persist over how precisely to define classic Hollywood *noir* and where to erect narrative boundaries. For the picture to qualify as *noir*, it is often held that central characters must be criminals or transgressors. Applying this rule, Mann's *Raw Deal*, *Side Street*, and *Desperate* fit comfortably into the *noir* category. *Strange Impersonation* is psychological *noir*. On the other hand, if the central characters are policemen or undercover agents, as in *He Walked By Night* and *Follow Me Quietly*, the *film policier* classification is more appropriate. *T-Men*, *Railroaded!*, and *Border Incident* each contain elements of *policier* and *noir*. Crimes and murders are committed in the rest of the films studied in this book, but their genre categories run the gamut from comedy/thriller/mystery (*Dr. Broadway* and *Two O'Clock Courage*) and gothic melodrama (*Strangers in the Night*) to psychological melodrama (*The Great Flamarion*) and period thriller with *noir* overtones (*The Tall Target*).

Anthony Mann was not entirely ashamed of his early output. Aside from *Desperate*, he did go on record expressing a fondness for *T-Men*. Had he lived to see how highly regarded his underrated earlier work would become, perhaps Mann might have reassessed its value. Or he might have just shrugged off the acclaim and scolded us for finding too much artistic meaning in what were routine assignments. No matter, no one who has experienced an Anthony Mann picture, regardless of how early or cheaply it was made, can ever forget it. Clearly I do not share Mann's disdain for most of his monochromatic crime melodramas; rather, I believe they are no less worthy of serious study than *The Naked Spur* or *Men in War*.[6]

Often faced with substandard projects for which he had little or no control, Mann was neither passive nor confrontational with studio front offices or supervising producers during these early Hollywood years. He moved from one assignment to the next and treated each with a gravity that made one believe he was as passionate about the material as his corporate overseers. Even the weakest Mann enterprises (easily outnumbered by his triumphs) contain brilliant passages reminding us of the commanding talent behind the camera. Equally apparent is the directorial signature of restrained anguish that has come to symbolize an Anthony Mann picture along with an economical use of the camera in emphasizing emotions.

Mann was not the larger-than-life figure we associate with a Huston, Welles, Preminger, or Lang. An engaging interview subject, he was not as media savvy as Alfred Hitchcock and Billy Wilder in terms of shaping his image before the press and public. Described in a 1939 newspaper interview as "a shy, nervous looking chap," in a 1950 account as "a good-looking, good-natured chap," in a separate 1950 interview as "an intense, volatile man with a keen profile and a high forehead," and in a 1956 studio press release as "[a] sharply intense man," Mann had to have been a tough customer during the production stages of his filmmaking.[7] No director of Hollywood westerns, war films, costume epics, or violent crime melodramas can be otherwise. This was, after all, a man who had to deal with tyrannical Columbia Pictures boss Harry Cohn on two of his 1950s westerns. Yet Mann was not a cantankerous fighter who ruled by fear and intimidation, nor did he bear grudges, factors which lead to his eventual ruination in the hands of massive productions and massive egos.

Uncovering precisely who is responsible for a studio success can only be determined by returning to primary sources, which I have made it my mission to do whenever possible. By now, it is a cliché to say that film is a collaborative medium, and when considering the assembly line mentality of U.S. movie production of the 1930s and 1940s, it is dangerous to assign credit or blame exclusively to the director. In many cases, Mann was brought in after a film had been written and cast, and he most likely departed for subsequent projects before editing began. This was how the system operated, as renowned English film director Michael Powell tersely reminds readers in his memoirs:

> There has been so much yapping over the years about the film director, the film *auteur* . . . that it is very difficult for the general public, and even for the informed public, to realize that making a film is an industrial process and it is perfectly possible to edit, alter, present and have a resounding success without the director having anything more to do with the film from the moment he stops shouting at the actors.[8]

To illustrate this theory, we should recall that Mann directed five major features for three leading Hollywood studios between early 1949 and early 1950. After shooting *Border Incident* at M-G-M in January and February of 1949, the studio assigned him to the "documentary" thriller *Side Street*, which began filming in late April. When that picture finished filming two months later, Mann was immediately put to work on his first theatrical western *Devil's Doorway* (also M-G-M), which entered production on August

17. Once the Robert Taylor western finished sixty-four days later, Mann headed to Paramount and producer Hal Wallis for a November 8 start date on *The Furies*. No sooner had this Barbara Stanwyck picture finished in December than Mann relocated to Universal-International to begin work on *Winchester '73*, whose cameras began turning on Valentine's Day 1950.[9] It would have been physically impossible for Mann to supervise editing on all these productions (although he does appear to have been present for at least a portion of the process on some of them). In late 1950, he admitted to a newspaper reporter that while he felt editing was the core of a motion picture, the director working in the current Hollywood studio climate had to battle to remain involved in the process.[10] Whatever Mann's involvement was in preproduction and postproduction on the pictures covered here, it is clear from the results that he took each assignment seriously and maximized his time on the set. His work stands out from other 1940s and 1950s directors whose eagerness to race through low-budget projects led them to lose sight of cinematic potentiality.

Anthony Mann was not without some critical supporters in the United States, but glowing reviews were a rarity for most of the films discussed here. Influential *New York Times* critic Bosley Crowther, who had already expended considerable ink in savaging the RKO chillers of producer Val Lewton, was not a fan of the 1940s Mann thrillers. Reviewing the 1950 masterpiece *Side Street*, Crowther's brief review concluded: "It can only be fully recommended to those who have a deep and morbid interest in crime." Even French leftist critic Georges Sadoul, who should have known better, dismissed Mann's entire 1940s output as "mediocre B-pictures."[11]

It is my objective to put to rest such dismissive assessments of this mercurial Hollywood director's early body of work. The Mann crime pictures are not exceptions in our comprehension of a fully realized Anthony Mann production: like the later films, they are inhabited by psychologically complex, volatile, emotionally scarred protagonists prone to erratic and violent behavior. With only a handful of exceptions, his pictures do not rely on simplicity and sentiment except in situations beyond his control. The violence depicted (as is standard in any Mann movie) is never glamorized or romanticized, even when brutally portrayed. "I'm the most unsadistic guy in the world, personally," Mann said in the aforementioned 1953 interview, "but I've done so many westerns and gangsters I don't know how to kill a man any more."[12]

Killing men on screen was never the motivating factor behind the filmmaker and his art. Even in these early crime melodramas, where the director seems to be biding his time, there are clear indications of a desire to examine deeper psychological and philosophical aspects of humanity. As Missiaen states,

> Tony knew a lot about the camera (lenses, deep or short focus) but he was also aware of the human condition. That's why he was a *superlative director of actors*. They often gave him the most of what they had to offer. Tony was careful not to tire them: *two simple shots* of Richard Basehart [in *He Walked By Night*], wounded, when the bullet goes out . . . *one striking shot* of Dennis O'Keefe's face when he is about to watch Alfred Ryder's death in *T-Men*.[13]

Simplicity is often the key to unlocking the secrets to Mann's power as a filmmaker. More a disciple of the John Ford directorial technique than the Alfred Hitchcock method, Mann was protective of his camera. When he used close-ups they were to exemplify highly emotional moments in a story (examples of which appear throughout this book). In general, he favored the medium shot where the camera was placed below eye level in order to achieve what journalist Ezra Goodman described as "intimacy and identification with the focal character in a scene."[14] A 1950 newspaper interview quoted Mann on the topic of camera movement:

> Some directors like to move a camera all over the place. That way they can create a certain suspense with an unknown thing that is moving around; but more often the spectator is conscious of a feeling of false movement that has no relation to the scene, a feeling of technicians "pushing" . . .
> I never use moving shots—except to dolly along with a player or players who are engaged in some critical action. I can get much more value by bringing my players downstage and close up—and by dramatic cutting.
> Also, I can save money. It is much less expensive to light one area than the many areas covered by a moving camera.[15]

Anthony Mann saved a lot of money for his producers in the many crime thrillers under study here, but, as Missiaen indicates, even the director's economizing did not stop his concerns for the human condition from emerging. What Mann wrote in 1964 could easily apply to certain aspects of his 1942–51 crime melodramas:

> I believe in the nobility of the human spirit. It is that for which I look in a subject I am to direct. I do not believe that everybody is bad, that the whole world is wrong. The greatness of Shakespeare's plays is the nobility of the human spirit, even though he may destroy the character.[16]

CHAPTER 1

FROM LOMALAND TO BROADWAY

Anton Bundsmann was a show business professional long before "Anthony Mann" ever existed. Bundsmann was Mann's stage name prior to 1941 and the name he continued to live by after unofficially changing it. He was not a teenage immigrant eager to Americanize himself but a thirty-five-year-old San Diego native with impressive entertainment credentials. At the time Paramount Pictures hired him in 1941, Bundsmann had acted on Broadway and directed stage plays with film stars of the past, present, and future. He had served as talent scout and screen test director for Hollywood producer David O. Selznick and directed live television plays for the National Broadcasting Company.

Nevertheless, there have been isolated efforts to distort or ridicule his pre-Hollywood background. Screenwriter Philip Yordan, who contributed to seven Mann pictures, including *God's Little Acre*, *Men in War*, and *El Cid*, provided a muddled account of the director:

> I knew Tony in New York when he was with Selznick, one of a dozen directors testing girls for *Gone With the Wind*. Tony never graduated from grade school. He was an orphan. He and I were about the same age, but ah [he was] very poorly bred. He loved the theater. He used to sleep in the theater at night. He was an assistant stage manager and maybe he directed one or two plays, I really don't know.
>
> Then when he came to Hollywood, he called me. I avoided him because I figured, jeez, this is a no-talent guy. You couldn't even have a conversation with him, he was so ignorant.[1]

While it is true that Mann later did test actresses for Selznick's Civil War epic, there is little truth in Yordan's summations of Mann's early life, education, stage experience, and intellectual capacity.

In an April 1992 interview for the home video release of *Spartacus*, British actor Peter Ustinov briefly reminisced about Mann, the director originally assigned to the Universal-International spectacle:

He was an astonishing character because he belonged to some kind of vague religious sect, his parents did, in the Californian hills in which he never wore clothes at all, I think, until he was about twenty-one. And when something disastrous happened to the sect—they went bankrupt and they all had to go to work!—Tony Mann was plummeted from a nudist existence and sun worship straight into the garment district in New York as an apprentice. If he survived that, I think he was tough enough to survive most things.[2]

As a great raconteur and wit, Ustinov had an active imagination and his recollections likewise have no basis in fact. The "vague religious sect" to which Ustinov referred was no nudist colony, but Lomaland, a Theosophical commune founded in 1900 in Point Loma, near San Diego in Southern California, and the childhood home of Anthony Mann, born Emile Anton Bundsmann on June 30, 1906.[3]

LOMALAND

The seeds of Lomaland were planted in 1897, when Katherine Augusta Westcott Tingley, a prominent Theosophist, purchased land in Point Loma as the site for the School for the Revival of the Lost Mysteries of Antiquity, to be built by the Theosophical Society. It was the first step in establishing a utopian enclave and cultural Mecca for promoting the Theosophical doctrine, a principle based on studying human beings and the universe through, among other sources, the teachings of the Greek philosopher Plato, the Egyptian philosopher Plotinus, the German mystic Jakob Böhme, the German-Swiss alchemist Paracelsus, and the doctrines of Buddhism and Hinduism.[4] The Theosophical movement, founded in late 1875 by a group which included Helena Blavatsky, studied Islamic, Christian, and ancient Persian (Zoroastrianism) religious ideologies. It was similarly attuned to the Gnostic doctrine preaching salvation through knowledge rather than strictly through faith. Its convoluted theories about religion, the occult, mysticism, and race were offset by progressive views of international cultures as well as modernistic concerns for conservation, prison reform, capital punishment, and animal protection. But these concerns, too, had limitations. The Theosophical Society stated in 1910 that its students at Point Loma "are not after any socialistic utopia of sharing goods and promoting physical comfort for all, and do not adopt strange habits and modes of life." While not a feminist institution, the Society stressed femininity, and at Point Loma, women outnumbered men 60 to 40 percent.[5]

Figure 1.0. Lomaland, the Theosophical commune in Point Loma near San Diego, 1903. Anthony Mann lived here from infancy until age fourteen (San Diego History Center).

There is no doubt that Emile Anton Bundsmann experienced an atypical upbringing of intensive cultural indoctrination at Lomaland. Tingeley viewed the dramatic arts, along with dance and music, as "providing a means of depicting man's nobler side before the general public." Through her efforts, the San Diego community experienced Lomaland's Rāja Yoga Academy students performing Greek and Shakespearean dramas, in the nation's first Greek open-air canyon theater (constructed in 1901), which overlooked the Pacific Ocean, and professional concerts.[6] Photographs and articles about Lomaland during the 1900s suggest a veritable Shangri-La environment for a growing child. Visitors to Lomaland would enter through a magnificent arched gate bounded by Roman columns. Sliding wooden doors allowed passage for automobiles and carriages, while pedestrians entered from either one of two doorways that flanked the archway. In the vast distance, across a stunning landscape, lay the imposing Loma homestead grounds, resplendent with beautiful gardens and palm trees, yucca plants, fields of chrysanthemums, a grove of eucalyptus trees, all set against a spectacular backdrop of the Pacific Ocean. By the time young Emile Anton was born, Lomaland had grown to accommodate living quarters for 500 people and was functioning as a self-contained community outfitted with stables, a blacksmith, carpentry and machine shops, tailoring and textile facilities, a bakery, a Tent Village communal dining area, and a Theosophical publishing house with bindery. Food for the community was produced in Lomaland orchards and vegetable gardens.[7]

Yet beneath this idyllic façade lurked an undercurrent of oppression. In October 1901, a scandal erupted after the conservative *Los Angeles Times* published a report accusing Lomaland of treating women and children like convicts, applying starvation and solitary confinement as punishment. A woman who allegedly escaped from the commune told the paper of forced labor in fields and of being "shut up in a cell and guarded as if she were a raving maniac." The woman claimed that marriages and families were intentionally broken up at Lomaland and family members forbidden from interacting with one another, including parents with their own children, the latter of whom were kept in separate guarded cells. The *Times* alluded to "gross immoralities" taking place at night in Madame Tingley's "spookery."[8]

Tingley sued the newspaper and won her case after the *Times* could not substantiate its claims and, in ensuing years, she worked diligently to court San Diego journalists and education bureaucrats.[9] Given the unconventionality of Lomaland during the post-Victorian era, it is unsurprising that a reactionary newspaper would try to discredit it. Regardless, several years after the discomforting *Times* article appeared, Lomaland's official society magazine, *New Century Path* (later *Century Path*), edited by Tingley, reveals contradictory ideologies. While readers encounter an occasional editorial condemning child labor, compulsory work for Lomaland children and strict regimentation of their activities are in evidence. For example, one magazine photo of a young girl and boy standing on a field path is identified as "Little Rāja Yoga Workers at Lomaland," although the type of "work" these "workers" perform is not mentioned.[10] The magazine also reported a daily military drill for male students designed to instill in them "an erect carriage, an alert mind and eye, and the habit of obedience." Other children took part in "drill and exercises" in the Greek theater and the Lomaland environs. Photos of boys from the Rāja Yoga Academy depict them in West Point-style uniforms; and another issue features four photographs of nine Rāja Yoga Cadets going through maneuvers, complete with rifles.[11]

As intellectual followers of the Theosophical Institute, Anton Bundsmann's parents, Professor Emil Theodore Bundsmann and his wife Bertha (née Waxelbaum/Weichselbaum), were deeply involved with the Theosophical movement. An Austrian immigrant Catholic with a doctorate in chemical engineering from Vienna, Emil taught mathematics, science, and

German at Lomaland, while Bertha, a native of Macon, Georgia, and the only child of a wealthy Bavarian-Jewish cotton mill owner, taught drama at the commune's conservatory of music and drama. The Jewish-Catholic couple had married in 1900, much to the dismay of Bertha's parents, and soon thereafter gave up their respective religions and their money to join the Point Loma commune.[12]

Like other children of Lomaland Theosophists, Emile Anton grew up under the control of the commune and its spiritual and cultural teachings influenced him. The adult Anthony Mann did have religious beliefs but not beliefs exclusive to Catholicism or Judaism. In a 1965 interview, Mann employed religious terminology to describe his uses of color and location filming ("God makes so much colour, makes such magnificent things, that it's difficult not to capture what He has if you go out on locations").[13] The director's daughter Nina Mann reported in an e-mail that "no particular religious emphasis was made during our childhood" but that she and her sister Toni briefly attended a Christian Scientist Sunday school:

> We each remember his saying, "Heaven and Hell were here on earth." He wanted to be cremated in a somewhat Hindu fashion ... He had some mystical traditional beliefs ... reincarnation ... although we never talked about that. My mother remembered his seeing a psychic re [sic] his future career and learning he'd be successful, but die relatively young![14]

The fact that Lomaland had separate group homes (known as "lotus houses") and bungalows for children, as well as its Rāja Yoga Nursery and Home of the Little Tots, lends credence to charges that Theosophical members had limited interactions with their children. Nina recalls Emile Anton's parents only visiting him on weekends. "My childhood memory of my father's description was that it was this horrible place. Obviously his own childhood experience was straight out of Charles Dickens."[15]

It was at Lomaland, however, that the young Bundsmann began his acting life, performing with other children in the Greek theater where his roles included Puck in Shakespeare's *A Midsummer Night's Dream*. Sadly, the boy did not benefit from his mother's dramatic teachings because his parents abandoned him after the elder Bundsmann became ill in 1909 and Bertha took her husband back to Austria to convalesce. The father's health only worsened, and the couple returned to the States on the eve of World War I. With her sick husband now institutionalized and herself financially destitute, Bertha moved to New Jersey to live with her sister. Nina Mann has stated that after her father's parents had fled to Austria, Emile Anton was essentially left behind at the commune from the age of three until he was fourteen, in all likelihood living in the children's quarters at Lomaland. He was placed under the care of a schoolmaster named Forbes who would routinely mete out punishment for misbehavior. Nina explained in a 2008 radio interview:

> I had a sort of jolt when I was watching *The Furies* [1950] because my father used to tell the story that when he was being naughty so to speak this Scot schoolmaster would pick him up by his feet and dunk his head in a pail of water until he knocked it over, which is pretty horrific if you can say that. And years later I was talking to somebody at this Society and the woman said, "Oh, well, that was to get your attention." I thought: "Well, okay." And then lo and behold there's this sequence in *The Furies* where Barbara Stanwyck is acting up and Wendell Corey grabs her by the scruff of the neck and dunks her face in a bowl of water. And you know [for me] it was really, "Oh, okay, I get that one. I know where that came from."[16]

Later in a telephone interview, she had an additional recollection about her father. "As a child I remember that if we were at a friend's house and going swimming he did not want to put his head underwater."[17]

Anthony Mann never publicly discussed his unconventional childhood, and so we can only speculate as to what extent the eccentricities of a communal living experiment influenced his career and art. In some of his films, the connections are clear. Nina Mann believes that the creation of her father's secretive hero characters—"outcasts"—was influenced on a certain level by how outsiders viewed the peculiarities of the Theosophists.

Although not born into wealth, Mann was the product of cultivated, intellectual parents; and while he chose a career in lieu of a university education, Mann possessed a knowledge base as substantial as that of the graduate of any Ivy League school. Not many Hollywood directors could boast, as Mann did in the 1960s, that he had seen "nearly all of Shakespeare's plays," including approximately fifteen stage versions of *Hamlet*. Outside of his thorough cultural education, however, Anton Bundsmann knew nothing of day-to-day living. "My father by the age of fourteen had never seen money and never eaten meat," admitted Nina.[18]

Bundsmann might have well remained in social limbo for years had it not been for his mother's cousin who visited Lomaland and subsequently issued Bertha an ultimatum about her son: "Go get him or he will be ruined for the real world." According to Nina's mother, the director was fourteen when Bertha came to collect him, a claim that appears to dispel previous accounts of Bundsmann as having left Lomaland at age ten. This myth originated in a *New York Times* obituary from Reuters on Anthony Mann. The year he would have actually arrived in New Jersey, 1920, would have also been around the time his father died in the public institution. Bertha spent a week traveling by train from New Jersey to California and then another week returning east with her son. According to Nina, the pair sat in their seats throughout the entire cross-country journey because they could not afford berths. It was a silent voyage east for mother and son.[19]

ANTON BUNDSMANN ON THE STAGE

In New Jersey, Emile Anton attended elementary school in East Orange and high school in Newark but dropped out to go to work. The *New York Times* obituary reports him leaving high school at age sixteen, but the Central High School transcripts indicate a January 1925 dropout date, when Emile Anton was eighteen. His age naturally raises questions as to how far behind he was in grade.[20]

In Newark, Bundsmann acted in amateur theatricals at public schools and even appeared in the Athenian tragedy *Alcestis* alongside future RKO Radio Pictures and Metro-Goldwyn-Mayer production executive Dore Schary, who played King Admetus. One of the more outrageous Anthony Mann myths has him playing the title character, a princess and the devoted wife of King Admetus. This legend originated in a 1956 Warner Bros. press release in connection with the film *Serenade* and has since appeared in more reputable cinema books. However, a photograph from the school production clearly shows Bundsmann in an unidentified male role (fig. 1.1). This fact, along with the presence of female cast members, confirms the absence of cross-dressing of the Old Globe variety.[21]

Throughout his acting and schooling, Bundsmann toiled to make ends meet, working as a messenger boy for Bamberger's department store, where, as Nina Mann explained, "he would take shoes to New York three and four times a week but he would use the carfare and food money to go to the movies, the theater, and anything else that was involved with the theater in New York." Bundsmann also took on a night shift job at the Westinghouse Electric factory on Plane Street in Newark.[22]

Bundsmann's professional theatrical career gained momentum at age seventeen, when he staged the George S. Kaufman–Marc Connelly comedy *Dulcy* under the name "Anton Bundsman." The play premiered on May 9, 1924, at the Proctor's Roof Theatre in Newark, where attendance was

Figure 1.1. Central High School production of *Alcestis* in Newark, NJ, circa 1924. Future RKO and M-G-M production executive Dore Schary (toga, far left) and Emil Anton Bundsmann (far right) pose with the rest of the cast.

reported to have been "far less than the Dramatic Club had the right to expect, but despite this fact the D.C. earned fame and its individual members covered themselves with glory." No later than two months after he dropped out of high school in 1925, he was hired by a Manhattan theatrical company called The Stagers, which paid him ten dollars a week (approximately $133 in 2013) to double as a general handyman and actor.[23]

Through most of the 1920s, Emile Anton Bundsmann performed as Anton Bundsman, earning his first professional credit with his performance as a bodyguard and Chinese man in the maiden Stagers production, *The Blue Peter* (1925), starring future Warner Bros. talkie idol Warren William. In the Hindu drama *The Little Clay Cart* for the Neighborhood Playhouse (1926), Bundsmann played a herdsman, and in a revival of *The Dybbuk* (1926–27), a wedding guest. In the spring of 1927, Bundsmann received a major acting break when he inherited the role of Pedro in the hit Broadway staging of Jean Bart's *The Squall*, directed by Lionel Atwill.[24]

From this point on, there are gaps in our knowledge of stage actor "Anton Bundsman." (A 1945 Republic Pictures publicity note indicating that he wrote Broadway plays under the nom de plume Stephen Lane is without merit.) Nina Mann's mother placed him at Walter Hartwig's theater camp in Peterborough, New Hampshire, in 1928, where, for a $400 enrollment fee, he participated in a production regimen similar to the one at Lomaland, involving acting, lighting, designing costumes, and building sets. Back in New York, he did receive credit in May 1929 for his role as a workman in a revival of *Uncle Vanya*, which had a limited two-performance run at the Morosco Theatre. The following summer, "Bundsman" acted for Hartwig's Manhattan Theater Colony in plays presented at a high school in Bristol, Connecticut. It was through the Hartwig organization that he met Mildred

Kenyon, the first of three wives, from whom he studied dance. They married in 1931.[25] It has been erroneously reported that Kenyon was an "executive" at Macy's, a myth first appearing in late 1940s trade accounts and 1950s Paramount and Warner Bros. press releases. Macy's records do not substantiate this claim. Kenyon was a Macy's employee but not an executive. In a December 2011 telephone conversation, a Macy's staff member reported locating a photo from the April 1932 issue of the house organ *Sparks* depicting Mildred Kenyon in a maid uniform standing alongside other women and identified in the photo caption as working in the china and silverware department.[26]

The couple had two children, who were introduced in press releases as a son named Anthony Jr. and a daughter, Nina. In truth, both children were girls. "Anthony" was the name inexplicably misapplied to the first daughter, Toni, an error originating in the 1950 Paramount press release and repeated ad nauseam by academics and scholars.[27]

The year Bundsmann married Kenyon was also the year he restored his professional name to "Anton Bundsmann" and subsequently appeared in more prominent roles for the New York Repertory Company, including parts in Dion Boucicault's *The Streets of New York; Or, Poverty Is No Crime* (1931), Will Cotton's *The Bride the Sun Shines On* (1931–32), featuring Dorothy Gish, and a failed staging of Henrik Ibsen's *The Pillars of Society* (also with Gish), which closed after two performances. Bundsmann later recalled learning his role the night before performing it for the first time:

> No doubt of it, the response was very fine. With all due modesty I was a big success. But when the producer [Lawrence Langner] brought the play into Broadway he said I was too young for the part and fired me. From that day on I have sworn never to appear again as an actor. So far I've stuck to that bargain with myself.[28]

At the time he gave that interview, Emile Anton Bundsmann had already crossed over from acting to directing. He never appeared on stage again.

CHAPTER 2

FROM BROADWAY TO HOLLYWOOD

ANTON BUNDSMANN, DIRECTOR

With the Depression ravaging the United States economy in 1933 and Anton Bundsmann the actor having retired from public view, Bundsmann the director appeared on the New York scene. The play *Thunder on the Left* was not a political tome but "a fantasy in three acts" by Jean Ferguson Black, based on the 1925 Christopher Morley novel. This production opened at Maxine Elliott's Theatre on October 31, 1933, and ran for thirty-one performances. The play was about a ten-year-old boy experiencing the world in an adult body.[1]

Thunder on the Left received mixed newspaper reviews, but Morley praised the playwright, director, and setting designer, providing clues as to how Bundsmann handled a key scene with two characters:

> Some spectators of the play will notice that that thunder heard by George and Phyllis comes from stage right. We had to choose whether the actors or the audience should hear it from the left. It seemed better to put it on the left of the audience. Besides—Maxine Elliott's Theatre was built that way.[2]

In 1934, Bundsmann directed three summer stock plays for the Red Barn Theatre in Locust Valley, Long Island, two featuring twenty-six-year-old James Stewart on the eve of his departure for Hollywood. John Stuart Twist and Catherine Emery's *We Die Exquisitely* premiered on July 2, 1934, and was a dramatic piece about several passengers making a suicide pact aboard an airplane. Stewart had a memorable role as a drugged-out pilot, foreshadowing the unstable men he later brought to life with Anthony Mann directing in the 1950s. John Van Druten's *All Paris Knows*, an adaptation of Alfred Savoir's French farce, opened to a capacity crowd of 500 on July 23, 1934. Stewart received second billing and a brief reminder to playgoers in the "Who's Who in the Cast": "You remember JAMES STEWART from 'We Die Exquisitely.' He played the hop-head co-pilot to rounds of applause."[3]

Following several theatrical setbacks, Bundsmann was then hired to direct sketches for the Leonard Sillman musical comedy review *New Faces of 1936*. Mindret Lord, screenwriter of Mann's *Strange Impersonation* at Republic Pictures ten years later, wrote four of the *New Faces* sketches. The humor in the show ranged from the comic antics of Imogene Coca and the drag sketch "Women in the White House" to "Marian [sic] Never Looked Lovelier," a satire of William Randolph Hearst's Hollywood gossip columnist, Louella Parsons. In this sketch, Elizabeth Wilde played "Louella Parsing" and was shown constantly praising, on the radio, actress and Hearst mistress Marion Davies. The Hearst papers were not amused, prompting a brief retitling of the sketch to "Mary Lou Never Looked Lovelier" with "Louella Parsing" changed to "Beverly Hills." (Sillman soon restored the sketch and even added another one, "Five Star Final," which lampooned the Dionne Quintuplets and included a character called "Mrs. William Randolph Hearst.") *New Faces of 1936* got off to a bad start with critics and was immediately reworked without Bundsmann within a month of the Broadway premiere.[4] The director by then had moved on to more intellectually challenging projects.

CONTROVERSY ON THE NEW YORK STAGE

In 1935, the Works Progress Administration (WPA) of President Franklin Roosevelt inaugurated the most ambitious federal government arts funding in United States history. The Federal Theatre Project (FTP), for which Hallie Flanagan was National Director, joined the Federal Music Project, Federal Art Project, Federal Writers Project, and other units in employing 40,000 people during the Depression years. The risk-taking FTP enterprise embraced left-wing social themes, producing plays challenging fascism, racism, and capitalism, eventually facing right-wing attacks in Washington, D.C. Among FTP's productions in 1936 were Orson Welles's *Macbeth* for the Negro Unit, *The Revolt of the Beavers* (featuring Elia Kazan) for the Children's Unit, *It Can't Happen Here* (featuring twelve-year-old Sidney Lumet) for The Jewish Theatre, and the Living Newspaper's *Ethiopia*. In addition, the FTP Classic Theatre Branch staged Welles's *Horse Eats Hat* and, in other FTP-affiliated companies, Gilbert and Sullivan operettas.[5]

Bundsmann found work at the Teaching of Theatre Technique Unit of the Federal Theatre and directed the Lynn Riggs play *The Cherokee Night*, staged during July and August at the Provincetown Playhouse in Greenwich Village. In episodically addressing the subject of a vanishing tribe of Southwest Cherokees, this controversial play anticipated the Mann westerns

Figure 2.0. *The Cherokee Night*, by Lynn Riggs, presented at the Provincetown Playhouse by the Federal Theatre Project, 1936. Director: Anton Bundsmann.

Devil's Doorway (1950) and *The Tin Star* (1957) in its sympathetic treatment of American Indians facing assimilation and destruction.[6]

What were Bundsmann's politics in 1936 and subsequent years? Having spent over a decade in the New York theater, he naturally affiliated with left-wing artists, but he did not join any radical political organizations. Bundsmann's theater work nonetheless exhibits a concern for urgent political issues and sympathy for the disenfranchised. Throughout his Hollywood career during the 1940s, 1950s, and 1960s, the director crossed paths with leftist artists, many of whom were future or past blacklistees. "We never had any problem with Tony about our views," recalled Norma Barzman, who fled the United States with screenwriter husband Ben as a result of House Committee on Un-American Activities purges in the late 1940s. "He wasn't what I would call progressive, but he was liberalish, easygoing about what happened and what was happening. Those years we lived through Vietnam and everything, so he was always on the right [moral] side." Although the Barzmans were Hollywood left-wing expatriates, Mann repeatedly hired Ben to assist with his 1960s screenplays. Norma asserted, "We never had any disagreement with him on anything . . . He was what I would call a good liberal." During World War II, Mann leant his name to an October 2, 1944, trade advertisement supporting the reelection of President Roosevelt.[7] The director's daughter, Nina Mann, confirmed in an e-mail that her father voted the Democrat ticket.

Bundsmann attracted more controversy with Joseph M. Viertel's anti-military school play *So Proudly We Hail*, which had tryouts at the Red Barn (under the direction of "Anton Bundsman") before moving on to Broadway in September 1936 for an aborted fourteen-performance run. The psychological and physical violence later seen in films of Anthony Mann can be traced to this play. The setting is the Stone Ridge Military Academy whose motto, "You Give Us the Boy, We Return the Man," serves as a warning to all young men entering its gates. In the play, young cadet Jim Thornton (film actor Richard Cromwell) evolves from a likeable and sensitive figure into a full-fledged sadist. After turning a blind eye to the death from pneumonia of a classmate and being rewarded with a promotion to sergeant, Jim quickly transforms into a brute. *Time* magazine described a scene where Jim supervises the torture of a fellow cadet "who failed to salute the War Dead":

> An officer who might have intervened leaves the room with the admonition: "Be careful, fellows." The victim is then tied to a double-deck bed, burned with a cigarette, given 18 lashes with a whip, hospitalized.[8]

Had the play been filmed in the late 1930s, Jim would have been punished. On stage, however, he receives the highest honors at the school commencement address. While the lack of female audience interested in the play may have been a contributing factor, a competing military school play, the comedy *Bright Honor*, opening at a theater two blocks away, sealed the fate of *So Proudly We Hail*. Both plays ultimately canceled out each other at the box office.[9]

SELZNICK INTERNATIONAL PICTURES

In late 1936, Hollywood entered Anton Bundsmann's life. Motion picture producer David O. Selznick, a former Paramount and RKO Radio Pictures production executive, having formed Selznick International Pictures in 1935, was now preparing his big-budget production of *Gone With the Wind*. The Selznick company hired thirty-year-old Bundsmann to accompany eastern representative Kay Brown in late November on a southern talent scouting tour in search of potential Scarlett O'Haras. The two interviewed hundreds of young women at several universities and drama clubs. While seated at a table piled high with letters, photos, and applications, Brown explained, "All these will have to be read by Mr. Bundsmann and myself." In an *Atlanta Constitution* photo, Bundsmann is identified as "a director of the organization," even though he was never a full-time Selznick staff member.[10]

Throughout 1937 Bundsmann freelanced as a Selznick East Coast talent scout. He auditioned hundreds of young boys for *The Adventures of Tom Sawyer* before settling on twelve-year-old Thomas Kelly. He secured veteran stage actress Minnie Dupree for her first screen role in *The Young in Heart* (1938), and in the fall returned to *Gone With the Wind* casting obligations and screen tests, which West Coast executives reviewed.[11] Years later, he told an interviewer,

> I had made a lot of film tests for David Selznick. I made all the tests for *Gone With the Wind*, *[The] Young in Heart*, *Tom Sawyer* and so on, and I was able to cut them as well. When I went to the Coast, I had some knowledge of method and technique.[12]

An inspection of talent culled from local radio stations for the *Gone With the Wind* auditions resulted in people "pictorially unsuited for picture work," Bundsmann wrote in a memo. With the aid of cinematographer Rudolph Maté (who photographed Carl Th. Dreyer's *The Passion of Joan of Arc* and was a future Columbia Pictures cameraman and director), he directed "silent close-ups" of seven actresses for the roles of Belle Watling, Melanie, Scarlett, and Aunt Pittypat. His freelance work for Selznick throughout 1938 and into 1939 included tests for Gregory Ratoff's *Intermezzo* and Alfred Hitchcock's *Rebecca*. The Selznick assignments subsidized Bundsmann's stage activities and enabled him to reject inferior theatrical properties.[13] He also could now afford to direct two more Federal Theatre plays, the first without credit.

William (W. E. B.) Du Bois's revolutionary play *Haiti* was credited to director Maurice Clark but the *New York Times* reported Bundsmann being brought in as "consulting director."[14] The main characters were a black rebel hero (Rex Ingram, alternating with Canada Lee) leading a Haitian revolt against French troops in 1802 and a Frenchwoman of mixed race who joins the Haitians. The play had a triumphant six-month success in Harlem but soon became cannon fodder for more rightist attacks on the Federal Theatre. On the small Harlem stage with only a few dozen actors, Bundsmann and his technicians created the effect of Haitian soldiers "sweeping down from the mountains with cannons and muskets and spears" to fend off 50,000 of Napoleon's troops, only twenty actors playing Napoleonic forces. Three stage managers controlled a panel of signal lights alerting two sound technicians when to signal a "Marseillaise" chorus or play a sound record of 2,000 shouting voices, and two stagehands fired revolvers. There were explosion effects high up on the theater fly floor and from ignited stage level smoke pots. A stagehand achieved a fire effect by blowing through a long tube connected to a large pot of burning powder. A man backstage simulated thunder by beating a drum and thunder sheet while another conveyed a falling tree by pulling a trip cord dividing the tree into vertical sections.[15] This type of theatrical training would serve Anthony Mann well in his "Poverty Row" films of the 1940s.

The final Bundsmann play for the FPT, Theodore Pratt's Deep South racial drama *Big Blow*, opening late in 1938 and running through early 1939, employed hurricane sound effects from a Samuel Goldwyn–John Ford movie, *The Hurricane* (1937). Although *Big Blow* was staged in other U.S. cities, it was not performed in the South where a scene with the white Celie (Amelia Romano) throwing her arms around a Negro man (Doe Doe Green) framed for rape would have been deemed incendiary.[16] Actress Romano later reported,

> Now that embrace got a lot of flak, although Dodie was delighted; lot of his friends, an awful lot of blacks, came to the theatre for the first time because of [that scene]. There were occasional hisses from the audience, but I refused to change it, because it seemed eminently right to me.[17]

The U.S. government soon prepared to deliver a death blow to the Federal Theatre Project. By that time, Bundsmann was commuting to New Jersey to freelance at the 1,400-seat Maplewood Theatre.[18] In Maplewood, New Jersey, he directed at least a dozen plays with prominent stage and film stars. The talent pool included Dorothy Mackaill, Jane Wyatt, Jean Muir, Milton Berle, Phillips Holmes, Ruth Chatterton, Frances Farmer, and, in the new Thornton Wilder play *Our Town*, the young up-and-coming actress Teresa Wright. That he shuffled as quickly as he did between dramas, comedies, farces, and literary adaptations illustrates how the future Anthony Mann was able to achieve so much within the confines of Hollywood low-budget filmmaking and move from picture to picture and genre to genre without disorientation or exhaustion.[19]

By June 1939 the director had moved on yet again. Contrary to previously held belief, he did not depart for Hollywood that year to begin work at Paramount Pictures.[20] This is yet another myth in the legion of Anthony Mann myths. In actuality, he found a yearlong assignment in the embryonic field of television. This facet of Mann's background, so vital to our comprehension of his subsequent motion picture career, has until now either barely been acknowledged or completely ignored.

BUNDSMANN AT NBC

It began with a papier-mâché Felix the Cat doll rotating on a phonograph turntable. This was the first image televised in the late 1920s at W2XBS, the experimental Radio Corporation of America/National Broadcasting

Company television station. On April 30, 1939, the station began airing regular programming, commencing with President Roosevelt opening the New York World's Fair. Television being in its infancy, the W2XBS programming was confined to approximately five hundred TV receivers, but RCA-NBC still produced live dramatic and music events.[21]

As a director at W2XBS from 1939 to 1940, Anton Bundsmann was among the very first television directors in the world. In the original scripts for these productions (on microfilm at the Library of Congress in Washington, D.C.), which ranged from ten-minute segments to full-length productions, his handwritten technical notes for the cameras appear on the right side of every page. Bundsmann was acquiring additional moviemaking technique via the live television experience.[22]

The first, airing live on the afternoon of June 20, 1939, was a ten-minute interview with two young female 4-H Club winners. Other summer segments featured singers, musicians, novelty acts, dry interviews with the World's Fair Television Beauty Contest Winners, "an eminent authority on Sleep," makeup experts, and a table-setting specialist. A ten-minute July 25 interview with celebrity World War I veteran Sergeant Alvin York (the subject of Howard Hawks's 1941 film *Sergeant York*) proved disappointing. "[Interviewer] Glenn Riggs did an excellent job," wrote Bundsmann in a report, "but Sgt. Yorke [sic] had practically nothing to say—mostly monosyllables in reply to Riggs' questions."[23]

There were career low points for Bundsmann at W2XBS. In *Oddities in Hat Wear* (aired on the afternoon of August 25), wisecracking hostess Frances Hidden demonstrated how to make hats out of breadbaskets, parasols, and vegetable strainers.[24] There was also the first of several shoe commercials, airing on August 16, in which *So This is New York* host George Ross flirted with a female model:

> ROSS: Well, Miss [the model's name was to be inserted here] . . . you certainly look happy . . . and . . . er . . . comfortable.
> MODEL: Yes, I *am* happy . . . *because* I'm comfortable.
> ROSS: Happy because you are comfortable?
> MODEL: Yes! You see, Mr. Ross, so many of we women sacrificed foot comfort because we failed to realize the importance of "quality" . . .
> (*Camera focused on Model's feet—close-up*)
> MODEL: *My* shoes are Andrew Geller shoes . . . the smartest footwear *any* woman could wish for . . . really tailored to the foot.
> ROSS: They look good to me!
> MODEL: And they're not expensive. They are really "chichi."[25]

Figure 2.1. *The Streets of New York; Or, Poverty is No Crime*, 1939. One of the few surviving fragments of Anton Bundsmann's live 1939 NBC television play.

Women's shoes continued to torment Bundsmann. On March 3, 1940, he directed the twenty-five-minute *Coward Shoes-Fashion Show*, which was doomed from the moment the comic announcer promised "a round half dozen of the loveliest, most charming specimens of feminine pulchritude you've ever seen in your life" in order to prevent male viewers from reaching for their dials. At one point, the host brought his unfortunate director into the proceedings by comically scolding the shoe models, "It really is too, too bad that you've all failed to take the opportunity I've been offering with my seemingly aimless conversation, because Tony Bundsman [sic], television director, is out front here and he *might* like you!"[26]

Not all the TV assignments were of such low caliber. On the night of July 18, 1939, Bundsmann directed a one-hour edition of the E. B. Ginty play *Missouri Legend*, his first feature-length media project, first western, and a play staged at the Maplewood Theatre the previous January. This biographical comedy about Jesse James (Dean Jagger) had a cast that included Norman Lloyd and Mildred Natwick.[27] Lloyd, a distinguished Broadway actor whom Jagger and Natwick encouraged to participate, later elaborated on these early NBC television efforts:

> It was an experiment by NBC. They took over some radio studios they had in the NBC Rockefeller Studios there in New York. And they tried to do a couple of plays in these radio studios. In other words, the sets were up against the wall and [for] the next set the camera moved over along the wall facing another set, then it moved over to another set . . .[28]

Missouri Legend and all of the Bundsmann W2XBS plays were photographed with three enormous Iconoscope cameras. Because they were aired live and technology to record them for posterity did not yet exist, all but one of these television efforts is lost. The one exception is a one-hour adaptation of Dion Boucicault's *The Streets of New York; Or, Poverty is No Crime*, which aired live on Thursday night, August 31. Bundsmann again cast Lloyd along with George Coulouris and the twenty-year-old Phyllis Isley Walker, who later became Jennifer Jones.[29] Only eleven fragmented minutes of this sixty-minute program survive, minus the soundtrack, thanks to an unknown technician who filmed a television monitor with a spring-wound 16 mm camera. As a result, it is the only Bundsmann television project existing in any form.

Reviewing the surviving fragments, film historian Richard Koszarski notes the deliberately broad silent comedy-style acting lampooning Victorian-era melodrama. "What exists reveals the camera work as surprisingly fluid and reasonably complex," Koszarski writes. "At least two cameras were used in some of the scenes, which appear to have been carefully rehearsed to take full advantage of camera mobility." (The original teleplay for the production indicates three cameras in use throughout.) Lloyd, who hated his own performance, vividly recalled cast members wearing heavy winter coats in hot August weather. "On the air we were sweating, shiny thespians, and, as the snow fell, it stuck to our faces like the confetti it was," he told the Paley Center for Media.[30]

In the fall of 1939, Bundsmann directed two live broadcasts of *Jane Eyre* (October 12 and December 6) and an adaptation of *Little Women* (December 23), which he previously directed on stage at Maplewood. There was also another teleplay airing that season which for our purposes is worth investigating. It is the sixty-minute murder mystery *A Criminal at Large*, broadcast on the evening of Friday, November, 17.[31]

This television play, previously filmed in England in 1932 as *The Frightened Lady*, was a drawing-room whodunit set in a little village in Sussex, England, and photographed on three interior sets in NBC Studio 3-H. Although mostly theatrical in terms of presentation, it does contain serious attempts at visual storytelling. The opening business in the Edgar Wallace script indicates that the director is already attuned to the importance of the camera establishing vital elements to a scene. After the opening titles, the action fades in to a window and the camera tracks over to show Lady Lebanon (Nance O'Neil) and Dr. Leicester Amersham (Charles Gerard) pantomiming an argument. The camera pans with the action over to a door and from camera #2 Dr. Amersham appears in close-up as Lady Lebanon remarks,

> Nobody would believe you if you told them. Tell them if you dare. And don't forget you are as deeply in it as anybody. You've always wanted to handle Willie's money.[32]

The teleplay explains the action from here, which Bundsmann recorded from cameras 1 and 3:

THE SOUND OF DOOR CLOSING
THE DOCTOR STANDS AT THE DOOR—PUTS ON HIS HAT AND COAT AND SLOWLY GOES DOWN THE WALK. HE PASSES THE WINDOWS WE HAVE BEEN LOOKING AT. WE SEE THE FIGURE OF A MAN BEHIND HEDGE. THE DOCTOR PASSES THE HEDGE AND AS HE PAUSES TO LOOK AT HIS WATCH, TWO ARMS HOLDING A STRIPED INDIAN SHAWL ARE SEEN AROUND THE THROAT OF DR AMERSHAM. THE SHAWL TIGHTENS—THE FACE IS DISTORTED—THE SOUND OF STRANGULATION AND WE FADE ON THE HEAD OF DR AMERSHAM FALLING BACKWARD INTO THE HEDGE.[33]

A gripping opening no doubt, but *A Criminal at Large* falls into more conventional trappings once two Scotland Yard detectives (one played by Dennis Hoey, the actor cast as Mr. Rochester in both *Jane Eyre* airings) visit a mansion with secret panels and conspiring aristocrats, one of whom ends up shooting himself. Bundsmann kept his three cameras fairly mobile and seems to have done what he could within the physical limitations of the material. In a scene at the end of Act II, the detectives encounter the sleepwalking Isla (Frances Reid) at night. Handwritten instructions in the script called for the #1 camera to pan down to the floor to reveal shadows on a nearby desk; the camera then panned up and dollied over to the stairs to follow the sleepwalker as she moved to the desk to open a drawer in search of the cloth murder weapon.[34]

Bundsmann handled more interstitial segments through the end of 1939, including a twelve-minute version of *Pinocchio* featuring the Sue Hastings Marionettes, which aired on the afternoon of December 30, several months in advance of the RKO-Disney feature cartoon. The subsequent narrative plays in 1940 became more elaborate. The intelligent Helen Jerome teleplay *Charlotte Corday* (February 9) ran sixty minutes and anticipated Mann's 1949 Eagle-Lion costume adventure thriller *Reign of Terror/The Black Book* in its portrayal of 1793 revolutionary Paris (although the dialogue here is truer to the eighteenth century). The biggest disappointment was the artistic license taken with the material, as when Mademoiselle Corday (Frances Reid) stabs the radical Jean-Paul Marat (José Ruban) in his workroom rather than bathtub.[35]

Bundsmann collaborated with actress Reid a third time two weeks later when W2XBS aired *Prologue to Glory* (February 23), adapted from the successful Federal Theatre E. P. Conkle play about Abraham Lincoln (staged from March through November 1938), with Reid playing Ann Rutledge. The most ambitious of the Bundsmann television plays, this drama utilized seven sets during the course of its seventy-eight minutes and like *Missouri Legend* was heavy on dialect-laden dialogue ("There's whur you're mistooken bad, Linkern. This-here country is the hopes of Americy").[36] During *Prologue to Glory*'s original 1938 staging, New Jersey Republican congressmen J. Parnell Thomas of the Dies Committee (forerunner to HUAC, of which Thomas was later chairman) cited the play and several other FTP productions (including *Haiti*) as having "communistic leanings." The limited reach of W2XBS in 1940 prevented Representative Thomas from paying much attention to Bundsmann's adaptation or several other television programs of the time.

The sixty-five-minute news digest *See! Hear! A Visual Digest of the Month, Issue 1—March 24, 1940* aired on March 27, 1940, and was an odd collection of reenactments, ranging from the history of plywood to the story of Easter (featuring Reid as Mary Magdalene). Future *Raw Deal* screenwriter Leopold Atlas wrote the program. Opening in the television studio after smoke from an explosion has cleared, an editor (Clancy Cooper, the sadistic detective Chubb in *Railroaded!*) rehearses his introduction and then asks, "How does that sound, Tony?" A voice (presumably Bundsmann's) responds, "Good. Sounds fine." The editor asks, "Shall I say it that way, then?" The voice proclaims, "You've said it. You're on the air!"[37]

In addition to constituting Anton Bundsmann's first official screen credit (as "Bundsman"), which a comic character named "Iko" read aloud, *See! Hear!* contained a subversive Dutch Nazi spy episode. The Atlas script bravely mocks FBI chief J. Edgar Hoover's thirst for enemy spies by mentioning a Hoover article urging citizens to inform on "any person whose actions might seem to indicate that they are connected with any foreign government." This prompts Iko (the actor's name is not recorded in the script) to question his existence in a monologue that satirizes not only the U.S. political climate of 1940, but the type of crime movie dialogue Atlas and others later wrote for Anthony Mann:

> IKO. You see? One out of every six is a possible spy. And it might be you, it might be him, and it might be me—Me? A spy? That can't be? I'm Iko! How do I know I'm not a spy? Maybe I ought to investigate myself. I'm acting mighty suspicious to me. O-O. Maybe I ought to turn myself in. If I'm a spy they'll throw me out of the country. But they can't do that to me. I'm an American citizen—I'll stand on my rights. I'll fight. I'm a tax payer. O-O. What if they

find out I aint [sic] paid my income tax? I aint got no income to pay a tax for but that don't make any difference to them. They'll arrest me—give me a number—they'll fingerprint me. I aint got no fingerprints. They'll think I'm tryint [sic] to hide from some crime. They'll send me to the hot-seat. I didn't do it, I tell you! I'm innocent! I didn't kill him. I swear I didn't do it. I didn't even know the guy. I wasn't even there on the night of Jan. 16th. O-o. [sic] Where was I the night of Jan. 16th. [sic] How'd I get into this mess? Everything happens to me. Here I was, walking down the street innocently and suddenly I'm a spy—an income-tax evader—a murder-suspect and who knows what else.

(*the rat-tat-tat of the punching bag is heard*)

The Cops! They're after me—they're shooting.³⁸

Clearly the writing of a left-wing author. In 1944, Atlas joined the Communist Political Association and by the end of the decade was being harassed by the federal government for his radical affiliations.³⁹ There never was an *Issue No. 2* of *See! Hear!*

The final Anton Bundsmann TV play, *Ode to Liberty*, was even more daring. Produced and aired on April 5, it was a sixty-minute condensation of Sidney Howard's 1934 adaptation of a Michel Duran play, *Liberté Provisoire*. The only credited screenwriter on *Gone With the Wind*, Howard had died in an accident the previous August. *Ode to Liberty* was of a different political stripe than *GWTW*: it was a comedy of manners about a French bourgeois woman (Mady Christians) who shields from police a radical communist (Walter Slezak). The play is as far removed from the anticommunism of Ernst Lubitsch's *Ninotchka* (released in late 1939) as one could imagine. Not only does the rich woman fail to convert the fugitive red, she bids him *adieu* from her balcony by offering the communist salute.⁴⁰

Two months later, NBC announced it was temporarily shutting the station down for the duration of the summer to make technical adjustments to its Empire State Building transmitter.⁴¹ As things turned out, World War II interfered with the network's television experimentation, and NBC did not resume original production until the late 1940s. With his television commitments complete, Bundsmann briefly returned to directing plays in Boston, Washington, D.C., and Philadelphia.⁴²

On January 22, 1941, Bertha Waxelbaum Bundsmann died in East Orange, New Jersey, and the death impacted her thirty-four-year-old son's future. With no parental ties holding him to the East Coast and with theatrical work unsteady, Anton Bundsmann sought to reinvent himself in

California. In March the director drove west with two friends in a used Ford, arriving in Los Angeles after six days of straight driving. Wife Mildred and three-year-old daughter Toni remained in their Greenwich Village apartment until Bundsmann was able to send for them in mid-1942 as he was preparing his second feature film under the new professional name of Anthony Mann.[43]

As usual, it did not take long for an opportunity at complete reinvention to present itself. One month after leaving New York, a simple notice appeared in the *New York Times*: "Anton Bundsmann, stage director, has been added to Paramount's studio staff." Contrary to later publicity accounts claiming him to have spent "an entire year studying the methods of top directors" at Paramount, the Manhattan transplant was directing screen tests for his first motion picture within six very short months of his Hollywood arrival.[44]

BUNDSMANN AT PARAMOUNT PICTURES

In Hollywood, Anthony Mann began at the top by working for one of the oldest and largest motion picture concerns. Although proclaiming its thirtieth anniversary in 1942, Paramount Pictures was younger than that, having started as a distributor in 1914 for such showmen as Adolph Zukor, Jesse L. Lasky, Samuel Goldfish/Goldwyn, and Cecil B. DeMille. Two years later, Zukor seized control of operations in a giant merger and during the 1920s was overseeing the biggest film organization in the world whose largesse was to be diminished after the 1929 stock market crash and in subsequent government antitrust decisions.

Throughout the years, Paramount mastered the art of promoting glamorous sexual sophistication through such stars as Rudolph Valentino, Gloria Swanson, Clara Bow, Louise Brooks, Marlene Dietrich, and Gary Cooper. The studio's 1930s anarchistic comedies of W. C. Fields, Mae West, The Marx Brothers, and Harold Lloyd are exemplary studies in cinematic drollery. At the time Bundsmann arrived in 1941, the Paramount celebrity roster included Claudette Colbert, Dorothy Lamour, Ray Milland, Bob Hope, Alan Ladd, Veronica Lake, and Bing Crosby. But in spite of its intimidating executive structure, Paramount was considered a director's studio, having over the years spawned DeMille, Josef von Sternberg, George Cukor, Mitchell Leisen, Henry Hathaway, and Dorothy Arzner. Paramount was also where Ernst Lubitsch, Rouben Mamoulian, and Leo McCarey made their finest Hollywood pictures and where immigrant writer Billy Wilder was able to reactivate his directing career in 1942. But as far as the studio was concerned, 1941 belonged to writer-director Preston Sturges, the brilliant mastermind behind *Christmas in July* (1940), *The Palm Beach Story* (1942), *The Miracle of Morgan's Creek* (1944), *Hail the Conquering Hero* (1944), and *Unfaithfully Yours* (1948). Anton Bundsmann was assigned to shadow Sturges.

Sturges at first seems an odd choice for such a mentorship. He specialized in highbrow madcap comedies, worshipping meticulously constructed dialogue as much as the future Anthony Mann despised it. Mann later made it clear that he believed a motion picture had to be visual while Sturges, although not resistant to occasional dalliances with complex camera technique, preferred the spoken word to dictate the design of a film. In truth, the two men were ideally suited to a temporary alliance. Both were products of eccentric upbringings in which cultural immersion had been carried out to near-suffocation.

Sturges's experiences in Paris as a boy with a mother who counted Isadora Duncan as a close friend were not unlike those of Bundsmann at Lomaland. In a scenario similar to the childrearing practices at Point Loma, the Isadora Duncan School of the Dance in Berlin had arranged with parents for the school to raise their daughters between the ages of four and seventeen. As a child, Sturges had worn Greek dresses and sandals, observed rehearsals of *Tannhäuser* and *Parsifal*, enrolled in experimental schools, and experienced the Greek tragedians and Shakespeare. It is not difficult visualizing Sturges sharing with his New York charge childhood memories in Florence, Italy, where at age six young Preston and his mother danced over Dante's Bridge with Isadora.[45] Sturges, too, gravitated towards the Broadway stage of the 1920s.

Sturges was at the pinnacle of his success at Paramount when Bundsmann arrived in spring 1941. *The Lady Eve*, starring Barbara Stanwyck and Henry Fonda, two actors later to appear in westerns for Mann, was drawing sizable crowds at theaters. Sturges was about to embark on the riskiest venture of his directing career, a lacerating satire on Hollywood in which broad slapstick intertwined with soulful dramatic passages. *Sullivan's Travels* (1941) was filmed between May and July 1941 on the Paramount lot and at various locations, and Bundsmann was witness to a masterpiece in the making. The searing film deals with a demoralized Hollywood director (Joel McCrea) of crude commercial films who masquerades as a hobo in order to study poverty up close for a proposed prestige film about humanity, "O Brother, Where Art Thou?"

Mann said in his last interview:

He let me go through the entire production, watching him direct—and I directed a little. I'd stage a scene and he'd tell me how lousy it was. Then I watched the editing and I was able gradually to build up knowledge.[46]

Looking at *Sullivan's Travels* with the benefit of hindsight poses the question of whether the observer's involvement went beyond staging a few "lousy" scenes. As a writer first and foremost, Sturges created a cinema of delirious verbosity where the camera primarily recorded what the actors were saying. Unlike his previous pictures, however, *Sullivan's Travels* contained a number of extended dialogue-less sequences uncommon both in the director's work and in 1940s Hollywood cinema. One of these depicts a vagrant (George Renovant) beating and robbing McCrea at night at a Kansas City railroad yard and an approaching freight train killing the vagrant. The scene would not be out of place in one of Anthony Mann's Eagle-Lion thrillers.

Did Sturges influence his student or did the student influence his mentor? None of the available production files on *Sullivan's Travels* mention Anton Bundsmann. Of the five assistant directors cited in daily production reports, his name is not among them, but this does not mean he was not present on set. The evidence shows that Sturges directed the freight yards sequence, filmed with two cameras late on the night of July 17, 1941, at the Union Depot in Los Angeles. Bundsmann was in all likelihood present for the filming—watching, studying, learning from a master.[47]

It was Sturges who urged Bundsmann to direct pictures:

Preston insisted I make a film as soon as possible. He said a lot of guys stall, and hesitate and falter, and you may never become a director. And I think he was right. They'll say, "What have you done?" . . . He said it's better to have done something bad than to have done nothing, and this was very sound advice. This was his advice; so the first picture, good or bad, that came along, I decided to do. And this was *Dr. Broadway*.[48]

Figure 3.0. *Dr. Broadway*, 1942. Macdonald Carey and Jean Phillips (Photofest).

CHAPTER 3

DR. BROADWAY (1942)

Although not a *film noir*, *Dr. Broadway* does take place over a twenty-four-hour period and mostly at night. The comic thriller features dark rooms, shadowed back alleys, and a supporting cast suitable for a police lineup in any 1940s crime picture. Reminiscent of the writings of Damon Runyon, Anthony Mann's first film is populated with big city working-class (and underclass) eccentrics fighting and sometimes beating the odds through a collective spirit. The most diverting of the Mann crime pictures, *Dr. Broadway* provides a pleasant counterbalance between humorous antics and an atmosphere of intrigue.

The film was the second to star Macdonald Carey, best remembered for portraying a dull detective in Alfred Hitchcock's *Shadow of a Doubt* (1943). The twenty-eight-year-old actor is cast as a physician whose adoptive family, a likable gang of Times Square hooligans, took him in as a boy after the death of his father, a newspaperman covering the Broadway beat. The young doctor is a Great White Way fixture who counts peddlers, policemen, vagrants, and con artists among his motley circle of friends; he barters his medical services to local politicos and is not above removing bullets from wanted killers. While the smiling, friendly faced Carey appears on the surface to be an aberration in the lengthy list of Mann screen antiheroes, his Dr. Kane is not out of place in this troubled cinematic universe. On screen, Kane will slug a woman one minute and then defend her honor in court the next. In the first two instances when female protagonist Connie (Jean Phillips) is in need of rescuing, Kane is cavalier in his attitude toward her safety. When Connie is eventually kidnapped, Kane again seems lackadaisical as he attempts to humor crook Venner (J. Carrol Naish) into revealing information about the latter's crime operations. Perhaps these qualities are what led the uncharitable *Variety* reviewer to classify Dr. Timothy Kane as "a combination Superman and jerk."[1]

Kane's adventures over twenty-four hours are of an agreeably exaggerated nature: interceding in police efforts to talk Connie from jumping off the ledge of a hotel building; agreeing to assist a recently paroled and dying gangster (Edward/Eduardo Ciannelli) into locating the mobster's missing daughter so she can receive $100,000; fending off police pursuers after he is suspected in the murder of the gangster; and, finally, soliciting his Broadway adopted family to help rescue Connie from Venner, who wants the murdered killer's money.

The director was not entirely dismissive of the production, and the film puts to rest any notions that Mann's evolution as a craftsman occurred gradually during the 1940s. *Dr. Broadway*'s director clearly has a handle on all aspects of studio filmmaking. Had Paramount not decided to abandon "B" production altogether, thus declining to retain his services, Mann would have risen in the studio ranks quicker than he did.

THE MAKING OF *DR. BROADWAY*

Paramount did not delay in offering Anton Bundsmann a directing job. As production on *Sullivan's Travels* was concluding in July 1941, the studio purchased three Borden Chase stories: *Dr. Broadway, Calling Dr. Broadway,* and *Death Across the Board*.[2] (Chase later wrote the 1950s Anthony Mann-James Stewart westerns, *Winchester '73, Bend of the River,* and *The Far Country*.) Bundsmann was paid $2,600 (over $41,000 in 2013) to bring the first of these comedic mysteries to the screen. When Paramount announced him as a studio director in late September, *Variety* indicated that "Bundsmann will change his name to Mann when he starts his picture work."[3] Removing the Germanic sting from a surname during World War II was not a requirement for Hollywood directors. Ernst Lubitsch, Fritz Lang, and Otto Preminger saw no need to Americanize their names. On the other hand, "Bund" had a negative connotation after the German American Bund propagandized on behalf of Nazi Germany during the late 1930s. In 1941, a director with "Bund" in his name could function in the East Coast theater world but was considered a public relations liability to movie studios dependent upon less educated and enlightened cinema audiences.

Bundsmann was unconcerned about his transition from stage to cinema directing. "I hate dialogue," he told a reporter in 1950. "The camera is the most exciting part of the medium for me. It can get anything over in one flash: you can experience a great shock or great beauty or any great moment simply by seeing it pictorialized." Asked how he was able to reconcile his stage training to the requirements of filmmaking, Mann explained, "They are less different than you think. I believe in placing the camera so that all the characters come to it, to you—not so different, really, from having the characters in a play advance down stage center, or what in vaudeville we used to call 'a drop in one.'"⁴

On September 15, 1941, Mann assembled actors Rod Cameron, Betty Jane Rhodes, and William Wright at Paramount's Stage 4 for *Dr. Broadway* sound tests. Charles Lang, a studio cameraman with experience working for Henry Hathaway, Lubitsch, and Fritz Lang, photographed the six-hour session. One month later, another round of afternoon tests were made (this time on a living room set on Stage 10) with the two actors eventually cast in the film, Macdonald Carey and Jean Phillips.⁵

Mann had bittersweet memories of the production:

> I think it had some good things in it. I remember very warmly the cameraman, an oldtimer name of [Theodor] Sparkuhl, who had done many films for UFA and Lubitsch, and he was a great help. Nobody else cared a damn about the picture. They said: "Don't build sets; don't do anything. You have to get finished in 18 days and, if you don't, the cameras are taken from you and 'OUT.'"⁶

(The film was actually shot in twenty days with an additional day for retakes.) Sparkuhl, an exile of the German film industry who had photographed the silent British version of *The Informer* (1929) and Jean Renoir's *La Chienne* (France, 1931), the latter of which featured modern approaches to early talkie photography, including handheld camerawork, was ideally suited to the dim rooms and alleys of the 1940s crime genre. Mann regretted not working with Sparkuhl again because "he was really a very fine cameraman and was doing nothing at that time so the studio let me have him. He didn't care how many hours I spent at night with him, discussing how to shoot the scene next morning."⁷

For the director, Sparkhul was a welcome respite from studio brass. On the afternoon of October 16, four days before the official start of principal photography, Mann attended a production meeting with twenty-six others at which the studio made it clear their desire to control costs on the picture. After the director indicated that he wanted the district attorney's office in the film to be "good," art director Hans Dreier told him that the real New York DA office was "unimpressive—very simple." Studio production manager Edward Ebele recommended saving money by utilizing a standing set from the Alan Ladd-Veronica Lake thriller, *This Gun for Hire*. The budget was set at $174,000 and exceeded that figure by $1,000. By the time *Dr. Broadway* began filming on October 20, Paramount's in-house process photographer Farciot Edouart had already completed background shots of

Manhattan locations for rear-projection effects. The director in charge of the rest of the picture was now identified as "Anton Mann."[8]

The production was filmed entirely on the Paramount lot and Mann made use of practical locations at the studio. The scene in a gymnasium where fighters are being recruited to assist Dr. Timothy Kane (captured in a brief uninterrupted camera take) was filmed on Day Three of production at the studio gym. A night scene where Jean Phillips follows Joan Woodbury into an alley and to a stage door was filmed outside the studio's editing building.[9] Mann recalled Paramount making conditions difficult for him:

> I'll never forget one experience—I was in the middle of shooting a scene on the backlot of Paramount. This was the first sequence in the picture and I was supposed to have three days out there. And about the middle of the very first day, one of Paramount's head production guys came out and said, "You're through here by tonight. Cecil B. DeMille wants to come out. You got to clear the set."[10]

Mann had already planned his filming schedule accordingly and "marked off some interesting angles" but was left with no choice but to comply. Presumably Mann is referring to the exteriors of the Surrey Arms Hotel from which Jean Phillips's character threatens to jump. These were filmed on the New York Street backlot on November 4, the fourteenth day of production. However, it is questionable whether the intervening party was DeMille since the latter's upcoming Paramount release *Reap the Wild Wind* had completed its retakes two months earlier. Sol C. Siegel, who later clashed with Mann at M-G-M over the calamitous big-budget remake of *Cimarron* (1960), was the supervising producer issuing the insulting command.[11]

The behind-the-scenes friction is not evident in the finished product, a polished piece of entertainment benefiting from superior Paramount production values. An example of this is a restaurant scene filmed on Stage 4 on the sixth production day, which features an ambitious tracking shot (or "master dolly shot") of Carey entering and walking past tables and potted palms until reaching his adversary's table. The settings are far and above what subsequent Mann underwriters Republic Pictures, PRC, and Eagle-Lion could afford. Mann accomplished this shot in seven takes, and it remains one of the very few such camera moves in his crime movie cycle.[12]

The opening titles to *Dr. Broadway* are the most inventive of any Mann picture, establishing the tone with charm and capturing the director's passion for Manhattan. The Paramount logo dissolves to nighttime stock footage of Broadway/Times Square as Irvin Talbot's jazzy, urban, Gershwin-like score accompanies the images. An art deco neon title treatment appears with the film's copyright information. Rising studio art director Hal Pereira directed the next shot of Carey exiting a taxi in front of a rear projection screen of Times Square, which was filmed on New York Street on November 29.[13] Carey's name appears in superimposed deco letters, and after he looks up to screen right there is an edit to the *Times* electronic sign scrolling on two sides of the dark building, the lighted names of Jean Phillips, J. Carrol Naish, Richard Lane, Edward Ciannelli, and Joan Woodbury optically printed to scroll along. The first screen credit of Anthony Mann appears over a night shot of Manhattan, in appropriate neon lettering. Although he had continued to be known on the lot as "Anton Mann" as late as November, the name "Anthony Mann" appears in studio memoranda by December 5, 1941.[14] Even though he never legally changed his name from Anton Bundsmann, he shall, for the sake of clarity, be hereafter referred to by his screen name.

From a directorial point of view, *Dr. Broadway* makes the strongest impression in the very first scene to be filmed: the introductory sequence (shot on Stage 7, as well as Paramount's Stage 2 transparency stage for rear-projection effects) in which Kane joins Connie on the building ledge, only to find out that her threat of jumping is part of a publicity stunt. With Kane and Connie perched between the building's imposing columns and the black city sky, occasional searchlights hitting them from below, Mann creates, under the restrictive big studio filming conditions, his first stylized film scene. Of equal merit are the darkly lighted scenes of the doomed gangster desperately confronting Kane in the doctor's office at night. Their dialogue offsets the surrounding gaiety and prefigures both the foreboding Mann crime melodramas and the director's refusal to abandon emotional dimension when depicting unsavory characters:

> TELLI. I'm up to my neck in my own grave. There ain't many people who get asked to do a favor by a dead man—you know it. (*Referring to his hands.*) See, the nails are blue. There's no blood in it!
> KANE. There's blood *on* it!
> TELLI. Not on this![15]

Mann's camera tracks in to Telli from a medium shot to a close-up as he turns away from Kane to stare past the camera, neon blinking on and off against his face:

> TELLI. Help me to do one square thing. I don't know how to pray. I'm afraid of what's out there. My wife killed herself. Hymie Peters—Dutch

Anderson—Maxie Sherman. You don't forget the people you've killed! They stay with you, they don't go away—they wait for you! Help me! I've got to do one square thing!

Dr. Broadway is an agreeable and likable diversion, but it would have benefited from a more consistent tone. This is a factor common in many if not all crime pictures of the pre-*noir* period. Some film reviewers in 1942 were aware of the common problems of using comedy as a crutch in tales of murder and intrigue. An unusually observant *Los Angeles Times* critic (most likely Philip K. Scheuer) noted that

> *Dr. Broadway* is soft-boiled where it could have been hard-boiled. It has the ingredients—a physician who is the pal of everybody on the Big Street, a girl poised on a skyscraper ledge, a paroled killer, and so on—but they all keep going movie on you all the time. This is because the studios still consider it necessary to hoke up any scene that threatens to become serious for more than three minutes. The result here is a continuous build-up, tear-down process that negates all feeling of physical danger as fast as it is created.[16]

Without realizing it, the newspaper critic was craving *film noir*.

Mann brought *Dr. Broadway* in within the allotted schedule. He completed most scenes in fewer than five takes, but a number of complex and less complex shots required more.[17] The scene in which Kane and a police detective discover Telli's corpse (filmed on Stage 10) consists of a pan and dolly through the dark outer office over to the dim room where Kane swings open a door to reveal an ultraviolet ray lamp:

DOYLE. What is it?
KANE. It used to be Vic Telli.

The camera tracks in to the burning light of the lamp. This shot alone required ten takes and was further delayed when the light in the lamp had to be changed (Mann took advantage of the break to rehearse his actors). Four other shots required eleven takes, including one incorporating a camera dolly in the hotel room where Connie is held prisoner. The studio gym was used again in the scene at Benny's Steam Baths in which Kane briefs his merry band of hooligans on their assignments in rescuing Connie. The lengthy camera take begins with a right pan of the gathered throng before the camera tracks back on a boom to include Kane addressing them, continuing backward for a long shot. This involved camera movement required eight takes and was eventually broken up in editing with inserted reaction shots of Kane and other characters.[18]

Mann initially completed *Dr. Broadway* on November 11, after twenty days of shooting that amounted to well under the allotted 80,000-feet of camera negative. Two weeks later, the company reconvened on Stage 13 for one day of retakes, including the scene in which Kane defends Connie in night court and a difficult scene of a woman knocking him unconscious as he enters a cheap hotel room. The latter sounds simple enough, but it originally required eight takes on November 8 and clearly had not proven satisfactory to studio superiors.[19]

Even as innocuous a project as *Dr. Broadway* could not avoid altercations with Joseph I. Breen's Production Code Administration, a studio-controlled entity whose job was to rigidly enforce the nineteenth-century values of its chief Catholic censor and that of the Code itself. Breen organized the PCA in mid-1934 to serve as an enforcer of the 1930 Motion Picture Production Code of Ethics, which the censor and such reactionary groups as the Catholic Legion of Decency felt the Hollywood studios were virtually ignoring. Beginning in 1934, Breen and his office became involved in censoring projects starting at the screenwriting level, demanding approval of all scripts before any film stock could be exposed. The completed pictures then needed PCA blessings before being distributed, but even these Breen-approved productions faced challenges from city and state censorship boards as well as those of other countries. Some examples of Breen's objections are typical of what producers, directors, and writers contended with on a daily basis from the mid-1930s onward. Words such as "hell" and "geez" were to be removed from the script prior to filming.[20] Another Paramount executive, based on Breen office instructions, advised producer Sol Siegel,

> In this scene showing Connie waking up in Dr. Kane's room, she must be clad in at least a slip. It is unacceptable to suggest that Dr. Kane has taken Connie's dress, in order to keep her from leaving the room, but nothing else.[21]

The producer was also instructed that in Connie's three speeches, "the word 'clothes' should be changed to 'dress.'" The censors also became technical advisors when they instructed Siegel to "[p]lease handle Red's slapping of Connie across the face in two cuts, as it will otherwise be deleted by certain boards here, in Canada and Great Britain." The studio ignored this demand. In the released film, the thug commits the act in an unbroken medium shot (his back to the camera, blocking her), the first tough moment in an Anthony Mann picture. The censors also spoiled some of the fun, shortening a Times Square newsvendor's line, "Taxes are up—*pants are down* ... Read all about it!"[22]

THE SELLING OF *DR. BROADWAY*

Not long after Mann completed his first feature film, Paramount dissolved the studio's "B" production division. Mann was not retained and now found himself unemployed in Hollywood.[23] The completed *Dr. Broadway* collected dust for six months, an inordinately long time for a low-budget project. When Paramount finally granted the picture a Manhattan booking in late June 1942 at the Rialto on Broadway, the director was already preparing to direct his second film, the musical *Moonlight in Havana*, for Universal Pictures.

"He's everybody's pal and nobody's fool!" the newspaper ads proclaimed. "Doc's a smooth operator and can break or mend a jaw! ... And What [sic] a bedside manner ... he knows all the angles—and all the curves!"[24] The picture performed unpredictably at theaters around the country. At the Rialto, *Dr. Broadway* opened with what *Variety* deemed a "weak" $5,000 gross, even though in current dollars that amount translates to nearly $71,000. The fact that the Rialto never advertised in any of the daily Manhattan newspapers did not help matters. Another two months elapsed before *Dr. Broadway* reached Los Angeles. The film was the top attraction at two Paramount theaters for one week, paired with Paramount's Ray Milland-Betty Hutton comedy, *Are Husbands Necessary?*, for a combined "meager" and "so-so" $12,500 gross. The Paramount box office musical smash *Holiday Inn*, with Bing Crosby and Fred Astaire, hugely benefited *Dr. Broadway* when booked in a double feature as the main attraction. At the Paramount in San Francisco, the combination earned $69,000 (nearly $1 million adjusted) in four weeks. In Boston, the three-week earnings for the two films reached $82,000. Live entertainment helped fill the void of Crosby and Astaire on screen. In Philadelphia, a house record was broken thanks to the appearance of the Tommy Dorsey Orchestra, resulting in a one-week engagement of $46,700. In Indianapolis, the film benefited from the support of the Sammy Kaye Band and its "Want to Lead a Band?" audience participation stunt. Elsewhere, business was reported "strong" in Seattle, "healthy" in Buffalo, "not so bad" in Chicago, "fair" in St. Louis, and "above average" in Providence, Rhode Island.[25]

Paramount still was not impressed. Matters were not helped by the presence of Universal's *Broadway* and Twentieth Century-Fox's *Just Off Broadway* in the marketplace, which must have confused many moviegoers at the time. In the end, the director was correct: Paramount did not care about his picture. The remaining movies in the trilogy of Borden Chase stories, *Calling Dr. Broadway* and *Death Across the Board*, were never produced.

ANTHONY MANN, FREELANCER

These early Hollywood years for Anthony Mann were plagued with bouts of unemployment, which were particularly difficult on his wife Mildred after she relocated to California with their daughter Toni. According to Nina Mann, her father used his spare time to attend movies, bet the horses, and play bridge, which exacerbated domestic tensions. Unlike the streets of New York, Los Angeles was not a city where Mann could casually encounter people offering professional assistance. He waited for the phone to ring in their Sherman Oaks home.[26] Being cast aside by Paramount, one of the leading film companies in the world, was a dismal beginning for any Hollywood director. It would be eight years before he would return to the Paramount lot in grand fashion to direct his second theatrical western, *The Furies*.

But in 1942, Mann was lagging behind his contemporaries. Billy Wilder remained at Paramount after directing his first Hollywood feature, *The Major and the Minor* (1942), and was rewarded with more lavish assignments. John Huston, who made his directing début with *The Maltese Falcon* (1941), was busy on a follow-up Warners feature with Humphrey Bogart before beginning his wartime film service. After *Citizen Kane* (1941), Orson Welles was directing several projects at RKO Radio Pictures. Meanwhile, Mann's mentor Preston Sturges was preparing his next Paramount comedy, *The Palm Beach Story* (1942).

Without a studio employing him, Mann was left to fend for himself. He labored to get another film project afloat, something closer to his heart and experiences. In 1942, he and Large Hargrove wrote an engrossing twenty-seven-page treatment called *To Men As They Need . . .* , which brought together themes from Mann's experience: religion, theater, political, and social commentary. This story of Manhattan's Little Church Around the Corner, at 1 East Twenty-Ninth Street near Fifth Avenue, was his most personal project, making it all the sadder that it failed to find a corporate benefactor.[27]

Of course, Mann did find employment again as a picture director, but the projects offered him were not of his choosing and well below his talents and abilities. His next several freelance assignments were in fact low-budget musicals. Anthony Mann might have remained a prisoner of this bygone genre had a property more suited to his atmospheric and psychological artistic skills not reached him in 1944.

Figure 4.0. *Strangers in the Night*, 1944. Edith Barrett and Helene Thimig (Photofest).

CHAPTER 4

STRANGERS IN THE NIGHT (1944)

The gothic melodrama *Strangers in the Night* is the strangest and shortest Anthony Mann picture. The film's running time of fifty-six minutes barely qualifies the project for "B" classification. William Terry stars as a wounded U.S. marine searching for a woman named Rosemary with whom he had corresponded while serving in the South Pacific. After military discharge, he travels to California to meet Hilda (Helene Thimig), Rosemary's elderly mother, who assures him that her absent daughter will be returning soon to meet him. As the days pass, the veteran suspects that something is amiss and that Hilda and her repressed female friend Ivy (Edith Barrett) are concealing secrets.

Hilda's idea of a constructive day is to sit in her living room chair with a glass of sherry, toasting the painted portrait of Rosemary, whom she believes to be "the most beautiful creature in the world." Hilda is distrustful of Leslie (Virginia Grey), a recently arrived woman physician, the notion of a female doctor challenging the sensibilities of the Old World recluse. Leslie proclaims unapologetically, "I'm sorry, but if they're going to take all the men into the service, I'm afraid we women'll have to learn to put up with each other."[1] (This fascinating character anticipates the spirited female cabbie of Ann Rutherford in *Two O'Clock Courage* and the starkly independent scientist of Brenda Marshall in *Strange Impersonation*.) Taking the hint from Hilda's rudeness, Leslie departs, promising not to return without invitation. Hilda justifies her rude behavior as a necessary antidote to Leslie's jealousy. "I could see the way she looked at Rosemary's picture," she tells Ivy. "She hated her for being prettier than she is."

The perplexing screenplay of *Strangers in the Night* relies heavily on narrative exaggeration: Johnny noticing Leslie reading *A Shropshire Lad*, the book Rosemary gave him, during a train ride to San Francisco; a calamitous train crash (depicted with a miniature train jumping the track) serving as an excuse for Leslie to display her medical skills. There are nods to Alfred Hitchcock's *Suspicion* (a glass of poisoned milk) and *Rebecca*, the David O. Selznick production for which Mann directed screen tests. Evoking the eerie memory of Mrs. Danvers, Hilda leads Johnny into Rosemary's perfectly preserved room, sliding open closet doors to reveal her daughter's scented clothes: "Can you smell the perfume? The rarest I could get for her." As the camera pans with Hilda hobbling screen right, she comments on how the perfume makes her feel "almost as if she were here, right with us in this room. Can you feel her presence here, Johnny?" (Originally, Johnny was meant to feel more than Rosemary's presence. The May 10, 1944, shooting script has Hilda showing him a fringe of black lace, an item Hollywood censor Joseph I. Breen insisted be removed.)[2]

Strangers in the Night is peculiar enough to prompt one to wonder for whom it was intended. Then we are reminded that it is a Republic Pictures production, the first crime drama Mann directed for the independent studio. As outlandish as this little film is, it cannot be dismissed as a Republic aberration. All three of the Mann Republic crime dramas are compelling oddities needing to be placed within the context of the studio's production history.

Among the hundreds of Republic releases during the 1940s and 1950s are outrageous, stylized, offbeat, low-budget melodramas, which seem to defy genre conventions. Released two years after *Strangers in the Night*, William Thiele's *The Madonna's Secret* (1946), which John Alton photographed in classic gothic *noir* fashion, has a fanatical European central character obsessing over the women's portraits he paints. With equal peculiarity, this film continues some of the twisted themes explored in the Mann picture. Directors of great prestige who had encountered career setbacks injected their own artistic personalities when hired to visualize Republic properties. Frank Borzage's *Moonrise* (1948) follows the tortured path of a young man whose father was hanged for murder. Fritz Lang's *House by the River* (1950) is an extreme gothic melodrama about an arrogant bourgeois writer who murders a woman. *Strangers in the Night* is part of this cycle of Republic Pictures productions.

Mann had no difficulty adapting to the eccentricities of Republic tastes, generating cinematic expression amidst such narrative lunacy, but he was miserable at the studio. "I wouldn't want to say any of my happiest days were spent there," he said many years later. "I would say they were fairly grim! Grim, grim days."[3]

REPUBLIC PICTURES AND *STRANGERS IN THE NIGHT*

Having been dropped by Paramount, Anthony Mann was reduced to freelancing as a director. With the reactivation of the wartime draft and pressures being brought to bear on motion picture industry personnel to support the World War II effort, Mann maintained a low profile, even managing to avoid directing any overt propaganda pictures. (Although his RKO Radio Pictures musical *The Bamboo Blonde* contains elements of propaganda, it did not enter production until after the war officially ended.) The director's second assignment came from Universal Pictures in late summer 1942, the pleasant if routine musical comedy, *Moonlight in Havana*.[4] With another child on the way, he was not in a position to refuse a directing offer from Republic, the largest of the independent Hollywood film factories.

In the Hollywood production-distribution hierarchy of 1944, there were seven major film studios (Paramount, M-G-M, Twentieth Century-Fox, Warner Bros., RKO Radio Pictures, Universal, and Columbia) and one leading independent (United Artists). These so-called "majors" accounted for 270 film releases out of a total of 442. But even the majors could not meet the demands of all 20,355 United States cinemas, so it was left to smaller independent operations to fill the void. Benefiting from the rise in double features during the Great Depression and the fact that only around 7,000 theaters booked single feature programs, these film companies focused, with rare exceptions, exclusively on low-budget pictures that could be distributed on a flat rental basis. Regarded as "B" films, they would be booked into theaters to accompany costlier "A" productions from larger studios.[5]

Hollywood cynics unflatteringly labeled the independent film companies specializing in such "B" product "Poverty Row" operations. Although Harry Cohn's Columbia Pictures was classified as a Poverty Row studio for years, his facility was levels above the others. Other smaller companies had, compared with the majors, microscopic production facilities without backlots. Many owned booking offices and none owned theater circuits. Filming schedules were tight and budgets were miniscule. In 1945, for example, when the average Hollywood feature film cost $554,386 (over $7 million in 2013), Edgar G. Ulmer directed his PRC Poverty Row *film noir Detour* for slightly over $117,000.[6]

Republic Pictures had achieved financial stability through low-budget westerns with Roy Rogers, Bob Steele, and Wild Bill Elliott; movie serials ranging from *Captain America* (1944) to *The Lone Ranger* (1938); and hour-long programmers designed as flat rentals for double features, including *Tahiti Honey* (1943), starring future Mann actor Dennis O'Keefe. Herbert J. Yates, a former American Tobacco Company executive, ran the production end of things, having entered the picture trade in 1915 by launching several film processing laboratories, which eventually crystallized into Consolidated Film Industries (CFI).[7] Republic was successful at this juncture, but the studio was a big comedown for a director who had served a brief apprenticeship at Paramount and had just completed a picture for Universal.

The five Mann Republic films made between 1943 and 1946 had production schedules of one to three weeks. Republic began by handing Mann the musical *Nobody's Darling* (1943), a putting-on-a-show tuner centered on a Hollywood movie star couple's singing-and-dancing daughter. Mann and wife Mildred had their second child, Nina, not long after the release of the picture.[8] Before directing the other Republic musical, *My Best Gal* (1944) with Jane Withers, Mann made *Strangers in the Night*. Although he disliked the latter film as much as he did others preceding it, this Republic melodrama at least steered him back towards the type of suspense material for which he had demonstrated a knack in *Dr. Broadway*. This time, however, there were to be few intended laughs.

Strangers in the Night entered production as *The House of Terror* and filmed for roughly two weeks (perhaps less than that), with production finishing on May 26, 1944. At fifty-six minutes, the movie was among the shortest of Republic's 1944 releases, barely exceeding the length of the average Republic western. Mann benefited from having Reggie Lanning as director of photography. With fifteen film credits in 1944 alone, Lanning was accustomed to working rapidly. Since the seven- to fourteen-day Republic productions were allocated between 23,000- and 45,000-feet of film negative, there is little reason to doubt such restrictions being placed on this Mann picture, particularly during wartime.[9]

Strangers is typical of the get-to-the-point structure of 1940s low-budget production. In the film's first three minutes, we see stock footage (a Republic specialty) of U.S. soldiers battling artillery fire in the jungles of the South Pacific; a newsreel view of soldiers running with a wounded man on a stretcher; the wounded soldier, Sergeant Johnny Meadows (William Terry), diagnosed with a bad back, dispatched to the base hospital where a friendly nurse learns he has been corresponding with Rosemary Blake whose name he discovered scribbled inside *A Shropshire Lad*.

From this point forward, most of the action takes place in the oppressive cliff top mansion of aging dowager Hilda Blake and her timid companion Ivy. It is in these scenes that Mann and Lanning make the most of the material, using reflected firelight to add intensity to the proceedings and occasional low-angles giving the women (particularly Hilda) a sense of menace. Austrian actress Thimig, whose theatrical director husband Max Reinhardt had died in Manhattan the previous October, plays Hilda with bombast and affectation. The pitiable grotesqueness of Hilda's overbearing demeanor, exemplified in piercing eyes, a twisted smile, and a crutch with which she can hobble about her mansion, are the source of unwanted laughter in dramatic moments. What needs to be emphasized, however, is that the modern audience response was present in 1940s cinemas as well, a factor lost on contemporary viewers of ancient movies who cannot conceive of audiences from earlier eras being savvy enough to detect bogus emotions or preposterous narratives. "This little number misses fire on the melodramatic side and, when reviewed yesterday, aroused much unintended laughter," wrote *Daily Variety* after screening it at the Orpheum Theatre in downtown Los Angeles in January 1945.[10]

Thimig's heavily accented English gives a stilted tone to most of her recitations, and actor William Terry's stiff readings only add to the dilemma. Although Mann could not have been enamored with her final performance, he must have had an affinity with the actress due both to her Austrian roots and her legendary husband's world-renowned reputation. The influence Mann had over her hiring cannot be ruled out even if the material may not have been of his choosing.

Mann does what he can to make the project palatable. A well-planned and executed extended camera take (running one minute) in Leslie's office during a visit from Ivy helps explain how Mann was able to shoot the film within such a tight production schedule. Mann and Lanning rise to the occasion in subsequent uses of the grand staircase in the mansion where actors are strategically arranged during dramatic moments or when hard light casts high-contrast shadows on the wall at night. Only in a living room scene where Hilda chastises Ivy for confiding in Leslie does Mann show a lapse in directorial judgment. The camera films them from inside the fireplace, a flame shooting upward, an archaic cliché Hitchcock and Billy Wilder ridiculed. This device fortunately never reappears in an Anthony Mann crime picture. (In his interview with Hitchcock, François Truffaut mentioned a British film attempting a "Hitchcock touch" by filming from inside a refrigerator. When asked if he would have directed it that way, Hitchcock responded, "Certainly not. That's like shooting through the fireplace, behind the flames." Wilder told Cameron Crowe, "I never shoot through the flames of the fireplace in the foreground, because that is from the point of Santa Claus.")[11]

The denouement occurs in the living room when Leslie and Johnny confront Hilda beneath Rosemary's portrait. As closet skeletons are divulged, Helene Thimig, presumably through Mann's careful manipulations, does an eloquent and touching acting turn. In a single take lasting one minute and thirty-three seconds, her soliloquy begins in long shot as she stands beneath the painting, talking painfully about her deceptions as the true author of

Rosemary's letters. With the camera gradually tracking towards her, stopping in wide-angle medium shot, she recalls the joy she experienced knowing that Johnny loved Rosemary's mind: "You gave me the happiest day I've ever known. Because it was *my* mind you were talking about. You were loving *me*, Johnny."

Regretfully, the proceedings unravel from this point, with Thimig returning to her over-the-top acting technique as she attempts to turn the tables on Johnny and Leslie, going so far as to sabotage their car brakes. The raucous finale between Hilda and her Rosemary portrait must have created gales of laughter among 1944–45 ticket holders, much as it does for current audiences.

Strangers in the Night barely escaped the Republic Pictures film laboratories. Its fleeting running time guaranteed it virtual obscurity in the marketplace and a lower stature than a majority of second-tier releases lasting ten to fifteen minutes longer. Consequently, it is the most difficult of the Mann crime films to trace. The earliest reported major city engagement for the picture was in various Chicago theaters where it shared the bill with Columbia's *They Live in Fear* and the Warner Bros./Raoul Walsh/Errol Flynn wartime drama, *Uncertain Glory*. The film did not play New York City in 1944 but did appear in a second-run cinema in Brooklyn where for three days in November 1944 it supported the adaptation of Eugene O'Neill's *The Hairy Ape* (United Artists). At another second-run Brooklyn house the following week, it took bottom billing to a Republic programmer of similar length, *Hidden Valley Outlaws*. In Boston, Anthony Mann's film was brilliantly teamed at two cinemas with the recent Paramount release from his mentor Preston Sturges, *Hail the Conquering Hero*, although it is doubtful the bookers were aware of their own cleverness.[12]

At other second-run cinemas, it accompanied a high-end Republic musical, *Atlantic City* (photographed by John Alton), Jean Negulesco's *The Conspirators* (Warner Bros.), and Rowland V. Lee's unpopular adaptation of Thornton Wilder's *The Bridge of San Luis Rey* (UA). Finally, at the very end of December 1944, the picture made an appearance at one theater in the Ventura County suburbs, sixty miles outside Los Angeles. Later in January, it appeared at an Oceanside, California, theater before its belated release at the Orpheum in downtown Los Angeles. As the sole film supporting Duke Ellington and his Orchestra on the Orpheum stage, *Strangers in the Night* was finally a success. Even if the audience found the film underwhelming, the presence of Ellington guaranteed "boff" business at $39,500.[13]

CHAPTER 5

TWO O'CLOCK COURAGE (1945)

"I am somebody—but who? I am accused of murder, but I have lost my memory. My innocence depends upon who I am. If you know—help me!"[1]

Thus stated the publicity tack card for theater owners promoting Anthony Mann's *Two O'Clock Courage* in 1945. Tom Conway appears on the card pressing a handkerchief to the side of his head, an image taken from the opening scene. The Conway character has a Kafkaesque name, "The Man," for most of the narrative because he is an amnesiac. At the start of the film, the screen is completely black following the credits until The Man staggers away, with his back to the camera, and we find ourselves on a dark, foggy, *film noir*-like street. A foghorn sounds in the distance and The Man grabs onto a street lamp and looks up, the camera craning upward to reveal the

Figure 5.0. *Two O'Clock Courage*, 1945. Ann Rutherford and Tom Conway (Photofest).

Figure 5.1

street signs before returning to a medium shot of the protagonist. He notices blood trickling down the side of his face (fig. 5.1) and moves to step off the curb until, in wider shot, he narrowly avoids walking into an oncoming taxi.[2]

This is where the basic *film noir* aspects of *Two O'Clock Courage* cease. As soon as the taxi screeches to a stop and whimsical cab driver Patty (Ann Rutherford) introduces herself, the picture's tone shifts dramatically from suspense tale to comic mystery. The couple soon learns that The Man fits the description of a chauffeur accused of murdering a famous theatrical producer. Convinced of The Man's innocence through her incessant spirited banter, Patty is determined to clear him and assist in uncovering his true identity. The Man and Patty spend a long night together in apartments, nightclubs, mansions, and "Harry," Patty's taxi, unraveling a labyrinthine plot involving a mysterious actress and her suitor, a writer of sinister character, a sarcastic female fortune hunter, and a stolen stage play.

Produced for RKO Radio Pictures, *Two O'Clock Courage* was Mann's first major studio assignment since Universal's *Moonlight in Havana* two years earlier. That the film is a remake of a 1936 RKO programmer dilutes the assignment's prestige. The earlier movie *Two in the Dark* starred Walter Abel as The Man and Margot Grahame as the woman, and was based on the 1934 Gelett Burgess novel *Two O'Clock Courage*. Both pictures are typical of 1930s and early 1940s light suspense fare emphasizing good-natured thrills rather than darkly motivated violence and tension associated with *film noir* and the *film policier*. Broad caricatures and even broader comic relief tend to neutralize what little genuine anxiety reaches the screen. As happened with *Dr. Broadway* in 1942, some *Two O'Clock Courage* critics were aware of the drawbacks of such formulas. An anonymous 1945 trade reviewer warned that "[t]oo much talk and an excess amount of mugging doom this entry to the lower half [of double features]."[3]

Indeed, Mann's 1945 remake, despite crime screenwriter Robert E. Kent's participation, is more comical in tone and contains more slapstick than the 1936 version from director Ben Stoloff. No matter, the Mann version has the advantage of modernizing its female lead from a stranded actress to a taxi driver, a change inspired either by World War II manpower shortages or perhaps the influences of left-wing writer Gordon Kahn.[4] Taking into account the extreme conditions under which Mann was toiling at RKO, *Two O'Clock Courage* is a smooth and efficient entertainment whose confident tone, winning lead performances, and infectious good nature obscure the hastiness in which it was produced. While hampered at times by a conflicting narrative tone, this is the least intense and most "fun" of the Anthony Mann crime pictures.

MANN AT RKO RADIO PICTURES

RKO Radio Pictures was the newest of the eight major studios, the result of a series of 1928 distribution and exhibition mergers involving, among others, Radio Corporation of America, the Rockefellers, Joseph P. Kennedy, and Pathé Exchange.[5] Despite David O. Selznick's production leadership in the early 1930s, the successes of the 1931 *Cimarron* (which Mann remade at M-G-M in the late 1950s), *King Kong* (1933), and the escapist musicals of Fred Astaire and Ginger Rogers (1933–39), financial crises plagued the studio during the Great Depression. RKO began to reverse monetary losses after a large investment trust bought out RCA and the Rockefellers. With George Schaefer installed as president in 1938, RKO attracted Samuel Goldwyn, Orson Welles, and Alfred Hitchcock, but the critical and artistic successes of Schaefer's régime (*Citizen Kane* being the pinnacle) coincided with a new downturn in profits.[6]

RKO Theatres executive Charles Koerner replaced Schaefer in 1942 and pursued a profitable budget-conscious slate of exploitable pictures, including the atmospheric 1942–46 chillers of producer Val Lewton (*Cat People, The Seventh Victim, I Walked with a Zombie*). Presumably Welles's nemesis Koerner was ignorant of Mann's similar left-leaning New York theatrical pedigree when the studio boss approved Mann remaking the *Two O'Clock Courage* story.[7] Judging from Mann's initial RKO projects (this comic mystery and the two musicals which followed), studio management viewed him as little more than a director for hire on pictures already in advanced stages of development.

The *Two O'Clock Courage* production schedule was stricter than that of the 1936 version. *Two in the Dark* had been given twenty-five camera days, not counting pickup shots, but Mann's remake was limited to sixteen days. In August 1944, Mann directed the picture on seven RKO studio stages. He may also have directed two hours of retakes on September 20, provided his commitments to *The Great Flamarion* did not prevent him. RKO supplied a paltry budget of $138,587 ($1,830,000 in 2013) and 50,000 feet of black-and-white camera negative. Mann ultimately exceeded the footage allotment by 5,790 feet.[8] Even with his shorter filming schedule, Mann was able to integrate showy technical touches, including a more mobile cinematographic approach to several key scenes.

Analyses of both the 1936 and 1945 films invite positive and negative comparisons. The Stoloff edition does benefit from having RKO cinematographer Nicholas Musuraca behind the camera. Mann never collaborated with Musuraca, a master of dark lighting and shadows who photographed not only *Two in the Dark* but some of the key RKO crime melodramas of the 1940s and early 1950s.[9] Musuraca's opening shot in *Two in the Dark* demonstrates the cinematic impact he brought to an otherwise pedestrian mystery: an extreme close-up of the eyes of The Man as background music plays. Blood runs down from a forehead injury as he moves his head screen left before turning and walking toward the background. But what Mann was able to achieve in a single camera movement, Stoloff and technicians assemble in three separate shots, the third being a tilt and rack-focus (not a crane movement) from the injured hero to the street sign. On the other hand, the park scene immediately following this, where The Man encounters the actress and arouses the suspicions of a beat cop (Ward Bond), is superior to that of the 1945 remake. There is no dialogue between the two leads at first, only the background music, and inspired uses of point-of-view and reaction shots seldom seen in a Hollywood movie of the late 1930s (including a striking POV angle of the actress filmed through The Man's open hands).[10]

The rest of *Two in the Dark* is unable to surpass these opening minutes. In terms of major narrative elements and scenes, *Two O'Clock Courage* follows the 1936 picture fairly closely but with far more energy and panache. Unlike Walter Abel and Margot Grahame, both of whom are rigid performers, Mann's stars Tom Conway and Ann Rutherford display screen chemistry. The remake is also adjusted to accommodate the woman's new vocation as in a taxi scene where Patty is the driver, not a passenger.[11] Another example of where Mann asserts himself despite RKO's suffocating budget is the scene in which Patty escorts The Man to the police station. The 1936 version films their arrival in two simple stationary shots (following the usual establishing shot of the precinct sign), culminating in a stack of newspapers being tossed from a passing truck, revealing a murder headline.

In comparison, Mann opts for a stately display of in-camera exposition through a virtually unbroken camera take. His shot begins on a lighted precinct sign, the camera craning down to show cops and civilians entering and exiting the police building before the camera pans over to Patty's parked taxi as a newsboy announces the slaying of stage producer Robert Dilling. Patty exits her cab with The Man, the camera panning left until she stops to buy a paper. An insert of the *Daily Mirror* headline, "ROBERT DILLING MURDERED! Famous Stage Producer Slain at Ocean View Estate," aborts Mann's *plan-séquence*, which he will invoke six years later when Dick Powell enters a train station early in *The Tall Target* (see Chapter 16). When we return to the master shot, the couple opts not to meet with police.[12]

Two O'Clock Courage jeopardizes the gripping amnesia premise through applications of broad comedy when the couple seeks to determine whether The Man is or is not the suspected ex-chauffeur. An overacting maid (Maxine Seamon) at the chauffeur's apartment building establishes the tone for the introduction of two characters best suited for installments of *The Saint* or *Charlie Chan* than an Anthony Mann murder saga. Inspector Bill Brenner (Emory Parnell) and churlish reporter Haley (Richard Lane) nearly drag the picture down to Abbott & Costello levels during an eleven-minute stretch that is of interest only to those curious to observe how Mann navigates undiscerning slapstick. Between the puns, the shenanigans, the corny quips, and the aforementioned mugging in scenes in which these two men appear, viewers may be forgiven for wishing to abandon *Two O'Clock Courage*. These two characters are present in the 1936 edition, but actors Alan Hale and Wallace Ford (as inspector and reporter) appear to be underplaying compared with Mann's two actors. Unfortunately, things get worse before they get better. In a prolonged bit of tomfoolery in the murder victim's living room, Brenner orders Haley to pretend to be a corpse so that The Man can get a better sense of what happened on the night of the killing. The scene has vaudeville-style slow burns, pratfalls, grimaces, and banal comic dialogue not evident in the 1936 screenplay (Brenner: "Oh, why didn't I stay a simple cop walking my beat leading children across the street by the hand?").

Through some miracle, *Two O'Clock Courage* recovers from these eleven minutes. Although Brenner and Haley do not disappear, they are wisely shifted to the background as Patty and The Man return to their rightful central positions. The audience belatedly warms up to the two central protagonists in a new scene written for this version where Patty brings The Man to her townhouse apartment so that she can change out of her working clothes. The comic complications involving her eavesdropping landlady Mrs. Tuttle (Sarah Edwards), complete with double-entendres, elicit genuine amusement. There is witty sexual innuendo when Mrs. Tuttle overhears Patty modeling an evening dress with a rabbit skin wrap and asking The Man if she looks better with her suit off. When The Man responds that he cannot remember ever seeing anyone prettier, the landlady has a disgusted reaction to Patty's response: "Now that's a fine compliment considering you can't even remember what happened two hours ago!" Joseph I. Breen of the Production Code Administration did not find this dialogue very funny and issued his usual warnings to the studio. RKO assured the Hollywood censor that "Mrs. Tuttle's reaction will be played on a quizzical note and shot in such a way that it can be conveniently deleted if necessary."[13] This sequence, culminating with the couple sneaking out through a separate door and Patty jolting Mrs. Tuttle with a "Boo!," demonstrates that the comic elements of *Two O'Clock Courage* can work if not performed too broadly.

The film is also enlivened during an extended scene at the Blue Room supper club (filmed on Stage 5 at RKO) where Jane Greer (billed Bettejane), revealing an underused comic persona, brightens the proceedings as flirtatious society snob Helen who recognizes The Man. The future femme fatale of *Out of the Past* (1947) achieves a delicate balance of acerbic wit and menace, her sarcastic interactions with the two leads being among the high points of *Two O'Clock Courage*. With delicious putdowns peppering her dialogue, one wishes Greer had a more prominent role in the picture. The supper club scenes easily surpass those from the 1936 version.

As The Man and Patty continue their investigative work, the narrative moves conventionally from one interior setting to the next. Mann's directorial approach, no doubt hampered by tight scheduling conditions, is conventional to a point and generally adheres to the 1936 screenplay structure and content. But Mann knows when to distance himself from the earlier film. An atmospherically lighted and suspenseful scene where The Man breaks in at night to the murdered producer's house in search of the *Two O'Clock Courage* play manuscript is directorially superior to the previous version but RKO editorial intervention weakens it. Beginning with an establishing shot of the Dilling house (originally to have been a practical location but dropped for budgetary reasons) and coinciding with a music cue, the action cuts to the interior of the dark study where a light shines through a curtained window. The Man is outside shining the light and the camera moves across the dark study to the French-style window from where he enters, and follows him over to a desk. A cut to a double door reveals a turning knob and the door opening automatically, prompting an eerie music cue. The Man searches through papers until he finds the manuscript. At this point, the studio abruptly inserts an earlier close-up of the manuscript cover page during which The Man is heard off-screen reciting the printed words on the page. This is an obvious RKO postproduction addition that does not appear either in the shooting script or the 1936 version's filmed scene.[14]

Mann surpasses the 1936 version in his handling of the flashback following The Man getting shot while attempting to leave with the manuscript. An image of the playwright arguing with The Man, photographed through a superimposed gauze-like resolution, appears over an extreme close-up (incorporating a partial zoom at the flashback's open and close) of the half-conscious Man. There are more twists and gunfire between the unseen killer and Brenner's cops before Dilling's murderer is revealed at the plagiarist's apartment.[15] Mann predictably shines in this sequence as his camera tracks with Brenner and The Man moving quickly across the apartment patio, bullets and shattered glass soon startling them. The 1936 version of this scene is staged in a more pedestrian fashion.

By the time it reaches its satisfactory resolution, *Two O'Clock Courage* has succeeded in engaging the audience. Even the final phone alert between reporter Haley and his annoyed editor elicits an authentic laugh.

SELLING *TWO O'CLOCK COURAGE*

RKO Radio Pictures treated *Two O'Clock Courage* as a "B" release, but the top billing of Tom Conway, brother of actor George Sanders and star of RKO's popular *Falcon* series, got the film slightly more attention from the sales department. RKO arranged for a national magazine advertising campaign for Trimz Ready-Pasted Wallpaper ("The New Miracle Wallpaper you just dip in water and apply!") featuring Ann Rutherford.[16] The studio suggested theater owners exploit the picture by publishing a classified newspaper ad:

> WANTED—information! Anyone who can identify the man wearing a pinstripe suit, weighs 160 lbs., has dark hair and brown eyes, looks like Tom Conway and wears a hat with the initials "R.D." Please communicate with the

Palace Theatre. His true identity will prove him innocent of murder in "Two O'Clock Courage" starring Tom Conway and Ann Rutherford.[17]

RKO recommended that theaters print fake newspaper headlines with "Robert Dilling Murdered!" in large typeface, items from the exhibitors' pressbook accompanying it:

> Fold the newspaper in half and have it carried so that the headline can be plainly seen. For a greater effect have newsboys shout the usual sensational jargon used by paper peddlers. Distribute the newspaper free on the streets, in hotels and in the theatre lobby.[18]

Theater managers were advised to build a large clock face in their lobbies with the hands pointing to two o'clock and the heads of Conway and Rutherford in the center. For "Eye Catching Ballyhoo" (the industry term for flamboyant publicity gimmicks) exhibitors were encouraged to dress a man up as a walking alarm clock, a giant bell atop his ahead, to "intrigue the public."[19] The exploitation department also suggested the "swell stunt" of arranging for a "mystery man" to appear on the streets near a theater during the film's engagement:

> Run his photo in the newspapers, and in your lobby, wearing a mask. On the opening day of the picture and for three continuous days during the run, have this man appear on the streets without his mask. Offer prizes to anyone who recognizes him. Tie in this stunt with your merchants by having the mystery man appear in their stores at specified times. Play this up in a big way, as it will create plenty of curiosity. The mystery man and those who recognize him should be introduced from your stage.[20]

The sudden death of President Franklin Roosevelt on April 12, 1945, affected the film's Manhattan release, many New York cinemas going dark for all or part of the following day, when *Two O'Clock Courage* opened at the Rialto. This resulted in only a "mild" $5,500 gross at the Rialto, which, as was its custom, declined to purchase any newspaper advertising. RKO teamed *Courage* with Walt Disney's animated *The Three Caballeros* in the ensuing weeks and rotated the double feature in its circuit of cinemas within the five boroughs. In Los Angeles, the city that permanently established multiple theater engagements for most commercial releases, the picture played at two RKO cinemas, supporting RKO's *The Enchanted Cottage*, for a strong $45,600 opening week before dropping the second week to $26,300. In

Boston, a box office-killing heat wave harmed the picture despite on-stage appearances of Eddie "Rochester" Anderson, the Johnny Richards Orchestra, and big-band singer Nan Wynn. (Even in 1945, the $21,000 gross for the week was considered "sad" by *Variety*.) Chicago was kinder to *Two O'Clock Courage* where it supported Abbott & Costello's Universal comedy *The Naughty Nineties* for a "good" opening week return of $25,000 and an equally strong five-day holdover.[21]

Anthony Mann had barely gotten settled at RKO when the independent studio Republic Pictures beckoned him for another assignment. This time he would be directing one of the great screen personalities in all of Hollywood, and one of the most difficult.

CHAPTER 6

THE GREAT FLAMARION (1945)

The theme of a calculating female destroying a gullible male is a mainstay in motion pictures and popular fiction, in religious legends and Italian operas. In the early twentieth century, the morality films of the 1910s and 1920s frequently exploited this subject, most poetically in F. W. Murnau's 1927 expressionist drama, *Sunrise: A Song of Two Humans*, and in silent melodramas featuring female flappers (the "vamps" inspired by the 1897 Rudyard Kipling poem, "The Vampire") targeting weak men for destruction. Josef von Sternberg's *The Blue Angel* (Germany, 1930) and Jean Renoir's *La Chienne* (France, 1931) both addressed the subject at the dawn of the sound era. In 1945, Fritz Lang remade *La Chienne* in Hollywood as *Scarlet Street*, one of the major *film noir* melodramas of the decade. However, *The*

Figure 6.0. *The Great Flamarion*, 1945. Erich von Stroheim and Mary Beth Hughes (Photofest).

Great Flamarion, Anthony Mann's own variation on the theme, was released eleven months before *Scarlet Street*.

The Vicki Baum short story upon which the Mann film is based is barely visible in the finished picture. On September 19, 1936, *Collier's* magazine published Baum's "Big Shot," a tale of an aloof Swiss sharpshooter named Brandt who performs acts of derring-do with a traveling European circus. Obsessed only with his profession, Brandt trains Ria, the young daughter of a recently deceased circus performer, to be the glamorous stooge in his tense act, holding up playing cards and other items for him to shoot to smithereens. Brandt and Ria marry but the circus environment, coupled with his detachment, soon get the better of her. Ria meets the handsome Hungarian singer Guy during a European engagement and the young couple embarks on an illicit affair, which continues during the circus tour. Ria is excited when Guy watches her stage act "in a frenzy of nervousness," but Guy fears for her safety once Brandt learns of the affair. Brandt challenges Guy to a post-performance duel but shoots himself in the courtyard when he realizes the young man is willing to die for Ria. Circus employees discover Brandt's corpse and Baum's narration ends, "He was lying near the vines, and he looked contented."[1]

In the film version, Brandt is transformed into Flamarion, an aging, arrogant vaudeville sharpshooter who falls in love with sexy deceiver Connie, the woman who, along with her worthless alcoholic husband Al, is part of the marksman's stage act. Seeing Flamarion as the solution to escaping her spouse, the *femme fatale* flirts and seduces her way into the elder man's heart, convincing him of her love and manipulating Flamarion into "accidentally" shooting Al during a performance. Connie eventually double-crosses Flamarion, thus ushering in the sharpshooter's descent into personal and professional ruin, where he is reduced to pawning his cherished pistols while obsessively searching her whereabouts. All that remains of the Baum material are elements of the stage act where the sharpshooter's bullets sever cigarette tips and shoot away flowers on a wreath binding Connie's hair.[2]

It is coincidental yet intriguing that a second Mann Republic Pictures production has Austrian elements. Not only was Mann using the material of Austrian novelist Baum (whose 1929 novel *Menschen im Hotel* became M-G-M's *Grand Hotel* in 1932), he was again assigned an Austrian actor, and one of the most confrontational in the picture business. Cast in the role of the self-destructive, egomaniacal Flamarion is Erich von Stroheim. The writer/director/actor previously promoted as "The Man You Love to Hate" had clashed with studios during the 1920s over lavish budgets and epic running times on his grand cinematic achievements *Foolish Wives* (1922), *The Merry Widow* (1925), *The Wedding March* (1928), and, most famously, *Greed* (1924). Banned from directing after 1933, Stroheim won acclaim acting in Renoir's *La Grande Illusion* (1937) and Billy Wilder's *Five Graves to Cairo* (1943), but such roles became increasingly rare for the star who was at his lowest professional ebb when he starred in *The Great Flamarion* in 1944. Mann told Jean-Claude Missiaen:

> ... *The Great Flamarion*, produced by Billy Wilder's brother, was a little more ambitious. In fact, I still have a very bad impression of [Erich] von Stroheim: coat-collar turned up, monocle and shaven head, he certainly created a presence, but as an actor—oh my God! My only strong point was the shooting-gallery sequence, and also Dan Duryea [as Al], whom I'd just noticed on a Broadway stage! After that film and the two or three which followed, nobody wanted to hear about me ... [3]

Mann judged his fourth Republic film (and its temperamental star) too harshly. From a studio perspective, it was a step up from *Strangers in the Night* in that the picture boasted stronger production values and two reels of additional material. *Flamarion* also gave the director an opportunity to tap into his previous theater experiences while telling a backstage theatrical story with, given the censorship limits of the day, an erotic undercurrent.

Mann knew the show business terrain and how to visualize it. The subtly spectacular opening shot (lasting one minute and thirty-eight seconds) conveys the director's affection for the less glamorous side of the entertainment world. After stock footage establishes 1936 Mexico City, the action dissolves to the exterior of a theater, the camera following a group of people to the box office and then into the auditorium where a mariachi player sings "Cielito Lindo" on stage. The camera tracks behind latecomers roaming the central aisle, the audience applauding a male dancer and the singer. After the vaudeville curtain rings down and the women are seated, the pit orchestra strikes up and the camera moves closer to Tony the Clown (Lester Allen) performing comic antics to off-screen laughter. His vaudeville routine is interrupted by sounds of two gunshots.[4]

This may be the start of the movie, but it is nearing the end of the story. Flamarion has already taken out his revenge on Connie and is now crawling around the above catwalk, wounded from her gunshot and hiding from police. Flamarion plunges to the stage after everyone but Tony the Clown has left the darkened theater, and as he lies dying, he volunteers a "before I die, I wanna tell you, Tony, why I killed her" confession in order to set up the ensuing flashback. Stroheim hated flashbacks in films and tried unsuccessfully to talk the moviemakers out of using one in *The Great Flamarion*. Any project with Stroheim automatically guaranteed his input into the screenplay and a potential clash of wills if a director or producer were not amenable to his detailed recommendations. In this case, Stroheim was correct. The picture would have been superior had the narrative been told in a linear fashion. Instead, the ending is given away at the very start and the story proper does not begin until nearly twelve minutes into the film. (Billy Wilder blamed his brother William for copying the flashback structure of *Double Indemnity*, which had been completed the previous spring.)[5]

The Great Flamarion is an impersonal assignment for Mann with a subpar screenplay, but between the director's confident stylistics and the strength of the lead performers, the thriller transcends its limitations. Stroheim and costar Mary Beth Hughes (as the duplicitous Connie) were the most complicated of Mann's screen characters at that time, two sociopaths concealing their dark pasts and ulterior motives from each other. In this duel of self-destructive personages, the two performers, despite conflicting acting styles, share a series of pungent scenes. In particular, the lovely looking Hughes is a revelation. Eroding Flamarion's gloomy resolve, her predacious Connie (whose previous transgressions include insurance fraud and thievery) transitions from seduction to repulsion and from desperation to aggression with a fluidity that would have led most actresses to mental collapse. With Mann guiding her behind the camera, Hughes overcomes these acting challenges with astonishing ease. To cite one example, Flamarion, in a scene at a Chinese restaurant, reaches down to kiss her hand and her reaction is a smooth display of understated contempt, Hughes's face changing from warmth to coldness once his head is bowed, and then back again. In a park scene following Flamarion being cleared in Al's death, Hughes's eyes, seen behind a widow's veil, cautiously move in Flamarion's direction as she utters her final words of deception. It is no small achievement that Hughes endures such melodramatic methodology without making her character laughable. Unlike lesser talents, Hughes maintains her dignity despite such ungainly dialogue as, "Don't be a sap! That guy wouldn't be interested in Venus unless she had a coupla guns in her girdle."

The so-called shooting gallery scene for which Mann claimed to be pleased is actually a vaudeville act at the start of the flashback set in a dressing room. Two lovers are interrupted by, presumably, the woman's husband (elegantly dressed Flamarion), who blasts his way on stage and proceeds to fire bullets into a champagne glass and bottle held by the woman. When she puts a cigarette in her mouth, Flamarion lights it with another bullet before

Figure 6.1

Figure 6.2

blowing off the tip of her cigarette. In an erotically charged moment, the woman reveals a shapely leg with garter through the slit of her gown and as she attempts to fix her face with her compact, Flamarion fires again, causing the right strap on the gown to drop from her shoulder (figs. 6.1 and 6.2).[6]

The marksman's remaining bullets (he fires backwards while staring into the woman's compact) intended for the hidden lover shatter a potted plant and umbrella stand. As the discovered man bobs from side to side in front of the dressing mirror, Flamarion shoots out a series of mirror bulbs. Portions of the woman's headpiece are the next to be shot off (although these magically reappear for the curtain call) for a crowd-pleasing comic denouement.

Mann's criticisms notwithstanding, the performance of Stroheim is not to be taken at face value. The actor at first sounds a single note in his interpretation of Flamarion, reciting monotone and periodically clumsy line deliveries from a morose face with a permanently furrowed brow. The transformation of the character as Connie intensifies her psychological assault cancels out whatever conclusions we may have drawn about Stroheim's performance. Admittedly, this is not an unusual part for the actor whose self-effacing roles as show business has-been increased after he appeared in *The Great Gabbo* in 1929. Stroheim is nonetheless better suited to the material here, surrounded as he is by a director on the ascension (Mann), not the decline (James Cruze).

The sadomasochistic mind games between Flamarion and Connie, in which she gradually deceives him into believing Al is jealous of her alleged love for Flamarion, make *The Great Flamarion* unexpectedly compelling. An early apartment scene where she falsely confesses her love is laden with sexual symbolism to which Joseph I. Breen and his Production Code Administration paid no attention. Connie visits the sharpshooter at night as he sits in the dark firing at swinging targets with a long-barreled pistol, dressed in a fascistic black shirt. She feigns arousal while recounting the excitement of their stage performances, "facing the man who holds my life in his hands," whose bullet eventually causes her shoulder strap to fall. Barely recovering from the sensual thrill, she adds, "I tell myself that it was your hand. Every bullet is a caress."

The implicit eroticism intensifies in the next camera angle, a medium shot of Flamarion, his phallic gun pointing rightward (fig. 6.0). Once she looks longingly at him, he lowers the gun in symbolic surrender even though there is no physical intimacy that night. (Breen may have overlooked this, but he tried and failed to get Republic to cut Flamarion's subsequent narration, "It was three days from Pittsburgh to San Francisco and in all that time, she never went back to her husband." Nor was he able to prevent the filmmakers from showing Connie reclining on Flamarion's berth in the train compartment scene.[7]) After the affair begins, Connie examines one of Flamarion's pistols:

CONNIE. You're proud of these, aren't you?
FLAMARION. They were my only friends until I found you.

She playfully aims the pistol at him and soon begins massaging the gun barrel (another touch overlooked by Breen), informing him she "dreamed" Flamarion fired at Al and fatally missed (fig. 6.3).

The seed is planted in James M. Cain fashion, and her words will haunt him as they would any *noir* patsy: "Al stood before the mirror. You fired and missed ... fired and missed ... fired and missed."

Figure 6.3

The dimensionality of Stroheim's performance emerges after the coroner clears Flamarion. Spending great sums in a high-end Chicago hotel suite to await his love (who already has $10,000 of his money), Flamarion smiles, whistles, spins about the room, and admires himself in mirrors, unaware that Connie is off in Latin America with her new lover. According to *New York Post* film critic Archer Winston, these hotel scenes made certain 1945 audiences uncomfortable:

> [W]hen von Stroheim cuts a stately caper under the spell of her expected arrival, the audience titters. Passion can embarrass most people when seen activating the carcasses of the middle-aged.[8]

Ageist audience reactions aside, Stroheim's interpretation of a tortured and delusional man letting down his defenses only to suffer further pain and degradation, is persuasive. His own professional travails during the 1930s, which included pawning cherished possessions in order to support his family, were clearly brought to bear on the performance. Stroheim comprehended humiliation and ruination better than anyone in Hollywood.

The final confrontation between Flamarion and Connie, potently captured with dark lighting and a dressing mirror (the mirror being a favorite tool for Mann's key crime compositions) contains dialogue similar to the cruel words Joan Bennett hurls at Edward G. Robinson in *Scarlet Street*. The similarity in fact is enough to make one wonder if the Lang film plagiarized the Mann film. Hughes aims an ivory-handled pistol at Stroheim and unleashes a diatribe: "Why, you poor sucker! How could anyone love you? That fat bull neck! Those squinty eyes! You're old! You're ugly! Even the touch of you made me sick! I hated you and I've always hated you!" Bennett's words to Robinson are, "I wanted to laugh in your face ever since I first met you! You're old and ugly and I'm sick of you! Sick! Sick! Sick!"⁹

FILMING AND SELLING *THE GREAT FLAMARION*

The budget for *The Great Flamarion* was in the $150,000 range, or slightly under $2 million in 2013. Mann shot the picture in eighteen days under the working title *Dead Pigeon*, with filming beginning September 11, 1944, at the historic Chaplin Studios at 1416 N. La Brea in Hollywood. That RKO Radio Pictures ordered two hours of morning retakes for *Two O'Clock Courage* on September 20 confuses our understanding of the *Flamarion* production schedule. It is unclear whether *Flamarion* suspended production on that day; whether Mann juggled both assignments (the RKO lot was only a five-minute drive from the Chaplin lot); or whether RKO assigned another director to handle the *Courage* retakes.¹⁰ (*Flamarion* was the first of the two pictures to reach cinemas in 1945.)

Mann recalled his experiences directing another legendary director:

> Von Stroheim, to say the least, was difficult. He was a personality, not really an actor. He looked well on film. But he was a great director. I'll never forget one thing he said: "Tony, do you want to be a great director? Photograph the whole of *Great Flamarion* through my monocle!" I said: "That's a helluva idea, but I only have $150,000 and fourteen days." I said: "It might be a fascinating idea, but I'll let you do it."¹¹

There were challenges with the actor in the park scene between Flamarion and Connie. Mann remembered this scene being filmed entirely in fog:

> We had no money: couldn't do it outside or even inside. We didn't even have a park, so we decided to do it in a fog. We filled the studio with fog and had a bench and a light, and it looked like a park.¹²

Stroheim was to emerge from the fog and ask for her forwarding address, but the actor wanted to incorporate a pen and address book as his props. Mann reported Stroheim continuously failing to work with these props (either he could not access them easily or the pen was out of ink) and causing filming delays. "By this time, the fog had vanished, and it took another hour to fill up our bare stage with fog again."¹³

The results tell a different story. There is no fog in the scene. Hughes and Stroheim sit on a park bench in front of an artificial tree and shrubbery against a night backdrop with more trees, plus occasional passing extras. Stroheim, who fumbles his dialogue in this scene, reaches into an inside pocket for the address book and pen to jot down information. There is a cut to a single shot of Hughes as she continues telling him her address and warning him not to send her gifts ("widows shouldn't have admirers"), then a return to the master shot. By this time, Stroheim no longer has the pen and address book and instead reaches into a jacket pocket for the $10,000 to give her. In spite of Mann's faulty memory concerning the fog, the editing confirms that adjustments were needed to compensate for Stroheim's mishandling of props.

Despite Republic having ignored some of his censorship suggestions, Joseph I. Breen granted the film a PCA seal one day after viewing the completed work on November 7, 1944. Contrary to Mann's recollections, newspaper and trade reviews were mixed but not outright hostile, although a few Manhattan critics suggested that *Flamarion* was anachronistic and too much in the manner of "a pre-war continental film."[14]

The picture opened in January 1945 at Republic's showcase cinema in Manhattan. There were decent-sized newspaper ads ("He's GREAT with a gun—and he's got to kill!"), but business was fair to poor during the three-week engagement. In Kansas City, the film had mediocre returns leading a double feature in spite of a live stage act and the personal appearance of star Mary Beth Hughes, who grew up in the region. The picture did "modest" business in Indianapolis and was "oke" in Louisville, where it supported RKO's *Having Wonderful Crime* featuring future *Border Incident* costar George Murphy. On the other hand, business was "neat" in Baltimore as a single feature and in St. Louis at the giant five thousand-seat Fox, where it supported Warners' *Hotel Berlin*. Response was "great" in Seattle thanks to singing star Alan Jones performing on stage; and in Los Angeles the picture earned a satisfactory $26,600 in three cinemas as a supporting feature for the *Brewster's Millions* remake from future *T-Men* and *Raw Deal* producer Edward Small (and starring Dennis O'Keefe). *Flamarion* returned to Manhattan in early April as a top attraction with the East Side Kids comedy *Docks of New York* in two-day bookings at multiple RKO theaters. Returns were "good" in Boston when leading a double bill with Bela Lugosi's Poverty Row thriller *Black Dragons*, and "okay" in Buffalo, New York, when supporting Republic's Dennis O'Keefe musical *Earl Carroll Vanities*. But when *The Great Flamarion* finally reached San Francisco, the movie lasted only five days billed under Paramount's Veronica Lake comedy *Bring on the Girls*.[15]

Mann was both modest and forthright in his final assessment of Erich von Stroheim:

> He drove me mad. He was a genius. I'm not a genius: I'm a worker. Geniuses sometimes end up very unhappy, without a penny. That's what happened to Erich and Preston Sturges, too."[16]

CHAPTER 7

STRANGE IMPERSONATION (1946)

Anthony Mann's final Republic Pictures film, *Strange Impersonation*, was smaller in scale and budget than *The Great Flamarion* and must have felt to the director like a professional regression. Irrespective of his reservations and despite its unsatisfying conclusion, the picture is an ingenious and frenzied little thriller, an appropriate culmination of the director's association with the bizarre independent studio of Herbert J. Yates.

Consider the first thirty-eight minutes of the movie. As chemist Nora Goodrich (Brenda Marshall) experiments on a new type of anesthesia, her jealous assistant Arline betrays her. Arline has designs on Nora's fiancé Stephen (William Gargan) and deliberately arranges for anesthesia fluid to explode

Figure 7.0. *Strange Impersonation*, 1946. Brenda Marshall (Photofest).

as Nora sleeps. The explosion disfigures Nora, who is now reduced to concealing her face with dark glasses and a veil, Arline having deceived her into thinking Stephen does not wish to see his fiancée anymore. At this point, a woman whom Nora nearly injured weeks earlier with her car blackmails the scarred chemist at gunpoint. In the ensuing struggle, the extortionist falls from the apartment balcony to her death and lands on her face. The police identify the corpse as "Nora Goodrich," so Nora assumes the dead woman's identity and heads west for plastic surgery to alter her original appearance.

Putting aside its conventional musings about a woman choosing between career and marriage, *Strange Impersonation* unveils the most spellbinding female character to be found in an Anthony Mann picture, Dr. Nora Goodrich. In this role, Mann directed yet another underutilized actress, the stunning brunette Brenda Marshall, wife of actor William Holden, and a former Warner Bros. contract player whose few distinctive credits were *The Sea Hawk* (1940) and *The Constant Nymph* (1943). *Strange Impersonation* did not lead the thirty-year-old Marshall to stronger roles and would be her third to last film.

Dressed in high-collared white lab coat and highly layered hair, along with the obligatory eyeglasses designating her intellectual status, Marshall cuts an imposing and intimidating figure as a chemist obsessed with developing her anesthetic formula. *Strange Impersonation* winks at the audience from the outset as we learn that Nora's place of employment is the Wilmott Institute, founded in 1903 by "Mindret L. Wilmott." This is an in-joke to screenwriter Mindret Lord, to whom we will return shortly. Standing in front of an art deco glass brick window as the camera tracks leftward, Nora promises a room full of medical types that she will complete her experiments within a few days. In low wide-angle, she approaches an armless medical body model to point to the section of the brain where the reactions to her formula will occur (fig. 7.0). In an unusually Brechtian statement for a Mann film (calling attention to the film itself), Nora informs her audience, "The anesthesia should be complete for approximately one hour, during which time the mind may indulge in dreams or fantasies, normal or otherwise."[1]

The picture soon shifts into *film noir* when Nora accidentally backs her car into drunken Jane Karaski (Ruth Ford). Jane is unharmed, but Nora drives her home despite harassment from an ambulance-chasing attorney (George Chandler). Censor Joseph I. Breen of the Production Code Administration lost a battle with Republic to change this unsavory character into "possibly a process server, taxicab man, or some busybody" in order to avoid "widespread offense to the legal profession." (As it turned out, the portrayal of a shyster lawyer did upset a *New York Times* reader who also cited the 1946 films *The Postman Always Rings Twice* and *Ziegfeld Follies* for stereotyping attorneys. The reader no doubt attended any one of dozens of Manhattan double features that summer where *Ziegfeld Follies* was teamed with *Strange Impersonation*.)[2]

Jane lives in a classic 1940s *noir* efficiency apartment outfitted with a Murphy bed and a curtained window through which a Joe's Bar and Grill neon sign blinks aggressively ("Beautiful, ain't it?" Jane slurs). Nora leaves Jane money and her card, though it is unclear whether the inebriated woman is fully aware of what is happening. The next phase of the narrative is staged in Nora's elegant apartment where Arline assists in testing the anesthesia formula. After Nora gives herself an off-camera injection (at Breen's request) she drifts off into unconsciousness complete with blurry, shimmering special effects and harp music.[3] Unable to wake her, Arline seizes the opportunity to tamper with the nearby chemicals, prompting the explosion that disfigures Nora.

This is not the type of crime melodrama from which one expects to find logic or realism. Mann never mentioned the movie in interviews, so it is unlikely the results, especially the resolution, satisfied him.[4] This does not make *Strange Impersonation* any less entertaining, particularly in such moments as when Nora points an automatic at Arline:

> NORA. You know, Arline, there was a time when I might have used this on myself, but after what you've done to me I'd just as soon use it on you.

MAKING AND SELLING *STRANGE IMPERSONATION*

After completing *The Great Flamarion* at Republic, Anthony Mann briefly returned to RKO Radio Pictures to direct another low-budget musical, *Sing Your Way Home*, filmed in twenty-four days between November 28 and December 26, 1944, on a modest budget of $278,625 ($3,685,000 in 2013).[5] Months of unemployment followed until he resurfaced at Republic for the fifth and last time to direct this picture.

Strange Impersonation emerged from the dark mind of Mindret Lord, a sketch writer for *New Faces of 1936*, which Mann as Anton Bundsmann supervised on stage in New York. Under the name "Mindred Lord," the author penned the "I Had an Alibi" episode of the CBS radio series *Suspense* (January 4, 1945). A writer with a macabre pulp fiction imagination, Lord is rumored to have been related to murderer Richard Loeb of the notorious

Leopold-Loeb case that inspired the literary and theatrical sources for Alfred Hitchcock's *Rope* (1948) and Richard Fleischer's *Compulsion* (1959). His résumé of short stories includes such titles as "The Dinner Cooked in Hell" (1940), "Agony in Clay" (1939), "Naked Lady" (1934), "Prince of Pain" (1935), and "Satan Takes a Bride" (1936). Regrettably, Lord's life was as troubled as his storylines. Lord committed suicide in late 1955 not long after the release of his first produced big-budget studio screenplay, *The Virgin Queen*, starring Bette Davis as Elizabeth.[6]

Lord's previous radio and fiction work clearly impressed Republic and producer William Wilder (who directed Lord's screenplay for the 1955 *film noir*, *The Big Bluff*), but it is not unreasonable to consider Mann recommending Lord based on the director's theatrical collaboration with the writer. Whoever was responsible for bringing in Lord, his inventive script (based on a story by Anne Wigton, one of the *Great Flamarion* screenwriters, co-wrote), filmed under the title *You'll Remember Me*, brought out the tougher aspects of Mann and in many ways set the severe tone for all the director's subsequent crime melodramas.[7]

In June 1945, Wilder submitted the *You'll Remember Me* screenplay to Breen's Production Code Administration. Although a Republic release, William Wilder Productions made the picture and filming commenced on July 7 at the Producers Releasing Corporation studios on Santa Monica Boulevard. While the movie was still listed in *Daily Variety*'s Production Chart nearly two months later, it would logically have been completed in well under a month.[8]

Mann's directing style in *Strange Impersonation* confirms that the picture was filmed quickly. He employs a number of extended uninterrupted camera takes which have less to do with showcasing choreography of actors and camera (such as the introductory shot in *Flamarion*) than with conserving filming time. The prolonged take was common in low-budget productions as a cost-saving technique, but lesser directors failed to take advantage of its cinematic potential. While Mann at this time did not yet have the vast resources of other filmmakers noted for their extended takes (such as Orson Welles and Vincente Minnelli), his theatrical training gave him a strong sense of staging and timing. Mann's placement of actors within the frames, repositioning them like chess pieces to provide whatever movement the camera was being denied due to tight budgets, elevates his low-budget work from that of others incapable of seeing beyond financial limitations placed before them. (Mann's working relationship with cinematographer Robert W. Pittack must have been satisfactory given that the director's former mentor Preston Sturges hired Pittack to photograph his

Figure 7.1

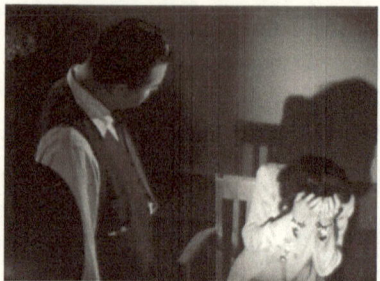
Figure 7.2

Figure 7.3

post-Paramount comedy, *The Sin of Harold Diddlebock*, aka *Mad Wednesday*, the following year.)

The first of Mann's long takes occurs in the initial hospital room scene where Stephen and an insincere Arline attempt to comfort the facially bandaged Nora. The camera movement is minimal and uncomplicated, the shot running uninterrupted for nearly one minute, forty-five seconds. The second such take, lasting just over ninety seconds, occurs in Nora's apartment when Jane awakens her. The lengthiest take (two minutes) occurs in Stephen's laboratory after Nora has returned from the plastic surgery makeover and is working for her unsuspecting former love. This stationary take is the longest in a Mann crime thriller.

There are other inspired shots and angles of brief duration amplifying Nora's emotional turmoil. After his first visit to Nora's hospital room, Stephen emerges into the hospital corridor and Arline's menacing shadow shares space with Venetian blinds shadows on the wall, the camera panning left to show her waiting for him. (Mann will take the menacing shadow to greater symbolic lengths in *Railroaded!* where he uses it to separate a killer and a future victim. See Chapter 9.) Mann and cinematographer Pittack showcase their skills in a climactic interrogation scene where a police inspector (Lyle Talbot) gives Nora the third degree. The darkly lit scene is a grueling collage of stark close-ups, expressionist low-angles, tilted medium shots, and high positions (fig. 7.1, 7.2), which lay the visual foundation for *Railroaded!*, *Desperate*, *Raw Deal*, *T-Men*, and other Mann artworks yet to come. There are three arresting montages in the film, the third occurring during the interrogation scene in which double images are continuously replaced with accusatory faces proclaiming variations of "You killed Nora Goodrich!" (fig. 7.3).

Strange Impersonation received a PCA seal on September 13, 1945, but six months passed before Republic released the film to cinemas. West Coast engagements were all but invisible as the film inauspiciously opened (in the earliest located engagement) as a supporting feature at a Pomona, California, theater. The East Coast, however, was kinder in the months ahead. Like *Strangers in the Night*, the thriller opened in Brooklyn before Manhattan, but this time supporting a second-run booking of M-G-M's all-star Technicolor musical *Ziegfeld Follies (of 1946)* for a profitable two-week engagement. From there, the film crossed over into New York City (again supporting *Ziegfeld Follies*) in seven second-run cinemas. The combination moved in early June to sixteen cinemas in Manhattan, Brooklyn, Queens, and Westchester, and then to another twenty-six (adding the Bronx) the following week. This final Mann Republic Pictures production was proof that in the world of motion picture economics, a "B" movie was only as good as the "A" feature it supported. Without such support, as was the case at the Tranx-Lux in Boston, the box office results were only "average."[9]

Immediately after completing *Strange Impersonation*, Anthony Mann returned yet again to RKO to direct the last of his low-budget musicals, *The Bamboo Blonde*, which cost $281,912. His participation lasted from September 4 until September 28, 1945, with Theron North directing retakes on January 7, 1946. By this time, World War II was over and Hollywood was entering its greatest box office year to date, with over 70 percent of the United States population attending cinemas weekly.[10] Nineteen forty-six would also be the pinnacle of success for the U.S. motion picture business. Decline in cinema attendance brought on by television set in quickly from 1947 onward.

Before he could be offered another cheap musical to direct, Mann wisely took matters into his own hands. He and Dorothy Atlas had a movie treatment called *Flight*, which was to be the foundation for his next RKO film project. It would also be the origins of *Desperate*, the first motion picture based on material of Anthony Mann's own creation.

CHAPTER 8

DESPERATE (1947)

In the couple-on-the-run film narrative formula, a man and woman are in perpetual escape from either sinister forces and/or misunderstanding lawmen. Living as fugitives, they are forced into transient existences, unable to put down roots, fearful of betrayal and exposure. Over the decades, Hollywood directors specializing in crime and suspense thrillers have displayed a fondness for this premise. Alfred Hitchcock popularized it in *The 39 Steps* (1935) and, to a lesser degree, *Saboteur* (1942). Fritz Lang visualized it in his

Figure 8.0. *Desperate*, 1947. Steve Brodie (Photofest).

pre-*film noir You Only Live Once* (1937), and Nicholas Ray and Joseph H. Lewis both used it powerfully in their respective *films noir, They Live by Night* and *Gun Crazy/Deadly is the Female* (both 1949). Anthony Mann's *Desperate* rightfully takes its place among the best of these pictures.

Gangster Walter Radak (Raymond Burr) cons working-class truck driver Steve Randall (Steve Brodie) into assisting Walt's gang on a night job that turns out to be a fur robbery. Steve alerts a policeman and attempts to flee the crime scene after more police arrive, but Walt's younger brother Al shoots a cop and gets arrested. The rest of the gang escapes and beats the innocent truck driver until he consents, under Walt's threats to disfigure Steve's pregnant wife Anne (Audrey Long), to confess to shooting the cop. Steve escapes and takes Anne to refuge on her relatives' Midwest farm, but once the policeman dies and Al Radak faces the electric chair, Walt goes on a hunt for Steve, first to force him into fulfilling his obligations, then, when it is too late to save Al, to avenge his brother's execution.

Desperate anticipates Mann's *Side Street* (1950) as both films center on struggling working-class newlyweds whose financial vulnerability makes them easy targets for criminals. Where the two pictures deviate are in their contextual approaches to the material. In spite of its moody and menacing trappings, *Desperate* is optimistic in tone compared with the bleaker *Side Street*, only in this instance the male protagonist is innocent of the charges leveled against him.

The film was a career turning point for Anthony Mann. Here was a picture that a studio did not arbitrarily assign to him but one whose story, the sixty-six-page treatment *Flight*, he actually coauthored.[1] It can be considered the first real Mann film in terms of themes and conditions prevalent in his most potent work. The hero of *Desperate* faces heightened and uncalculated brutality from his criminal adversaries and in his own desperation reveals violent characteristics. The comparatively wholesome working-class central characters counterbalance the inner suffering and pathos of a villain racing against time to save his kid brother from the executioners. Walt Radak is a pitiable figure, especially when lamenting the inevitable execution of his brother, "Al's just a kid."

Although *Desperate* flirts with sentiment as the Randalls seek rural protection away from the corrupting influences of the city at the farm of her immigrant relatives, there is more to suggest that country living is not devoid of exploitation. A smug, cigar-smoking used car dealer (Cy Kendall) swindles Steve and offsets any illusions about stalwart honesty in rural America ("The law of supply and demand. I've got it—you want it"). An ostensibly friendly traveler turns out to be the county sheriff (Dick Elliott) who attempts to bring Steve into custody at gunpoint. Steve's reaction to the sheriff in the film is muted. In the original treatment, as we shall see, it was not so muted.

Mann claimed that he and Dorothy Atlas wrote *Flight* in less than five days. In May 1946, the Nat C. Goldstone Agency submitted it to RKO Radio Pictures for consideration:

> The responsible people at RKO were immediately interested and offered me 5,000 dollars for the [treatment]. I told them: "The story is yours if I'm the director." They replied: "Anybody but you!" Just the same, I made the picture."[2]

The Atlas/Mann treatment commands interest as an exercise in the narrative underplaying that works best in crime fiction. Their tale opens on a passenger train after protagonist Steve and his wife ("Anna" at this early stage) are already on the run, which occurs eighteen minutes into the completed film. The next morning both overhear gossip about a warehouse robbery where a policeman and two innocent bystanders were killed. Steve swears he was not responsible for the killings.[3] In this initial version, Steve is not an unwitting participant in an underworld operation but a man with a criminal past who knows the police will not be able to protect him from the gangsters who are on his trail. At one point he refers bitterly to his former existence:

> I was the guy who was going to do it the easy way—Just a dumb truckdriver [*sic*] who thought he was smart—I should've broken away a long time ago—but I was soft—it's nice to have money in your pockets—[4]

Steve's dark history reveals itself early on with violent outbursts. Unlike the filmed scene, his roadside confrontation with the country sheriff predates the smoldering brutality of the Jim Thompson pulp novel antiheroes and of borderline sadist Dixon Steele (Humphrey Bogart) in Nicholas Ray's *In a Lonely Place* (1950):

> He [Steve] drags the Sheriff out and starts pummeling him—
> "I told you to let us go—" His breath comes in great gasps—"I didn't want no trouble—You should've let us go—"
> Suddenly, through his fogged mind he hears Anna's frightened cry as she shakes him—
> "Steve! You're killing him!"
> Slowly Steve relaxes his hold. The Sheriff falls limp.[5]

It is not until page thirty-one that the pursuers make their presences known through a large box containing a wreath of dead flowers. Across the wreath, in tarnished gold, is the date they plan to kill Steve: September 11 at 8:00 p.m.[6]

The screenplays prepared from the Atlas/Mann material, and Mann's handling of them, are structural improvements over the original narrative because they visualize unseen events from the *Flight* treatment. During the first six minutes of the film *Desperate*, Mann and his screenwriters establish the backgrounds and economic conditions of the married couple, their personal relationship and marriage, the wife's pregnancy, and the one phone call destined to change their lives for the worse: a $50 job offer from a man who turns out to be a criminal. This simple narrative device is enough to draw Steve into dangerous circumstances, but the Steve of *Desperate* is not the same Steve of the Dorothy Atlas/Anthony Mann *Flight* treatment. No longer linked to the criminal world, he is now a straightforward workingman in love with his new pregnant bride. Without the previous shortcomings of the character, the screen moments between the couple consequently lack tension. Mann will overcome this drawback in *Side Street* whose central married couple has a touch more complexity.

Yet the film does improve upon the structure and content of *Flight*. The chief beneficiary is villain Walt Radak who only appeared in the last six pages of the treatment, mostly to recount the facts of the robbery to Steve. The climactic shootout between Steve and Walt was to have ended with the hero shielding a boy with a bloody nose and then hearing a child's music box "gaily tinkling" the nursery song "Hey, Diddle, Diddle." Once he is safely in the clear and triumphant, Steve grins at a police detective and extends his hand, announcing his plans to head to California. Had the scene in the treatment been filmed, the hero's final line would not have been one of the stronger closing statements in crime cinema: "Why do you suppose that fool cow ever wanted to jump over the moon—" [sic].[7]

THE MAKING OF *DESPERATE*

Harry Essex, a screenwriter with an impressive crime genre résumé who went on to contribute to *He Walked By Night*, did the initial adaptation of the Atlas/Mann treatment *Flight*, and Martin Rackin, later an uncredited writer on *Follow Me Quietly*, was brought in for polishing.[8] Hollywood censor Joseph I. Breen of the Production Code Administration was not a fan of the resulting screenplay. In an October 17, 1946, letter to RKO Radio Pictures' Harold Melniker, Breen issued a warning:

We regret to say that in its present form, this basic story is not acceptable under the requirements of the Production Code, for the reason that, aided and abetted by a police officer, your sympathetic lead, Steve, takes the law into his own hands and kills Radak. Further, the police officer sends Steve off scot free [sic], with no suggestion whatever of due process of law. Before the basic story could be approved, it will be necessary to rewrite completely this unacceptable ending.[9]

Melniker submitted to Breen a revised draft of *Flight* on October 30 that still contained the violent confrontation between hero and villain. For reasons unexplained, this time Breen found the basic story acceptable. Unbeknownst to the makers of *Desperate*, the PCA was in the process of amending the Production Code to specifically target crime movies. In December 1947, half a year after the Mann film premiered, the PCA introduced an amendment, "Special Regulations on Crime in Motion Pictures." Many restrictions placed on the *Desperate* screenplay later appeared in the twelve statutes of this amended text.[10]

At RKO, *Desperate* (known as *Flight* until early 1947) was not viewed as a prestige item. The picture was filmed in twenty-seven days between November 21 and December 23, 1946, on a budget of $234,635 ($2,800,000 in 2013). Mann saw his directing salary adjusted downwards from $4,375 to $3,500. This revised budget also confirms theories about studio cost-cutting influencing dark cinematographic styles in black-and-white crime movies. The initial lighting budget of $14,381 was soon cut to $10,285.[11]

The original twenty-five-day shooting schedule allowed for twenty at studio facilities, four on local locations, and one paid holiday. Production ultimately finished three days behind schedule, a serious but not uncommon occurrence in the cost-conscious netherworld of low-budget studio filmmaking. Even more striking was Mann's profligate use of film stock, which far exceeded preliminary allocations. For *Desperate*, RKO supplied 75,000 feet of negative raw stock, which Mann exceeded by nearly 28 percent, or 20,880 feet. The total exposed negative of 95,880 feet represents a nearly fifteen-to-one shooting ratio (percentage of film exposed versus percentage used in the finished release) for a film eventually reduced in editing to 6,490 feet. This was not the first excessive footage intake for Mann at RKO. He had exposed 9,370 feet above the 75,000 provided for *Sing Your Way Home* (1945) and went 1,465 feet over for the same allotment for *The Bamboo Blonde* (1946). How did RKO feel about this? Judging from the work of other directors on the lot that year, Mann's overages would not have caused many alarms. Two Lawrence Tierney thrillers filming during 1946

Figure 8.1. From left: Raymond Burr and Freddie Steele (Photofest).

both exceeded their footage budgets. Robert Wise's *Born to Kill* (costlier to produce than *Desperate*) required 23 percent more footage than originally allotted, and Felix A. Feist's *The Devil Thumbs a Ride* (less expensive than *Desperate*) exceeded its amount by a huge 52 percent.[12]

The first scenes in *Desperate* to be filmed were those set in villain Walt Radak's apartment/hideout, a major location. Filming occupied five production days between November 21 and 26 in Stage 1B of the RKO lot. Before these scenes could be staged for the camera, censor Breen oddly instructed RKO "to avoid any suggestion that Walt and his henchmen are 'gangsters'" and that the villain's crew be limited to three men. After reading a subsequent script draft, Breen allowed a fourth member to be part of Walt's gang.[13]

Viewing the results, it is clear Mann was in his element as these hideout scenes are rich in atmospheric intensity and inspired compositions. To cite one example, the director frames Walt Radak in a symbolic low-angle shot through the "bars" of the wooden chair where he tosses cards. This prison motif will be used to even greater effect in a location scene with Farley Granger in *Side Street* (see Chapter 15). The warehouse fur robbery scene, in which the RKO wardrobe building loading dock doubled as location, benefited from the premature sunsets of late November and early December.[14]

The lighting scheme used was common for the monochromatic night-for-night cinematography of the era: unseen arc lights aimed diagonally at darkened warehouses, providing a half-lit silhouette of Steve's truck as it drives over to the loading dock.

In his October 17 letter to RKO, Breen warned against killing cops on screen and insisted that the scene where Al shoots the policeman

> should be shot in such a manner as merely to suggest that the policeman has been badly wounded. We recommend that . . . you use such an angle as will preclude the showing of the policeman's body. Later in the story it is established that he died.[15]

On film, the cop winces from the bullets, and when we return to this angle, other policemen are helping him up from the ground.

How Walt Radak convinces Steve to take the blame for the shooting of the cop was a source of anxiety for Breen. In the film, two hoods brutally beat Steve off-camera as the overhead light swings and scatters shadows in all directions. During this off-screen violence, Walt and henchman Reynolds (William Challee) observe under stunning high contrast lighting conditions, their faces awash in whiteness and shadow from the swinging light (fig. 8.2, 8.3).[16]

With the beating having failed to sway Steve, Walt smashes a bottle and walks up to the camera, the jagged edge of the glass shown in close-up as the gangster says calmly, "Say, I'll bet that new bride of yours is pretty. How about it, Steve?" With Walt's orders to "pick her up!," Steve relents and Walt reminds the trucker that Anne "ain't going to be so good to look at" if Al does not walk out of the police station by midnight.[17]

While even the suggestion of an off-screen beating was discouraged by censorship regulations, the suggestiveness is more rattling.[18] The potential use of a bottle weapon is surprising considering the controversy it caused when Breen read the script in October 1946. In his initial letter to RKO, Breen urged and recommended that the studio "omit the breaking of the bottle and the dangerous suggestion of using the jagged edge as a weapon." RKO ignored him. In a subsequent October 29 script draft, Breen reminded the studio that "the smashing of the bottle will not be acceptable. Some other form of threat should be substituted."[19] RKO again ignored him. Breen repeated his order a third time after reading the November 13 draft:

> As we have heretofore advised you, this action of smashing the bottle and the threat of disfigurement will not be acceptable. Something else must be substituted.[20]

Figure 8.2

Figure 8.3

RKO retained the bottle-smashing and Breen did not challenge the occurrence after editing was complete. There is no record indicating whether RKO reminded Breen of the PCA approving a broken beer glass weapon for Monogram's Lawrence Tierney *noir*, *Dillinger*, released a year-and-a-half earlier (fig. 8.4).

Breen also had issues with the interactions between Walt and smarmy detective Pete Lavitch (Douglas Fowley), whom the crook hires to locate the fugitive couple. In the film, it is not clear how Pete confiscates a letter linking Steve to Anne's Minnesota farm relatives, but the October 11, 1946, script draft reveals that the investigator bribed a neighbor boy to steal it from the couple's apartment mailbox. Breen insisted this reference be "completely eliminated," however, the released film does show neighbor boy Richard (Teddy Infuhr) observing, from the stairwell, Steve departing for the train station to meet Anne. There is no mention of bribery in the Harry Essex versions of the script, only that "a kid in the building told me." When Walt asks how Pete got hold of the letter, Pete says, "It was in the wrong box. But I picked every mail box in the house ... You never know."[21] These lines do not appear in the completed film.

Walt's killing of Pete was another challenge for the censor, who urged the producers to devise a substitution. The crime remained in the October 29 draft and Breen accepted it under certain technical conditions:

> One [gun]shot should suffice for the killing of Pete. If more than one shot is fired, you are likely to lose the scene at the hands of political censor boards. Also, for reasons of political censorship, the two men should be in separate frames when the shots are fired.[22]

RKO adhered to the demands of this letter. Breen also wanted to make clear that a corridor shootout between Walt's gang and police did not indicate that one of the cops was "any more than wounded."[23]

Figure 8.4. Lawrence Tierney in *Dillinger* (1945).

Walt and Reynolds eventually locate Steve in Minnesota. On the day of Al's scheduled execution, the criminals attempt to shoot Steve from a passing sedan. In this scene filmed at the RKO Ranch, the camera actually photographs through a car passenger window as the gun fires, panning right to show Steve diving in time to miss the bullet. Cinematographer George E. Diskant repeated this realistic style of photography for Nicholas Ray's *They Live by Night* (RKO 1949) and in several night locations on the Gordon Douglas *film policier Between Midnight and Dawn* (Columbia, 1950) and John Cromwell's *The Racket* (RKO, 1951), for which Ray was a contributing director.[24] If one is to accept RKO publicity, which was more than likely pure fabrication, the crew achieved the scene at considerable risk to actor Steve Brodie:

> ... Brodie took a chance by allowing a special effects man to shoot real bullets through a newspaper he held during the filming for a scene in "Desperate."
>
> According to Jack Lannan who did the shooting, there was only a space of two inches between Brodie's head and the bullets, because of the angle at which the shots had to be fired to penetrate the newspaper and break a plate glass window before which Brodie was standing.
>
> When asked about taking the chance with the bullets in order to save a four-hour wait to set it up with squibs set in the glass, Brodie said:
>
> "If Lannan says he can do it safely, it's okay with me. I'd have to change my name if it leaked out that I refused to take a chance."[25]

Jason Robards Sr., whom Mann previously directed for RKO in *The Bamboo Blonde*, plays, with caustic detachment and dry humor, jaded Detective

Lieutenant Louie Ferrari. Archly filing his nails in his major scenes, Ferrari allows Steve to obtain a gun permit once it is clear the trucker is innocent and Anne and child are safe. It is instructive to note the minute but influential changes in dialogue Breen made to the film after perusing the October 11 script draft. In the picture, the hero tells the cop:

> STEVE. All right, you want to see Walt and Reynolds locked up—so do I. They're no longer interested in my wife and they're too late to help Al. All they wanna do's get even with me!

It was Breen who inserted the words "locked up," and Steve's "get even" line replaced the written dialogue, "I've got to get them before they get me." This dialogue substitutes for Ferrari, in the October 11 draft, giving Steve a gun and instructing him on how to use it.[26]

The final memorable phase of *Desperate*, filmed on December 16 and 17 on RKO Stage 1A, is the confrontation between Steve and his two pursuers in the victim's apartment. The tense standoff is a triumphant cohesion of cinematic technique. Eleven tightly composed camera angles are intercut as tensions pile up, augmented by the anxiety-provoking ticking of a clock and music. In medium shot, Walt holds his gun on Steve before taking a drink from the latter's milk glass. In medium shot, Steve sweats, eyeing the men on both sides of him. As he watches Walt, cigarette smoke floats upward. In close-up, the ticking alarm clock approaches ten to midnight. In a wide-angle close-up of Steve, his eyes shift between the two men and then downward as the ticking gets louder. Walt is seen in a wide-angle close-up as he tensely watches Steve. The close-up of Reynolds is more distorted and the remainder of the standoff consists of extreme close-ups of the three men's eyes.

The intensity of this montage proved too much for Australian censors in 1947. To appease them, Breen instructed RKO to "[r]educe considerably suspense scenes showing close-up of ticking of clock, close-ups of men's faces and eyes, and close-ups of faces showing fear and perspiration."[27]

The final stairway showdown between Steve and Walt is an expressionistic tour-de-force covered in thirteen camera angles and running two minutes and twenty-one seconds. The two frame enlargements from this sequence (fig. 8.11, 8.12) confirm that Mann was fully in command of the medium even before his affiliation with cinematographer John Alton.

Steve emerging elated rather than emotionally bruised at the end of *Desperate* sounds a false note. His cheerful willingness to relay Lieutenant Ferrari's family greetings is also not to be believed considering that the police

86 | DESPERATE (1947)

Figure 8.5

Figure 8.6

Figure 8.7

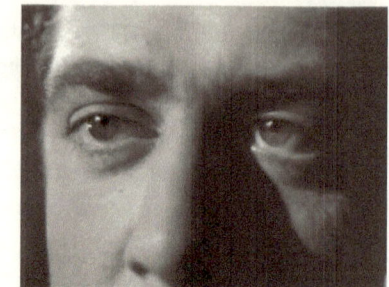

Figure 8.8

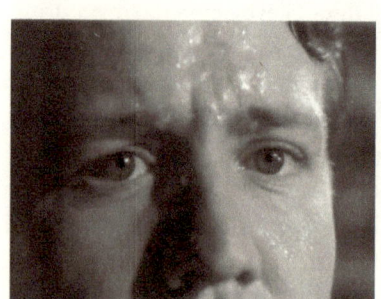

Figure 8.9

Figure 8.10

Figure 8.11

Figure 8.12

would have punished him severely had a gang member not cleared Steve. Contrast this Hollywood ending with the Alberto Cavalcanti British *film noir* of the same year, *They Made Me a Fugitive*, in which gangsters refuse to clear the man they framed (Trevor Howard) and police return him to jail, leaving his girlfriend to walk off alone down a dark night street.

THE SELLING OF *DESPERATE*

As *Desperate* was prepared for distribution, the RKO publicity department devised typically brassy suggestions for theater owners to use in promotions. The studio encouraged adventurous exhibitors to hire an attractive girl to carry a suitcase and display a sign that read:

> I am in a desperate hurry to reach the Palace Theatre to see "Desperate" with Audrey Long and Steve Brodie.[28]

The following note was recommended for daily newspaper personal columns:

> ANNE! We must elude Radak. We'll be safe at the Palace Theatre in the crowd attending "Desperate." STEVE.[29]

Finally, there was a radio/newspaper letter contest suggestion inviting listeners to reply to the question, "When did you ever feel desperate?"[30]

Promotional ideas notwithstanding, RKO released *Desperate* as an afterthought. Its first reported showing was in June at San Francisco's Golden Gate theater where, supported by live vaudeville from Dick Haymes and Helen Forrest, it played one week for what *Variety* termed a healthy gross of $40,000. This proved to be the only instance of the film having fortuitous timing: a transit strike the following week badly crippled cinema business in that city. For the duration of the film's theatrical life, RKO relegated it largely to double bills. One month later in Los Angeles, *Desperate* was a supporting feature at two theaters, including the Pantages, competing awkwardly with Universal-International's *Brute Force* on five screens. In Chicago, *Desperate* supported U-I's *Slave Girl* at RKO's Palace in a two-week engagement that grossed nearly half of what *Brute Force* earned at another RKO cinema. In Providence, Rhode Island, *Desperate* had a "fairly steady" one-week booking as second bill to the U-I comedy *Something in the Wind*. In Omaha, Nebraska, business was "stout" through unusually low ticket prices, but audiences were likely drawn to the main attraction *Down to Earth*, starring Rita Hayworth and Larry Parks. Conditions briefly improved in Baltimore when *Desperate* played solo at the Hippodrome with a Louis Prima Orchestra stage show. The film finally reached New York in early October when RKO circulated it throughout the five boroughs to its own circuit of sub-run theaters as a barely visible supporting feature for the hit Cary Grant-Shirley Temple comedy *The Bachelor and the Bobby-Soxer*.[31]

Unsurprisingly, Anthony Mann was gone from RKO by the time *Desperate* was completing distribution. The prolific Mann had already finished two new crime thrillers, *Railroaded!* and *T-Men*, and was well on his way to commercial success. On the eve of falling into the hands of Howard Hughes, RKO Radio Pictures, Inc., was less fortunate.

CHAPTER 9

RAILROADED! (1947)

On December 9, 1932, two robbers shot and killed Chicago police officer William Lundy during the robbery of a delicatessen. The woman who owned the establishment, the sole witness to the killing, identified two men in a police lineup as the criminals, one of whom was twenty-four-year-old Joseph Majczek. Both men received opprobrious prison sentences in 1933, but it was not until October 1944 that an enterprising reporter at the *Chicago Times* initiated a campaign to clear Majczek after suspecting something amiss in the case. Investigations uncovered corruption ranging from police intimidation of the alleged witness to political "war on crime"

Figure 9.0. *Railroaded!*, 1947. Ed Kelly (foreground left) and Hugh Beaumont (foreground right). Standing, left to right: Clancy Cooper, Peggy Converse, Jane Randolph, Charles D. Brown (Photofest).

pressures that a city government eager to promote tourism for Chicago's 1933 Century of Progress Exposition brought on the local court system. None of these disclosures would have been possible without the diligence of Joseph Majczek's mother, who spent a decade scrubbing floors in order to raise $5,000 as a reward to anyone providing information on the real killer. Majczek received an official governor's pardon in August 1945; five years later, the other convicted man, Theodore Marcinkiewicz, was exonerated.[1]

John C. Higgins, the screenwriter of Anthony Mann's *Railroaded!*, based his script on the travails of Mrs. Tillie Majczek. Although Higgins changed character names, the similarities were sufficient for Twentieth Century-Fox to protest to Eagle-Lion Films prior to producing Henry Hathaway's 1948 docudrama on the Majczek affair, *Call Northside 777*. Mann lamented the outcome:

> Fox found that the picture would hurt the box office returns of *Call Northside 777*, and paid Eagle-Lion a sum greater than the returns on my film; so the film had a very short run on a limited circuit. At least I made the acquaintance of John Higgins![2]

Due to the Twentieth Century-Fox entanglement, *Railroaded!* underwent script and editing revisions prior to release. Even with these changes, there are remnants of the Majczek story along with inevitable compromises. New York City is never mentioned by name, but brief stock footage of Times Square helps to establish the Club Bombay setting of the gangsters in the story. In the introductory four minutes following the main titles, two masked gunmen with shotguns rob a bookie joint affiliated with a beauty parlor. Clara (the adroitly cast Jane Randolph), the owner of the parlor, has signaled the gunmen, but the robbers catch employee Marie (Peggy Converse) by surprise. One of the men backs Marie into the dark salon, lurching toward her with his double-barreled weapon. Marie's scream attracts a policeman and the second gunman begins shooting at the cop who returns fire and seriously injuries the first gunman. The second gunman, who turns out to be the despicable Duke Martin (John Ireland), kills the officer.

As is to be expected, Mann's staging of the robbery is of a high caliber, carefully constructed and edited with gripping close-ups and subjective points-of-view angles accentuating the anxiety. The gunman terrorizing Marie approaches the camera in medium shot from her perspective, and in a reverse point-of-view, the camera tracks from medium shot to a close-up of her frightened face. Cutting back to Marie's point-of-view, the gunman continues lurching toward the camera, double-barreled shotgun aimed

Figure 9.1

Figure 9.2

Figure 9.3

directly at the lens to swelling music. The outside presence of the beat cop O'Hara is visualized through a classically lit *noir* silhouette.

Duke and injured cohort Cowie Kowalski (Keefe Brasselle) stole Steve Ryan's laundry truck for their getaway and plan on having Steve (Ed Kelly) take the blame for the crime. Clara does her part to distract the law by giving them a phony description of Steve. Even the dying, hospitalized Cowie identifies to police the unfortunate young man as his partner in crime. Meanwhile, erudite and pompous nightclub owner Jackland Ainsworth (Roy Gordon), who also controls Clara's bookie joint, is oblivious about his own muscleman Duke having masterminded the robbery. The police come down hard on Steve Ryan, ruthlessly refusing to believe his innocence and threatening him with execution to avenge the officer's death. The story then switches its focus to his sister Rosie (Sheila Ryan) as she searches undercover for the real killer. Sheila's nightclub flirtations with Duke are convincing enough for the murderer to let down his guard with her.

Anthony Mann was dissatisfied with this 1947 crime melodrama. When asked about his earliest directorial work, he responded, "I think one of those films is as bad as the other, but *Railroaded[!]* may have been bad in a more personal way: by that I mean its faults are more directly imputable to me."³ Mann did not expound on those faults and indicated that the studio felt him to be "hopeless," but presumably he felt he had not done justice to the John C. Higgins screenplay.

ANTHONY MANN ON "POVERTY ROW"

Hollywood's Poverty Row was in decline by 1947. Although Republic Pictures was functioning comfortably, Anthony Mann's next Poverty Row employer, Producers Releasing Corporation, was on the verge of collapse. If Mann described his time at Republic as his "grim, grim days," one can only imagine how he felt about PRC. Although he had no way of knowing in the spring of 1947, his decision to direct a PRC project immediately following *Desperate* at RKO Radio Pictures would be the first step in strengthening his flagging Hollywood career.

Eagle-Lion Films released *Railroaded!* after absorbing PRC, so the picture is a "phantom" PRC production in the minds of scholars.⁴ PRC's origins date to 1939 when an ex-film salesman formed Producers Distributing Corporation, but within a year the company was in debt and creditor Pathe Laboratories reorganized the studio. Under the new name PRC, the revitalized company released thirty-six pictures in 1945, running the gamut from budget-conscious westerns and jungle films to comedies and gangster melodramas. PRC filming schedules made Republic's appear lavish by comparison. "Most of my PRC pictures were made in six days," Edgar G. Ulmer famously told Peter Bogdanovich. "Just try to visualize it—eighty setups a day." Ulmer had a system where at least one wall of the set was barren of decorations and then used as a backdrop for all close-ups of actors, which were saved for the final day of filming. "I had to cut with the camera, because I was only allowed 15,000 feet [of camera negative] for a feature. No more. Two to one, nothing more."⁵ Even under such a rigid system, Ulmer was able to create his cult *Detour* (1945) and the impressively stylized *Bluebeard* (1944).

This atmosphere must have been depressing for Mann, who had already had a taste of major studio facilities and operations. Screenwriter Stewart Stern (*Rebel Without a Cause*) served as dialogue director on *Railroaded!* and suggests that the filmmaker adapted skillfully to Poverty Row conditions:

> He had a great sense of how to be able to shoot once he had the camera focused in one certain direction. He would just shoot almost everything in that direction in the schedule for that day that had to be shot. In other words, if he lit one

wall that had a door in it, he could find five scenes that he could shoot against that. He would rehearse in the master [and] could see ahead through the day so that he could see everything in that [camera] position and not change the lights because it would be the same. Maybe it would be [filmed] night-to-day,[6] but the camera stayed right there until he got through shooting in that direction. Then he would turn it around and light the other way and then shoot everything that happened that way. I don't think I ever saw him looking at notes.[7]

Located near the Samuel Goldwyn Studios in West Hollywood, the Producers Releasing Corporation studio stood at 7324 Santa Monica Boulevard. Stern recalled that the administration building was outfitted with a large dining room, although food was also ordered from the Chinese restaurant next door. The lot was without a water tank or backlot street, but it did have several soundstages.

THE MAKING AND SELLING OF *RAILROADED!*

Canadian screenwriter John C. Higgins, who contributed to four more Mann projects, was a superior crime writer and author of low-budget features and shorts at M-G-M, including James Stewart's feature début *The Murder Man* (1935) and the initial U.S. features of directors Jacques Tourneur (*They All Come Out*, 1939) and Fred Zinnemann (*Kid Glove Killer*, 1942). Higgins was adept at meticulously detailing the crime-solving techniques of hard-working detectives and forensics men. He could also propagandize effectively on behalf of federal law enforcement agencies. On the other hand, Higgins had a skill for exposing the excesses and inhumanity of the legal system. In *Railroaded!*, police bully and threaten an innocent man and in the Edmond O'Brien-Howard W. Koch thriller *Shield for Murder* (1954), which Higgins cowrote, they torture and kill with impunity. It is for these reasons that Higgins's screenplay *Tomorrow You Die* (the pre-release title of *Railroaded!*), adapted from a Gertrude Walker story, encountered opposition from the Production Code Administration of Joseph I. Breen.

In late March 1947, PRC submitted the script to Breen for approval; the Hollywood censor immediately tagged the project "unacceptable." Aside from his concerns about the use of illegal shotguns, the depiction of criminals killing a policeman, and "an excess of killings," Breen was alarmed that "the administration of justice in contemporary American life is shown to be ineffective" and that a district attorney, a drunken lawyer, police officers, and detectives were being presented unsympathetically.⁸ Breen was directing his correspondence to Eagle-Lion Films despite the independent distributor not officially taking over PRC until after *Railroaded!* was completed, and Eagle-Lion had cleverly installed Joseph I. Breen *Jr.* in its story department.

A meeting at the E-L studios to discuss a revised draft of *Tomorrow You Die* therefore occurred between father and son, a ritual that continued during *T-Men*, *Raw Deal*, and *He Walked By Night*. After the two Breens met in conference, Breen Sr. reminded an E-L executive "that all police shown in this story should be presented favorably," in particular Detective Chubb (Clancy Cooper) whom Higgins portrayed as a sadist. Breen Sr. revealed a disquieting statistic about 1947 censorship conditions in the United States:

> You will have in mind that approximately 300 censor boards in this country are in the hands of the police departments of the various cities and for this reason, as well as the social implications, offense should be avoided in portraying law enforcing officers.⁹

Breen Sr.'s anxieties were eventually confirmed when the Chicago Board of Censors attempted to ban *Railroaded!* on grounds that "it shows the police prosecuting an innocent man and further, there are excessive killings." Eagle-Lion fought and won a lifting of the ban several weeks later.¹⁰

Breen Sr. was unsuccessful in removing the overall tone from the Higgins screenplay. Like any competent crime writer, Higgins was drawn to the psychology and machinations of the criminals from whom his screenplay drew sardonic humor and this naturally made him an ideal creative collaborator with Anthony Mann. Club owner and avid reader Jackland Ainsworth torments a girlfriend with misogynist quotations, including an inaccurate citation of Oscar Wilde: "Women should be struck regularly, like gongs." (The correct line, "*Certain* women should be struck regularly, like gongs," is from Noël Coward's *Private Lives*.)¹¹ Psychopath Duke Martin has his own share of cheap philosophy:

> DUKE. You know, in this racket, you meet a lot of characters. Some are good, some are bad. Some are right guys, some are wrong—okay, you learn what they want you to learn. Sometimes you learn what they don't want you to learn.¹²

When introducing the Steve Ryan character, Higgins establishes the boy's naïveté in a self-reflexive breakfast table scene where the young man, unaware of the horrors awaiting him, debriefs his sister Rosie about a crime movie she attended the previous evening:

> ROSIE. And then right at the end of the picture the cops got him. Gee, I felt sorry for him.
> STEVE. Good picture, huh?
> ROSIE. Yeah, I cried and everything. But they had no right to do that . . . just because they had the law on their side.
> STEVE. Well, maybe some guys need a goin' over.

The censors failed to suppress the most unyielding dramatic moments where Steve is stripped of his dignity and forced to endure accusations from the vengeful police. Playing bad detective to actor Hugh Beaumont's good detective Mickey is the obtuse Chubb whose gleeful sadism so distressed Breen Sr. While not observed "playing with the 'hand-sap'" (a small baton) or pushing Steve into a chair as he was caught doing in several April 1947 screenplay drafts, Chubb remains thoroughly dislikable as he verbally abuses the young man and Steve's family.[14] Even Mickey, a role in need of a more hardboiled actor than Beaumont, displays contradictory and cruel qualities customary in an Anthony Mann protagonist.

Under pressures from the PCA, the filmmakers do their utmost to humanize Mickey. As police ransack the Ryan household in their fanatical search for the gun that killed the cop, the detective insists, "I'm not paid to persecute people." Not convincingly, Rosie softens and is innocently about to ask if Mickey thinks her brother committed the crime. Mickey cuts her off: "Feelings don't count in my racket—just evidence." (The film deserves credit for preserving "racket," a word associated with organized crime.) Mickey hardly comes off better in the following interrogation session where he stands silent and impotent as fellow lawmen persecute Steve with questions, threats, and accusations.

Mann positions his actors masterfully in the frames to capture the mental violence of the interrogation, such as a wide-angle view of the towering Mickey and his supervisor, Captain McTaggart (Charles D. Brown), standing on both sides of Steve (fig. 9.4); a medium shot of Chubb chewing gum (fig. 9.5); Steve's frozen reaction to McTaggart crying out for the gas chamber (9.6). The hospital scene in which Cowie implicates Steve by hand and eye gestures is grueling in its construction of suspense and another illustration of Mann's keen eye for arranging actors within the frame and employing close-ups to maximum effect. The barely conscious Cowie,

Figure 9.4

Figure 9.5

Figure 9.6

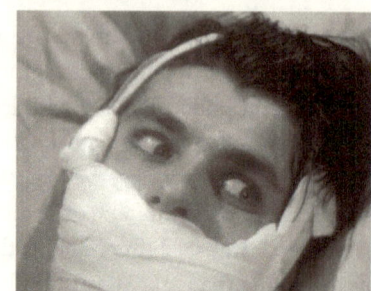

Figure 9.7

suffering under a shattered lower jaw and a brain with an inoperable bullet, menacingly shifts his eyes towards Steve (fig. 9.7) before using a clenched right hand to signal Mickey that Steve is the cop-killer.

Such technical and compositional craftsmanship are what isolates Mann from many Poverty Row directing peers unable to see beyond the tight budgets forced upon them.

If Hugh Beaumont proves insufficient as the kindly police detective, John Ireland supplies abundant compensation as Duke Martin. In the first of his two crime film appearances for Mann, the rugged character actor of *Red River* and *All the King's Men* (and later Mann's *The Fall of the Roman Empire*) takes possession of all his scenes. Ireland tosses out abbreviated morsels of John Higgins sarcasm with aplomb while obsessively polishing his revolver, perfuming bullets (Breen Sr. would not allow garlic to be used to demonstrate how it makes bullets fatal in their effects), or toying with a butter knife.[15] But Ireland's Duke does not need to say anything to show his contempt for an adversary. When Mickey insults him in one scene, Duke responds simply by breathing on the cigarette case he is polishing. Ireland creates malevolence in ways that are both unobvious and unsettling.

Director of photography Guy Roe later brought an economical and atmospheric look to the low-budget Budd Boetticher suspense drama *Behind*

Figure 9.8

Locked Doors (1948) and employed diverse photographic methods in Cyril Endfield's harrowing *film noir*, *The Sound of Fury/Try and Get Me!* (1950). The association continued briefly when Roe was brought in to film three days of *Raw Deal* retakes one year later. During the course of this production, Mann and Roe bathe Duke Martin in darkness to visualize his brutish personality. In the scene in Steve's dark van following the initial robbery where Duke orders Cowie to implicate Steve, a single source from the rear lights both silhouetted men (fig. 9.8). This visual theme continues throughout the picture, in a scene where Duke's shadow either separates him or shrouds him from his forthcoming victims (fig. 9.9–9.12), culminating in the final nightclub standoff between Rosie and Duke that leads to the inspired choreography of gunfire between him and Mickey on a dance floor of stacked chairs. (This partially compensates for an earlier farcical wrestling match between Rosie and the drunken Clara that is not one of Mann's stronger directing moments.)

The first edition of *Railroaded!* (still called *Tomorrow You Die*) was shot in ten days beginning on April 23, 1947. If we apply Edgar G. Ulmer's PRC footage statistics, this would have allocated Mann a paltry 25,000 feet of film negative for the production. In light of the fact that he was coming off of a picture for which he exposed nearly four times that much negative, Mann likely exceeded these front office limitations. On June 6, 1947, Breen Sr. screened the first cut of the picture. Two months later, Twentieth Century-Fox complained on behalf of *Call Northside 777*, and Eagle-Lion was required to invest an additional $25,000 ($258,000 today) on new scenes and retakes for the film now being called *Railroaded!*. Although it was announced at the time of the retakes that the actress playing Steve Ryan's mother (Hermine Sterler) was to be cut entirely from the picture, this did not occur.[16]

Figure 9.9

Figure 9.10

Figure 9.11

Figure 9.12

The question remains as to how involved Mann was in these changes. *T-Men* had already entered production on July 31, 1947, and the Breen office approved the rewritten script scenes for *Railroaded!* on August 6. Nearly a month later, Breen Sr. screened the re-edited results and approved a release.[17] The *Railroaded!* retakes needed to be filmed after August 23 (the official completion date for *T-Men*) in order for Mann to have directed them. This would give Eagle-Lion nine working days to film new material and re-cut the footage into the earlier version. Other options were for E-L to arrange a *T-Men* hiatus so that Mann could complete *Railroaded!*, or for simultaneous filming on certain days. E-L could also have assigned another director to the *Railroaded!* retakes just as Mann would later secretly take over from Alfred Werker major portions of *He Walked By Night*.

Rosie's improbable romantic feelings for Mickey (at one point they kiss to strains of violins) lead to a ludicrous half-minute finale in the Ryan living room. Backed by an upbeat music score, Mrs. Ryan and others greet her children and Mickey. Rosie, who has miraculously recovered from Duke having shot her, has an arm in a sling. Mickey and Rosie share this closing dialogue:

MICKEY. Did you change your mind about cops just a little?
ROSIE. Well, I suppose you have to make a living somehow. Yes, I . . . I think I've changed my mind.
(*They kiss.*)

One has to believe that both Higgins and Mann loathed this resolution. Since the conclusion has a very tacked-on feel to it, one also wants to believe that Mann was too busy with *T-Men* to have directed the scene.

SELLING *RAILROADED!*

As *Railroaded!* was being readied for release in August 1947, Eagle-Lion Films, Inc., acquired the thirty-one film exchanges of Producers Releasing Corporation. E-L had been organized in June 1946 as a U.S. subsidiary of J. Arthur Rank's British film operations, and PRC handled physical distribution of E-L productions under the supervision of nine separate sales and publicity personnel. After the takeover, the Poverty Row producer/distributor PRC passed into history. The emerging film company Eagle-Lion took over the PRC studio lot and inherited twelve unreleased PRC productions, including *Railroaded!*[18]

This merger, coupled with the aforementioned legal skirmish with Twentieth Century-Fox over *Call Northside 777*, presented obstacles for the Mann picture. Most of the major theatrical playdates for *Railroaded!* occurred between October and December 1947 and the commercial reception varied from situation to situation. At Detroit's huge Michigan Theater, the picture supported Paramount's Marlene Dietrich melodrama *Golden Earrings* for what *Variety* branded both a "comfortable" and "trim" $25,000 in the first week and a "passable" $15,000 in the second. In Buffalo, New York, the thriller supported the Eagle-Lion comedy *Out of the Blue* with "good" business. In Los Angeles, the picture opened in three theaters (once again supporting *Out of the Blue*) but Robert Rossen's *Body and Soul*, with John Garfield, showing on four screens, exceeded it financially. In Boston, Mann's film did only "routine" business when teamed with a notorious Ronald Reagan-Shirley Temple fiasco, *That Hagen Girl* (Warner Bros.) At two theaters in Denver, supporting Universal-International's Robert Cummings-Susan Hayward drama *The Lost Moment*, business was "nice" and "fine." As was demonstrated with *Desperate*, *Railroaded!* performed decently when supporting a major live stage act. In Louisville, Kentucky, the film played unchallenged with the Henry Busse Orchestra and other stage performers for a "brisk" gross. In spite of the politics involving *Call Northside 777, Railroaded!* was even booked into numerous theaters within the Fox circuit.[19]

In the end, Mann was his own worst enemy when it came to the movie's lackluster commercial reception. The competing appearance of one of the first major releases from the newly reorganized Eagle-Lion Films dashed whatever opportunities his low-budget thriller had to gradually attract a larger segment of moviegoers in late 1947. The film was *T-Men.*

CHAPTER 10

T-MEN (1947)

> This is what I really call my first film. I was responsible for its story, for its structure, its characters and for actually making it. This was my first real break towards being able to make films the way I wanted.[1]

Anthony Mann is speaking of his 1947 crime thriller *T-Men*, a film of many firsts. *T-Men* is Mann's first breakthrough commercial success, his first collaboration with cinematographer John Alton, his first use of extensive location photography, his first motion picture to garner sufficient critical acclaim (including a pictorial in *Life* magazine), and his first to open commercially in France. It even received an Academy Award nomination (Best

Figure 10.0. *T-Men*, 1947. Alfred Ryder (right). Background from left to right: Dennis O'Keefe, John Wengraf, Charles McGraw, and Jack Overman (Photofest).

Sound, Jack R. Whitney), the second for a Mann picture.[2] *T-Men* did not have to support a so-called "A" release from a major studio but held its own as a leading theatrical attraction around the United States. After twelve low-budget features, Anthony Mann had finally captured the attention and respect of influential Hollywood decision-makers.

In a scenario foreshadowing *Border Incident* two years later, *T-Men* follows Treasury agents Dennis O'Brien and Anthony Genaro (Dennis O'Keefe and Alfred Ryder) as they go undercover to penetrate and smash a Detroit counterfeiting ring. O'Brien is accepted into the gang only after enduring a beating and convinces the criminals that his set of counterfeit plates are superior to those of their regular supplier, The Schemer (Wallace Ford). The counterfeiters eventually become aware and make conditions miserable for both the undercover agents and others within their criminal syndicate.

T-Men is a cohesion of three different popular crime drama styles of the time period. The "semi-documentary" was a narrative movie style striving for authenticity through the incorporation of newsreel techniques (impersonal, authoritative narration) and vivid location filming. By taking cameras outfitted with black-and-white film stock (the epitome of 1940s newsreel realism) to actual localities where true stories occurred, wartime and post-World War II moviemakers believed they could combat conventional studio artificiality. *T-Men* was not the first film to apply this semi-documentary technique, which Mann acknowledged back in 1947:

> Pictures such as *The Lost Weekend*, *T-Men*, *Boomerang* and *The House on 92nd Street* have gripped a public which wants realism in its screen fare. The only way you can make a factual screen drama is to go to the actual locations to make the picture. That's why we went to actual scenes of crime as revealed by Treasury records, to re-enact the crime which provides so much of the impact in *T-Men*.[3]

In addition to a semi-documentary, *T-Men* is a *film policier*. The heroes of the story are Treasury agents whom we observe taking meetings at law enforcement agencies, researching their assignments, and secretly passing on the results of their undercover work. There are scenes at Washington, D.C., crime labs where technicians explain the resistance, endurance, and fiber composition of counterfeit currency paper. And there are more scenes in offices with governmental higher-ups processing information they have just received from the two undercover agents.

Finally, *T-Men* becomes a *film noir* when the criminals take center stage, conspiring, torturing, and murdering in an atmosphere of oppressive shadows, blinking neon, and all-encompassing camera angles. The narrative

Figure 10.1. John Alton, 1950 (Photofest).

hurls the two agents into dark streets, back alleys, transient hotels, gambling dens, steam baths, smoky Los Angeles Caribbean-style clubs, and, ultimately, the waterfront, where the familiar procession of con men, icy blondes, and gunmen hold court. The fact that the film avoided depicting the "fancy-pants night club life" of other contemporary crime thrillers won it praise from the Communist Party newspaper, the *Daily Worker*.[4]

In grouping together the semi-documentary, the *film policier*, and the *film noir*, T-Men cannot avoid becoming lopsided and there are times when one is interfering with the other. Typical of the shortcomings is the narrator stating the obvious during a superbly cinematic scene hardly in need of verbal embellishment ("Having found The Schemer, Agent O'Brien became his shadow..."). At the same time, the picture seldom releases its grip on the viewer. The Eagle-Lion publicists were not exaggerating when they assured theater owners that "it hits ... and hits ... and hits—like a piledriver!"[5]

Hungarian-born cinematographer John Alton was Mann's key collaborator, and his impact on the director's pictures from this point forward cannot be overstated. Alton achieved unconventional angles and virtuoso visualizations of tenseness through expressionist uses of wide-angle lenses and harsh convergences of light and shadows. He understood what Mann was after and knew how to achieve it. Theirs was to become one of the most momentous director-cinematographer collaborations in Hollywood history.

Mann and Alton met while both were employed at Republic Pictures. Since Alton had photographed two Erich von Stroheim productions at Republic, Alton could have recommended Mann for *The Great Flamarion*. In his introduction to Alton's *Painting with Light*, Todd McCarthy writes that Republic had placed Mann in the hands of the cinematographer "to learn the ropes of filmmaking," but this contradicts the fact that Mann had already directed two features by that time, both for major studios.⁶ Perhaps Alton gave the recent arrival helpful tips on achieving top results with zero resources. In any case, the two men got on well enough for Mann to request that Eagle-Lion secure Alton from Republic.

"I found a director in Tony Mann who thought like I did," Alton recalled many decades later. "He not only accepted what I did, he demanded it."⁷ As for Mann, he revealed the tendency in some directors to offer conflicting sentiments on a cinematographer achieving equal fame and cult appreciation:

> He was a very talented and imaginative cameraman. He could get all sorts of effects with very limited budgets. And this is what we were working on. And actually we shot this one all outdoors, in the shops, and so on: like they do now, and everybody says is a new move. But *T-Men* was twenty years ago.⁸

In a separate interview around the same time, Mann commented,

> I don't think that John revolutionized photography technique whatsoever, but he knew how to use the means you gave him to the maximum."⁹

Whether or not Alton revolutionized cinematography, all of the subsequent thrillers, costume dramas, and westerns that the two men collaborated on (*Raw Deal, He Walked By Night, Reign of Terror/The Black Book, Border Incident, Devil's Doorway*) would not have been the same without Alton.

T-Men was conceived as a promotional vehicle for the Treasury Department and functions within the limitations of such a framework. Mann would again have to submit to government cooperation with *Strategic Air Command* (1955), and what he later said about that James Stewart film could apply to this one as well:

> [T]he co-operation of the Air Force was vital, and we were held within the bounds of what they wanted. The story itself was restricted and the whole concept of its shooting was confined to what they would let me show, which is perfectly all right. I went into it purely as a service to the Air Force, and as Jimmy Stewart was of the Force, we accepted this handicap and just tried to make an exciting film . . .¹⁰

Truman-era pomp and circumstance influence the beginning of *T-Men* as federal buildings, clangorous Gayne Whitman narration, and military-style music serve, however inadvertently, to assure Cold War audiences of the patriotic credentials of the film's makers.¹¹ From the Washington, D.C.,

Figure 10.2

Figure 10.3

Figure 10.4

landmarks the action shifts to lifeless Elmer Lincoln Irey, former chief coordinator of Treasury Department law enforcement agencies, who sits behind his desk, preparing to set the stage for the film we are about to see. Irey supervised production on the picture and had achieved fame for his arrests of gangsters Al Capone and Waxey Gordon, and Bruno Hauptmann, whose alleged killing of the Charles Lindbergh baby is still being disputed. Ironically, Irey also imprisoned the corrupt leadership of IATSE, the International Alliance of Theatrical Stage Employees and Moving Picture Machine Operators, who had demanded payoffs from Hollywood studios in the late 1930s. *T-Men* not only used IATSE film technicians, the film's associate producer Aubrey Schenck was nephew of Joe Schenck, whom Irey's agencies jailed for being a liaison between IATSE and the studios during the payola scandal.[12]

After Irey introduces the composite Shanghai Paper Case, the real *T-Men*, an altogether different movie, begins.[13] We are now on location at night in an industrial section of Los Angeles, off Santa Monica Boulevard, as an agent emerges from the shadows to keep an appointment with a contact named Shorty. At the bottom of a tall water tank-like structure familiar to viewers of such Los Angeles crime melodramas as Samuel Fuller's *The Crimson Kimono* (1959), we see Shorty's silhouette (fig. 10.2). Lit in

Figure 10.5

Figure 10.6

Figure 10.7

wide-angle medium shot from a side lighting source is the face of the killer Moxie (Charles McGraw), appearing from a mostly dark screen (fig. 10.3). This shot evokes memories of William Conrad's gunfire lighting up actor McGraw's face (fig. 10.4) in Robert Siodmak's *The Killers* (1946).[14]

Shorty staggers over to a loading dock as Moxie observes in the foreground, Shorty's face moving from shadow to light and then into darkness (fig. 10.5). Music swells as we cut to a quintessential John Alton shot of Moxie silhouetted in a doorway, the left side of his body outlined by light, as he holds a revolver, turning to face the camera in an unnerving "rim-light" setup (light from behind outlining his figure) for an explosion of gunfire and a surge in music (fig. 10.6). Shorty is hit twice, then in the next angle (filmed between Moxie's legs) more bullets hit the informer, his shadow meshing with his silhouetted form (10.7). Moxie removes a roll of bills from the victim and drives off.[15]

Imagine the disappointment of such a gloriously staged and conceived sequence preceding a series of uninspired office scenes involving Secret Service and Treasury Department agents planning their next moves. As is typical of the average *film policier*, law enforcers sitting in bland offices trading quips, inquiring about family members, and dispensing expository data makes for unexciting viewing. Even Mann and Alton are unsure as to how

Figure 10.8

Figure 10.9

Figure 10.10

to make these scenes visually compelling, and who can fault them? They are eager to move on to the transgressors, as are we. In *T-Men*, the action gathers momentum after agents O'Brien and Genero are recruited for "a roping job, all undercover" to crack the Vantucci mob in Detroit which is using revenue stamps from "a tough, tight outfit" in Los Angeles. Remove Mann and Alton from the confines of federal agency offices and suddenly their cinematic imaginations flourish. As Vantucci (Anton Kosta) questions the two agents in his produce warehouse, the agents are framed from a side angle, Genero's face three-quarters in shadows and O'Brien's illuminated by a hanging light. As two of Vantucci's men later give Genero a beating during their boss's interrogation, a low wide-angle shot beneath another unseen hanging light frames the uninterrupted one-minute, sixteen-second take (fig. 10.8).

The semi-documentary approach in *T-Men* is stylishly used in various Los Angeles locations where O'Brien searches for The Schemer, the agent filmed through a wooden "X" from behind a porch or through carefully controlled uses of foreground and background staging (fig. 10.9, 10.10).

Mann expressed satisfaction with at least two sequences in the picture.[16] Moxie's beating of O'Brien is an example of where *T-Men* switches from *policier* to *noir* mode. It begins inside a (soundstage) hotel room with blinking

Figure 10.11

Figure 10.12

Figure 10.13

Figure 10.14

letters from the "hotel" sign casting faint light into the room. O'Brien is jumped in the dark, a scuffle ensuing in total blackness until Moxie turns on a light switch. The grinning Brownie (Jack Overman) handlocks the agent and, in a trademark Mann low-angle shot, holds him down in the foreground while Moxie sits and twists O'Brien's fingers in his quest for answers (fig. 10.11). Gasping in pain, O'Brien insists, "I can't hear a thing you're sayin'," at which point Moxie angrily boxes his victim's ears. O'Brien's agonized reaction is presented in a wide-angle medium shot as the window behind him briefly lights up from the unseen neon (fig. 10.12). Moxie asks off-screen (in McGraw's unique gravel-voiced elocutions), "Ya hear any better now?"

In scenes such as this, Alton employs so-called "Criminal Lighting," a technique dating from the silent film era. This occurs where an actor is lit from a low light aiming upward for an unusual angle. Alton wrote in his 1949 book *Painting with Light*,

> It distorted the countenance, threw shadows seldom seen in everyday life across the face. This light, which exaggerates features, became so popular that even in our films of today [the late 1940s], when we want to call the attention of the audience to a criminal character, we use this type of illumination.[17]

Figure 10.15

Alton cited two *T-Men* scenes, one in which O'Brien first confronts The Schemer, the sole lighting source from a table lamp below them; the second with blonde photographer Evangeline (Mary Meade) visiting a counterfeit bill supplier (William Malten) in a photographic darkroom, both characters lit from a table light (fig. 10.13, 10.14).[18]

Mann was also rightfully pleased with Wallace Ford's on-screen demise as The Schemer, staged in a steam bath. The baths are a recurring theme in *T-Men*, each depiction building in intensity and providing Mann and Alton with an ideal economical lighting and composition strategy (fig. 10.15). Alton, an enthusiast of live fog for dramatic atmosphere, compared the steam of Turkish baths with fog effects:

> Fog is particularly suitable for outstanding light effects in the form of shafts of light. Backlight should be carefully employed, because the rays of lamps pick up easily. If possible the entire field of vision should be covered with backlight instead of just an arc ray here and there.[19]

The Hollywood Athletic Club served as the key location for the steam bath segments. To prevent fogging, the lens of the camera had special glass plates treated with glycerin attached.[20] According to publicity accounts, never to be taken at face value, Mann was dissatisfied with the levels of steam during a scene with Dennis O'Keefe. Attendants indicated that the pipes could not provide any more for the scene:

> The ingenious Mr. Mann then ordered a cake of dry ice placed at O'Keefe's bare feet. A jet of air was directed to blow gently upon the ice. In no time at all, a satisfactory facsimile of steam, actually carbon dioxide, was wafting across the room.
>
> "Feels kind of cold against my feet," complained O'Keefe, whose body was covered with perspiration.

Figure 10.16

Figure 10.17

Figure 10.18

"That's all right," Mann encouraged him. "We'll get the shot in a minute."
Mann was almost right. The scene was filmed in a minute—or maybe two or three. But by that time, it was too late. O'Keefe's toes were frost-bitten.[21]

Moxie's killing of The Schemer clearly influenced a gory steam room murder in David Cronenberg's Russian mob thriller, *Eastern Promises* (2007). In *T-Men*, however, Mann constructs agonizing tension without blood, brutality, and graphic nudity. The killer's shadow envelops the victim's face amidst all the steam, tension building in alternating close-ups, low- and high-angles exquisitely lit through the steam, as The Schemer gradually realizes Moxie's intentions. The dialogue is appropriately minimalist and Paul Sawtell's music evokes a dream-like state of subdued intensity before starting to build.

Another memorable scene in *T-Men* went unmentioned by Mann and almost did not make it past censor Joseph I. Breen Sr.: the killing of agent Genero.[22] The confrontation leading to this moment is a continuation of the composition and editing tactics Mann used during the final act of *Desperate*: wide-angle subjective close-ups, extreme close-ups lit from single light sources, eyes shifting in one direction (fig. 10.19, 10.20). Breen Sr. would not allow a federal agent to be killed on screen, so Moxie's gunshot is heard

Figure 10.19

Figure 10.20

Figure 10.21

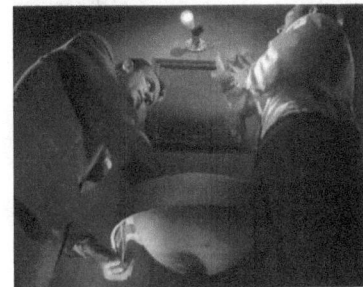

Figure 10.22

off an extreme, agonizing close-up of O'Brien. Genero grimaces and in a smoky low-angle shot, Moxie fires another bullet. Returning to O'Brien, we hear Genero whisper the last of his two final words ("you . . . suckers"), O'Brien looking downward until the brim of his fedora casts a shadow over his face and we hear the corpse dropping to the floor (fig. 10.21).

As demonstrated above, Mann had a fondness for low camera angles as a means of generating tension and discomfort. One of the most intelligent of these occurs in the final portion of the narrative when O'Brien washes his hands at a bathroom sink where Moxie is shaving (fig. 10.22). The agent has received a message to leave town with his counterfeit faceplate because the counterfeiters can now identify it. The plate is hidden beneath the sink and Mann prolongs our expectations as O'Brien tries not to act conspicuous while groping around for the plate, at one point abandoning his efforts when Moxie drops a shaving towel.

These are the kinds of showcase scenes that made the best crime thrillers of the post–World War II years so unforgettable. Rudy Behlmer recalled hearing Anthony Mann deliver an address to a group of students at the University of Southern California-Los Angeles in which the director explained part of the reasoning behind such sequences in his 1940s low-budget pictures:

His approach to them at the time was that he'd get a script and look through it to find maybe one or two sequences that lent themselves to doing something interesting directorially. Then he would plot his schedule so that he could do everything else as quickly as possible, allotting himself time for those one or two sequences that would show him off a little bit, or allow him to develop the material somewhat.[23]

Once a film was completed, Mann persuaded executives unaccustomed to watching "B" movies to view one or two sample reels containing a showcase scene. "Their comments were, 'Look what he was able to do on a very tight schedule.'"[24]

THE MAKING AND SELLING OF *T-MEN*

Mann gave his account of how the *T-Men* project started:

> I'd gone to Washington to see the authorities of the Treasury Department, and they had furnished me with abundant documentation on the Treasury Men's organization and their working methods. I then developed the idea with Johnny Higgins, insisting on his help with research, and surrounded myself with excellent actors like Dennis O'Keefe, Alfred Ryder and Wallace Ford.[25]

In typical show business fashion, William Irey had his own account. Irey told the *New York Times* that the *T-Men* project emerged after the Hollywood censorship office refused to permit production of a film about the government's arrest of gangster Al Capone on tax evasion charges. Undeterred, Irey had long conferences with John C. Higgins on ways to bring other Treasury success stories to the screen.

> Since we could not make the Capone picture as originally planned, we reached a compromise. From my personal files and from memory I embodied in Mr. Higgins' script three cases that were an integral part of the Capone investigation.[26]

Others nonetheless predated the involvement of Mann and Higgins. In October 1946, as Mann was preparing to direct *Desperate* at RKO Radio Pictures, Producers Releasing Corporation contracted Henry Blankfort to write the screenplay *T-Man*. (Producer Edward Small soon took over the project from PRC.) Virginia Kellogg is credited with the story for the film, so it is presumed Blankfort adapted her material. Writer George Brickner either replaced or assisted Blankfort one month later, and in January 1947 writer Robert B. Churchill was brought in to work on the script. In early March 1947, as Mann was embarking on *Railroaded!*, Higgins replaced Churchill.[27] Mann felt that Higgins's input was significant enough to warrant another screenwriting in-joke when villainess Diana Simpson (Jane Randolph of *Railroaded!*) informs a hood about the location of a shipment of currency paper: "It's aboard the *Higgins* right now."

Budgeted at $400,000 (nearly $4.2 million in 2013) for a three-week shooting schedule, *T-Men* eventually cost $466,300, making it the most expensive Mann picture so far, although still below the industry average. Locations (many filmed second unit) do play an essential part in the film, but so do Hollywood soundstages. Many interior scenes were filmed on stages, including a hotel room set later recycled for *Raw Deal*. On this picture, Mann, contracted under the name Anthony Bundsmann, drew his biggest paycheck since arriving in the film colony: $14,267.[28]

The largest line item was the salary of star Dennis O'Keefe[29] who, if we are to accept the usual press agent hyperbole, worked hard for his money. The publicists for distributor Eagle-Lion most likely invented this O'Keefe quotation for the film's pressbook:

> Half the film heavies in Hollywood punched my face somewhere during the eight reels, and Anthony Mann, the director, kept screaming for realism.
>
> I was scalded in a steam room, slapped, kicked and tossed around like a basketball. Mann had the cute idea of having one killer grab me by the hair and yank my head back while another belted me in the stomach. It was particularly interesting when they put a lead pencil between the fingers of one hand and then pressed.[30]

Eagle-Lion publicists assumed theater owners and journalists were unaware screen violence was simulated.

Filming began on July 31 and initially finished on August 23, 1947, with four additional days in September for retakes, new scenes, and inserted material. Mann and Alton exposed 86,160 feet of camera negative, approximately 30 percent over the budgeted amount of footage.[31] Alton described filming conditions at the time:

> The studio and Anthony Mann, the director, said they had confidence in me and that I was to photograph the story exactly as I saw fit. So we shot scenes just

as they came along. We shot under all conditions. Our night shots were made with almost no lights.

I know some people thought the scenes wouldn't match and it would be a horrible mess. Fortunately, it turned out as I was sure it would. It's natural and real and that's what makes it dramatic. That's exactly what we wanted.

In addition to our almost 100 per cent [sic] natural photography, we had another element that added to the feeling of reality. Neither Dennis O'Keefe, who is starred in the film, nor any of the other [male] players wore make-up. We did all our street scenes with masked cameras and in more cases than we expected the action was so natural that passers-by never realized they were in the middle of a movie scene.[32]

This apparently was not the case in scenes filmed outside the Detroit Public Library where the two Treasury agents research their criminal targets. As hidden cameras filmed O'Keefe's arrival at the library from the rear of a laundry truck, three bobby-soxers spotted the actor due to his dark glasses. Others besieged O'Keefe for autographs (again, if we are to believe Eagle-Lion publicists) and the scene was abandoned for the day. Convinced that the dark glasses caused the interruption, Mann ordered O'Keefe not to wear them during the next day's reshoot.[33]

Aside from Detroit and Washington, D.C., Mann and his camera crew paid visits to Montreal, Chicago, and the Los Angeles port district San Pedro for background sequences. Three special trucks outfitted with Treasury Department-style Belgian glass enabled cameras to achieve the desired semi-documentary look.[34] According to publicity accounts,

> The glass, a wartime invention, looks like mirror from the outside but permits vision with plate-glass clarity from the interior of the truck. Cameras, turning inside the trucks, recorded on film movements of star Dennis O'Keefe, the feature cast and hundreds of street passers-by who will thus become part of a motion picture.[35]

By late November, *T-Men* was finished and being trade-shown. Max E. Youngstein, Eagle-Lion's director of advertising, publicity and exploitation, sent producer Edward Small a Western Union telegram:

> THE REACTION OF LAST NIGHTS SCREENING T-MEN ON THE PART OF REPRESENTATIVES FROM SALES ADVERTISING AND PUBLICITY DEPARTMENTS WAS THE MOST ENTHUSIASTIC REACTION THAT I HAVE EVER SEEN. THIS IS NO LINE OF BULL. THIS IS A FACT.

THE PERSONNEL FROM MY DEPARTMENT RETURNED TO MY HOME AFTER THE SCREENING AND WE TALKED UNTIL THREE OCLOCK THIS MORNING ABOUT IT. WE KNOW WE HAVE A GREAT PICTURE IN T-MEN AND I PROMISE YOU ONE OF THE GREATEST CAMPAIGNS YOU HAVE EVER SEEN.[36]

Youngstein kept his word. A massive magazine campaign primarily aimed at movie publications (but also including *Parent's* and *Varsity*) featured full-page advertisements with lurid illustrations and blasting copy:

TOUGH! ... TENSE! ... TERRIFIC! ... and TRUE![37]

NAKED FURY! SAVAGE VIOLENCE! TERRIFIC ... *and true!*[38]

THIS ONE IS LOADED!
SEE Killers trapped the way it hurts most – through their women! SEE A squealer get his ... scalding death with live steam! SEE Hammering fists of vengeance batter a man to death! SEE Screaming bullets of vengeance mercilessly riddle a killer![39]

The exhibitors' pressbook recalled previous crime box office hits as it assured theater owners that

"T-MEN" is a bare-fisted, hard-hitting, tough-as-horsehide power package of the type which put the "move" in the movies! It has All the authenticity of "G-Men" ... PLUS the newsworthiness of "House on 92nd Street" ... PLUS the shock of "Brute Force" ... and the power of "The Killers!"[40]

There were explosive twists on previous ad copy:

The underworld's "Big Guys" ... plundering, torturing, murdering to build an illicit empire ... only to be betrayed by a woman's lovely lips![41]

She knew all the answers ... even how to make men die![42]

Eagle-Lion also arranged for "ten smash tieups" with such nationally advertised products as Albolene Face Cream, the Ritz Electric Broiler, American Limoges China Company, Handi-Bag (a combination handbag and umbrella), and Emerson portable radios. Dennis O'Keefe posed in a Jeep, was photographed using a Remington Rand typewriter, and advertised

Caxton Hats. The saga was also sold to children via "T-Man Shield Buttons," featuring a full-color action photo of O'Keefe.[43]

Public reaction to *T-Men* was enthusiastic. During Christmas week 1947, Eagle-Lion opened the picture at six theaters in Los Angeles and surprised observers with a strong gross of $53,300. In January 1948, the picture did "giant" business in Philadelphia where it set a house record of $22,500. At the State-Lake in the Chicago Loop, it earned a rousing $43,000 during the first week, sharing the stage with the Mills Brothers and singer Jan August, but subzero temperatures prompted a drop in income for the second week. Despite fifty-two inches of snowfall in Manhattan, the picture was strong in Times Square and ran for four weeks. E-L capitalized on New York police capturing a local counterfeiting gang, and offered a $25 reward bond to anyone correctly identifying a real "T-Man" in Times Square (it is unknown whether there were any claimants). Business was "sock" in San Francisco and Cincinnati (the latter engagement benefited from E-L tying in publicity to a local police manhunt) and "big" in Pittsburgh. By 1949, Eagle-Lion's Arthur Krim expected *T-Men* to gross over $1,250,000 in U.S. cinemas, a comfortable figure for a programmer at that time and a new record for an Anthony Mann picture.[44]

Infighting ensued between various producers eager to take credit for *T-Men*. In March 1948, Edward Small wrote a heated letter to associate producer Aubrey Schenck, accusing the latter of discrediting Small's involvement and downplaying Small in *T-Men* press materials. Small assured Schenck, "In order to avoid such a petty incident in the future, however, I have decided to change the billing on *Raw Deal*."[45]

And so the next Anthony Mann crime picture was promoted as "Edward Small's *Raw Deal*."

CHAPTER 11

RAW DEAL (1948)

If ever a case could be made for the viability of creating cinematic art from an artistically bankrupt literary source, *Raw Deal* would be it.

The story of this Anthony Mann triumph begins with *Corkscrew Alley*, a virtually unreadable sixty-two-page film treatment by Arnold B. Armstrong and Audrey Ashley. It is told in the first person by antihero Tex Lester who, with friend Bitsy Morgan, escapes from a southern chain gang where Tex is serving a sentence for armed robbery. After liberating Tex's girl "Lady" from the women's reformatory, the troika carries out a series of robberies until Tex finds legitimate work with the respectable Millicent Dillon. Lady hates Millicent for pursuing her man and becomes impatient. In one of her pithier moments, Lady tells Tex,

Figure 11.0. *Raw Deal*, 1948. Dennis O'Keefe and Raymond Burr (Photofest).

Well, dip your needle in this, Tex Lester, and shoot it in the main line: if you think I'm going to settle down in a dull little berg where nothing ever happens except Rotary on Wednesdays, Chamber of Commerce on Fridays, and Knights of Pythias on Saturday nights you're coked up for fair.[1]

In short time, Lady is out carousing and gambling away Tex's honestly earned money before heading off with Bitsy to initiate a new crime rampage as the Santa Claus Bandits, complete with Santa suits. In the end, the sheriff's posse guns down Bitsy before Tex turns Lady over to the authorities.

The *Corkscrew Alley* treatment is as dreadful as it appears, with "gritty" pulp dialogue and slang exceeding self-parody. Further evidence of this:

Bitsy was born full of tarantula juice and the only lug in this world he liked was me.[2]

In the escape car, Tex reminds Lady of her previous sickness. Lady's response:

Sick! I was going stir-simple. I've been chewing bars for two years. Let me wrap my stranglers around that wheel, and I'll show you how sick I am.[3]

During an argument with gangster Rick Coyle, Lady snaps,

You, Rick Coyle, are nothing but a Hitler. This is a free country, bub, and there's no room in it for a dictator like you.[4]

Tex describes his fight with Coyle:

Rick had sprawled on the floor. He wasn't out but he was plenty wingdingy. He sent a paw crawling toward that bulge under his left shoulder, and tried to get up. I yanked him to his feet and pulled his stinger.[5]

(A "stinger" is a gun, this slang word dating back at least to William Wellman's 1931 Warner Bros. gangster thriller, *The Public Enemy*.)

In December 1946, Eagle-Lion purchased the treatment for $1,250 (roughly $15,000 in 2013) as a Richard Basehart vehicle with *Railroaded!* producer Charles F. Riesner, a former comedy director whose credentials included Buster Keaton's *Steamboat Bill, Jr.* (1928), attached. After *T-Men* producer Edward Small took over the property, the plotline was discarded, with only the film's temporary title and villain's name retained, as well as its promotion as the "story of a chain gang."⁶

Between January and May 1947, Don Stafford wrote the first *Corkscrew Alley* screenplay. John C. Higgins replaced Stafford through the end of May, and in October and November Leopold Atlas polished the script.⁷ Under these writers, the new film narrative has Pat (Claire Trevor in the film) helping her boyfriend Joe Sullivan (Dennis O'Keefe) break out of prison. Gangster Rick Coyle (Raymond Burr), who was an accomplice in the original robbery that sent Joe to the penitentiary, has engineered the breakout. What Joe does not realize is that Coyle, not wanting to share the stolen money, anticipated Joe being killed in the robbery. Now Joe wants his $50,000 portion of the cash. After Ann (Marsha Hunt), his lawyer's secretary, threatens to go to the police, Joe takes her hostage with Pat's assistance, intending to flee with Pat to South America as soon as he gets his share of Rick's money.

Edward Small and the Eagle-Lion publicists were convinced that the film that became *Raw Deal* was not only a love story but, to quote the pressbook, "a WOMAN'S PICTURE."⁸ This is not as delusional as it seems. There is more of a woman's angle to this self-described "bullet-blazed melodrama of love and vengeance on the wrong side of the law" than customary patrons of the crime genre would expect. Claire Trevor's Pat Cameron is the storyteller, her softly spoken words of desperation accompanied by the theremin of composer Paul Sawtell, himself freed from the commercial constraints of *T-Men*. A fine, understated actress with an elegant voice who specialized in hardened roles in which she was usually the loser in a love triangle, Trevor has a magnetic screen presence ideally suited to such brawny melodrama. It would have been gratifying to discover which of the three hired writers had been responsible for Pat's sparse, hazy narration that is tastefully and unobtrusively scattered among the narrative. Regrettably, only the final Leopold Atlas drafts of the *Corkscrew Alley* screenplay are preserved among the Edward Small papers at University of Southern California, making it difficult to determine the contributions of Higgins and Stafford.

Pat's words are first heard over a shot of a "State Prison" sign, which dissolves to a full view of prison gates facing California mountains as her open sedan approaches a guard.⁹

> PAT (V.O.). This is the day. This is the day—the last time I shall drive up to these gates. These iron bars that keep the man I love locked away from me.¹⁰

The action dissolves to a subjective tracking shot courtesy of cinematographer John Alton, simulating Pat's walking, with slight shakiness and the sounds of her footsteps, as we approach a castle-style building where a uniformed man stands, his back toward the camera.

> PAT (V.O.). Tonight he breaks out of these walls. It's all set. Eleven-thirty. That's the word I'm bringing him.

In the shadowy corridor of the prison office (filmed on Stage F on the Samuel Goldwyn lot in West Hollywood), Pat, dressed in black with a bizarre veiled hat, turns the corner, walking in our direction to a low wide-angle shot at the guard's desk.

> PAT (V.O.). I don't know which sounds louder: my heels or my heart. It's always this way when I go to see . . .

The theremin theme abruptly cuts off as Pat gives the desk guard a name: "Joe Sullivan."

From this opening, the picture has differentiated itself from the average prison break thriller. It is not told through the perspective of an inmate or police detective, but from the woman who has stuck by her convict. The theremin, for once used by a film composer in a non-sensationalist fashion, only contributes to the deconstruction. During Pat's existential road trip with Joe and his pretty hostage, Pat and her theremin periodically return as she agonizes over her lover's growing attraction to Ann and begins second-guessing her own feelings for Joe. At night parked outside the prison, Pat's thoughts are again vocalized, her final words in an anxious whisper:

> PAT (V.O.). Waiting . . . waiting. All my life it seemed as if I'd been waiting for Joe. Joe . . . Joe, be careful . . . careful. . . .

Her reverie resumes at night in the car as the threesome evades police roadblocks. They sit in the front seat, Joe at the steering wheel and Ann between them:

> PAT (V.O.). We've made it all right. We've gotten out of town. But for some strange reason, I feel worse than before . . . like a two-time loser . . . Maybe it's the letdown, though there is still the roadblocks up ahead. Or maybe it's because of her, sitting next to Joe where I should be. Where I *would* be if she weren't there. If she weren't . . .

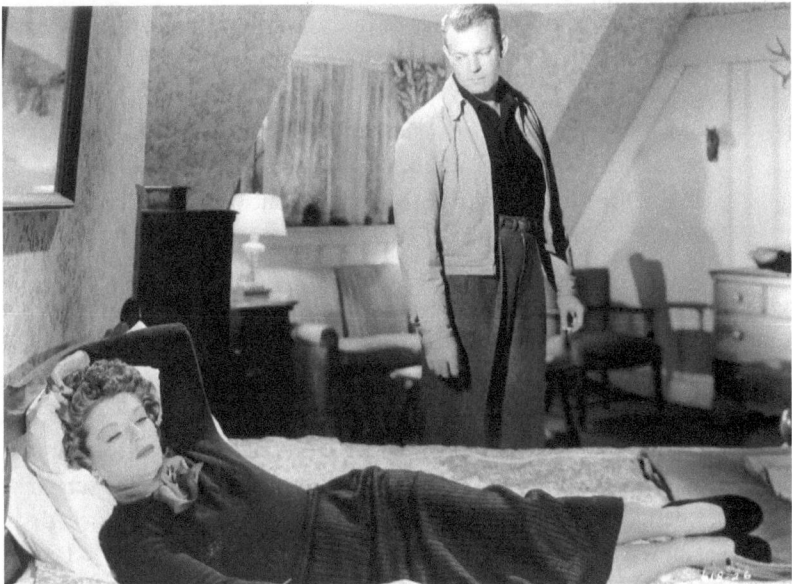

Figure 11.1. Claire Trevor and Dennis O'Keefe. This posed still repositions O'Keefe from his original position at the background window (Photofest).

Later, when the trio camps out in the forest, the camera tracks over to the campfire, Pat reclining on the ground at the center of the frame, staring up at the sky, her words emerging slowly:

> PAT (v.o.). There was the smell of the pines ... in the sky. I suddenly felt, I don't know, big and small at the same time.

Staying overnight in a tavern in the woods, Pat has another internal monologue as she reclines in bed in a beautifully composed wide-angle deep focus shot (followed by a dramatic close-up of her), Joe standing in the background, lost in thought as he stares out the window into darkness.

> PAT (v.o.). Deep down I guess I have no real beef with what I know is happening. Watching him ... one thing keeps ringing inside of me. He's never really told me he loved me. Funny how that keeps coming back now. I hadn't minded it before. I'd always been more than ready to take him at any terms.

Hollywood censor Joseph I. Breen Sr. tried and failed to get this last line of dialogue deleted.[11]

Later, when Joe and Ann are parted and the two women walk past each other on a beach road, Pat's reaction is muted:

> PAT (V.O.). I suppose I should feel some kind of victory, but I don't. I even feel sorry for her, passing her like this. She too is a dame in love with Joe, and she's lost. I've been behind that eight ball too often myself ... I ought to know how she feels ... how she feels....

One thing is indisputable: the screenplay that became *Raw Deal* was unrecognizable from the *Corkscrew Alley* treatment. Gone were characters named Bitsy and Lady. Gone were the Santa Claus Bandits. What emerged was a harshly poetic and tragic love triangle between a doomed escaped con and two very different, needy women. Under Anthony Mann's direction and John Alton's often astonishing images, the screenplay reached the screen as a bleak, woeful, fiercely beautiful cry of *film noir* despair. That it reached the screen at all is a considerable achievement.

BATTLES WITH JOSEPH I. BREEN SR.

On October 14, shortly after Mann was signed to direct the *Corkscrew Alley* project, Leopold Atlas delivered his draft of the screenplay. The script shook the foundations of the Production Code Administration. In a stern letter to David Stephenson of Eagle-Lion Films, PCA head Joseph I. Breen Sr. insisted that the screenplay was

> completely and utterly unacceptable under the provisions of the Production Code, and a motion picture developed from this screenplay could not be approved by us.
>
> The unacceptability of this story stems from its overall low moral tone. It is a sordid story of crime, immorality, brutality, gruesomeness, illicit sex and sex perversion, without the slightest suggestion of any compensating moral values whatsoever.
>
> Every one of the identifiable characters in this story is a criminal, and for a number of them there is no indication of any punishment whatever. There is not the slightest suggestion throughout this story that the forces of law and order are operating; the leading male character is shown to be a vicious criminal, successfully outwitting and thwarting the law. His death is in no way brought about through the efforts of the police and is a result merely of poor judgment

on his part. His mistress and partner in crime walks off at the end of the story scot-free.

The characterization of Rick Coyle is that of a sex pervert and a sadistic beast who is portrayed deriving sexual ecstacy [sic] by setting fire to a human being.[12]

"Sex pervert," it should be remembered, was Breen Sr.'s term for a homosexual. The industry censor ended his letter on a discouraging note:

> The general nature of this story being, as it is, fraught with so many major problems, we earnestly suggest that you dismiss considering developing this present material into a motion picture to be submitted for our approval.[13]

Eagle-Lion was not easily deterred. On November 11, 1947, a meeting took place at the E-L studios between Breen Sr., Mann, Aubrey Schenck (the uncredited associate producer), and PCA officers Harry Zehner and Eugene Dougherty. Changes were agreed upon, including in the Rick Coyle character. Breen confirmed in his follow-up letter that

> There would not be the slightest suggestion of sex perversion or perverted sadism in the characterizing of Rick Coyle. It was plainly understood that the merest suggestion of sex perversion would force us to withhold our approval of the finished picture.[14]

The Edward Small papers do not contain copies of these objectionable screenplay drafts, preventing our comprehension of what precisely made Rick Coyle appear as such a "sex pervert" to Joseph I. Breen Sr. The only clues the censor provides are confusing fragments of dialogue in a party scene where Coyle's gunman Fantail (John Ireland of *Railroaded!*) remarks to the boss during some verbal jousting, "You ought to try my way for a change." Of page 118 of the Atlas draft, Breen Sr. indicates, "Following the lines of our agreement concerning the change in the character of Rick, please eliminate his line (spoken with distaste), 'Dames!'"[15]

While Breen Sr. was successful at suppressing this aspect of the script, Eagle-Lion selectively addressed or diluted his other complaints. Rick Coyle may not have reached the screen as a homosexual, but he remained a sadist. Joe Sullivan also remained a hardened criminal. The police were relegated to cameo appearances and appear briefly in insignificant scenes.

After the November 11 meeting at Eagle-Lion, Breen Sr. was convinced that "[a] strenuous effort would be made to lift the overall flavor of the present story to a much higher plane ..." This, he was convinced, could be achieved by making Ann "the voice for morality" who would not "desert her stand for morality and accept the philosophy of Joe, but rather she would convert Joe to her way of thinking and thereby initiate his regeneration." Continuing with such wishful thinking, Breen Sr. believed arrangements were made

> to indicate to the audience in some way that Joe does not really intend to flee the county with Pat, but in some manner it will be clear that he intends to return to San Francisco and submit himself to the police.[16]

Breen Sr. was pleased "that the element of intelligent police activity would be injected into the story and continued throughout." He eagerly anticipated police waiting at the boat scheduled to take the two fugitives to Panama so it was clear Joe had not outwitted them.[17] By the time the Hollywood censor became aware of the fact that many of his key points were being downplayed, *Corkscrew Alley* had already begun production.

On November 18, first unit filming began, and on December 4, Breen Sr., having seen a revised draft of the script, sent Eagle-Lion a furious letter stating his anger over Ann not having been transformed into the "eloquent voice for morality." Breen Sr. was appalled to find Ann "radiantly happy when she learns of his [Joe's] love for her and that she is crushed and heartbroken when he sends her away from him." In this new draft, Joe was still outsmarting the police.[18] Rick Coyle was also causing new concerns for reasons explained below.

THE MAKING OF *RAW DEAL*

Between November 14 and December 13, 1947, *Corkscrew Alley* filmed second and first unit photography. Three extra days of March 1948 retakes brought the total number of production days to twenty-six. The film cost $522,039 with O'Keefe's increased salary accounting for over 10 percent of the budget, but Mann took a pay cut, earning $11,200. Location filming included Mount Wilson, Chatsworth (including the Susana Susanna Pass near the Iverson Movie Ranch), Canoga Park, Paradise Cove in Malibu, and Santa Monica Beach. Three soundstages at the Samuel Goldwyn Studios in West Hollywood housed interior sets. Not counting the second unit production work, Mann exposed 76,750 feet of camera negative.[19]

An added but dangerous perk, extravagant for a Mann production at the time, was the rental of a camera crane for six days. On December 11, the

Figure 11.2. Marsha Hunt and Anthony Mann during production of *Raw Deal* (Photofest).

final week of studio filming, the crane became overbalanced and collapsed on the set. At the time of the accident, O'Keefe and crewman Bing Hall were standing under the crane and received leg lacerations, but Alton and camera operator Lester Shorr fell sixteen feet to the ground. Alton was knocked unconscious, suffering hip bruises and a slight concussion while Shorr received a lacerated hand along with head and leg contusions. Production of *Corkscrew Alley* shut down for the day while the men were treated at the studio hospital.[20]

On April 13, 2012, Marsha Hunt attended a 35 mm screening of *Raw Deal* at the TCM Classic Film Festival in Los Angeles. During the post-screening audience questions, film researcher Chuck Willett asked the actress about her memories of working with Mann. Hunt recalled,

> Only that it was totally congenial. In our case, he did not direct our performances. He directed, I think, what you saw. He directed where the camera was, the lighting, the mood, the pace. But performance? Well, he was working with three pros—more than three, Raymond Burr and John Ireland were pretty good actors, too!—and we kind of knew our craft by the time we worked together in that film. He turned us loose assuming that we would have our

characterizations ready. I'm sorry, I really don't recall any specifics about performance direction, only that it was a very compatible set. And I think his glory as a director was probably... as I said, lighting and mood were splendid, but he didn't give the performances, the actors did.[21]

It could be that Mann allowed the actors to fend for themselves while he expended energies on the technical side of the picture. It could also be that Hunt and the others were not as conscious of his directing methods, which may have been more sedate than that of most Hollywood directors. Mann was a veteran stage actor and former theatrical director, so it is unlikely he would have been indifferent towards his actors, regardless of how tight the filming schedule or seasoned the players. Yet there is no question that he had moved beyond being burdened with "actors who can't be made to say lines" and was now experiencing the comfort of maneuvering screen professionals who required less guidance.

Cinematographer John Alton establishes angst and atmosphere with a variety of wide-angle lenses and expressionist lighting strategies when Claire Trevor's Pat and Marsha Hunt's Ann visit Joe separately. In the visiting room where Ann converses with the prisoner, Alton films Joe through the wire screen in a wide-angle diagonal shot, another prisoner visible in the background, shadows and prison bar patterns in the left of the frame (fig. 11.3). In his book *Painting with Light*, Alton described the methodology behind the symbolic lighting techniques of the old studio era:

> There is nothing romantic about the drab, gray prison scene. The prison mood can best be presented with display of lights and deep shadows. Black iron bars are the traditional symbol of captivity. It is sufficient to show the black shadows of bars on a wall to indicate that the scene is laid in a prison.[22]

In the moments leading up to Joe's night prison break, Mann and Alton construct edginess through shadow and illumination effects as Pat sits in the getaway car. The camera films her from behind, as shadows of a passing train are projected on the building, the top of her face visible in the rearview mirror. In a continuation of a brief technique he used in *Desperate*, Mann places the camera in a real car as it drives in the direction of the searchlights and gunfire.

Plans for a one-way trip to Panama in three days go awry when police bullet holes put the getaway car out of commission and the duo resorts to stealing Ann's car, with Ann as their hostage, to throw off the dragnets. This is where the love triangle begins in all its savage futility. A scene challenging

Figure 11.3

everyone involved (filmed on Stage A at Goldwyn) occurs when Joe sneaks into Ann's bedroom at night to kiss her as she sleeps, stifling her scream with a hand. The publicists cited O'Keefe as contributing to this scene that called for Joe "literally to yank the sleeping beauty out of her slumber, caveman style, because that's how this rough-and-rugged character would act." As a concession, Mann apparently filmed it both ways.[23]

The sexuality of the Ann character led to further PCA anxieties. Once she is out of bed (Marsha Hunt wore a new fashion of strapless nightgown) she tries reasoning with him by saying, "If I had a gun, I'd stop you." His response in the film is, "You don't need a gun, baby." In the script, after her dressing gown came open, Joe was to have added, "You've got a lot more. And twice as deadly." Several pages later, Joe was to have admired Ann in a mirror as she wore only her underpants, but Breen Sr. put a stop to that as well. The fugitive's dialogue, "You keep your eye on Miss Law and Order here. She might go soprano on us," was also adjusted, at the censor's insistence, from the original reference to the hostage as "Miss Cutie-pants." Furthermore, Breen insisted on an erotically tinged scene of Joe observing Ann swimming at night being replaced with a chaste dialogue exchange between them, which it was.[24]

As the threesome continues on the road to San Francisco, Alton and his second unit crew begin economizing by resorting to day-for-night location photography, which involved filtering the camera lens during daytime filming to simulate nighttime as the sedan drives along country roads and mountains. This photographic device is rarely convincing in any motion picture (especially those photographed in color) but reduces time and costs. For monochromatic film, these shots are achieved with red filters or by combining pink and green filters in front of the camera lens.[25] In a majority of situations, they are as convincing in simulating nighttime or twilight as a pair of sunglasses. One day-for-night angle that does work in *Raw Deal*, however, occurs after an unsuspecting forest ranger on horseback trots away from Joe in what is the first real "western" image (filmed in Chatsworth, California) to appear in an Anthony Mann film.

The action shifts on occasion to the villain of the piece, Rick Coyle, with Raymond Burr resuming his unsavory characteristics from *Desperate*, albeit in a more mercenary and caustic manner. Early in the story, Rick speaks to fellow hoodlum Fantail (John Ireland) about Joe:

> RICK. He was screaming he wanted out. When a man screams, I don't like it—especially a friend. He might scream loud enough for the DA to hear. I don't wanna hurt the DA's ears. He's sensitive.

In a party scene in which Rick is on edge because Joe is still running loose and demanding the $50,000 owed him, the villain hurls a flaming chafing dish at his girlfriend Marcy (Chili Williams). Not surprisingly, Breen Sr. wanted this portion of the script eliminated. A few days before it was to be filmed, Joseph Breen Jr. of the Eagle-Lion story department wrote his father,

> We will not show the flaming dish hitting Marcy. We will show Rick throwing it and then cut to the reactions of the crowd; or we will show Rick throwing it and then go to a Closeup of Marcy and show her reaction, without showing the flaming dish hitting her. We feel this can be done without being excessively brutal. Please advise on this.[26]

In a final show of familial subservience, Breen Jr. added,

> Maybe I'm just full of Thanksgiving turkey which may cause my brain not to function, but I do feel this script has been pretty well cleaned up – thanks to all your constructive help.[27]

In late November 1947, the scene went before the cameras on Stage F at Goldwyn.[28] In the *Raw Deal* pressbook, Eagle-Lion publicists engaged in their usual exaggerations of fact:

> The screenplay by Leopold Atlas and John C. Higgins called for Raymond Burr, as a sadistic gangster, to drench Chili with flaming brandy, turning her into a burning torch. Director Anthony Mann explained the script requirement to the departments and they turned up with the small clothes which, they assured Mann, would be fireproof, comfortable and non-transparent.

Figure 11.4

Junoesque Chili appeared on the set ready for her scene and wearing the panties, bra and a worried look. "The script says the scene's a closeup," Chili worried, "so what happens when the burning brandy hits my exposed midriff?"

"That's easy," Mann said, "I'll spray it beforehand with asbestos paint." And that's what he did.[29]

This bears no resemblance to the filmed results. At the party, Marcy drunkenly dances with another man and accidentally bumps into Rick, spilling her drink on his back. There is a cut to an unsettling low wide-angle medium shot of Rick looking in their direction while brushing the booze from his suit (fig. 11.4). In a master shot, Rick turns to grab the chafing dish and the action cuts to a jolting subjective angle of him tossing the contents directly into the camera.

The next cut is a quick low-angle medium shot of Rick staring downward as we hear Marcy's scream. Interviewed in 1953, Mann observed of a new Fritz Lang thriller,

> I saw *The Big Heat*, in which Gloria Grahame got a pot of scalding coffee in her face. I had THAT in a picture released five years ago, *Raw Deal*.[30]

(Complicating arguments against male filmmakers of the post–World War II era suggestively visualizing such screen violence against women is the fact that two years prior to *Raw Deal*, producer Joan Harrison depicted a more explicit coffee-hurdling scene in her RKO release *Nocturne*. In that 1946 *film noir*, George Raft scalds villain Bernard Hoffman with coffee during a fight—and the camera actually shows the latter's face in close-up as the liquid splatters him.)

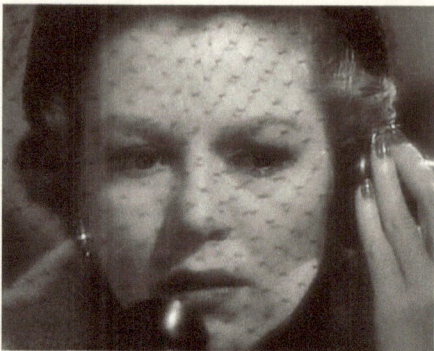

Figure 11.5

The tavern in the woods section of the film features a forceful sequence of an escaped murderer (Whit Bissell) seeking refuge from the police. This character is introduced to give Joe an idea of what he will face if he continues his criminal path. Fortunately, there is too much intelligent writing, acting, and staging for the scene to be anything other than an exemplary instance of how Mann and his creative team gave emotional and psychological dimension to melodramatic devices. Breen Sr. was never fond of the scene, particularly

> the action of the police shooting the man who has left the tavern to surrender. This is nothing more than cold-blooded murder on the part of the police. The police, we believe, should be shown merely arresting this man.[31]

A compromise was reached. The murderer breaks free from the tavern, delirious and insistent upon not being able to go on living without his dead wife, firing into the air before the police gun him down.

The final cataclysmic round of San Francisco night scenes occur as Joe and Pat prepare to escape on a freighter bound for South America after she has dissuaded him from demanding his money from Rick. The veil Pat wore in the opening prison scene now covers her face and Alton uses it to magnificent advantage in an extreme close-up as she ponders suppressing from Joe news that the gangsters have captured Ann with intent to harm her at 12:30 a.m. unless he shows up to face Rick.

The veil also dominates the most artistically startling and gut-wrenching scene in the picture, which takes place in the dark ship's cabin with light coming in from a port window. As the couple waits for the boat to shove off (Breen Sr. had failed to arrange for the police to surprise them at the dock),

Joe finally talks himself into marrying Pat. Staring out at the fog, his back to the camera, he begins a minimalist soliloquy in an attempt to convince them both of their future in South America. With Paul Sawtell's softly frenetic music and John Alton's images of Pat in silhouetted profile or reflected in the cabin clock, one is hard-pressed to recall a melancholy scene in the entire *film noir* canon whose conceptual elegance matches this one.

> JOE. Lights of Frisco. Embarking out in a minute . . . You know, I've been doing a lot of thinking lately—no laugh. In five or ten minutes we'll be pullin' out. Pullin' out for a new country. Leaving everything behind. Maybe . . . maybe we can make a different life for ourselves in South America. A good life. A fella could, I hear. I never been there myself but some friends of mine told me. (*He lights a cigarette.*) They say it's a good place . . . a new place. Might be able to get a little . . . little ranch, or . . . or little business or something . . . Start fresh. Decent. Have a house, kids maybe, bring 'em up right. Scrub 'em all up, send 'em off to school. (*Engine sounds.*) It's the engines. Five, six minutes we'll be shoving off.

His soliloquy is intercut with Pat and the cabin clock, whose time registers 12:14.

> JOE. You know, with everything we got on the ball we oughta be able to make something out of ourselves . . . something, something *decent*, something not always afraid of the daylight.

It is not clear who among the three credited writers was responsible for this sublime scene. The matter will remain a mystery until the initial drafts of the screenplay are located. Mann certainly maximizes the talents of his two actors, as does Alton the resources of his limited sets and lights, each camera angle a work of photographic perfection (fig. 11.6–11.10).

In November 1947, undisclosed problems arose for Mann during filming on Stage F at Goldwyn of the final battle between Joe and Rick in the latter's burning apartment. This was among several scenes retaken on March 15, 17, and 19, 1948, and Guy Roe of *Railroaded!* lit and photographed them. By late March 1948, Edward Small informed Eagle-Lion that the retakes had been inserted into the picture "besides making some other editorial changes." Small's response was restrained. "I believe the picture is a good solid piece of entertainment and with O'Keefe in it following *T-Men*, it ought to get some money."[32]

Figure 11.6

Figure 11.7

Figure 11.8

Figure 11.9

Figure 11.10

THE SELLING OF *RAW DEAL*

Eager to capitalize on the success of *T-Men*, the Eagle-Lion publicity machine established promotional tie-ins with Marsha Hunt and Emerson portable radios via twenty-four-sheet billboard advertisements in seventy-five cities and 15,000 window display cards. Hunt and O'Keefe appeared on the advertising pages of *Life*, *Look*, and other weekly magazines, promoting Inner Sanctum Wallets in connection with the E-L release. The studio capitalized on the violent crime comic book wave by arranging with *Mysterious Traveler Comics* to produce a sixteen-page comic strip version of *Raw Deal* in its first issue scheduled for June 1948, just as the film expanded its release. As things turned out, the issue did not reach newsstands until November and only then as an eight-page strip (with Bob Powell illustrations), so momentum was lost.[33]

Eagle-Lion publicists devised their usual circus midway-style showmanship tips for theater exhibitors. Theaters were encouraged to hold contests where entrants submitted twenty-five-word letters on the worst raw deals they ever had. E-L encouraged exhibitors to station reporters outside cinemas the day before *Raw Deal* opened to ask exiting patrons, "What's the worst raw deal you ever got?"[34] E-L also had a sense of civic responsibility:

> Contact local safety authorities with an idea for a poster to be tacked to street light [sic] poles or placed in schools which can use "Raw Deal" title to punch across a safety message. Art for poster can show an accident and copy can read:
> DON'T GIVE YOURSELF A RAW DEAL
> OBEY TRAFFIC SAFETY RULES![35]

In the advertising copy, E-L's anonymous copywriters did not disappoint:

> BULLETS! WOMEN!
> CAN'T HOLD A MAN LIKE THIS!
> Guns couldn't scare him—
> Cops couldn't stop him—
> He's out to kill or be killed in the screen's most startling story of revenge ... a dangerous guy who couldn't stay away from guns ... or women![36]

> DOUBLECROSS HIM ... and die! A dangerous guy in a deadly game—where a woman's kiss could be loaded—with death![37]

> GUNS or WOMEN—HE COULDN'T STAY AWAY FROM EITHER ... even if it meant his life! ...[38]

Some ads focused on the woman's angle with a drawing of Hunt holding a gun:

> "I KNOW HE'S A KILLER ... BUT HE'S MINE—and no one can take him away!"[39]

> IT'S TWICE AS TERRIFIC AS 'T-MEN'![40]

In many ways, it is.

In the end, *Raw Deal* was a pleasant success but not as big as its predecessor. In May 1948, it shared the bill at five theaters in Los Angeles with Eagle-Lion's *Assigned to Danger*. This double feature earned nearly $20,000 less its first week than *T-Men* had during the previous Christmas holiday, and only the downtown Orpheum (location of the negative audience response to Mann's *Strangers in the Night* three years earlier) generated a "hefty" figure. In Boston, where the companion feature was the Allied Artists release, *Song of My Heart,* box office was "mild," and in Times Square and Chicago the openings were "good" and "big." The Hippodrome in Baltimore played it as a solo attraction with live vaudeville, but response was only "fairish." In Cincinnati, business was "zippy," but the biggest returns were in Cleveland with a live warm-up act that included comedian Henny Youngman, leading the film to an "okay" $25,500 box office take at slightly higher admission prices. By early 1949, *Raw Deal* was expected to gross $1 million in the United States, a significant amount for a downbeat thriller.[41]

Raw Deal was the last screen credit for writer Leopold Atlas, soon to be pursued by the House Committee on Un-American Activities in the wake of his Communist Political Association affiliations. On March 12, 1953, Atlas testified as a cooperative witness in Los Angeles before HUAC, informing on others as he recanted his past. The experience killed him: he died of a heart attack on September 30, 1954, at age forty-six.[42]

For his part, Anthony Mann was en route to a third consecutive crime thriller success at Eagle-Lion. But unlike *T-Men* and *Raw Deal*, he would not receive credit for his work and would be all but invisible in the eyes of publicists, reporters, and promoters.

CHAPTER 12

HE WALKED BY NIGHT[1] (1948)

The 1948 Eagle-Lion thriller *He Walked By Night* is the most confounding event in Anthony Mann's career. Mann is not credited in the film but is believed to have either directed the production in full or in part. Before addressing this conundrum, let us first return to the scene of a crime.

Figure 12.0. *He Walked By Night*, 1948. Richard Basehart (Photofest).

THE CASE OF "MACHINE GUN WALKER"

On the night of June 5, 1946, California Highway Patrolman Loren Roosevelt, the former Arcadia police chief, had a violent altercation with twenty-eight-year-old William Erwin Walker. On his hospital deathbed, Roosevelt testified that he had chased speeding motorist Walker and that the latter began firing a gun at him. Roosevelt shot back despite (according to a newspaper account) being hit at close range with nine .45 caliber bullets. Walker's 1942 sedan was later found abandoned not far from the crime scene, the car's contents containing a submachine gun stolen from a government surplus store, dynamite caps, a nitroglycerine bottle, and burglary tools.[2] Roosevelt died as a result of his bullet wounds.

Walker told a different version of the night's events. He claimed Roosevelt accosted him as Walker was loitering in front of a Los Feliz market at Los Feliz Boulevard and Brunswick Avenue:

> He called me over to his car. I saw he had a gun in his hand. He shot at me and I dodged and shot him twice. After I shot him, he asked me to call an ambulance. I told him I wouldn't do anything to help him.[3]

Walker later admitted that Roosevelt had surprised him in the midst of a burglary. During his getaway, Walker dismantled and tossed portions of the murder weapon into a canyon along Griffith Park.[4]

Walker himself had a police background. Before serving in the army in the Pacific, the radar and sound technology expert worked between 1940 and 1942 as a radio dispatcher for the Glendale, California, police department. Deciding against resuming his police job after his 1945 army discharge, Walker went on a $70,000 robbery spree in Los Angeles, which included holdups and safecracking. On the evening of April 25, 1946 (more than a month before the slaying of Roosevelt), two detective sergeants on a stakeout traded gunfire with Walker while attempting to apprehend him outside the home of a man to whom the thief was planning to sell $40,000 in stolen electronics equipment. Shot in the stomach and left leg, Walker rushed home to treat his own wounds.[5]

On December 20, 1946, Los Angeles police raided Walker's Argyle Avenue apartment in Hollywood. Walker was asleep at the time, a .45 caliber pistol at his bedside and a submachine gun (one of at least half a dozen he owned) on the bed next to him. Captain Jack Donahoe and detective sergeants Earle Rombeau and Marty Wynn of the homicide division led the intrusion, which woke up Walker. The *Los Angeles Times* newspaper account reads like a John C. Higgins film treatment:

> The suspect, awakened by officers as they turned the door key in the lock, arose and crouched in the darkness of his bedroom to hide. He reached for his submachine gun, grasping it too late to fire at the officers bearing down on him....
>
> In the struggle that ensued, Walker lost his grip on the weapon temporarily. Though Capt. Donahoe fell on the gun, the suspect, undaunted by head blows administered by Wynn, wrested it from beneath the officer and once more became a threat to the police.
>
> He was subdued only after Wynn shot him twice, once through the shoulder and once through the back. Even the wounds, however, failed to end the fighting immediately, Walker continuing to combat his captors until his strength ebbed.[6]

Once in custody, Walker allegedly told of two motorcycle policemen pulling him over the previous week on Hollywood Boulevard for a minor traffic offense. Walker had a hidden submachine gun at the time, so the cops were fortunate to have let him off with a warning, thus avoiding a deadly confrontation. This was how William Erwin Walker soon came to be known as "Machine Gun Walker."[7]

TRANSLATING THE WALKER CASE TO FILM

He Walked By Night is based on the Walker case and is generally faithful to the aforementioned events. The film reshuffles certain aspects (on screen, the killer's robbery spree occurs after the cop-killing) and censorship restrictions concerning machine guns prevented the Walker character ("Roy Morgan") from possessing such weapons. There is also the glorious artistic license taken with the climatic police pursuit of the killer, one of the greatest of all crime film sequences, through the Los Angeles storm drain system. This historic cinematic chase was invented for the picture.

The portrayal of an intelligent and skilled criminal psychopath whose brilliance leaves law enforcers baffled for much of the story makes *He Walked By Night* unusual for its time. As in the case of *T-Men*, the film incorporates both *film policier* and *film noir* elements into the narrative structure. There are two stories being told continually, one from the police perspective and the other from that of the killer. The police sections utilize a deep-voiced narrator who speaks with newsreel intensity and are heavy with dialogue as detectives confront one another, compulsively examine forensics evidence, employ dragnets to snare and interrogate suspects, and come close to suffering emotional collapse in their tireless searches for suspects and clues. Detectives Brennan and Jones (Scott Brady and James Cardwell) playfully call each other "Junior" as their fatherly superior (Roy Roberts) inquires about family members and repeats information already visualized in previous scenes. Despite the Roy Morgan character, like Erwin Walker, being a former police department worker, the film wants the audience to differentiate between policemen and police department staff. As a detective closes in on the killer, a police clerk reminds him, "And remember: he was a *civilian* employee!"[8]

In contrast, the camera has an assertive presence in the stark scenes with killer Roy Morgan (Richard Basehart) where dialogue is kept to a minimum and tension builds relentlessly. (In fact, Basehart was so concerned about the lack of dialogue in his scenes that it was necessary for Eagle-Lion to assure him that screen time was more valuable to an actor than the number of spoken lines.) The more pedestrian aspects of *He Walked By Night*, the *policier* aspects, inspired actor Jack Webb, who plays Lt. Lee in three forensics scenes. Webb secured the role after attracting industry attention on the San Francisco mystery radio series *Pat Novak for Hire*. During production of *He Walked By Night*, Webb befriended Detective Sergeant Marty Wynn, who was hired to be the film's technical advisor.[9] Dialogue director Stewart Stern (later screenwriter of *Rebel Without a Cause*) was present when the two met on an Eagle-Lion soundstage:

> Webb came over and in my presence (I was just standing there) he had the idea for *Dragnet*. It happened right on the set at Eagle-Lion! He and this cop immediately had a conference and they found in themselves the means of going ahead and doing that thing.[10]

Indeed, *He Walked By Night* clearly inspired the general structure of Webb's *Dragnet* television series (NBC-TV, 1951–59 and 1967–70). The opening statement in the 1948 film even assures us that "only the names are changed—to protect the innocent." The narrator then speaks over an introductory panoramic view of flat Los Angeles and other candid city scenes:

> NARRATOR. This is Los Angeles—Our Lady the Queen of the Angels as the Spaniards named her. The fastest-growing city in the nation. It's been called

a bunch of suburbs in search of a city, and it's been called the glamour capital of the world.

The next image is recycled footage from *T-Men* showing Dennis O'Keefe outside Union Station preparing to cross the street over to Chinatown. The narrator continues,

> NARRATOR. A Mecca for tourists. A stopover for transients. A target for gangsters...

After sharing population and geographical statistics, the narrator takes us to downtown police headquarters where dispatchers read handwritten notes from a conveyor belt familiar to viewers of another Jack Webb TV series, *Adam-12* (NBC-TV, 1968–75). This is where blatant similarities between *He Walked By Night* and Webb's television programming end.

ALFRED WERKER VS. ANTHONY MANN

Eagle-Lion credited Alfred Werker with directing *He Walked By Night*. A July 1949 *New York Times* account of a Swiss film festival jury voting the thriller best crime picture of the year refers to the winner as "Alfred Werker's *He Walked By Night*."[11] A *Times* article the following month about Werker reported,

> By 1948 he was ready to accept a job directing *He Walked By Night* at Eagle-Lion for $5,000, even though preparing, shooting and editing the picture took nearly twenty weeks.[12]

Anthony Mann never mentioned this movie in his handful of published interviews, an odd occurrence considering it earned as much as *T-Men* at U.S. box offices. Yet the underlying assumption is that Mann is the creative brains behind *He Walked By Night* and at the very least directed the unsurpassed chase and shootout in the underground Los Angeles storm drains. There is also the dominant presence of creative and technical staff from either *T-Men* or *Raw Deal* (screenwriter, cinematographer, camera operator, editor, assistant director, art director, set director, musical director, photographic effects, special art effects) and even *Desperate* (contributing writer Harry Essex), not to mention the aforementioned inclusion of *T-Men* footage, to convince us of Mann's participation. Moreover, given his ability to rush from one project to another while barely catching a breath, Mann could have found a way to direct the film between *Raw Deal* and *Reign of Terror/The Black Book*. John Alton photographed all three pictures, so Mann could likewise have directed all three. But where is the evidence to support this and how did rumors of Mann's involvement originate?

In the December 1987 issue of the British film magazine *Film Dope*, scholar Michael Walker mentions four specific scenes in *He Walked By Night* (one third of the film) attributable to Mann.[13] When contacted, Walker indicated that others had researched this information but recalled the same data appearing in the May 1967 *Cahiers du Cinéma* interview with Mann, credited to Patrick Brion and Olivier Eyquem. Eyquem was then contacted in France and explained that he and Brion only assembled the accompanying filmography and did not conduct the actual interview. It was Jean-Claude Missiaen, author of the first book written on Mann, *Anthony Mann* (1964), who interviewed the director. According to Eyquem,

> Missiaen visited Mann on the *Heroes of Telemark* set for a few days and had several conversations with him at that time. Mann did not recall *He Walked By Night*'s title per se, but his indications were quite clear and the actors and scenes (notably the sewer sequence) quoted left NO doubt as to the identity of the film. None of us had seen *He Walked By Night* at that time, and watching it later at the Cinémathèque left little doubt.[14]

Several months later, Missiaen confirmed in a handwritten note his conversations with Mann about *He Walked By Night*. In the meantime, other eyewitnesses were pursued. Screenwriter Stewart Stern, who as dialogue director witnessed the filming in the storm drains back in 1948, was reached by telephone and confirmed that Mann not only directed that sequence but others as well. "I don't remember the reason Tony took over," he said. "I think Werker got sick. I think I got a call telling me that I would have to replace Werker the next day. Then Tony appeared and I've never been more relieved in my life!" Stern added, "I don't think Werker worked a day on that, but I'm not sure."[15]

Other routes led to impasses. Although eager to assist in the search for clues, the Los Angeles Department of Public Works was not able to locate any data in the city archives pertaining to Eagle-Lion location filming in the summer of 1948 for *29 Clues* (the working title of *He Walked By Night*). There was hope that a box among the Eagle-Lion papers at the Wisconsin Center for Film and Theater Research in Madison, Wisconsin, would

Figure 12.1. Scott Brady (left), Roy Roberts (second from left), and fellow policemen in the Los Angeles storm drains sequence, one of several Mann directed without credit (Photofest).

contain the solutions to this mystery, i.e., payroll information or daily production reports. Two Milwaukee researchers made the journey to Madison only to discover that the box contained nothing other than mortgages, contracts, and financial correspondence. "The documentation for [the 1948 Robert Kane production] *Canon City* was much more complete than for aka *29 Clues*," wrote researcher Dr. Richard Brigham. "It was almost as if the documents that would have definitively answered your question were lifted from the files."[16]

A quick perusal of Alfred Werker's 1928–57 filmography suggests an open-and-shut case in Mann's favor. Most Werker pictures are inexpensive programmers with occasional titles, including *The House of Rothschild* (1934), *Kidnapped* (1938), and the live-action sequences for Disney's *The Reluctant Dragon* (1941), that were more than ordinary studio hackwork. Werker's involvement in the ruination of Erich von Stroheim's only talkie as director, *Walking Down Broadway*, which Werker and others re-filmed at the insistence of Fox executives as *Hello, Sister!* (1933), further tarnishes his legacy Even so, there are a few *noir/policier* entries in Werker's otherwise bland filmography. The seventy-minute Twentieth Century-Fox insane asylum *noir* melodrama *Shock* (1946) demonstrates a knack for stylish suspense horror-thriller material. Werker's 1947 Eagle-Lion picture *Repeat Perforamnce*, in which a woman (Joan Leslie) relives the year 1946 after committing a murder, features occasionally atmospheric lighting to visualize the clever premise.

On the other hand, Werker's 1952 Columbia-FBI *film policier Walk East on Beacon!*, the closest in conception to *He Walked By Night*, is a compendium of poor performances and slipshod direction that is salvaged only by Boston location photography. Another Columbia potboiler, *The Young Don't Cry* (1957), Werker's last film, is erratically directed and, with few exceptions, amateurishly acted. When placed alongside these efforts, *He Walked By Night* does not appear to emanate from the same director.

In comparing the directing styles of Mann and Werker, it is evident that even the best Werker thrillers are plagued with uneven direction of actors. Vincent Price and Lynn Bari, for example, effortlessly overshadow their rigid costars in *Shock*. The acting in *Repeat Performance* is of a generally affected style seldom encountered in a Mann production of this period. This unevenness is also evident in *He Walked By Night*, where little effort has been made to elevate weak actors (Scott Brady, brother of Lawrence Tierny) to the levels of the film's more accomplished and confident performers (Richard Basehart, Whit Bissell). The flatness of most of the dialogue scenes in which Basehart and Bissell do not appear makes it extremely unlikely that Anthony Mann was the sole director of this thriller.

There is no reason why Mann would have lied to Missiaen about his involvement in a low-budget picture whose title he could not recall. Although Stern was eighty-nine years old when interviewed via telephone, he was a sharp interview subject, even if he admitted to having only a selective memory of his Eagle-Lion days. The available evidence supports theories that Werker and Mann directed different sections of *He Walked By Night*. Even so, why did Eagle-Lion decline to give Mann credit? As strange as it may appear today, in an age where screen credits are seemingly out of control, there was nothing conspiratorial on Eagle-Lion's part back in 1948.

A director under contract to a studio (as Mann was to Eagle-Lion) could expect to be shuffled from picture to picture whenever the schedule demanded, even if it meant directing portions of someone else's project. During the silent era, Josef von Sternberg worked without credit on Frank Lloyd's *Children of Divorce* (1927) just as Nicholas Ray was not credited when he took over direction of Sternberg's *Macao* (1952). Richard Fleischer was brought in to direct revised sequences for the John Farrow RKO comedy-thriller *His Kind of Woman* (1951) just as William Cameron Menzies was brought in to direct retakes for Fleischer's *The Narrow Margin* (1952).[17] Fleischer rationalized the process in his 1993 memoir:

> I'd get my chance to work with stars at last, and, since I would not be getting any screen credit, there was no risk as far as the final outcome of the film was

concerned. If I did a lousy job, John Farrow would get the blame. If I did a great job, I'd be a hero. There was nothing to lose and everything to gain.[18]

This was the common attitude among contracted directors, especially if the film in question was a low-budget programmer.

THE ANTHONY MANN SCENES

Mann filmographies in *Film Dope* and *Cahiers du Cinéma* mention his directing the Richard Basehart exteriors, but *Film Dope* specifies these as including the first murder sequence. If *T-Men* unofficially began with the ill-fated rendezvous between the agent and the informer, then *He Walked By Night* commences with the opening two-minute, forty-five-second crime sequence, which begins with a high contrast long shot of Roy Martin crossing a tree-lined street in silhouette. A background street lamp casts his figure in long shadow. Peerless applications of harsh source lighting and bold wide angles continue to enhance this example of Mann and Alton's monochromatic artwork. Roy and his shadow reach a closed Radio Television Supply store. From an inside window filmed from a low-angle (fig. 12.2), Roy removes a small zippered case with gloved hands, which, in close-up, contains lock-picking tools. Roy abandons his burglary after noticing a sedan with an off-duty policeman (fig. 12.3). In a tracking shot unusual for a Mann crime picture, the camera moves with Roy as he walks past shrubbery, half-looking over his shoulder and tossing the tool case and gloves. Roy walks toward a corner lit by a street lamp casting more long shadows (fig. 12.4).

In a reverse angle from around the corner, the sedan stops alongside the suspect. "Hey, fella, c'mere," says the officer. Through the passenger window of the sedan, grinning Roy walks toward the camera, explaining he was on his way home. When asked to show identification, Roy smiles before realizing he has forgotten his wallet. The cop politely persists, and Roy responds, "How about my army discharge? I got it right here . . . !" Roy's identification is a revolver and three bullets. A music cue is heard. The barely conscious officer crashes his sedan into Roy's car. Neighbors gather and Roy runs across a dark field, away from the camera until he becomes a distant figure.

Another engrossing Mann section, running close to four minutes, occurs approximately half an hour into the film when Roy makes a late-night appearance at an electronics store whose meek owner Reeves (Whit Bissell) has inadvertently served as a fence for the killer's stolen equipment, which

Figure 12.2

Figure 12.3

Figure 12.4

includes a television projector. Unbeknownst to Roy, Detectives Brennan and Jones have staked out the store. Each Mann and Alton image in this section builds upon the atmosphere of anxiety without intrusion of background music. The lighting design, depicting Roy as both a silhouette and a partially lit face, accentuates the tension (fig. 12.5, 12.6) and there are two impeccable darkly lit long shots of the two detectives and Roy watching the nervous Reeves.

In a similar vein, the paranoia of the killer as he senses himself in a trap is conveyed in masterfully composed low- and high-angles (fig. 12.7, 12.8).

Figure 12.5

Figure 12.6

Figure 12.7

Figure 12.8

The third scene attributed to Mann occurs after Brennan shoots Roy. It is the two-minute scene where the killer performs surgery on himself at night in his apartment. This dialogue- and music-less scene makes full use of the dramatic close-up as we see perspiring Roy, shirtless and with a towel tossed over his right shoulder, mirror in his right hand, gritting painfully and panting, steam floating up past his face. This indelible image is a bravura application of suggestion, Roy almost fighting back tears before finally gasping and trembling as he holds up a portion of a bullet (fig. 12.9, 12.10).

The true-life Erwin Walker story seemed to have all the elements of an exciting police drama, even the violent apartment arrest scene where police bullets fail to deter the crazed antagonist. But this was not enough for the producers. The killer's capture demanded something bigger than an apartment. It needed a prominent location. Mann's most noted contribution to *He Walked By Night* is the heralded storm drain sequence that is the film's climax and predates Harry Lime's escape through the Vienna sewers in Carol Reed's *The Third Man*, released the following year. The underground sewers first appear thirty-eight minutes into *He Walked By Night* following Roy's liquor store robbery. In one of the sequence's innumerable well-composed images, he enters a circular passage and crawls out of a pipe, partially

Figure 12.9

Figure 12.10

Figure 12.11

Figure 12.12

Figure 12.13

Figure 12.14

silhouetted in the circle of the pipe (fig. 12.11), before dropping from view. In the pitch-black sewer, the silhouetted Roy runs toward the background, following the beam of his flashlight until he is a tiny figure in blackness.

During the final eight minutes of the picture, a police dragnet, having cordoned off the outlets, pursues Roy through the storm drains. The sequence is a cinematic gallery of single source lighting bouncing off wet brick walls, bobbing flashlights in dark, foggy tunnels, echoing footsteps pounding concrete, tunnel tracking shots behind and in front of police pursuers, and more bobbing police flashlights in the black distance (fig. 12.12, 12.13, 12.14).

The film cuts back and forth between Roy's fleeing silhouette and the distant bobbing police flashlights until the eventual showdown within the confines of a drainage system crossroads, which may or may not be a studio set (fig. 12.15, 12.16, 12.17).

With this storm drain pursuit, Mann and Alton substantiated that expressionist cinematography was not limited to interiors lighted with 2000-watt bulbs. Dialogue director Stewart Stern recalls the location filming below the streets of Los Angeles:

> John Alton I remember very well, just really loved [him]. His contributions and discoveries on that set were unprecedented. I do remember shooting in

Figure 12.15

Figure 12.16

Figure 12.17

the sewers and the magic that he did in there just using flashlights. He had had no patience with old-fashioned methods . . . He saved our lives. I don't know how many hours of work he saved for Tony . . . They were indispensable to each other. Most of the stuff [photographic methods] was pretty flat, studio shooting. But it all had to happen so fast because of the brevity of the schedule.[19]

According to Jean-Claude Missiaen, "Tony was often looking for what he called 'daring shots' (his own words). John Alton, Ernest Haller[20] and Robert Krasker[21] had sometimes a hard time with him."[22] Missiaen remembered Mann alluding to friction between Mann and Alton during *He Walked By Night*:

> Alton did not appreciate the shots in the sewers. Why? Because one can have a glimpse at the *wires* going from Basehart to the electric generator. Remember we were back in 1949!! Tony wanted to keep the slam-bang of this striking sequence, made before Carol Reed's *The Third Man*.[23]

These above sequences are those credited to Mann, which account for nearly 22 percent of *He Walked By Night*'s seventy-nine minutes.

HE WALKED BY NIGHT BEFORE ANTHONY MANN

Screenwriter Crane Wilbur, inspired by the Erwin "Machine Gun" Walker case, wrote *The L.A. Investigator* for producer Bryan Foy as an Eagle-Lion project. Aiming for a realistic "documentary" style, Wilbur approached local police departments to interview people connected with the Walker affair, using a wire recorder during interviews, which was an unusual method at the time.[24] Wilbur's commitments to direct the E-L prison break melodrama *Canon City* caused him to depart the Machine Gun Walker project. John C. Higgins took over the screenplay in early 1948, with *29 Clues* becoming the new title.

In March, Joseph Breen Jr. of Eagle-Lion submitted a version of the script to his father, Joseph I. Breen Sr. of the Production Code Administration. Breen Sr. had no objections to the Walker tale as long all references to machine guns were eliminated. As in the case of Mann's *Railroaded!*, Breen Sr. indicated he would not allow the picture to "graphically show a police officer dying at the hands of a criminal," but the completed film does show the policeman getting shot three times and falling back against the car seat.[25] Having a character named Breen in the screenplay probably helped diffuse PCA anxieties. The script originally opened with a "Walter Breen," Captain of Detectives, Homicide, addressing the audience and setting the stage of the narrative over the next four pages. The narrator is faceless in the finished film, but Captain Breen (Roy Roberts) remains a key figure in the *policier* scenes. Whether this was an Eagle-Lion in-joke honoring Junior Breen of the studio or a shameless political appeal to the PCA chief is open to speculation.

One week after Breen Sr. received the initial script, Eagle-Lion announced Alfred Werker as director of *29 Clues*. Werker was still identified as director once filming began sometime between April 19 and 26. Mann's *Raw Deal* retakes were completed on March 19, so he could have begun working on this thriller provided he was not distracted with the postproduction of *Raw Deal*. Nevertheless, a trade notice on May 11 reports Werker embarking with his Eagle-Lion crew to Montebello for location filming.[26] The screenplay, however, did not yet contain the storm drain chase climax.

In John C. Higgins's February 11, 1948, screenplay, Captain Breen and Detective Marty Brennan force their way into the suspect's apartment, but the killer ("Kent" in this version) is not home. A secret passage leads them to the next-door apartment where they take a man and woman by surprise. The action shifts locales to a recognizable Los Angeles landmark, but not the Los Angeles storm drains. With the last seven pages of this version of the script as our guide, here, for the first time, is the reconstituted ending of *He Walked By Night* prior to Anthony Mann's involvement in the project.[27]

After the apartment incident, Captain Breen and his detectives receive an all-points bulletin that the murder suspect is heading south towards the Los Angeles Memorial Coliseum. Outside Exposition Park, Kent runs across the grass. The next angle was a natural for John Alton:

> EFFECT SHOT A RUNNING FIGURE
> *It runs toward CAMERA, then stops in a CLOSEUP. It is KENT. His eyes are wild, desperate. He is breathing gaspingly, sucking his breath through his teeth . . . He has an automatic in his right hand.*[28]

In a subjective long shot, a radio car sweeps the grass with a searchlight, "making long shadows of the tree trunks." Kent turns and runs but is captured by the light, rushing off despite gunfire. Kent fires at radio and detective cars converging on the Coliseum. Breen's car, with detective Chuck Jones at the wheel, careens to try and cut Kent off, but the killer scrambles over a wire fence "like a wildcat." There is a cut to a low camera angle:

> *As KENT dashes under the Olympic arch into the Coliseum. A spotlight cuts under the arch and picks him out. He ducks OUT of sight.*[29]

Police cars converge on one end of the Coliseum in a fan-shaped formation. In a high-angle, light from the cars illuminates part of the Coliseum playing field. The tiny figure of Kent runs across the gridiron to a darkened section and leaps the barrier. Breen's car cuts Kent off inside the Coliseum tunnel, forcing him to reverse his tracks. The car crashes the gate and the detectives jump out in pursuit.

The ensuing gun battle between Kent and the police in the lower tier seats of the Coliseum interior is absurdly exaggerated, but hardly more so than the original *Los Angeles Times* account of police arresting the crazed Erwin Walker in late 1946:

> CLOSEUP KENT
> *He is concentrating on his closest enemy—Marty. He takes careful aim.*
>
> CUT TO:
>
> EFFECT SHOT SHOOTING DOWN

as MARTY works his way slowly up the aisle toward Kent . . . There is a SHOT off scene. A FLASH of FLAME from the drum of Marty's TOMMYGUN, and several EXPLOSIONS. Then it is enveloped in FIRE. Marty throws it sideways from him with both hands. It continues to BURN fiercely.

CUT TO:

TWO SHOT MARTY AND KENT
latter in the b.g. He lets out a yell of triumph, starts down toward Marty, FIRING as he comes . . . Marty hurls himself between two rows of seats, draws a snub-nosed combat gun . . . Bullets tear splinters from the benches near his head . . . Marty fires back, and suddenly Kent topples down, head over heels, in a tumbler's roll, toward Marty . . . He comes into a sitting position, trying to get his bearings, searching with eyes and gun muzzle for the man who brought him down. Marty rushes him, as Kent FIRES. The bullet catches Marty in the side, whirls him half around, but the momentum of his rush carries him into Kent . . . Kent raises the gun for another shot, but Marty bears down on Kent's gun arm, hammering at him with the barrel of his bellygun . . . Kent raises Marty bodily in the air—showing his amazing strength, slowly bringing the gun around. Marty crunches down on him with all his strength . . . Then suddenly falls back and down, hurling Kent over in a wrestler's roll . . . Lights shine on the two battlers, and suddenly they are engulfed in a wave of manpower, one of them Breen. Kent is grabbed by FIVE MEN, and yanked to his feet. In spite of his wound, of his battered condition, he hurls his captors back and forth, like a bear shaking off a pack of dogs. Then superior weight tells, and stands glaring at his captors, and at Marty. Both Marty and Kent are breathing hard, their clothing torn and bloody. Kent rages at Marty.

KENT (almost hysterically through his teeth). Why'n't you kill me! Why'n't you kill me! You coulda!
MARTY (glaring back at him). You'll get it! The way you deserve![30]

The action faded out. From there, the film returned to Captain Breen addressing the camera from his office:

CAPT. BREEN. And he'll get it! As he deserved—in the gas chamber at San Quentin. By the time you hear this, David Solon Kent will have been paid off . . . There was a young man who had everything! Talent. Education. Personality. Intelligence. Good upbringing. A young man who could have succeeded in almost any field of endeavor. But instead, he chose to put those God-given talents to work against his fellow men as a murderer, a burglar, a robber, and

> a thief. It is a pity that a youth with so much to live for should so deliberately spread death and suffering... The world will not miss him![31]

Alfred Werker, until alternative evidence surfaces, directed this script draft of *He Walked By Night* during spring and early summer 1948. Few would argue that it is superior to the released film. The producers and Eagle-Lion must have been similarly unimpressed because new scenes, including the storm drain sequence, were quickly written and inserted into the script. The film went back into production on July 21 for seven to ten days of retakes. Although Werker was initially announced as retakes director, his name does not appear in subsequent trade notices. The likeliest scenario, pending the discovery of the original daily production reports (which have yet to resurface), is that Anthony Mann directed these new sequences. *Reign of Terror/The Black Book* was not scheduled to start filming until August 17, so there would have been time for him and Richard Basehart (who plays Robespierre in the costume thriller) to complete the added material.[32]

Accounting for the seamlessness with which the Mann and Werker segments are woven is cinematographer John Alton having remained on the show throughout production. His stylistic consistency and originality prevents the conflicting directorial styles from appearing jarring. The final "Mann" version of *He Walked By Night*, containing all the retaken sequences, was screened for Joseph I. Breen Sr. on August 13, 1948, and the PCA gave a seal of approval on September 7.[33]

Regardless of its dubious authorship, *He Walked By Night* remains one of the outstanding *film policier/film noir* thrillers of the post-World War II years.

SELLING *HE WALKED BY NIGHT*

Eagle-Lion Films devised inventive promotional techniques to promote *He Walked By Night* by capitalizing on the post-World War II climate of paranoia. Satirizing the then-popular "Raffles" routine, the distributor encouraged theater owners to "help publicize the relentless hunt for the crazed cop-killer" through cooperation with local newspapers running stories "with clues as to the identity of the wanted man" in advance of the film opening. The E-L publicists also recommended a public safety campaign in which a reporter and photographer accompanies a policeman on his beat to photograph examples of negligence:

Wherever a door or window is left unlocked; where a fire has not been extinguished properly; where a car is left with the keys in, a picture can be taken and a story written.

To further promote the picture, a card can be placed wherever negligence is discovered with the following copy:

"*You have been negligent in protecting yourself against he who WALKS BY NIGHT!*"[34]

Merchant and home protective services were seen as viable promotional outlets to distribute cards as their watchmen made the night rounds:

> Your store has been checked by the Blank Burglary Protective Agency. We protect you against those who WALK BY NIGHT! See "He Walked by Night" at the . . . Theatre.[35]

Radio stations could likewise be approached about doing live remote interviews with "those who walk by night" such as police, servicemen, and watchmen. Newspapers would be targeted for interviews with such night workers as milkmen, firemen, and farm produce deliverymen. The studio encouraged theater owners to conduct cooperative campaigns with stores selling guns, burglar alarms, fire extinguishers, and window and door locks.[36] For exhibitors with solid local connections, a police siren was recommended to attract passersby to the lobby:

> Calling all Cars, Calling all Cars! Lookout [sic] for Richard Basehart—he is a dangerous killer—he can be found slashing his way to stardom in "He Walked by Night" at this theatre, starting next Tuesday (Siren).[37]

In November 1948, *He Walked By Night* opened in Los Angeles and grossed $40,300 (nearly $390,000 in 2013) at five cinemas where the thriller was top bill to RKO's *Indian Agent*. Four of the venues performed at "nice" to "okay" levels and only the downtown Orpheum achieved "sock" business, accounting for more than half the earnings. Business was robust in New York, Chicago, San Francisco, Boston, and Kansas City, where several engagements were solo bookings. In Philadelphia, the picture came close to shattering the previous house record, but business was only "okay" in Baltimore. In the end, *He Walked By Night* was profitable. The picture cost $361,865 to produce and by February 1949 Eagle-Lion was anticipating more than a $1,250,000 gross.[38]

To appease the censors, cop-killer Roy Martin meets a violent death on screen. In reality, the authorities took Erwin "Machine Gun" Walker alive and put him on trial. Walker was found guilty and in June 1947 sentenced to death, but a subsequent suicide attempt spared him from execution. Having been declared insane following a psychiatric evaluation, Walker remained incarcerated until obtaining parole in 1974 and eventually found work as a chemist. He died in obscurity in 1982.[39]

Had the film industry's censorship requirements in 1948 not insisted upon vengeance in dealing with murderous characters, and had the makers of *He Walked By Night* adhered more to the facts, the picture might have ended differently. Imagine Anthony Mann, a director eager to explore human contradictions and complexities, restaging Erwin Walker's December 20, 1946, ambulance trip following the violent police apartment raid. Detective Sergeant Earle Rombeau shared the ambulance ride with wounded Walker. En route to the hospital, Walker asked the cop, "Are you a married man?" Rombeau confirmed he was married and the father of two children.

"Then you're very lucky," said Walker. "You nearly missed going home tonight. My advice to you is that you're in a tough business. You'd better get out of it if you want to enjoy your children."[40]

Figure 13.0. *Follow Me Quietly*, 1949. William Lundigan and the Dummy (Photofest).

CHAPTER 13

FOLLOW ME QUIETLY (1949)

The serial killer film is not a recent phenomenon. Mentally ill murderers targeting random victims have fascinated directors of various stripes and nationalities, from Fritz Lang and Joseph Losey (the 1931 *M* and its 1951 remake) to Edward Dmytryk (*The Sniper,* 1952) and Michael Powell (*Peeping Tom,* 1960). Richard Fleischer explored the theme on numerous occasions in his fluctuating filmography, most significantly in *The Boston Strangler* (1968) and *10 Rillington Place* (1971). However, these two films were not his only forays into the grisly genre.

In 1949, early in his Hollywood career, Fleischer directed *Follow Me Quietly,* a one-hour police thriller (ignored by Fleischer in his 1993 memoir) about an urban slayer known as the Judge. Killing indiscriminately on rainy nights, the Judge leaves cryptic reminders of his ordained right to murder. Francis Rosenwald and Anthony Mann cowrote the story upon which this low-budget RKO Radio Pictures *film policier* was based. Other writers adapted the 115-page treatment into screenplay form.[1] Like Mann, Fleischer was biding his time in the low-budget programmer field, but his work lacks Mann's directorial finesse. Performances in this picture are below the standards of even Mann's "Poverty Row" melodramas, and Fleischer is more conventional in his camera placement and staging of actors. These issues still do not detract from the positive components of *Follow Me Quietly,* whose narrative tightness and meticulous layering of tension supersedes the underdeveloped characters.

Follow Me Quietly adheres to the basic Rosenwald/Mann treatment, with significant exceptions. The scaling down of the production during studio development prevented the picture from becoming one of the major crime thrillers of the late 1940s. The invigorating uses of Manhattan locations alone would have predated Mann's *Side Street.* Once Howard Hughes's new régime took control at RKO, a prominent *film policier* was slenderized to programmer levels, although not enough to eliminate all interest and suspense.

Running a scant fifty-nine minutes, *Follow Me Quietly* does not have much time or eagerness to delve into psychology and pathology, a problem partially attributable to the screenplay adaptations made of the treatment. There are three central figures in the story, two cynical police detectives and an overzealous woman tabloid reporter, each pursuing the Judge for different reasons. Police Lieutenant Grant (William Lundigan), having studied the murderer from every angle, is obsessed with trying to keep one step ahead of the criminal while his jaded partner Sergeant Collins (Jeff Corey) treats the situation as a standard part of a daily routine. Gadfly tabloid magazine reporter Ann Gorman (Dorothy Patrick) sees the case as a way to boost circulation and negotiates with Grant to pay him $500 for an exclusive story (the police retain prepublication approval and the money goes to their fund). Theirs is an alliance fraught with bitter distrust.

Both the film and the treatment begin and end in a cheap bar where the two detectives regularly unwind. When Ann enters the establishment, the Rosenwald/Mann treatment supplies ribald details absent from the picture:

> Two fat-breasted mermaids look down at her from either side of the bar mirror—She pulls the top of her suit close.[2]

On paper, the bartender makes a memorable first impression:

> This is Don. He has a nude tattooed on the back of one hand—standing on her head—thighs disappearing under the shirt cuff.[3]

Ann's introductory dialogue with Sergeant Collins is faithful to the treatment and consistent with the film's superficial tone:

> ANN. Hot case.
> COLLINS. If it gets any hotter—it'll sizzle.
> ANN. Funny thing calling himself the Judge.
> COLLINS. The Judge is a funny kind of guy. Killin' people's a funny kind of business.
> ANN. I could use a few facts. Any slant on a likely motive?
> COLLINS. I once knew a man who used to cut off cats' tails. He didn't like cats. The Judge cuts off people's wind. He don't like people I guess.[4]

In the film, the Judge's motives are never explained beyond this or Collins's quick observation to his partner en route to a crime scene, "Maybe he likes rain. Must be a fish." The presence of Ann nonetheless enables Lieutenant

Grant ("Garant" in the treatment) to condemn tabloid journalism. The following treatment dialogue was cut from the screenplay:

> ANN. Our circulation is better than half a million a month.
> *(Grant downs his drink.)*
> GRANT. I didn't know there were that many morons.[5]

Grant's other remarks about tabloids made it into the film. At a crime scene, the detective criticizes her editor for pursuing this type of police story:

> GRANT. Just the kind of stuff that guy would go for.[6] How the Judge kills—and why—and what it feels like to be a killer—spicy, isn't it? Just think of all the gory pictures you could use for illustrations.
> ANN. Well, our readers want to know what's going on! The Judge is a menace, isn't he?
> GRANT. Yes, and so are you! Polluting minds until some poor dope gets ideas and goes on a homicidal holiday![7]

(Perversely, the released film gets to have it both ways. A police headquarters scene features several graphic photos of what appear to be actual murder victims.)

An unnecessary flashback introduces the Judge in both the film and the Rosenwald/Mann treatment. The killer has thrown McGill (Frank Ferguson), a newspaper editor, out of an office window, and the man lies dying on an ambulance stretcher. Logically, this section of the film should have begun with the attack on McGill but instead begins with Grant and Collins questioning the editor at the crime scene as a newspaper copy man takes down details. An antiquated camera-defocusing device frames the flashback. Even if the decision to employ a flashback here was poor judgment by Rosenwald and Mann, the treatment is superior when first placing the detectives in the editor's vandalized office:

> They go in—Grant[8] first: a swivel chair in front of the roll top desk is overturned—its tripod pointing at the door—an eyeshade dangling pathetically from one of the three short legs—Papers scattered over the floor—An inkwell in a dark pool—Broken eyeglasses—One of the high windows shattered and thrown wide open—
> The monotonous beat of the rain mingles with the pulse of the presses.
> The group moves to the window. It faces the dark shaft of a court. Four stories down—a skylight—brilliantly lit up by improvised floodlights. A stocky

gray-haired man lies on his back—A white-coated interne kneels beside him—readying a hypo.

The man in shirtsleeves clears his throat—"McGill[9] jumped clear from this room—"

Collins glances at Grant—"Some jump—"[10]

(In the film, a weaker variation of the scene appears after the flashback and Collins's remark is, "Some drop.")

Fleischer's staging of the Judge's late-night attack on McGill is uninspired compared with the Rosenwald/Mann treatment. In the film, the Judge enters the editor's office as McGill is writing, sneaking up behind the journalist and, moving around to the front of the desk, putting his hands around the victim's throat. The two men struggle around the room before the Judge hurls McGill through an open window into the rain. The treatment describes the action more inventively:

> The office on the eighth floor—McGill sitting at the roll-top desk editing an article—he pays scant attention to the footsteps approaching down the hall outside. Unhurried footsteps. Somebody whistling—softly. McGill catches it—it's an old tune—a familiar tune—Brahms—The Lullaby. McGill smiles.
>
> The footsteps pause just outside the door. McGill doesn't notice this. His back is toward the glass door—his eyes focused on the article in front of him.
>
> Suddenly the lights go out.
>
> All the lights.
>
> Darkness.
>
> Only a faint glow outside the windows—And a trickle of light seeping through the frosted glass door.
>
> McGill pivots in the swivel chair.
>
> Somebody moves in the room.
>
> The tip of a cigarette glows.
>
> A pair of hands finds McGill's throat—Tightening—Cutting off his breath—Pushing him back—
>
> McGill hangs on to unseen wrists—Twisting—Gasping—
>
> Not a sound from the figure.
>
> The chair overturns. McGill rolls across the floor—Rolls on toward the window. He raises himself on hands and knees—heading straight for the window. He smashes it. Crashes through it. Screaming—Jumping—Falling—.[11]

In the film, after McGill dies on the stretcher, the detectives investigate his office, where they find the Judge's latest cut-and-paste note: *"I have BEEN*

ORDained to destroy ALL EVIL. BEWARE!" Back at police headquarters the following morning, Collins finds another "crank letter": "*YOU ARE not THE law. I am the Law! I am the Judge. You will Never Live to catch me. The day of Judgment is at HAND!*" (This was changed from the treatment, which featured a similar note proclaiming, "THE JUDGE IS NOT A CRIMINAL. THE JUDGE HAS BEEN ORDAINED BY THE ALL POWERFUL TO DESTROY EVIL IN SPIRIT AND FLESH."[12])

A glass display case in an adjoining office contains bits and pieces of Judge artifacts, and Grant is frustrated knowing all the physical details about the killer except for the face. In fairness to director Richard Fleischer, *Follow Me Quietly* was constrained by a small budget, so this scene in the film is limited to Grant pacing in frustration before walking toward the camera for a close-up. In the Rosenwald/Mann treatment, the display case items trigger a memory montage:

Dissolve:
 Night—Rain—A vacant lot—Searchlights. Grant[13] and Collins examine the rigid form of a dead man—strangled by "loaded" hands—hands that have crushed the larynx. Cigarette butts—The impression of a footprint—
Dissolve:
 Another night—A staircase—A living room—the landlady of a rooming house—strangled. Grant and Collins searching—finding—cigarette butts—the killer's impression left on a seat cushion—a note saying THE JUDGE—saying with the victim's lipstick—
Dissolve:
 A radio station—A control booth. A disk jockey slumped over the microphone—strangled. A pile of boogie-woogie records smashed—A pigskin glove—
Dissolve:
 Rain—Wind—Darkness—A dead man lying under an El-structure—strangled—in a puddle of water—the killer's hat pulled over his face—
Dissolve back to ...
The office at headquarters.
Grant wipes his brow—wipes away the spectre of the past—[14]

A life-size dummy designed by police to facilitate identification of the Judge is the most memorable aspect of *Follow Me Quietly*. Outfitted with a suit and hat, the Dummy has a blank face, and two of the film's genuine chills feature this creation. The first, edited down from Rosenwald and Mann's text, is during a police briefing where the Dummy is positioned on a stage, back to the audience. Collins "interviews" the Dummy on stage and receives answers from a voice heard over a public address system. The scene quotes from the treatment when the Dummy rationalizes his crimes ("I was ordained to sit in judgment on sinners") and his reasons for leaving notes ("I want people to know—I enjoy being talked about").[15] The camera is tracking in to a medium shot of the back of the Dummy's head as the life-size doll "answers" a question regarding rain's deadly inspiration:

VOICE OF THE DUMMY.[16] Rain makes me restless. I get excited.
COLLINS. What do you do when you get excited?
VOICE OF THE DUMMY. I kill!

The Dummy abruptly turns 180 degrees to face the camera for a close-up. The Dummy's face is blank. The film added this jolting pivot to good effect.

Uncredited screenwriter Martin Rackin (*Desperate*) is responsible for the second memorable chill involving the Dummy, which was not in the original treatment. Lieutenant Grant, frustrated by all the false leads, is alone on a rainy night in his outer office, staring out the window at the dark city. He enters his dim office where the Dummy, back to camera, is propped up in a chair. Grant speaks to the Dummy, wanting to know where he is tonight, seeking a "blind date." Collins arrives and worries that the lieutenant is losing his mind. Suspecting that "Deadpan" will be going on the prowl again, Grant exits, Collins soon following him. There is an edit to the back view of the Dummy, which now starts to move. It is the Judge himself. The Judge stands up from the chair and replaces the Dummy before slipping out through a side door.[17]

The Judge's next strangulation victim is a woman, but this time the killer leaves behind a clue: a crime magazine. Film editor Elmo Williams confidently assembles several montages depicting the detectives showing Dummy photos at bookshops, barbershops, pool halls, and other gritty locations, after which a waitress makes a positive identification. The man they are looking for is Charlie Roy, and he resides in a working-class neighborhood, filmed on the RKO backlot. Roy, however, senses the trap has been sprung and runs off, but Grant chases him to a gas plant, and soon police cars arrive as backup. The gas plant finale where Grant traps the Judge was filmed on location in downtown Los Angeles and was the last scene photographed in the picture.[18] With Grant in pursuit, the killer runs up the steps of the boilers and past piping, climbing desperately, like a cornered animal, until he reaches the top of the structure. Collins is injured during a shootout between the Judge and police. Police machine gun fire punctures pipes and sends water pouring. The Judge is trapped, and Grant approaches him with handcuffs and a simple instruction, "Follow me quietly." But the falling water, reminiscent of rainfall, causes the handcuffed killer to panic, and an intense fight between him and Grant begins.

FOLLOW ME QUIETLY: THE ORIGINAL CONCEPTION

Certain authors have cited sequences in *Follow Me Quietly* to either confirm Anthony Mann's participation in the story or even to suggest he might have directed portions of the *policier*. William Darby, unaware of Martin Rackin being the author of the scene, cites the section of the Dummy coming to life at night in the office as evidence of Mann's involvement:

> This shocking kind of reversal is a tactic we have seen repeatedly in Mann's noir films, and here it is used to suggest several thematic points.[19]

In a similar vein, Jeanine Basinger argues that the final shoot-out in the gas plant "clearly reflects Mann's individual input" because of its similarities to the ending of *T-Men*:

> Without access to RKO studio files, it's difficult to know how much input Mann had in shooting this finale, but it certainly looks as if he himself might have directed it.[20]

Basinger wrote these remarks in 1979, eight years before RKO Pictures donated studio papers to UCLA Special Collections, but she failed to provide any updates in the new introduction for her book's 2007 edition.

Mann did not and could not have directed this sequence for several reasons. Filming occurred between 9:00 a.m. and 5:50 p.m. on September 2, 1948, while Mann was at work directing *Reign of Terror/The Black Book* for Eagle-Lion, which entered production on August 17 and finished on October 10. Contemporary newspaper accounts confirm that Mann was involved in editing *Reign of Terror*, so he would not have had time to film the climax of *Follow Me Quietly*. Fleischer is also listed on the RKO daily production chart as director of the gas plant filming. Moreover, as gripping as the gas plant pursuit may be, the absence of the "Anthony Mann touch" is evident in terms of camera composition and angles, which were superior even in his Republic Pictures melodramas of 1944–46.[21] The gas plant climax also does not appear in either the Francis Rosenwald/Anthony Mann treatment or in subsequent

Follow Me Quietly screenplays on file at UCLA in the RKO studio papers. In truth, *Follow Me Quietly* as Rosenwald and Mann conceived it, was to have ended quite differently, and more spectacularly.

The S. Bergerman Agency submitted the original film treatment to RKO Radio Pictures on June 30, 1947, and Allied Artists (the upgraded brand name for Poverty Row producer-distributor Monogram Pictures) soon announced the property as a $650,000 production ($6.8 million in 2013) from producer and Texas oilman Jack Wrather for star Don Castle. Wrather pursued Dorothy Lamour for the female lead as the budget approached $1 million. Wrather then sold the story to RKO for $8,000, and the studio assigned *Murder, My Sweet* producer Sid Rogell and *Desperate* screenwriter Martin Rackin. The writer labored until late March 1948 until Lillie Hayward, author of Robert Wise's *noir* western *Blood on the Moon* and several spirited Warner Bros. comedies and melodramas, took over for the next two months. In May 1948, financier Floyd Odlum sold RKO to Howard Hughes for $8.8 million, which immediately affected *Follow Me Quietly*.[22]

The Hughes régime slashed the film's budget, to the detriment of the project. Kent Smith was announced as star and William E. Watts, a dialogue director on *Crossfire* and *The Locket*, as director, but RKO soon replaced them with William Lundigan and Richard Fleischer. On August 18, 1949, the picture entered production under producer Herman Schlom, a specialist in cheap westerns. In keeping with the selective frugality of the new Hughes administration, *Follow Me Quietly* was filmed in sixteen days with a drastically reduced budget of $259,437.[23]

To get a sense of what was lost in the transition from a $1 million Dorothy Lamour event picture to a $260,000 second-tier feature, it is important to compare the completed movie with the overall Rosenwald/Mann treatment. The treatment is set in New York City but the film makes no mention of Manhattan. Most of the film's action (with the exception of the finale) is staged on traditional studio backlots. While the philosophical musings of the treatment are shallow at best, there are attempts to comprehend the Judge and what he represents on a deeper level than what the Fleischer film is ultimately capable of achieving. At the first crime scene, the treatment melodramatically depicts the dying newspaper editor being carried via stretcher into the pressroom where he dictates his harrowing tale to a heavyset man at a linotype machine. Nevertheless, the victim places the Judge's crimes in a social context:

> The man who calls himself The Judge has struck again. Psychiatrists have linked this maniac to a cycle. A post war [sic] phenomenon. Our own brand of Golem reflecting a world gone mad.[24]

Later, the exasperated Lieutenant Grant tells Inspector Mulrooney, his supervisor,

> GRANT. This Judge is not an ordinary criminal—He is a by-product of our time—like the train wrecker Matuschka—the woman butcher Landru. A man setting himself up as The Judge—in a world he no longer understands—
> MULROONEY. His tough luck.[25]

(Rosenwald and Mann are referring to Szilveszter Matuschka, the Hungarian killer who derailed passenger trains in Austria and Germany in 1930–31; and the French murderer Henri Désiré Landru, aka "Bluebeard.")

Screenwriter Lillie Hayward wrote a scene for *Follow Me Quietly* that was filmed and later deleted from the release version depicting Ann arguing with her editor over the staging of a lurid photograph of a female murder victim wearing a flimsy negligee.[26] This replaced a fascinating passage from the Rosenwald/Mann treatment between Ann and a tough woman named Louise, which served to illustrate how tabloid journalism distorts the truth. The scene also exemplifies how Anthony Mann sought to examine the root causes of certain violent crimes.

Louise lambastes Ann for the magazine article "Born Bad" in which the woman was described as "Sweetheart of Killer Combs." Louise denies being romantically linked to the accused:

> LOUISE. You say he was born bad—that he hated everybody—that he got a great kick out of killing. Willie—Mr. Combs that is—never hated anybody—and he didn't harm a fly until things got too much for him. I know—I picked him up sick as a dog and not a friend in the world. That's all there is to the sweetheart stuff—that's what I said in court—[27]

Louise now refuses to accept the money she was promised from the tabloid but is told it is too late to cancel the deal. Noticing Ann's slender, well-groomed hands, Louise asks:

> LOUISE. How do you keep them so clean—digging in other people's dirt—You don't get that off with no lotion—[28].

The woman's voice breaks.

> LOUISE. I didn't come here to threaten you. I thought being a woman you'd understand—about him and me. Why did you have to dig up that picture of

us in bathing suits—? Why throw mud at a fellow who's going to die—and me who wants to stick by him—Why—?²⁹

Her parting words to Ann:

> LOUISE. You're worse than a cop. They only run you in—but you—you run people down and over them. You and your smooth talk about Combs getting a decent funeral out of my story—You certainly buried him for good—right in the dung heap.³⁰

In addition to voicing social concerns, the Rosenwald/Mann treatment contains surrealism. The Judge Dummy psychologically torments Lieutenant Grant in two scenes in which the overworked detective becomes delusional. At a police target range Grant imagines the Dummy grinning at him, the vision making it impossible for Grant to pull the trigger on his gun.³¹ Even stranger is a bar scene in which the drunken Grant, stressed by his inability to locate the Judge, hallucinates while staring at a liquor bottle:

> The bottle—
>   It takes on the shape of The Dummy.
>   It walks away in the slanting rain—the gray hat sits at a jaunty angle—the cigarette sticks in the corner of its mouth—the back heaps ridicule upon Grant—³²
>   If he could only see the face.
> The rain turns to snow—
>   The Dummy walks away in the swirling snow—the gray hat sits at a jaunty angle—the coat collar is turned up—the cigarette sticks in the corner of its mouth—the back heaps ridicule upon Grant—
>   If he could only see the face.
>
>   The Dummy walks into the wintry horizon—its footprints forming in the snow—in an endless trail from nowhere to nowhere—³³

When Grant finally catches up with the Judge in Rosenwald and Mann's *Follow Me Quietly* treatment, the confrontation is different from that of the motion picture. The treatment concludes in Manhattan on New Year's Eve during snowfall where the police lieutenant pursues the slayer on foot as merrymakers celebrate on Greene Street. At a subway station, Grant monitors an incoming train but sees no sign of the killer. Grant boards an uptown train:

> The train moves—
> Faster—the rear lights grow smaller—
> Eyes in the tunnel—
> They disappear—[34]

Police descend on the rapid transit traffic center:

> The heart of the subway system—trains are started from here—stopped—Every train is charted-moving across a huge illuminated map entirely of glass—showing stations—signals—trains—a beehive of transportation—[35]

The treatment describes the chaos:

> The glass map—stations—signals—trains—moving perpetually, uptown and downtown—fast—slow—stop. Somewhere on this map—The Judge—
>
> A subway station—
> An attendant and a plainclothes man enter the men's room—check it. Nothing—
>
> A subway barn—
> A train pulls in—officers board the cars—from end to end. No Judge—
>
> Subway track—
> A procession of searchlights
> Line detectives.
> They pass a repair crew.
> "Happy New Year..."
> "Happy New Year..."[36]

A policeman in a squad car contends with a jalopy of drunken sailors at a suburban intersection. They attempt to cajole him into a drink and he tells them to ease up. The police radio orders all units from 180th Street and adjacent areas to stand by. The target is reported heading east via the Beach Line.

Gears mesh.
　　Mounted on the traffic light is a police recall signal—It blinks on and off—Code 'Stand by'—
　　The car speeds off—
　　The sailors holler, "Wanna race—"[37]

The ensuing chase anticipates both *Side Street* and William Friedkin's *The French Connection* (1971), giving us a sense as to how Mann might have directed the *Follow Me Quietly* showcase finale:

A Highway—running parallel to the open tracks of the Beach Line—
　　Ahead is the gray ocean—
　　It is snowing—
　　A lonely intersection—the recall signal blinks frantically—
　　Every signal—telephone—radio in the area is in action—
　　[Inspector] Mulrooney closes in on the Judge—
　　A subway train—alongside the highway—
　　Sirens—
　　A police car—
　　Another police car—
　　Sirens—
　　A motorcycle—
They're racing the train—ready for action—in constant communication with Headquarters.
　　The train is almost empty—hardly anybody in the lighted cars—nobody goes to the beach now—a short hour before New Year—
　　The whole city is whooping it up—loud enough to be heard out here—firecrackers—noise-makers—drivers blowing their horns—
　　Dress rehearsal for the big moment—
　　The train dives into the tunnel for the home stretch—
The train roars through the tunnel—
　　Grant[38] walks toward the first car—
　　Across the old-fashioned railed-in platform—every car is in service tonight—
　　He enters the first car—
　　A lone passenger—sitting near the engineer's booth—facing the tunnel ahead—
　　He wears a gray hat—muffler—dark overcoat—blue trousers—dark shoes—
　　No gloves—
　　A cigarette is sticking out of his mouth—cold—
　　Grant looks at the man—

If he could only see the face—
Now he is going to see the face—
The Judge turns his face toward him.
Grant looks at the face—
The shock is tremendous—
Not much of a face—
A very ordinary face—
The face of a middle-aged man—gray and lined—
He doesn't wear his glasses—
The eyes are circled with blueish shadows—
Sick eyes—
In a tired face—very tired—
The Judge smiles at Grant—
A very uncertain smile—timid—begging for a smile in return—
Grant walks toward the Judge—
The Judge doesn't move—
He waits—and smiles—
Grant taps him on the shoulder:
"Follow me quietly."
The Judge gets up—steadying himself—the train is going fast—
"Show me your hands," says Grant.
The Judge shows his hands—average—neither large nor small—round nails—clean—
The handcuffs snap shut—linking the Hunter to the Hunted.
The train crosses an intersection—
The lights dim—
The engineer signals the station ahead—
The whistle shrieks—
It frightens the Judge—
The cigarette drops from his lips—
He makes a wild dash for the rear of the car—
His maniacal strength is unbelievable—
He drags Grant with him—
He smashes back the door with his free left hand—
Grant struggles—
He can't hold back the Judge—nobody could—
The Judge is mad—violently insane—
He wants to jump off the platform—
He strains toward the gleaming rails—
The cinders rush past like black snow—

Nobody can hold the Judge—
He heaves Grant over the low rail—
This isn't the Last Mile—
It's the last couple of yards—
Down to the cinder bed—
Grant's right hand grasps the revolver—
Justifiable Homicide—[39]

Screenwriter Martin Rackin did not use the subway pursuit climax in his drafts of the screenplay, but Lillie Hayward incorporated the chase in her April 23, 1948, draft.[40] A subsequent Hayward draft makes a small but significant insertion:

EXT. STATION PLATFORM

MED. FULL SHOT. *The Judge sees the train coming, and with a superhuman effort tries to hurl himself and Grant off the platform. Grant struggles to hold back. The Judge makes a supreme effort. With a final maniacal burst of strength, he wrenches loose, whirls, leaps down toward the tracks.*

ANOTHER ANGLE—*as he hits the third rail. There is a blinding flash of blue flame—and the Express ROARS into scene with SCREECHING brakes. People SCREAM. Collins and a couple of cops run into scene from the stairs above.*[41]

The "third rail solution" eventually worked its way into the thrillers *City That Never Sleeps* (Republic, 1953), shot on location in Chicago, and both the Manhattan-filmed *Cry Terror!* (M-G-M, 1958) and *The Taking of Pelham One Two Three* (United Artists, 1974). As Richard Fleischer directed it, the gas plant climax of *Follow Me Quietly* preserves only Grant instructing the Judge to follow him quietly after the lieutenant checks the slayer's hands. Had the Howard Hughes austerity measures at RKO Radio Pictures not demanded a serious reduction in budget, the film of *Follow Me Quietly* would have been more of an enduring accomplishment.

SELLING *FOLLOW ME QUIETLY*

When *Follow Me Quietly* was ready for release in summer 1949, the RKO publicity forces maximized the serial killer theme. To spread word in their communities, theater-owners were given this suggestion:

Have a man walk the streets of town with his face covered with a piece of plain material to hide his features but thin enough so he can see where he is going. A poster on his back can call attention to your show: *I am called "The Judge." I strangle my victims in the rain! Try to identify me in "Follow Me Quietly"* now at the Palace Theatre.[42]

Follow Me Quietly was the sole feature booked into RKO's Palace on Broadway and Forty-seventh Street in Times Square, where it shared the billing with eight vaudeville acts. *Variety* reported "sock" business. The film/vaudeville policy had equally strong effect in Boston, Chicago, Buffalo, and Providence, Rhode Island. The thriller successfully supported the RKO releases *Easy Living* in Los Angeles and *Roseanna McCoy* in San Francisco.[43]

Anthony Mann and Francis Rosenwald collaborated on a subsequent crime project that was never filmed. In October 1949, the Rosenwald/Mann screenplay *Stakeout*, in which a police detective attempts to expose a corrupt political machine, was announced for Larry Parks and independent producer Louis Mandel. Joseph H. Lewis (*Gun Crazy*) was set to direct until a contractual dispute ended his involvement. Mandel, finding Los Angeles options unsuitable, embarked for New York in search of actresses to play the detective's wife and the femme fatale. "All the available leading ladies here have 'tired faces'—that is, too often seen in pictures," he told a reporter prior to his departure. By March 1950, Parks's wife, M-G-M actress Betty Garrett, obtained a release from her studio contract to play opposite her husband in the film, which was expected to begin production as soon as the actor completed *Emergency Wedding* for Columbia. This was the last anyone heard of the Mann/Rosenwald property *Stakeout*.[44]

CHAPTER 14

BORDER INCIDENT (1949)

By late 1948, Metro-Goldwyn-Mayer was soliciting Anthony Mann's directing services. *T-Men* had impressed M-G-M, and Mann had another John C. Higgins screenplay for the Culver City film factory to consider:

> Metro said: "Make whatever picture you want." John and I had thought of doing *Border Incident*, because the guys there were also involved with the Federal agents and T Men. Through the research we had made with *T-Men* we found the fantastic story of the *Border Incident* boys. We made it on location, but it was really not Metro's cup of tea. When it came out, they were flabbergasted. It wasn't anything they thought a motion picture should be![1]

Figure 14.0. *Border Incident*, 1949. Jack Lambert (background left), James Mitchell (center, standing), Ricardo Montalban (foreground left), and unidentified actors (Photofest).

On the surface, Mann and M-G-M were an ill-matched alliance. This was, at the time of Mann's arrival, the studio of such Arthur Freed Technicolor musicals as *Easter Parade* and *Words and Music* and a roster of stars including Judy Garland, Clark Gable, Robert Taylor, Walter Pidgeon, Van Johnson, June Allyson, Fred Astaire, Ava Gardner, Spencer Tracy, Esther Williams, Red Skelton, and Elizabeth Taylor. Studio production head Louis B. Mayer, a cultural lobbyist for screen glamour, wholesomeness, and opulence, disliked the types of gritty crime melodramas for which Mann was noted. A full-page advertisement in a 1947 issue of *Variety* for director Robert Z. Leonard's Elizabeth Taylor drama *Cynthia* establishes Mayer's views of the genre. The ad shows a photo of a hand clutching a revolver above a headline, "VACATION FROM GUNPLAY!" The ad copy continues:

> Imagine! M-G-M's "CYNTHIA" hasn't a gun or a gangster in it! Exhibitors tell us that while there's always room for those thriller-killer films their public is hungry for a change of pace in entertainment, at least *one* picture without murder and mayhem in it.[2]

Border Incident not only had guns and gangsters but also an abundance of murder and mayhem.

The film incorporates social justice issues into the violent *film policier-film noir* formats, focusing on illegal border crossings by *braceros*, Mexican migrant workers who are exploited, robbed, and occasionally murdered by racketeer smugglers. This thriller evokes in all its effective and artful brutality the memories of such topical Warner Bros. Depression-era working-class melodramas as Mervyn LeRoy's *I Am a Fugitive from a Chain Gang*. But Hollywood had changed since 1932. Post-World War II censorship was stricter and the reactionary Cold War climate made it increasingly difficult to make a serious social document, particularly for the old-fashioned studio M-G-M, without political compromises. That the film was made at all, and with a Mexican actor (Ricardo Montalban) in the lead, is, to say the least, impressive.

Border Incident continues the merging of crime melodrama and adventure-western cinematic technique that Mann and cinematographer John Alton initiated in *Reign of Terror/The Black Book* (1949). It is in fact a preparation for the Mann westerns that began with *Devil's Doorway* (1950), his third M-G-M film. There are sequences where the positioning of actors within the austere, arid landscapes more than suggests the western milieu. At the start of the picture, three exhausted Mexican braceros stagger across the Mexico-United States border, seven silhouetted bandits (photographed

Figure 14.1 Figure 14.2

day-for-night) observing them from horseback against a mountain backdrop. Galloping towards the foreground, the bandits line up in a row on their horses (fig. 14.1). During the grueling climax, where one of several unsavory villains (Charles McGraw) leads a group of braceros on a death march through the mountains, Mann continues his western-style cinematic compositions of low-angles and shallow depths of field (fig. 14.2).

Although hindered throughout by Alton's overuse of day-for-night filters, which are designed to make scenes filmed in broad daylight appear to take place at nightfall (see Chapter 11, *Raw Deal*, and the above two frame examples), *Border Incident* has all the emotional intensity and tough eloquence of the Mann Eagle-Lion films.

This picture opens inauspiciously with helicopter views of the All-American Canal and agricultural land in Southern California as a narrator makes dry industrial film-like observations:

> Out of this desert wasteland, Man's industry has made a flourishing garden. Farming in Imperial Valley is a great industry. Here a single field of prosaic carrots or lettuce or flacks or melons may be worth a half million dollars. This great agricultural empire is important to the entire United States.[3]

Eventually migrant workers are seen in the distant fields below and there is a potent dissolve to a barbed wire metal fence, the camera panning down to reveal dozens of male Mexican workers standing and waiting on the other side of it. The narrator completes his two-minute-and-forty-second semi-documentary introduction with assurances that "the following composite case is based upon factual information supplied by the Immigration and Naturalization Service of the United States Department of Justice." This is the equivalent of *T-Men* shifting from Elmer Lincoln Irey to the murder of Shorty since, in *Border Incident*, the transition ushers in a different picture altogether and a masterful sequence of conception and direction.

Figure 14.3

After the previously mentioned views of the three braceros and the introduction of the seven bandits on horseback, there is a high-angle location view of the braceros running across the sand away from the barbed-wire fence. Jim, a white man, watches them with binoculars from atop the mountain (filmed in a studio). The silhouetted horsemen stand in the foreground of the mountain. Jim picks up a signal light and flashes it into the camera for a major music cue. The horsemen see his signal and gallop in unison toward the mountain. The three migrants walk along a rocky mountain path, briefly looking back before the camera tilts upward to the sky. From another high-angle, the braceros ascend a steep mountain path past the camera. In a wider view, they walk across rocks toward shadows. Bandits lurk between boulders, one brandishing a knife, another a shotgun. The three braceros continue walking on rocks toward the camera, a bandit appearing in the background. The cutthroat Zopilote (Arnold Moss) stands on a rock, a knife in his right hand, his sombrero hanging by a string. He jumps toward frame right for another major music cue. In low-angle, two of the braceros turn to run but are cut off by bandits, then turn back and run past the camera. In a studio shot, bandits surround and attack the braceros as an armed bandit observes from behind a rock. Another bandit stabs one of the migrants, backed by frenetic music, and Zopilote slices open the clothing of the victim as others pick through baskets and pockets. One bandit holds a watch to his ear. Four bandits drag the three bodies over to quicksand and drop them in before walking off, in low-angle, through the bushes into the wilds. In a powerful close view, two dead or unconscious braceros, their heads above quicksand, slowly get sucked into the sandy abyss (fig. 14.3).

This is the first seven minutes of Anthony Mann's *Border Incident*.

The focus of the film, however, is not on the bracero migrant workers. Undercover agents, working on behalf of Mexican-U.S. government agencies committed (according to the film's ideologies) to protecting exploited braceros, are the protagonists. In a variation of the *T-Men* plot, Pablo

Rodriguez (Montalban) of the Mexican Federal Police and Jack Bearnes (George Murphy) of the Immigration and Naturalization Service combine forces and resources to infiltrate the bracero smuggling racket. Pablo will impersonate a desperate migrant eager to cross over illegally and Jack will assume the identity of a U.S. crook selling fake work permits.

The position the film takes on the bracero issue is stated at the Mexicali governor's palace following the quicksand killings as Mexican official Colonel Rafael Alvarado (Martin Garralaga) and INS assistant commissioner John McReynolds (Harry Antrim) discuss the border crossing problems:

> ALVARADO. We are not talking about bloody shirts or torn hats. We are not talking about that at all! We are talking about the people who lived and died in these clothes.
> MCREYNOLDS. I know that, sir, but if they cross illegally what is our responsibility to them?
> ALVARADO. Most of my people do not cross illegally.
> MCREYNOLDS. Those who come over with work permits we protect. And as a matter of fact, most of the ranchers on our side obey these work treaties. They take certified farm workers and pay them legal wages.
> ALVARADO. These things we know. But some of my people, they are not well educated. They allow themselves to be smuggled across.
> MCREYNOLDS. I know. And some of my people pay them half wages, conceal them from arrest, make them live in fear and send them back to the desert to be robbed and killed.
> ALVARADO. Since these people work together to break the law, we will work together to enforce the law.

Mexican braceros at the time did not share the film's views that life was easier for migrant workers obeying immigration laws. There was ample evidence for such distrust of U.S.-Mexico policies.

THE BRACERO PROGRAM

The Bracero Program was a timely subject for a 1949 feature film. Seven years earlier, in order to compensate for World War II employment shortages in non-military industries, the governments of the United States and Mexico arranged for Mexican nationals to enter the U.S. under contract to harvest agricultural produce. The first wave of bracero workers reached California in September 1942 with the two governments officially agreeing to terminate the program at the end of 1947. The United States had guaranteed Mexico that it would not draft Mexican nationals into military service or subject them to discriminatory policies, but also ensure that California work locations obeyed Mexican labor standards. A work contract was drawn up for prospective U.S. employers stipulating braceros be provided hygienic lodgings, risk insurance, sick pay, higher wages for specialized tasks, tools, affordable meals or a daily subsistence allowance, adequately heated living quarters, and other provisions. The braceros would be able to elect their own representatives and receive protection under U.S. laws. For those able to read, the contract held great promise. Yet as a bracero later remarked to a government investigator, "Some of us have read the contract but it cannot be mentioned to the boss. The contractor laughed and he said, 'The contract is a filth of a paper.'"[4]

As ranchers and agriculturalists profited from and became dependent upon Mexican labor, they successfully lobbied the United States Congress to extend the bracero program. At the time *Border Incident* was being prepared in 1948, there were 5,000 Mexican immigrant laborers living in thirty camps in Los Angeles, Orange, and Ventura counties in California. An approving *Los Angeles Times* account of migrant worker living conditions reported "untrained" braceros earning sixty-five cents an hour (around $6.30 in 2013) and experienced orange pickers fifty to seventy-five dollars a week.[5]

In reality, Mexican immigrant workers under the Bracero Program were no better off than those working illegally in the United States. This matter was made clear on January 28, 1948, one year before *Border Incident* began filming, when a chartered DC-3 plane of the United States Immigration Service crashed and burned in Western Fresno County, California, killing twenty-eight braceros, three crewmembers, and an immigration guard. The Mexican casualties included documented laborers returning home as well as undocumented workers the INS was deporting. It is symbolic that United States newspaper reports of the accident only published the names of the four U.S. victims. The radical folk singer Woody Guthrie memorialized the plane crash in his protest poem "Plane Wreck at Los Gatos (Deportee)."[6]

In 1949, at the time *Border Incident* was in postproduction, Latino newspapers in California were equating the Bracero Program with modern slavery and reporting inhumane exploitation of workers. In his 1956 U.S. government report, Ernesto Galarza provided extensive documentation on employer contract violations and overall exploitative treatment of braceros in the years immediately following the release of Anthony Mann's thriller. Mexican nationals spoke openly of grim and costly housing conditions, continuous contractual violations, extortionate charges for food and lodging, transportation safety hazards, and discriminatory wage policies. The *Los Angeles Times* report to the contrary, some "legal" braceros were having net earnings as little as $6.85 a week by the early 1950s.[7]

WRITING THE SCREENPLAY

Border Incident began as an Eagle-Lion Films property. From the outset, screenwriters endeavored to give dimension and humanity to undocumented Mexicans crossing the Mexico-U.S. border. There were also attempts to make the bracero Juan Garcia (James Mitchell in the film) the central protagonist and hero. George Zuckerman's initial twenty-seven-page treatment, *Border Patrol,* from October 1947 begins with three weary and tense Mexican laborers, including the married couple José and Delores, sitting near the edge of a brush awaiting a boat. The frightened woman crosses herself and her husband comforts her, both grateful to Jimmy, the man who guided them through the brush. José looks forward to returning to Mexico "a rich man," having earned $500 at a Texas fruit ranch. He advises Jimmy to find himself a nice wife and live a happy life. The couple boards a boat whose boatman is "a stolid, old Mexican," and when the boat reaches the Mexican side of the river, José notices two figures in the darkness but is assured they are friends. After the couple debarks, "both bend down to kiss their native soil, when suddenly the two 'friends' step forward and plunge knives in their backs." Jimmy briefly escapes but is knifed to death. Stripped of their U.S. money, the bodies of all three victims are dumped into the water. "Then before they leave, the assailants wash the blood from their knife blades in the Rio Grande."[8]

The Zuckerman treatment shifts to the Department of Justice in Washington, D.C., where INS officers meet with a Mexican government official to discuss the deaths of sixty-three Mexicans and four Border Patrol agents in recent months. Two U.S. agents are recruited to investigate, one of them, Jimmy Garcia, "posing as a Mexican wetback." The other agent, Larry, is determined to fight the ring of criminals after learning of the three recent murders. The rest of the Zuckerman story is radically different from the film and contains a female love interest that eventually accompanies Larry across the border to safety. In late October 1947, Zuckerman wrote a 151-page screenplay based on his previous treatments but he eliminated the murder prologue and shifted the initial government meeting to Mexico City. In this version of the script, the gang of smugglers kills Jimmy Garcia.[9]

In early 1948, after Zuckerman departed *Border Patrol*, Bryan Foy, producer of *He Walked By Night* (and former E-L production chief) announced plans to make the project under the title *Wetbacks*, but Foy did not remain involved for long. In the original *T-Men* prologue, Elmer Lincoln Irey cited "the Customs Agency Service with the Border Patrol" as one of the arms of enforcement for the Treasury Department, so Eagle-Lion renamed the project *T-Men on the Border*. Writer John C. Higgins joined newly assigned producer William Katzell in Mexico City to scout locations and collaborate on the script. Higgins wrote an "incomplete dialogue script" on June 16, 1948, under the title *Border Patrol*, which is substantially different from the finished production.[10]

Higgins established the tone of the picture from the outset:

> NARRATOR. This is the story of Juan Garcia, Mexican farmer . . . But it is much more than that, for it is also a story that proves that governments exist not to regiment men and to reduce them to serfs—but to serve men—to protect them—to raise their condition as individuals.[11]

In Higgins's September 3, 1948, version, the bracero Juan emerges as the main hero and turns over the surviving villains to a "Mexican Raiding Squad" headed by Rojas. The script ends on this note:

> ROJAS. Nice job, amigo mio. . . .
> JUAN (*seriously*): Maybe so, Señor Jefe . . . But it's hard work—(*looking down at Zopilote's body*) I think farming is more easy . . . (*to the group*) I think I will go back to Michoacán![12]

Once *Border Incident* became an M-G-M property, the character of Juan was gradually eased into the background and the project as a whole took on a more propagandistic tone. In Higgins's November 10, 1948, screenplay draft the opening narrator is first heard after the initial bracero killings:

> NARRATOR. Three men murdered in the desert. In Mexico . . . Below the Border, south of California . . . Just three men, returning illegally to Mexico, robbed and killed for their savings and their clothing. Unimportant men—now without identity—stripped—naked to the sky and the vultures. . . .[13]

Dissolving to a stock shot of a DC-3 at high altitude, the narrator offers an ironical addition:

NARRATOR. Unimportant, did I say? ... Those murders, the latest of many along the Border, set in motion the power of two governments.[14]

In subsequent script drafts this narration was rewritten to explain bracero farm workers seeking work permits in the U.S. Southwest where they hoped to earn enough money to return to Mexico

> to buy a farm—or a business—or a truck—or a few burros—or shoes for their children—or a sewing machine for the Señora ... And—where there is demand and supply—there are always the unscrupulous who connive—and prey—and kill out of avarice...."[15]

The October 18, 1948, script omits this ponderous narrator and opens without any dialogue as Zopilote and his gang murder the three braceros. In this version, Mexican police agent Pablo Rodriguez is introduced but killed on page 129, entrusting Juan with carrying out the government assignment. The harrowing tractor death of Jack Bearnes discussed below appears for the first time on pages 121–23, but there is no quicksand. Juan reunites with his wife Maria after a climactic winery shootout.[16] The December 9, 1948, draft inserts an end coda with Juan and Maria praying in church:

> JUAN. And I thank Thee for bringing us thru the peril of death—my friends and I—but mostly I thank Thee for bringing me safely back to the wife of my heart![17]

In the last image, Juan grips Maria's hand. In the December 18 draft, Juan has no dialogue in the church scene. A narrator replaces Juan's words:

> NARRATOR. And so, as Juan Garcia places his thank-painting in the Church, we can report that a number of crooked rangers were taken into custody through the permits that Bearnes[18] had planted, and they are now serving prison terms. ... Bearnes died in line of duty, but his work lives on—in a bettering of conditions for the Mexican braceros—in support of honest ranchers—and in proof of cooperation between two peoples of America. Thank you...."[19]

In terms of framing the basic thriller story, things deteriorated from screenplay draft to screenplay draft. The January 11, 1949, Higgins script virtually duplicates the leaden Elmer Lincoln Irey opening from *T-Men*. Fading up on seals for the Immigration and Naturalization Service and the federal seal of Mexico, superimposed text informs us that the film was made in cooperation with the INS, United States Department of Justice, and Mexican government, and that "Metro-Goldwyn-Mayer studio thanks the officials of both governments for their valued assistance." The action was to have dissolved to "the Honorable Watson B. Miller, Commissioner of Immigration and Naturalization" at his Washington, D.C., desk who, before introducing another composite case, stiffly promises the public "an opportunity to see in this factual picture how the men of the Immigration Service serve you and guard your interests as United States citizens." From here the action dissolves to something similar to the completed film: helicopter footage of southwest agricultural fields, a narrator explaining the operations of the vegetable and produce industries and how dependent they are on braceros.[20]

Either Mann or his M-G-M supervisors deleted Commissioner Miller from the released film, although the industrial film-style narrator remains during the opening sections.

ANTHONY MANN AT M-G-M

In late September, while Mann was in production on his French Revolution drama *Reign of Terror/The Black Book*, Eagle-Lion signed him to direct *T-Men on the Border* for a November 1 production start date. In early October, according to a trade account, Mann was to have accompanied John C. Higgins and production supervisor Aubrey Schenck to Calexico and Mexicali "to shoot footage of migratory Mexican laborers crossing the border." When Mann spoke of the production to the press, the approximate start of production had been moved to the middle of November on a budget of $450,000. At that time, the project was finally known as *Border Incident* but still perceived as a sequel to *T-Men*. Mann told the *New York Times* that 75 percent of the picture was going to be filmed in the Joaquin Valley and in Mexico's Lower California with sympathetic treatment of "the exploited braceros." (Mann simultaneously announced another E-L crime thriller, *Twelve Against the Underworld*, which was never produced.) In November, Joseph I. Breen Jr. of the Eagle-Lion story department submitted "two final scripts" to his father at the Production Code Administration. Joseph I. Breen Sr. offered an encouraging response but wanted E-L "to make certain that the finished picture contains nothing that would be offensive to Mexico, or the Mexicans."[21] M-G-M soon showed interest in the property.

Metro-Goldwyn-Mayer was on the verge of celebrating twenty-five years as the most prestigious and powerful of the Hollywood film studios. In 1948,

Loew's Incorporated, the leading cinema circuit that created M-G-M in 1924, still controlled the studio, which maintained distribution operations in fifty-six countries. Theater magnate Marcus Loew had masterminded the 1924 merger by acquiring and joining the production and distribution facilities of Loew's own Metro Pictures and rival Goldwyn Pictures (Samuel Goldwyn was no longer with that organization). In 1925, Loew's Incorporated purchased Louis B. Mayer Productions, whose namesake (a former distributor and Metro Pictures executive) was in charge of West Coast studio operations. Nicholas Schenck, uncle of *T-Men* and *Raw Deal* producer Aubrey Schenck, took control of Loew's Incorporated in 1927 following Marcus Loew's death. This new M-G-M was based at the former Goldwyn Pictures studio lot in Culver City, formerly Thomas Ince's Triangle studio, and instantly became the center of celluloid glamour throughout the reigns of Mayer (1924–51) and production executive Irving Thalberg (1924–36). With a roster of stars over the years including Gable, Jean Harlow, Greta Garbo, Norma Shearer, Robert Montgomery, Lana Turner, and Mickey Rooney, M-G-M catered to high-gloss fantasy and escapism with reality rarely encroaching upon motion picture subjects. Through comedies, musicals, and melodramas, M-G-M pictures glamorized wealth, respected authority, upheld western religious values, and promoted a middle-class morality with greater diligence than most of the other major Hollywood studios. Historically, M-G-M had been, with certain exceptions, a safe haven for conservatives and reactionaries.[22]

What appeal did *Border Incident* have to the M-G-M of Louis B. Mayer, a studio whose interpretation of Mexican culture seldom strayed beyond such Technicolor musical banalities as *Holiday in Mexico* (1946) and *Fiesta* (1947)? In truth, it was not Mayer but production executive Dore Schary, a former Mann schoolmate, who pursued the project for Metro. Mann and Schary both attended Central High School in Newark, New Jersey (see Chapter 1). In the late 1920s, Schary was also acting on Broadway but by the 1930s had relocated to Hollywood as a screenwriter. At M-G-M Schary shepherded such family entertainments as *Boys Town* (1938), *Young Tom Edison* (1940), and *Lassie Come Home* (1943), but he revealed a more serious, politically astute side at RKO Radio Pictures during his eighteen-month reign as executive in charge of production. Arriving at RKO shortly after Mann's *Desperate* entered production in late 1946, Schary encouraged the types of gritty crime-related melodramas now regarded as *film noir* as well as pictures addressing anti-Semitism (*Crossfire*, 1947) and other forms of bigotry (*The Boy With Green Hair*, 1948). In July 1948, after colliding with new RKO owner Howard Hughes, Schary returned to M-G-M as vice president in charge of production.²³

Despite nationwide political pressures stimulated by the 1947 House Committee on Un-American Activities hearings in Washington, D.C., Schary brought a liberal postwar sensibility to M-G-M. He was also anxious to introduce the profligate studio to more economical methods of production. Schary was particularly impressed with the Eagle-Lion model and the successful "documentary" style of programmer Mann and Higgins had created in *T-Men*. Within three months of Schary's arrival, M-G-M purchased *Border Incident* from Eagle-Lion for $50,000 and secured the services of Mann and cinematographer John Alton. Schary valued their experience in (to quote *Daily Variety*) "the quickie field," and Eagle-Lion's Arthur Krim was relieved to be rid of a project whose budget was approaching $650,000. The M-G-M budget was set at $550,000, but *Border Incident* ended up costing more than even Krim had estimated. With a filming schedule of twenty-eight days established (Metro features were averaging between fifty and ninety days), Schary advised Mann and Alton to produce *Border Incident* in a speedy fashion, "but not just for the sake of speed."²⁴ According to *Daily Variety*:

> Schary, it's been learned, hasn't put the finger on Mann and Alton to break any records in the making of "Incident." Deal is strictly an experimental one, in order to lay the groundwork for future product. He intends to prove that even at Metro a picture can be turned out at a reasonable budget without bypassing production quality.²⁵

Mann later said that this was the first picture on which he had more freedom "because they didn't even know what kind of animal I was."²⁶

There were benefits from an M-G-M affiliation for *Border Incident*. Mann had access to an actual Mexican star to play heroic Mexican agent Pablo Rodriguez. Latino actors were a rarity in starring roles for Hollywood productions of that era. Three years after *Border* was produced, Twentieth Century-Fox and Elia Kazan cast Marlon Brando as Emiliano Zapata in *Viva Zapata!* Nearly a decade after *Border*, Charlton Heston played a Mexican cop in Orson Welles's *Touch of Evil*. As late as the 1980s and 1990s, Al Pacino was playing Cubans and Puerto Ricans for Brian De Palma in, respectively, *Scarface* (1983) and *Carlito's Way* (1993). Thus, it was a revolutionary concept when M-G-M announced in December 1948 that contract player Ricardo Montalban was going to star in *Border Incident*.²⁷

After signing the actor to a contract in 1947, M-G-M relegated Montalban to Latin Lover roles in such musicals as *Fiesta* and the Esther Williams pageants *On an Island With You* (1948) and *Neptune's Daughter* (1949). According to studio publicity materials:

> The frustrated dramatic actor seemed destined for a Technicolor life of similar roles until Director Anthony Mann and Nicholas Nayfack, producer of "Border Incident," began selecting their cast. Tests indicated that Montalban in dirty blue jeans was even more compelling than in Technicolor spectacles. The fire he had whipped into his dances blazed through just as brilliantly in trigger-quick dramatic scenes.[28]

Casting contract player George Murphy as INS agent Jack Bearnes was another offbeat decision. Murphy was an underwhelming performer known for light comedy and musicals, but Mann wrenched a reasonable performance from the actor, even if Murphy's casting appears in retrospect designed to dilute potential political fallout from the film. Like his contemporary Ronald Reagan, during his career Murphy had shifted from the Democratic to the Republican Party and served two terms as president of the Screen Actors Guild. Murphy was active in the Hollywood Republican Committee and retired from pictures in the early 1950s to pursue politics. In 1964, he was elected to the United States Senate on the GOP ticket. If Montalban guaranteed *Border Incident* cultural authenticity, Murphy promised temporary political insurance.[29]

Border Incident began filming on January 27, 1949, and finished approximately one month later. Considering the complexities of physical design and structure and the challenges of balancing the "action" and social injustice elements, this is a major accomplishment. Mann barely had two months to prepare for filming *Border Incident*, yet the finished motion picture does not suggest a hasty preparation.[30] Shooting on border locations was to have begun in January, but three weeks of rainy weather required Mann and crew to remain in Culver City for the filming of interior scenes on M-G-M soundstages. On February 8, the crew belatedly left Los Angeles for two to three weeks of location filming in the Imperial Valley where their base of operations was El Centro. The grueling production schedule included eight consecutive night shoots from dusk to dawn, temperatures ranging from blazing heat of day to chilly evenings. Among the locales were Painted Gorge, twenty-two miles west of El Centro and east of the Coyote Mountains, and Superstition Mountain in Arizona. By early March, the film was completed and being assembled in M-G-M editing rooms with composer André Previn scoring the music.[31]

Since Mann was preparing for his next Metro feature, *Side Street* (which started filming the following month), his participation in editing would have been limited. Despite the picture ultimately costing $741,000, nearly $200,000 over the original budget, the studio still considered *Border Incident* an example of budget-conscious production.[32] But this did not prevent Metro from discarding the film in the marketplace in late 1949.

VISUALIZING THE BRACEROS

In a Mexicali plaza near the Mexican border, Montalban's Pablo befriends Juan (James Mitchell) who, unaware of Pablo working undercover, laments the shortage of available U.S. jobs for the dozens of gathered braceros. "For six weeks I have been here, waiting. Every day, waiting," Juan tells Pablo. The scene captures what Ernesto Galarza later described in his 1956 government report, which documented the travails of the bracero Perez:

> Every day, at designated hours, Perez stands by with possibly eight or ten thousand other hopefuls. Some days the list that is read over the loudspeaker may contain fifty names; other days there may be three hundred. Some days there are no lists at all.[33]

Mann and Alton visualize the atmosphere of desperation with impeccably arranged extras surrounding Juan and Pablo.

Figure 14.4

Figure 14.5

Figure 14.6

Figure 14.7

After Juan is not called, he insists on accompanying the impatient Pablo on an illegal border crossing into the United States. A church scene between Juan and wife Maria (Teresa Celli), featuring Alton's beautiful lighting and composition, provides a respite from the harsh visual reality of the enveloping material. As a one-armed peasant tells a priest of being robbed of his savings in the desert by killers, Mann and Alton bring to mind the dignified cinematographic emotion of Mexican cameraman Gabriel Figueroa: a side-angle view of Juan's hands clutching the flower that will serve as his ticket to an illegal border crossing, the camera tilting up to a wide-angle two-shot of the couple facing down in prayer, a stained-glass window and two lit candles behind them (fig. 14.5). A filtered profile favoring Maria, her face brightly lit in two thirds of the frame, has an almost Bergmanesque impact (fig. 14.6).

Pablo and Juan encounter disreputable profiteers in gritty night scenes set in dark shacks and rotting cafés. Their exploiters lend themselves to the oppressive low wide-angle shots for which Mann is renowned (fig. 14.7). Actors Alfonso Bedoya (Gold Hat in John Huston's *The Treasure of the Sierra Madre*) and Arnold Moss (given the wittiest lines as Fouché in *Reign of Terror/The Black Book*) expertly extract grim humor from the proceedings, their brutal natures appropriately jarring viewers as the narrative advances.

Figure 14.8

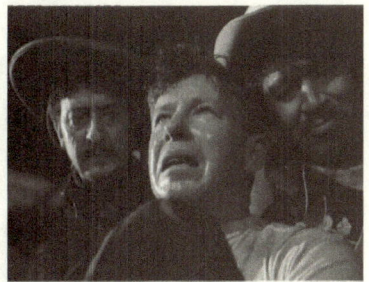
Figure 14.9

Figure 14.10

Border Incident thrives on taking the viewer off-guard, alternately invoking beauty and poignancy, tragedy, comedy, shock, excitement, and terror, a feat few commercial thrillers have ever achieved. In one of the most quietly moving scenes in all of Mann's pictures, Pablo and Juan witness the death of a sickly old Mexican man (Mitchell Lewis) while packed with other braceros into the lower part of a truck (fig. 14.8). Zopilote and fellow crook Clayton (Arthur Hunnicutt) discard the dead man in the desert as the braceros, joined by Juan and Pablo, recite a Spanish prayer. Contrast this with Zopilote and Cuchillo (Bedoya) torturing Jack in a dark garage, truck headlights aimed directly at him (fig. 14.9). Or a major suspense sequence in which Pablo sneaks up to a water tower at night where Jack is held captive, unaware that Clayton is edging his way up wooden steps toward them in yet another example of Mann's aptitude for fashioning and maximizing screen tension (fig. 14.10).

Mann admired but spoke little of *Border Incident*. He did remark on the sequence where a motorcyclist eludes police after retrieving Jack's package of fake work permits from an El Centro post office. Police pursue the motorcycle on a rural highway and along a dirt river road but the biker steers onto a railroad track and loses the car. Mann took credit for the motorcycle sputtering through a cabbage patch, filmed from several angles. "That was

Figure 14.11

me. I was down there in the lettuce fields and it looked like a wonderful way to do it."³⁴

Unfortunately, Mann never spoke of the terrifying demise of Jack Bearnes, a sequence few directors, cinematographers, and editors of the 1940s and 1950s crime genre-era surpassed. Unlike many scenes in *Border Incident*, this was actually filmed at night and illustrates the superiority of "night-for-night" photography over "day-for-night."

Owen Parkson (Howard da Silva), a criminal overseer who spends his spare time shooting a popgun at model birds on a wire, learns of Jack's INS connections, so Clayton and bigoted subordinate Jeff Amboy (Charles McGraw) take the agent for a night ride. Pablo and Juan attempt to save Jack but are helpless as Jeff shoots and beats the agent in a cabbage field with his rifle. Jeff takes his position behind the controls of a tractor parked against the pitch-black sky and activates the motor. For this sequence, film editor Conrad A. Nervig assembles forty shots as Jack tries to stir himself from the ground, the sputtering tractor moving toward him across the field. Wheels of the tractor grind up dirt and cabbage as Pablo and Juan observe in horror; Jack is shown in horrifying low wide-angle as the tractor, spouting smoke against the black night sky, heads in his direction. Clayton stands with a shotgun in the dark field as tractor headlights flash over him. It is a scene of almost unbearable intensity. While no substitute for the actual moving images and the accompanying music-less soundtrack of the grinding and squeaking tractor gears, and the coughing engine, the following selective frame enlargements provide a sense of the impact and the power of Anthony Mann and John Alton's camera placement.

Joseph I. Breen Sr.'s Production Code Administration did not interfere with this scene in most of the United States, but the tractor killing was ordered cut or trimmed in Ohio and Pennsylvania, as well as in the Canadian

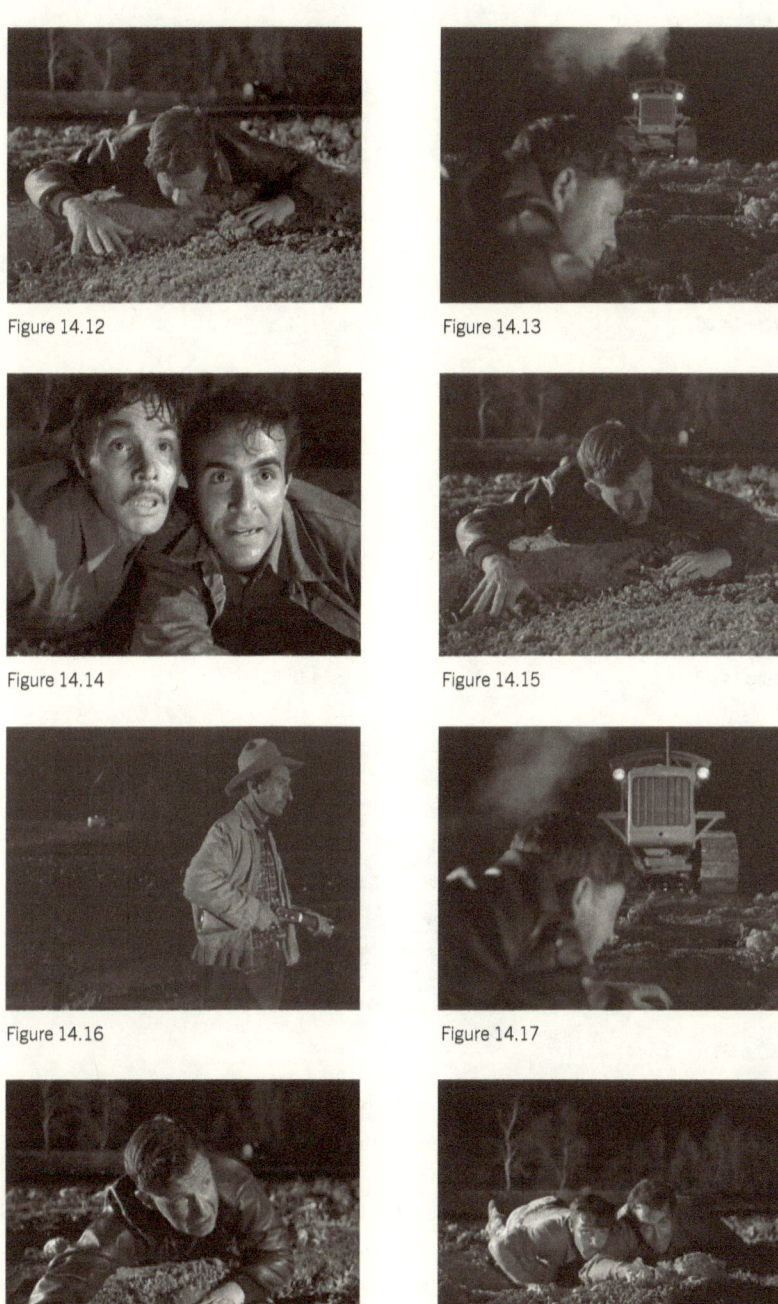

Figure 14.12

Figure 14.13

Figure 14.14

Figure 14.15

Figure 14.16

Figure 14.17

Figure 14.18

Figure 14.19

Figure 14.20

Figure 14.21

Figure 14.22

Figure 14.23

Figure 14.24

provinces of Alberta and British Columbia, and in Australia. The entire sequence was also censored in New Zealand and England.[35]

With nearly twenty minutes left to go, *Border Incident* cannot top what we have just witnessed, but Mann and his collaborators do not let up on the tension as Pablo metes out justice. The shamelessly thrilling quicksand fight between the agent and Zopilote was filmed on an M-G-M soundstage with a truckload of pulverized cork used to simulate the deadly sand.[36] Regrettably, producer Nicolas Nayfack inserted an end coda where the narrator returns with assurances, over footage of braceros toiling in the produce fields, that all is well among Mexican laborers who are "now safe and secure, living under the protection of two great Republics—and the bounty of God almighty."[37]

THE SELLING OF BORDER INCIDENT

In Los Angeles, M-G-M opened *Border Incident* in three cinemas, including the Egyptian on Hollywood Boulevard, where it supported the studio's Roy Rowland thriller *Scene of the Crime*. The advertising copy admirably got to the point:

> EXPOSED! THE ANGRY UNCENSORED STORY ... The shocking story—based on fact—of the notorious slave trade—and the men who risk their lives to stamp it out![38]

Response in Los Angeles was a "mild" combined gross of $32,400. By the time the picture reached Chicago, where it was improbably paired with *The Secret Garden*, starring Margaret O'Brien, the ads hit hard:

> SMUGGLING SENSATIONS! Not since the days of slave auctions—an evil like this! The story of a ruthless racket in human lives—and the heroes who blast out the flesh mongers![39]

Box office results in Chicago were "weakish," according to *Variety*. Business in Pittsburgh (leading the bill with the reissue of the 1941 *film noir Johnny Eager*) and Portland was "dull," but response was "about par" in Philadelphia, where it was the only feature accompanying a live stage act. In Boston, *Border Incident* was barely noticed as a supporting attraction to *Miss Grant Takes Richmond*, a Columbia Pictures comedy with Lucille Ball and William Holden. Manhattan was equally unkind. At the Globe in Times Square (currently the Lunt-Fontanne Theatre), Mann's thriller was a solo attraction, but in spite of studio endorsements ("M-G-M's DRAMATIC THUNDERBOLT!"), the picture was pulled after only six days. (Richard Fleischer's Eagle-Lion FBI thriller *Trapped* was the ironic replacement.) Denver proved to be one of the few major markets where the picture performed well, leading the double bill with the United Artists thriller, *Jigsaw*.[40]

Once the House Committee on Un-American Activities resumed its Hollywood hearings in March 1951, social documents of the *Border Incident* type became more difficult to produce, even if they were ultimately supportive of government agencies. The Truman-era political climate affected the *Border Incident* cast members in varied ways. Howard da Silva was blacklisted for refusing to cooperate with HUAC on March 21, 1951.[41] George Murphy, on the other hand, left pictures on his own accord to pursue aforementioned Republican Party politics.

Anthony Mann lamentably did not collaborate again with John C. Higgins, who had been such an important screenwriting contributor to *Railroaded!*, *T-Men*, *Raw Deal*, and *He Walked By Night*. Mann's next and final collaboration with John Alton would be on the M-G-M western *Devil's Doorway*. But first Mann had to return, without Alton and Higgins, to the city that had spawned his professional artistic skills, an urban metropolis brilliantly suited to the "semi-documentary" approaches to crime storytelling.

The result would be the director's last released crime masterpiece.

CHAPTER 15

SIDE STREET (1950)

M-G-M backlot views notwithstanding, Anthony Mann's *Side Street* is best remembered for its vivid Manhattan location filming. Through the evocative utilization of the streets, alleys, parks, and corridors of the monochromatic city of his stage and television background, Mann brought the sensibility of a displaced New Yorker to this *film noir*. In 1949, the director commented,

Figure 15.0. Farley Granger in *Side Street*, 1950 (Photofest).

There have been some fine pictures about New York City—*Naked City* to name one, which have captured the spirit of the city but which sublimated human factors in conveying that spirit. In *Side Street* we tried to get in much of the flavor but our principal concern was to tell a story of human beings, with the spirit of the city sublimated.[1]

The released version of *Follow Me Quietly* discarded the exciting climactic urban pursuit Mann had cowritten, but the director was not deterred. Even if he didn't ultimately stage an elevated train chase in his own feature *Side Street*, he found ways to maximize the intense cinematic potential of New York City's photogenic surface streets. This was apropos of the so-called "semi-documentary" approach to numerous late 1940s Hollywood thrillers and melodramas, which capitalized on an increased post-World War II moviegoer awareness and desire for actual locations rather than studio backlot reproductions. The crime thriller genre to which *Side Street* belongs lent itself perfectly to the semi-documentary format, although Mann had mixed feelings about the material:

> The semi-documentary school offers real possibilities. Filming in natural settings doubled the scenes' veracity and, consequently, shaped the film by giving it an often unexpected appearance and consistency. I liked the element of chance that could always be introduced. *Side Street*, for example: have you noticed the shift between the first part, uninteresting, and the whole second half, which takes place in Manhattan? It must be said too that Sydney Boehm's script wasn't very distinguished....[2]

In his memoir, star Farley Granger likewise dismissed the screenplay as "ordinary and predictable" and claimed "[f]or its time, *Side Street* was a good-looking, well-made film that was not able to rise above the banality of its story."[3] Directors and actors are not always the best judges of their work. Perhaps Mann and Granger were too enmeshed in their responsibilities on *Side Street* to recognize that it was a tour-de-force in the making.

Boehm's screenplay does have distinguishing characteristics if one accepts the exaggerated chain of events familiar to any effective crime tale. Although the uneven narration at the start and close lessen some of the emotional impact, the story itself is a serene commentary on post-World War II U.S. society. Granger plays Joe Norson, a temporary mailman who steals from an office of blackmailers an envelope containing $30,000. Joe's reform comes too late: the man holding the money disappears and is murdered. Police suspect and pursue the mailman, who becomes a fugitive in his own heartless city and separated from his expectant wife (Cathy O'Donnell).

Sydney Boehm was the skilled crime scenarist of Joseph H. Lewis's *The Undercover Man* (1949) who went on to write dark *film noirs* for Fritz Lang (*The Big Heat*, 1953), Roy Rowland (*Rogue Cop*, 1954), Hugo Fregonese (*Black Tuesday*, 1954), Richard Fleischer (*Violent Saturday*, 1955), and Henry Hathaway (*Seven Thieves*, 1960), among others. Boehm remained on the project throughout development and preproduction, and his departure harmed the picture. Despite some crime-movie clichés (such as a wisecracking blonde gun moll and monotonous police banter), Boehm's working-class protagonists and their perils have parallels to Mann's *Desperate* (1947). *Side Street*, however, is bleaker, darker, and hence more emotionally painful. Although, as we shall see, the social content became diluted as the script underwent revisions, the end result alludes to the Manhattan class divide. By comparison, director Jules Dassin was forced to witness Universal-International censor such themes from his original version of *The Naked City*.[4]

THE SYDNEY BOEHM SCREENPLAY

Side Street the motion picture symbolically begins and ends in the Manhattan financial district. After Mann's directorial credit there is a dissolve to a leftward high-angle panning shot from the Standard Oil headquarters to the New York Stock Exchange as police Captain Anderson (Paul Kelly) narrates:

> ANDERSON'S VOICE. New York City: an architectural jungle where fabulous wealth and the deepest squalor live side by side. New York: the busiest, the loneliest, the kindest and the cruelest of cities.[5]

In the next shot, a police car travels north on Broad Street past Federal Hall, the exact location of the film's melancholy conclusion. The last ten minutes of *Side Street* are a high-speed police chase going up and down the narrow financial district streets where radio cars pursue a taxi, which Joe drives under orders of a murderous adversary. The cars soar past the Lehman Brothers building on William Street and converge in the vicinity of the J. P. Morgan Building on the corner of Wall and Broad, opposite the Sub-Treasury Building and Federal Hall. The statement is as blatantly anti-capitalist as one is likely to encounter in a 1940s Hollywood crime drama—and in a Metro-Goldwyn-Mayer picture, no less.

This is a militant assessment of a commercial "cops and robbers" melodrama. There are admittedly dangers in applying political interpretations to unwarranted situations or those contrary to the creators' intentions, but such an interpretation of *Side Street* is not an abstract theory benefiting from hindsight. To deny the searing political symbolism in the film is to overlook Mann's astute awareness of the issues Boehm raises. The original drafts of the script make clear the author's exposure of capitalism's casualties.

Initially, the Boehm property was titled *Murder Is My Business* so as to echo the narrative words of the police narrator in the earliest drafts of the screenplay: "My name is Walter Anderson . . . New York is my home . . . Murder is my business!"[6] In early versions of his script, the writer acknowledges New York City as a living, breathing sociopolitical organism. The screenplay, like the completed film, is framed between the captain's narration, and the November 15, 1948, draft directly addresses social and racial polarity within Manhattan at the very start of the story over views of the City College of New York campus in Harlem ("knifed in two by CONVENT AVENUE and its fast-moving metropolitan traffic"[7]):

> ANDERSON'S VOICE. New York is no single city; it is an empire of cities—white, brown, yellow and black—a philosophy of tolerance, of racial and religious freedom, a United Nations grown into reality.[8]

The camera, positioned in high-angle at the entrance, moves through an open window into a classroom, where forty male students listen to their instructor:

> ANDERSON'S VOICE. Live here a while and you must feel the cohesion of its peoples—you must see its fifty creeds, welcome and living at peace within their shelters.[9]

The camera pans across the students, "identifying the mixture of races—Puerto Rican, Italian, Chinese, Negro, White, etc." The action then dissolves to a low-angle of a tenement shaft, filming directly up toward the roof.[10] Boehm vividly describes the setting:

> ANDERSON'S VOICE. New York is no panorama of skylines; nor any sequence of pretty pictures—
>
> *Somehow, pencils of sunlight have managed to penetrate the closeness of this typical "airshaft" between tenement walls. Clotheslines, sagging under their*

wet-wash burdens, interrupt the beams of light and give it an eerie, jagged effect. Wooden window "ice-boxes" and bundles of bedding, stuffed through open windows, contribute to the narrowness of the areaway.

ANDERSON'S VOICE. It is a restless city—a city of slums and miseries—[11]

The screenplay dissolves from the tenement to the corner of Wall and Broad Streets, "heart of the financial district, epitome of all that represents wealth." As Anderson briefly describes "countless wealth—locked away every night in vaults deep in the earth and brought to light each morning for the start of big business,"[12] Boehm documents a soulless daily Wall Street ritual:

CAMERA PANS DOWN AND PICKS UP one of the typical every morning "CHAIN GANGS," a procession of a dozen pairs of brokerage clerks, emerging from the NATIONAL CITY BANK vaults. A HALF-DOZEN uniformed and armed private PATROLMEN escort the "Chain Gang." Each pair of clerks carries a metal treasure chest by the simple but effective method of chain handles. One end of each chain is locked to the chest and the other end locked around the wrist of the carrier. They parade toward their brokerage office while hundreds of Wall Street workers pass by, completely impervious to this everyday sight.[13]

By the November 15–18 revisions, Anderson is focused more on educating out-of-towners about New Yorkers not being that different from human beings: "Here, too, they pray—and steal . . . make New Year's resolutions—and break them . . . touch wood, toss salt over shoulders—and defy death." To illustrate this, Boehm employs comical devices that are out of place with the rest of the story: a marital argument at a race track and a superstitious man calmly cleaning a skyscraper window.[14] Boehm's narrative additions introduce the New York Police Department in simplistic terms:

ANDERSON'S VOICE. To protect the good from the bad, an army of twenty thousand is needed. There is no perfect society and without this army, only the strong and evil would survive.[15]

Boehm amended Anderson's final comment that same day:

ANDERSON'S VOICE. Preponderantly, the good outnumber the bad. Most people are basically decent, inherently kind. But without this army, the strong and evil would devour the good.[16]

Figure 15.1

Figure 15.2

Figure 15.3

Anderson also changes from social commentator to humanistic statistician. Some comments survived the final cut with slight changes ("Three hundred and eighty babies will be born today in the City of New York—One hundred and ninety-two persons will die—").[17] Racial diversity absent from the film is still evident in the screenplay, which features candid night shots of 138th and Lenox Avenue in Harlem, a compelling dissolve between the Savoy Ballroom and the Stork Club crowds, as well as a daytime view of a mounted Negro policeman on 125th Street and Seventh Avenue.[18] The class aspects of the city were gradually supplanted with safer sentiments: a stoic mother preparing to give birth in a tenement as her children play in the adjoining room; a priest administering Last Rites to an elderly man in a comfortable apartment. Nevertheless, Anderson's words about the city remain potent: "Its adults suffer and die within sound of their neighbors' laughter. It is a city inarticulate despite its piercing cries."[19]

The political and class observations of Sydney Boehm's screenplay are less pronounced at the start of Anthony Mann's film, which focuses more on the police department's role as city protectorate. During a stunningly assembled montage of "semi-documentary" Manhattan views, Captain Anderson speaks of "an army of twenty-thousand whose job is to protect the citizens in this city of eight millions." There are direct edits between a

Figure 15.4

series of urban images: a motorcycle cop driving his cycle onto Park Avenue; a Times Square policeman evicting a street vendor not far from the Loew's Criterion, which is presenting M-G-M's Fred Astaire-Ginger Rogers musical *The Barkleys of Broadway* (fig. 15.1); a policeman in Central Park near Seventy-second Street attending to a little boy holding a pinwheel (fig. 15.2); a cop on horseback in the Fulton Fish Market; a staged low wide-angle close-up of a pickpocket lifting a subway passenger's wallet and rushing into a detective (fig. 15.3).

Anderson recites his city statistics. We see a nursery with babies and a young married couple with a marriage certificate descending the steps of a courthouse. In a solemn edit, several police carrying a casket-like box exit a building on a crowded industrial street. In his homicide squad office with Detective Simon (Charles McGraw finally playing a law enforcer), Anderson predicts in his narration that

> twelve persons will die violent deaths, and at least one of them will be a victim of murder. A murder a day, every day of the year, and each murder will wind up on my desk.

Cutting back to the Fulton market on the Lower East Side, women buy fruit from a sidewalk vendor as Anderson asks, "Which of these people will be the victims?" As the packed Staten Island Ferry floats towards a foreground dock, he asks again, "Which will be the killers?"

In stressing the captain's statement that "New York is all things in all places gathered into one community," a couple gallops on horseback in the southwest part of Central Park near Columbus Circle, a cop on horseback trotting in the opposite direction, looking at them. In the next shot, several tramps gather around a skillet, the Brooklyn Bridge looming in the distance (fig 15.4).

Figure 15.5

Outside a Catholic church in Little Italy, an older priest walks among children before encountering an elderly Orthodox Jew.

Sydney Boehm had left the project by the time *Side Street* began editing in late July 1949 and Captain Anderson's social commentary soon ended. Screenwriter Helen Deutsch was brought in to rewrite portions of the narration. Despite having contributed to Samuel Fuller's screenplay *Shockproof* that same year for director Douglas Sirk at Columbia, social observations were not Deutsch's forté. Her narration is designed to give the proceedings more heart, but instead it is blandly sentimental. As a well-dressed older man checks his watch against a window of antique clocks, Anderson asks, "This one. Does he secretly long to recapture his vanished youth?" We then see a cheerful Joe Norson pausing to admire a mannequin in a Saks Fifth Avenue window, upon which Anderson remarks, "And this one: a part-time letter carrier. Dreaming of the unattainable: a fur coat for his wife." As a man and woman sit at a window table in a real Manhattan restaurant, the captain inquires, "These. Are they tragedy or comedy?" When Paul Harvey's Emil Lorrison character (who sets Joe's problems in motion) enters a city bank, Anderson is unrecognizable from the social commentator of the early Sydney Boehm script drafts:

> ANDERSON'S VOICE. This man looks troubled. He has a problem. It might be helpful to a policeman to know the details of some of the problems that walk the streets of New York.[20]

Deutsch also supplied Captain Anderson's well-meaning but superfluous narration that surfaces elsewhere early in the picture:

> ANDERSON'S VOICE. Two hundred dollars in a filing cabinet. Great deal of money to a part-time letter carrier with fifty cents in his pocket. He's only human, and no stronger than most of us.[21]

Figure 15.6

Fortunately, the captain mostly forgoes further voice-over reflections until the very end of the picture.

VISUALIZING *SIDE STREET*

Farley Granger's Joe Norson is in a constant state of anxiety as he plummets to the depths of urban despair. Joe has too many expensive fantasies (i.e., a European trip with his wife in that mink coat) and is willing to steal for them. Over the course of five days, he experiences the full range of crime-thriller antihero degradation: from the sanctity and safety of the tenement apartment where he and his wife live with her parents to the grim isolation of a transient hotel; from conversing with a friendly beat cop in broad daylight outside the Criminal Courts building to walking South Street Seaport at dawn (fig. 15.6). He is alone and despondent, anticipating and fearing his capture or killing.

Prowling all corners of the city, from Midtown to Greenwich Village, in search of clues leading to the vanished money for which he is now being held accountable, Joe fraternizes with a hardened chanteuse (Jean Hagen, indispensable as always) and receives beatings from her gunman-lover (James Craig). Joe is reduced to sneaking into the maternity ward at night to see the wife for whom he stole the money. At home, he collapses onto a bed, face down on the sheets. In his skid row hideout, he turns away from a window to grip the ends of the bed, looking down in disgrace. Joe Norson lives in constant fear, which helps explain why Mann and Granger had difficulties with this project. At no point does Joe explode in a fit of violence to

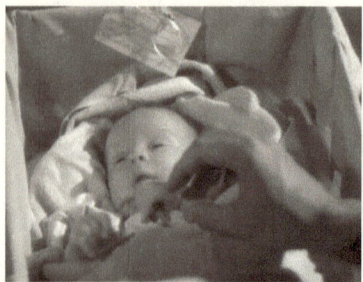
Figure 15.7

Figure 15.8

repel his pursuers as Steve Brodie did in *Desperate*. Nor is he a psychological amalgamation of contradictions and complexities as the Mann heroes we have seen in Dennis O'Keefe and later will see in James Stewart, Gary Cooper, and Victor Mature. He is an average man struggling to survive.

Mann recreates the delicate onscreen chemistry between Granger and Cathy O'Donnell from Nicholas Ray's RKO *noir* thriller *They Live by Night*, filmed in 1947 but held back from release until late 1949. The actress provides *Side Street* with its fervency, which, given the underdeveloped nature of the Ellen Norson role, is a significant accomplishment for O'Donnell. Her scenes with Granger are convincing and affecting. When Joe visits Ellen in Polyclinic Hospital after she has given birth, Mann overrides a potentially sticky M-G-M moment in which a newborn baby warms a criminal's heart. Through careful camera placement and direction of his actors, Mann makes the scene one of agony for Joe. In a close-up of the baby, Joe holds the tiny hand but the following shot is a return to the close-up of Joe's tormented face (fig. 15.7, 15.8).

There are linkages between Joe and Ellen of *Side Street* and Steve and Anne Randall of *Desperate*. After Joe discovers the corpse of the bartender who inadvertently agreed to temporarily store the stolen $30,000, Joe sneaks back at night for an unauthorized hospital visit with Ellen. His confessional scene has added impact when considering the subliminal references to *Desperate*'s endangered couple:

> JOE. Oh, I hated to admit I was a flop. A complete bust. Even after I lost the gas station I kidded myself I'd bounce back. Living with your folks was only going to be temporary.

The reference to a gas station seems to be an allusion to Steve Randall's California service station that he was eagerly planning to manage after

Figure 15.9

Figure 15.10

Desperate concluded. In that sense, Joe and Ellen Norson are a dire continuation of Steve and Anne Randall.

Mann benefits from O'Donnell's fragile nature to wring unexpected emotions from some of her scenes. When Captain Anderson visits Ellen in the hospital office, she professes her husband to be no murderer. Anderson promises they will help Joe if he is innocent. A phone call comes through from Joe:

> CAPT. ANDERSON. If you want your husband alive, keep him on this line. Answer it.
> ELLEN. You tracing this call?
> CAPT. ANDERSON (*nods*). Remember: we want him alive as much as you do.
> (*He picks up the receiver and hands it to her. The camera quickly tracks in to a close-up of Ellen screaming into the phone:*)
> ELLEN. Run, Joe, run! . . . (*Anderson grabs the phone.*) The police are tracing this call!

The shattering moment when the camera pushes in to Ellen's tormented face (fig. 15.9) is one of authentic heartbreak in *Side Street*. It serves as a potent reminder that Anthony Mann's cinema is not one limited to surface violence but a cinema capable of probing humanity and human suffering.

Since the semi-documentary school craved realism and authenticity, having an ex-New Yorker behind the camera contributed to the selected locales being skillfully maneuvered for full photographic impact. The Brooklyn Bridge is an ominous presence during the film, overlooking Joe's transient hotel (a studio set) and also the roof of his apartment (a practical location on the edge of Chinatown, since demolished) where he hides evidence of his theft. In addition, there are artistically framed snippets of Lost New York as Joe walks near a Third Avenue elevated bridge to a tavern (fig. 15.10).

Three police cars giving chase to the taxi in lower Manhattan during the last ten minutes of *Side Street* provide a sense of what Mann was striving to achieve in his *Follow Me Quietly* screen treatment. This sequence does not appear in early Sydney Boehm screenplays but, as indicated above, does serve to visualize the screenwriter's intentions.

In the film, Joe picks up the singer Harriet whom he has linked to killer Garsell. Suspecting his motives, she brings Joe to a tenement flat and directly into the clutches of Garsell and his cabbie accomplice Larry (Harry Bellaver). In the original screenplay, Garsell (named "Manny") gives Joe a beating as a prelude to strangulation but his plans are thwarted when the police captain has the building surrounded with fifty cops and firemen "armed with fire hoses, tear gas bombs and Tommy guns." A tear-gas bomb explodes in the room and Joe fights back through the smoke, taking two bullets in the shoulder, "but he keeps Manny from killing any more policemen until Manny himself is shot down." Having already featured tear gas prominently in the action finales of *T-Men* and *He Walked By Night*, Mann needed a substitution. This original script ends with a family reunion in the police infirmary, the captain informing the recovering Joe that no charges will be brought against the letter carrier. The captain promises to send Joe's family a Christmas tree. Thankfully, Mann discarded this conclusion.[22]

On April 14, 1949, Boehm submitted a new ending containing the high-speed chase, which producer Sam Zimbalist immediately approved. As was his fashion by now, Mann made certain it would be a showstopper on film. In the final version, Garsell knocks Joe unconscious, then, fearful of police locating him through Harriet the way Joe did, strangles the singer in the back seat of Larry's taxi. Joe is forced at gunpoint into the taxi with Larry and ordered to drive to the East River so that Garsell can simultaneously dispose of Joe and the woman's corpse.

The taxi departs M-G-M's backlot New York Street and is soon speeding along the cobblestones of Houston Street, turning and screeching north on West Street under the shaded West Side Elevated Highway. An all-points bulletin orders "all cars south of Fourteenth Street" to cordon off the area (in truth, the police are being sent in the wrong direction). A police car in an industrial part of lower Manhattan backs away from the camera and speeds off in pursuit. Cops jump into police cars overlooking South Street, outside the police precinct (presently the site of the New York City Police Museum). The taxi races past decaying dockside buildings on Twelfth Street as a perplexed vagrant observes from the sidewalk, then back down West Street beside the elevated highway (a location also used for Martin Ritt's *Edge of the City* in 1957), where it swerves to avoid an oncoming truck

Figure 15.11

Figure 15.12

Figure 15.13

(fig. 15.11). At Pearl Street, a police car spots the taxi and chases the cab through the Tribeca area. The taxi and police car narrowly avoid colliding in front of Honest Dave's corner tool store at the tip of West Broadway and Greenwich Street (fig. 15.12). A longer focal length lens photographs the action at Centre Street and Park Row, the decaying Park Row Elevated Station in the background, as the speeding taxi makes a shortcut at a Mobilgas station before steering back onto the road and under the Brooklyn Bridge (fig. 15.13). (The pursuing police car abides by driving rules.) On the other side of the Brooklyn Bridge industrial area, the taxi turns the corner onto Gold Street, barely missing a truck.

Garsell soon kills Larry for attempting to abandon them and orders Joe to take the wheel for the second half of the chase. The cab speeds up Jacob Street and down Exchange Place, crossing Broadway and soaring along the empty cobblestones of Warren Street before screeching past the old Federal Reserve Building near Maiden Lane and John Street. During this time, Mann and cinematographer Joseph Ruttenberg have filmed two astonishing high-angles of narrow financial district streets. The verisimilitude of the location filming is hampered by several studio insertion shots of policemen in mockup cars firing guns against rear-screen projected backdrops.

THE MAKING OF *SIDE STREET*

Side Street was filmed over a seven-week period beginning April 21, 1949, and the first ten days of production were in Manhattan. M-G-M scheduled the picture close to the filming of four other New York City projects: George Cukor's *Adam's Rib*, Curtis Bernhardt's *The Doctor and the Girl*, Gene Kelly and Stanley Donen's *On the Town*, and Mervyn LeRoy's *East Side, West Side*. Crews were in place to start filming shortly after arrival of West Coast talent so that Los Angeles *Side Street* players could go directly from the airport to location sites. In June, more New York and M-G-M/Culver City filming and retakes (the latter most likely with initial murder victim Adele Jergens) occurred.[23]

Side Street was the first Anthony Mann picture since *Railroaded!* without John Alton as director of photography. M-G-M cinematographer Joseph Ruttenberg, who had an impressive record of adaptability, was an excellent substitution. Ruttenberg's camera angles and lenses were less ostentatious than Alton's, but the Russian cinematographer, having already provided appropriately dark tableaus for *The Bribe* (1949), had no difficulty capturing dim tenement corridors and apartments. In a touch of self-referential humor, Jean Hagen's nightclub singer leads Farley Granger's Joe into the dimly lit foyer of her slum apartment and quips, "What some people won't do to save a dollar. You'd think one little light costs a fortune." This must have amused studio personnel accustomed to working with limited lighting resources on lower-tier projects.

Mann was still officially under contract to Eagle-Lion Films when M-G-M borrowed him for *Side Street*. Larry Parks (*The Jolson Story*) was the first choice to play Joe Norson but the studio ultimately borrowed Farley Granger from producer Samuel Goldwyn. The tense and stiff actor from the Alfred Hitchcock thrillers *Rope* (1948) and *Strangers on a Train* (1951) displayed a stark vulnerability in Nicholas Ray's début film *They Live by Night* and does so here as well. In spite of RKO Radio Pictures delaying the Ray film's release, enough people in the industry were familiar with that picture to see the value in re-teaming Granger with *They Live by Night* costar Cathy O'Donnell, whom M-G-M now had under contract. After seeing Jean Hagen in the Broadway play *The Traitor*, producer Sam Zimbalist gave the actress a New York screen test and air-expressed the footage to Metro on the West Coast. M-G-M immediately signed Hagen to a studio contract.[24]

Filming *Side Street* on location in Manhattan had its share of drama. During the location scouting process, M-G-M's William D. Kelly and several production officials took a police barge on the East River as a practice

Figure 15.14

run for an early scene in the film in which crewmen on a freighter discover the floating body of Garsell's first female victim. Kelly later told *Newsweek*, "We actually found a body, a man's though—it had been drifting around in the river a couple of months."[25]

Joseph Ruttenberg was responsible for the momentous introductory aerial views of 1949 New York, which appear under the main titles and were filmed during a three-hour blimp flight over Manhattan as the cinematographer, sitting on the edge of a plank inserted into an open door of the airship, operated the camera.[26] Night sequences on Eighth Street in Greenwich Village (where Joe searches for Garsell's girlfriend), attracted, according to M-G-M publicists, 3,000 onlookers:

> However, Director Mann actually welcomed the crowds, many of whom unknown to themselves appeared as "background," with the passersby and traffic adding a compelling authenticity to the New York story.[27]

Visual symbolism comes into play in a trenchant location shot filmed in the Stuyvesant Town housing development in the East Twenties: a low wide-angle photographed through the jail-like bars of a fence while Joe is observing children playing on a swing set (fig. 15.14). Mann filmed the children with a hidden camera in order to capture their playground activities naturally.[28]

The greatest location challenges were the police-taxi chase at the end. *Side Street* reaches a crescendo as the taxi starts skidding along Wall Street near Federal Hall. In a low-angle of Joe filmed from inside the taxi (a studio mockup) through the steering wheel, he pulls the wheel sharply to the left and ducks (fig. 15.15). In a low street angle, the screeching taxi skids and rolls over onto its side as police cars surround it, before bouncing back into normal position (fig. 15.16).

Figure 15.15 Figure 15.16

Within an hour of cameras and equipment being set up for this big scene on a quiet Sunday in early May, curiosity seekers were already present. Overturning the bulky Manhattan taxicab required twelve takes for stunt driver Frank McGrath and stunt passenger Carey Lofton. According to the *New York Times* account:

> On the first attempt it skidded within a few feet of one of the cameras, manned by Edward Hyland lying prone on the street. Ropes were then tied about both Hyland and his equipment, so that they could be jerked to safety if necessary. Another camera mounted on a platform and facing the direction from which the chase came was manned by Herb Fisher, and between them paced the head cinematographer, Joseph Ruttenberg, worrying over his men and equipment and the poor lighting.
>
> Time after time the cab, with Lofton as the uneasy passenger, would careen down the street, followed by police cars with screaming sirens. For ten attempts before lunch-time it would crash over the high curb, and then roll off, still on all four wheels.
>
> On each run the stubborn cab developed more knocks and rattles, to say nothing of three flat tires, one so battered that it had to be replaced. Then, on the second try after lunch, McGrath finally made it by succeeding in locking a rear wheel against the highest point of the curb. Over the cab went—but even then it wouldn't give up. It stayed on its back [*sic*] for a scant two seconds and, carried by momentum, slowly rolled back to land on all four wheels.[29]

The closing moments between Joe and Ellen, despite editorial tampering, are the most moving in all of the Mann crime melodramas. Ellen rushes out from another taxi as Joe is being wheeled on a stretcher to an ambulance, just as bells from Trinity Church are chiming (Mann told the press that the bells rang at the hour as if on cue).[30] She bends down to kiss his cheeks and mouth, alternating close-ups of the couple ensuing as the weeping Ellen

Figure 15.17

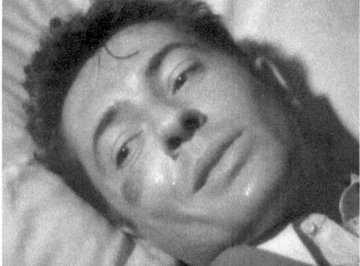

Figure 15.18

Figure 15.19

nuzzles his face (15.17). With Captain Anderson observing, the stretcher is wheeled to the ambulance. Joe attempts a smile from inside the ambulance while Ellen stares down at him through the window. The Trinity Church bells chime as he holds up bent fingers against the glass and she puts up her hand against the other side of the glass next to his (15.18, 15.19).

Staged and performed to perfection, the scene provokes curiosity as to how the couple's separation would have played had studio editors eschewed music and narration. Imagine the ambulance slowly driving away, Ellen walking beside it, her hand against the window, until, in the final camera angle, she is a distant figure in the street, the bells of Trinity Church chiming above her. There is no evidence to support the notion that Mann would have preferred such a conclusion, but he certainly could not have been enamored with M-G-M's additions. In the film, lighthearted music and the return of narrator Captain Anderson replace the Trinity bells. Screenwriter Sydney Boehm's closing narration in the April 14, 1949, script would have sufficed:

> ANDERSON'S VOICE. Today again, 380 babies will be born in the City of New York—192 persons will die—12 by violence—two of them victims of murder . . . and both murders will wind up on my desk . . . for murder is my business.[31]

This would have been a dignified link to his initial commentary. Instead, Anderson's final narration is weak enough for no writer to claim credit, and the anonymously written dialogue was approved in late July after Boehm (and presumably Mann) had departed from the project:

> ANDERSON'S VOICE. This is the story of Joe Norson. No hero, no criminal—just human like all of us. Weak like some of us. But foolish, like most of us. Now that we know some of the facts, we can help him. He's gonna be all right.[32]

Nevertheless, uninspired narration and swelling music cannot obscure the impact of the image of abandoned Ellen Norson standing alone in the street of mercenary finance, staring at the retreating camera as the ambulance carries her injured husband to an uncertain future.

THE SELLING OF SIDE STREET

Trade-screened in late December 1949, *Side Street* was among M-G-M's record backlog of nine completed, trade-shown, and unreleased productions. Months passed before it opened in cinemas.[33] This delay enabled RKO to release Nicholas Ray's *They Live by Night* and capitalize on the pairing of Granger and O'Donnell.

In selling *Side Street*, M-G-M went to manic-depressive extremes, from the ultra-violent to the sweetly romantic. "Exploitation" hints (outrageous attention-getting devices for theaters to carry out) included techniques to "Sock-Sell Action Fans!" by capitalizing on villain Garsell strangling his victims with clothesline. M-G-M advocated that cinemas "Sensationalize the 'CLOTHESLINE STRANGLER'!" by appealing to the basest natures of moviegoers:

> He kills his victims in SIDE STREET with a knotted clothesline. This object can be given action treatment by theatres whose patrons like their movies raw and violent. The "CLOTHESLINE STRANGER" is pictorially featured in all four litho posters.
>
> DANGLING CLOTHESLINE IN LOBBY. Suspend it from ceiling, with knotted noose at the end. Warn patrons to "Watch Out for the 'CLOTHESLINE STRANGLER'!"[34]

The studio devised this device for prospective patrons in the streets:

MASKED "CLOTHESLINE STRANGLER." Unusual ballyhoo of masked man carrying clothesline with a knotted noose. Sign warns the public he is coming to your theatre.[35]

Gentler exhibitors with less violent patrons were encouraged to focus on *Side Street*'s "Young Love Theme." Exploitation possibilities included posing such questions as "What would you do with $30,000?" or "What did fate drop into your lap?" Theaters could print cooperative newspaper ads promising free baby gifts to the first child born in town during *Side Street*'s theatrical run. Theaters were also urged to promote the movie in the side streets of their neighborhoods, photographing the "prettiest girls on a 'Side Street,'" offering free tickets to residents whose side street addresses are printed in the newspaper, and even a side street shopping campaign with stores located off the main streets.[36]

When *Side Street* did premiere in Manhattan in late March 1950 at the Palace in Times Square, live vaudeville accompanied the film for a one-week gross of $21,500 (nearly $208,000 in 2013), exceeding expectations. In Los Angeles, Mann's thriller was oddly used at two theaters to support Red Skelton's M-G-M comedy *Yellow Cab Man* (the studio promoted the program as "POSITIVELY L.A.'S HAPPIEST EASTER SHOW!"). In Washington, D.C., at the Loew's Capitol, the Xavier Cugat Orchestra guaranteed the Mann picture an even stronger opening week than in Manhattan. M-G-M had little interest from this point forward and subsequent double-feature engagements were reported as "skinny" (Indianapolis, where even Alfred Hitchcock's latest thriller, *Stage Fright*, was having "thin" results at a competing cinema), "hapless" (Chicago), and "dim" (Detroit). Instead of leading the theatrical bookings, *Side Street* was following the Red Skelton model by serving as a lower-tier "B" feature for such mainstream comedies as *Champagne for Caesar* (United Artists) and *The Reformer and the Redhead* (M-G-M). Appropriately, the only combination that partially succeeded outside of Los Angeles was in Boston where the picture had an "okay" reception teamed with *Black Hand*, Gene Kelly's M-G-M Mafioso melodrama.[37]

Anthony Mann had little time to take notice of *Side Street*'s commercial reception. As M-G-M erratically distributed the crime melodrama around the United States, he had already completed three more feature films, all westerns. *Side Street* was to be his last released contemporary crime feature until he incorporated the genre into the spy thriller *A Dandy in Aspic* nearly eighteen years later. As for the final crime melodrama completing Mann's 1942–51 cycle, it was not technically a *film noir* or a western but a combination of both.

CHAPTER 16

THE TALL TARGET (1951)

A Baltimore-bound passenger train pulls into the Jersey City terminal station on a cold winter's night. Police Inspector Reilly (Regis Toomey) boards the train to await the arrival of Detective Sergeant John Kennedy (Dick Powell). Meanwhile, the latter, having been tipped off about a murder scheduled to occur in Baltimore the next day, seeks help at headquarters from Police Superintendent Stroud (Tom Powers). Kennedy demands Stroud take immediate action, but the superintendent is too busy socializing with cronies in his dark, smoky office to take the sergeant's warnings seriously. The men present find the whole theory laughable. Disgusted with their indifference, Kennedy turns in his badge and storms out of Stroud's office.

Figure 16.0. *The Tall Target*, 1951. Left to right: Ruby Dee, Marshall Thompson, Paula Raymond, Dick Powell (Photofest).

Arriving at the busy Jersey City terminal, where wartime tensions are in the air, Kennedy sends a warning telegram to the governor's mansion. After searching in vain for Reilly, Kennedy buys himself another train ticket, barely catching the last car as it pulls away through white steam from the wet station platform. Once the train is in motion, Kennedy finds Reilly dead outside the baggage car—murdered. The corpse falls from the car as the train turns a sharp corner. Returning to his passenger car, Kennedy discovers the brutish Wilde (Leif Erickson) in his seat, identifying himself to the conductor as "John Kennedy." Later that night, Wilde seizes Kennedy at gunpoint and plans to kill the ex-detective as soon as the train stops in New Brunswick, New Jersey.

Anthony Mann's 1951 thriller *The Tall Target* has all the trappings of a taut black-and-white *film noir* along with the confined settings, as Mann himself attested, of an Alfred Hitchcock suspense entertainment:

> I tried to do a Hitchcock, or, if you will, an exercise in high voltage: the maximum suspense and tension, in action that was very concentrated in time and space. The film didn't do too badly, but I was only partially satisfied.[1]

This film, however, does not take place in 1951. There are no sedans or coupes, no penthouses, no telephone booths, no police cars, no pinstripe suits, no nightclubs, no neon signs, no radios, and no tear-gas canisters. The wartime tensions are not related to World War II or the Korean War but to the impending Civil War, for *The Tall Target* takes place on the night of February 22, 1861, the eve of President-elect Abraham Lincoln's inauguration. At the same time, *The Tall Target* is a crime thriller, as the above synopsis indicates, with serious *film noir* overtones, and Mann's last from this initial 1942–51 cycle.

In his police superintendent's office, Kennedy has failed to convince his supervisor to notify the secretary of war about the rumored assassination. Stroud tells the other men that Kennedy had been detailed for two days to guard Lincoln when the latter was campaigning in New York: "He thinks he's still on the assignment!"[2] Colonel Caleb Jeffers (Adolphe Menjou) of the Poughkeepsie Zouaves is among those men ridiculing Kennedy but offers the detective a patronizing handshake. Stroud warns Kennedy against going to Baltimore to contact higher authorities: "You cut across channels and I'll bust you!" This is vintage *film policier* dialogue, but as an interviewer suggested to the film's producer, Richard Goldstone, *The Tall Target* enters *film noir* territory as soon as Kennedy surrenders his badge.[3] The stage is set for

Figure 16.1   Figure 16.2

layman Kennedy to take his grueling train journey of continual confrontation, capture, and escape.

Anthony Mann stages the tense chaotic pageantry of the protagonist's preparation for departure with simple yet virtuoso choreography of camera and extras. This is evident in a thirty-five-second camera movement in the Jersey City Terminal: a two-shot of a man purchasing a newspaper from a newsman as a "Union Forever" banner with an illustration of Lincoln hangs in the background; a band performing George Frederick Root's "Battle Cry of Freedom" (a song not written until the following year), the camera panning with the newsman who turns to reveal the front page of the *New York Daily Blade* declaring Jefferson Davis the "Savior of the South" and Lincoln "An Enemy of the Human Race." The camera pulls back to show another man purchasing a paper, then retreats to a long shot of Kennedy entering from the background, band music becoming louder. The camera follows Kennedy to a telegraph desk, the military band marching behind him, and he writes his telegram. The camera then pans left with the soldiers who, cheered on by men and women, march behind windows toward the train platform. This is what Anthony Mann means when he says that a film must be visual.[4]

On the grueling southbound voyage where Kennedy's presence is unwanted and deemed threatening, *The Tall Target* communicates the culture shock and hostility the ex-detective experiences. The stoic Ginny Beaufort and her cadet brother Lance (Paula Raymond and Marshall Thompson) resent Kennedy's inferences that Lance may have murderous designs on the president-elect. Professing to be an ally, Colonel Jeffers offers Kennedy shelter in his compartment only to reveal his own deadly impulses. Through their effective underplaying, actors Powell and Menjou forestall any predictability from encroaching upon the proceedings. The static staging in Jeffers's compartment is at first reminiscent of Mann's low-budget Republic

Figure 16.3　　　　　　　　　　　Figure 16.4

Pictures melodramas, but inspiring ideas emerge as the turmoil intensifies. A medium shot of Kennedy resting in the bunk with a newspaper draped over his head, vocalizing his suspicions of Lance as Jeffers prepares to turn a gun on his visitor, illustrates Mann's rigid sense of building anticipation. When Kennedy outwits Jeffers, Mann uses his chess-piece staging as the two men switch places in the compartment (fig. 16.1, 16.2). When Jeffers again emerges the victor during a Philadelphia stopover, Mann displays his mastery of foreground/background staging, showing the colonel walking across wet pavement and stopping to look back at several plainclothesmen leading Kennedy away from the telegraph office.

In *The Tall Target*, Mann and his camera expectedly command authority in scenes of physical and mental confrontation. In the baggage car where Kennedy searches for Reilly but instead finds the murdered man's smashed glasses, Powell walks toward the camera from a wide low-angle, the camera panning with him as he picks up the glasses, ending in a low-angle of the protagonist (fig. 16.3). Kennedy's discovery of the corpse on the dark platform of the shaking baggage car is a suspenseful assemblage of close-ups intercut with nighttime footage of the passing train. Later on, the fight between Kennedy and Wilde on the New Brunswick station tracks occurs amidst a backdrop of white steam, Kennedy pressing Wilde's head against the track under the locomotive wheel while demanding information. The engineer (Victor Kilian), unaware of the violence occurring beneath his train, puts the locomotive in motion. In an uncomplicated yet dynamic camera movement, the silhouetted locomotive starts to move, the camera panning right to reveal Kennedy pinning Wilde on the track (fig. 16.4). From the perspective of pure physical tension, Mann is unable to surpass this sequence, and the climactic train-fight between Kennedy and confederate Lance Beaufort, with tacky rear-screen projection effects, pales in comparison.

THE MAKING OF *THE TALL TARGET*

In the fall of 1949, M-G-M signed Anthony Mann to a "long-term agreement," but the director was unable to report to the Culver City studio until fulfilling commitments to Paramount on *The Furies* and to Universal-International on *Winchester '73*. After directing the short episode *Load* for M-G-M's *It's a Big Country: An American Anthology* (see Chapter 17), the studio sent Mann, in the fall of 1950, to Italy for second-unit work on the spectacle *Quo Vadis*.[5] Back in Culver City, producer Richard Goldstone was preparing *The Man on the Train*. Metro had begun developing the property in spring 1946 from a George Worthing Yates treatment called *The Lonely Road*. The love triangle between the Southerner Lance, his Northern fiancée Clare, and his disapproving brother Cass (who falls in love with the woman) is set almost entirely aboard a train. Unbeknownst to other passengers, President-elect Lincoln and his party are traveling anonymously at the behest of bodyguard Allan Pinkerton, who has been warned of an assassination plot. Barely figuring in the narrative is New York Police Superintendent John Kennedy.[6]

By May 1949, the treatment and characters changed after Goldstone and Daniel Mainwaring (whose screen name was "Geoffrey Homes") discovered the book *Lincoln and the Baltimore Plot, 1861*. A subsequent treatment briefly retitled *An Instant in the Wind* (capitalizing on that other David O. Selznick-M-G-M Civil War movie) is closer to the finished film. In this version, Kennedy (a character name that obviously took on added significance in future years) is demoted to police detective and placed at the center of the story. The June 6, 1949, script-length treatment credited to Yates and "Homes" is told entirely from Kennedy's perspective. Director Joseph Losey (who had directed *The Boy With Green Hair* for Dore Schary at RKO Radio Pictures) was soon engaged to rework the treatment and possibly direct.[7]

Both Mann and Powell arrived late to the production. Their next M-G-M feature was to have been the newspaper thriller *This Is News* for producer Nicholas Nayfack, which was to star Powell as "a hard-bitten crime reporter of 'The Front Page' school" confronting a crime story. In early December 1950, Powell switched from *This Is News* to *The Man on the Train*, bringing Mann with him. Producer Goldstone gave himself credit for having Mann come over to M-G-M to direct *The Man on the Train*. In actuality, by that time Mann had already directed the M-G-M features *Border Incident* and *Side Street*, in addition to the unreleased short film *Load* and the second-unit material on *Quo Vadis*. *Border* began filming within a month of Goldstone arriving in Culver City from RKO Radio Pictures.[8]

Figure 16.5. Filming *The Tall Target*. Dick Powell (left), Anthony Mann (center), director of photography Paul C. Vogel (right)(Photofest).

What is indisputable is that Mann was a hired hand for *The Man on the Train*. "He had no involvement in the script," Goldstone told an interviewer in 1991. Mann confirmed that he had "less freedom (because Metro started to impose its will)" on both this and his next film for the studio, *Devil's Doorway*.[9] These factors indicate why the film that became *The Tall Target* is not as satisfying as other Anthony Mann crime thrillers. Mann's input would have improved the inadequate screenplay, which compares unfavorably with Daniel Mainwaring's superior scripts for Jacques Tourneur's *Out of the Past* (1947), Joseph Losey's *The Lawless* (1950), Phil Karlson's *The Phenix City Story* (1955), and Don Siegel's *Invasion of the Body Snatchers* (1956). While *The Tall Target*, as indicated above, contains exceptional sections, Mann's detachment is evident. His compositions are less inspired, and cinematographer Paul C. Vogel, while having composed starkly dramatic black-and-white visuals for the 1950 M-G-M thrillers *A Lady Without Passport* and *Black Hand*, fails to contribute as forcefully as previous Mann collaborators John Alton and Joseph Ruttenberg.

At first glance, *The Tall Target* would appear to have influenced Richard Fleischer's 1952 RKO *film noir The Narrow Margin*. Both take place during a crime-laden train ride and are without music scores. Both are compact in structure and suspenseful in execution, forcing the viewer to participate as a passenger caught up in the violent chaos. However, most of the Fleischer picture was filmed before *The Tall Target* (between May 27 and June 13, 1950) and held back from release until RKO owner Howard Hughes pondered the film's fate. William Cameron Menzies directed three days of *Narrow Margin* retakes in late December 1951, three months after *The Tall Target* opened in initial engagements. Richard Goldstone chose not to have background music in the picture because he had already produced a music-less thriller at RKO, Robert Wise's *The Set-Up* (1949).[10]

The lack of music gives *The Tall Target* an unusual semi-documentary feel for a nineteenth-century costume thriller. During the opening titles, a slow-moving passenger train enters diagonally from frame left, and as the last of the flowing credits moves up past the top of the frame, a distant figure is seen walking on the platform. As originally conceived on paper, *The Tall Target* was to have opened with views of Washington, D.C., but Goldstone explained that

> The moment that we saw the results of the first process shot, which was the station with the train pulling in, we threw those temporary images of Washington out right away. Obviously, as soon as you saw the old train on the screen, that was the beginning of the story.[11]

Goldstone's description of Anthony Mann is illustrative of the director's ability to fly under the political radar in the reactionary Hollywood climate of 1950–51:

> Well, personally he was an extremely articulate, genuine intellectual ... I mean in his approach as an artist. He was not only very acuitive [*sic*], but ... for example, with *The Tall Target*, he immediately immersed himself with the entire historical background. I'm sure he did the same with his French revolutionary subject [*Reign of Terror/The Black Book*]. He was extremely well-read. Technically, he had all the tools of an artist in every field of cinema. He never particularly expressed his own personal, political philosophy. I don't know what it was, as a matter of fact.[12]

Goldstone recalled M-G-M being the only studio facility in Hollywood where such a film as *The Tall Target* could be photographed entirely on a backlot. Back in 1951, the Culver City lot contained two miles of railroad track, and an 1860s Baldwin locomotive was stored in a Lot 3 shed adjoining the parking space for Clark Gable's trailer. After M-G-M craftsmen cleaned up the engine and attached a funnel-shaped smokestack, the train was pulled over to Lot 2 for filming. According to Goldstone, a narrow gauge track in the San Fernando Valley, where the train (transporting reporters) was run as part of an evening publicity stunt, was the only location scene in the picture.[13]

> The art director was Eddie Imazu, who was a little Japanese *genius*, he was wonderful! From the Army days, the Air Force days, I had developed a storyboard system, and Eddie actually storyboarded many of the sequences.[14]

Goldstone admired Mann's tendency for "the dramatic move to a big closeup by means of character movement. In other words, he was a very good director for this piece, because his style is somewhat of a stationary camera."[15]

The Man on the Train entered production at M-G-M on January 9, 1951, with, according to studio accounts, "martial music, parading Zouaves, a bunting-draped railroad station and pictures of Abraham Lincoln..." By the end of the month, the title was officially changed to *The Tall Target* and production ended on February 12.[16] Actor and dialogue coach Robert Easton was among the train characters, but his role barely survived final editing:

> I was playing this pompous aristocratic Southern guy. And I'm on my way back to the south to enlist in the Confederate army. Lou Nova was in it, [he] was an excellent boxer. I had no previous rehearsal. Mr. Mann wanted a complicated boxing thing. I hadn't been hired for that. Mr. Mann said to Lou Nova, "The kid doesn't know how to box. Take a half hour out to show him how to box and choreograph it for him." It didn't work out too well.[17]

There were historical benefits for Easton, even if much of his work was deleted: "The clothes that I was wearing were made for Clark Gable. He wore them in *Gone With the Wind*."[18]

The Baltimore Flyer Express train car set was constructed on M-G-M's huge Stage 15 where the studio previously erected the mockup of the USS *Hornet* for *Thirty Seconds Over Tokyo* (1944). In order to accommodate camera angles, the train cars, said Goldstone, were built so they could be pulled apart in sections.[19] This set serves as primary location in *The Tall Target* as Mann and Vogel's camera accompanies Kennedy through tight

Figure 16.6

corridors and cramped compartments. For a director whose first western, *Missouri Legend*, was staged entirely in one modest television studio back in 1939, such challenges posed little problem. The restrictive environment in the film works well until the end where studio frugality becomes difficult for Mann and his technicians to conceal.

Although Mann seems indifferent toward many of the train characters, he does get comic mileage out of two future Hollywood blacklistees, Will Geer's stern conductor and Victor Kilian's anxious engineer. Early in the film, Mann frames the two men from a wide low-angle with the engineer staring out of the locomotive window as the conductor stands in profile at the bottom. Mann continues such camera psychology during the final stages of the film, when cadet Lance pistol-whips John Kennedy in front of Ginny and their maid Rachel (Ruby Dee), Mann framing the action in a low, Orson Welles-style angle (fig. 16.6). More such compositions would have enlivened *The Tall Target*.

The New Brunswick train station fight between Kennedy and Wilde invigorated Mann. Filmed on one of the M-G-M backlot's oldest standing sets, which previously doubled as the Gare de Lyon in Ernst Lubitsch's *Ninotchka* (1939),[20] the sequence suggests the strongest moments of *T-Men* and *Raw Deal*. Goldstone recollected Mann's staging of the fight:

> As I recall it . . . he had a pencil in his hand a lot of the time . . . working with Eddie Imazu, where they very carefully laid out and drew in great detail the fight under the train. Shot for shot. And also, Paul Vogel was very involved with planning these camera set-ups. It was really a threesome with the art director, the director and the cinematographer.[21]

Perhaps, but Mann was already well trained in the staging of screen fights and this one is consistent in style with what had appeared in his previous work for Eagle-Lion and M-G-M.

HOLLYWOOD AND THE SOUTH

The Civil War of 1861–65 has long posed a problem for the motion picture industry. The southern market is a vital revenue source for Hollywood distributors, so from the outset studios avoided producing Civil War pictures offensive to white political leaders and audiences in the south. As late as the 1940s, distributors allowed pictures to be exhibited in racially segregated cinemas and for musical numbers with Lena Horne and other black entertainers to be censored from 35 mm prints of white-dominated movies projected in southern white cinemas.[22] It is for these reasons that virtually every major Civil War film portrays chattel slavery ambiguously, whitewashes it in sentiment, or views the subject as an aberration instigated by a handful of scoundrels. Into this troubled environment came Anthony Mann's *The Tall Target*.

The participation of Joseph Losey in the screenwriting process prompts one to attribute to him the humanistic content present in the completed film, specifically the cautious condemnation of slavery through the character of freed slave Rachel. Losey told Michel Ciment:

> The script which I wrote with George W. Yates was quite a different proposition, and I think much better than the film that was made. They wouldn't make the picture, then. We were writing it for Lena Horne, who was to be the Negro maid in it—it was a much bigger and better part then.[23]

Losey indicated that the studio would not consider Horne as an actress. The role instead went to Ruby Dee, who delivers a quietly heartrending performance as Ginny Beaufort's maid.[24]

In truth, Losey was less concerned with racial politics and more with atmospheric and period details. The June 9, 1949, working outline Losey cowrote with George Worthing Yates begins with socialist poet and Abraham Lincoln biographer Carl Sandburg introducing the story in present-day Washington, D.C. Sandburg was to utilize such National Archives props as canceled railroad tickets and an antique locomotive headlight, and his narration was to lead to the Jersey City railway terminal that opens the film.[25] Supplementary notes from Losey delivered on June 21, 1949, say little about

Rachel and instead list historical details and background characters in numerous scenes, including "wild Abolitionists and Yankee business men [sic]" in the Jersey City station. Losey proceeded to the screenplay stage for *The Man on the Train* and wrote several drafts through September 1949. A narrator and later an opening title crawl replaced Carl Sandburg. Richard Goldstone blamed M-G-M production executive Dore Schary for stressing the historic details in the original screenplay.[26]

By November 1949, Losey was no longer connected with the project, and in July 1950, Goldstone brought in RKO writer Art Cohn for a script polish. Cohn had written *The Set-Up* and was also English-language contributor to Roberto Rossellini's problematic *Stromboli* (1950). It was Cohn who ultimately gave dimension to Ruby Dee's Rachel. Although progressive by M-G-M standards, the Cohn treatment treads lightly on its corrosive subject by emphasizing her tolerance and patience. For example:

> A sensitive girl in her middle twenties, born in slavery, Rachel loves the South and its people, despite their intolerance, because it is her land and her people.
>
> Through the hurts she has suffered and the kindnesses she has received she has learned to understand the contradictory character of the benign, vicious, arrogant, vengeful, frustrated white people who govern the South.
>
> She would give her life to save Ginny and, were she white, would not rest until she married Lance [Ginny's brother]. But her devotion to Lance ends when she learns that he means to kill Lincoln.
>
> What can Lincoln mean to this semi-literate Negress who has been given her freedom and treated like an equal by a mistress she loves?[27]

According to the treatment, Lincoln criticizing the Dred Scott decision of 1857, which denied freed slaves legal rights, affected Rachel:

> This made sense to Rachel. She did not pretend to understand the political or economic implications of abolition but she grasped the full meaning of those words.
>
> All men, even Negroes should have the right to be left alone.
>
> All men, even Abraham Lincoln.
>
> Since there are people committed to kill him for those words she feels there should be others ready to kill in defense of them—and who more than she, one of the few of her people who has known the joy of freedom?[28]

Cohn remained as screenwriter throughout the filming process.[29]

At times the screenplay shackles Mann with stock characters and one-dimensional dialogue. Yankee chatterbox Mrs. Charlotte Alsop (Florence Bates) annoys everyone within listening range as she spreads her pro-Union/anti-slavery views, snarling "Secessionist!" or giving disapproving scrutiny through her lorgnette to those challenging her. One has to believe that Mann could have diluted some of the offensiveness in the script if he had more influence. In the released film, Mrs. Alsop interviews Rachel in the club car as the latter spins yarn with Ginny:

> MRS. ALSOP. I'm sure I'm very grateful to you for allowing me to talk to your slave, Miss Beaufort. After all, I've never talked to a slave before. We don't have them in Boston, you know.
> GINNY (*subtle sarcasm*). Oh, it's quite all right, Mrs. Alsop. I'm sure the experience is as novel for Rachel as it is for you.

After some club car distractions, Mrs. Alsop continues her interview:

> MRS. ALSOP. Tell me, my dear, how does it feel being beaten? They did beat you, of course.
> RACHEL. (*Softly.*) Yes, of course. (*Mrs. Alsop's face lights up and she takes some notes.*)
> GINNY. Rachel, don't be so absurd.
> RACHEL. They did too, Miss Ginny. Remember the Christmas ball when we slid down the banisters together?
> GINNY. You forgot to tell Mrs. Alsop (*to Mrs. Alsop*) we were ten years old. They spanked me, too.
> RACHEL (*smiling*). That didn't make me hurt any less. (*Ginny smiles back at Rachel as they continue spinning yarn together.*)

Moments such as these indicate why the director of the Federal Theatre plays *The Cherokee Night*, *Haiti*, and *Big Blow*, each of which dealt with bigotry and racial injustice in some way, was only partially satisfied with *The Tall Target*.

Fortunately, Ruby Dee's Rachel has more dignified moments later on. One hour into the film, Kennedy, arriving in the Beaufort compartment as Ginny sleeps, tries to convince Rachel to give him one of Lance's guns. Claiming to be neither Republican nor abolitionist, Kennedy cannot promise Lance will be unharmed. His mission to protect Lincoln, he suggests in a whisper, is based on kind encounters with the politician during the

 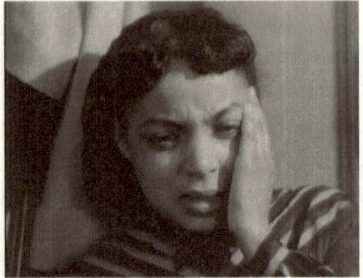

Figure 16.7   Figure 16.8

New York campaign. Ginny awakens, grabs the gun, and slaps Rachel, who cowers as her mistress trains the weapon on Kennedy (fig. 16.7). Ginny orders Rachel to locate Lance, but Rachel, looking away tearfully, offers the words of dissent, "No, Miss Ginny." Ginny repeats the order and in a searing close-up of Rachel, her left hand still pressed against the left side of her face from the slap she received (fig. 16.8), actress Ruby Dee provides the singularly most retching moment in *The Tall Target* when she repeats, "No, Miss Ginny."

Art Cohn wrote this exchange for the August 23, 1950, script draft, which went further than an M-G-M production taking place during the Civil War could expect to go. Ginny is disbelieving of Rachel's actions, reminding her that the two of them "grew up like sisters." As Rachel submissively utters, "I know that, Miss Ginny," Kennedy (sounding more like an abolitionist after all) comments strongly, "Like sisters. Only you're free and she's a slave." Art Cohen's dialogue continues:

> GINNY. Rachel is as free as I am! (*She looks at Rachel.*) You know that. That's why I never thought to ask for your freedom! And why I never thought of givin' it to you.
> RACHEL (*lowering her hand from her face, staring tearfully ahead*). Freedom isn't a thing you should be able to give me, Miss Ginny. Freedom is something I should've been born with.

This being an M-G-M production, backpedaling is inevitable. Once Ginny is aware of Lance's role in the plot against Lincoln, she turns against her brother. After Lance shoves Kennedy out the cabin door at gunpoint, the two women face each other and Ginny embraces Rachel.

Mann does his best to maintain levels of suspense once the train reaches Baltimore in daylight and Kennedy faces the conspirators. There are images which, like the earlier close-up of Rachel, haunt the memory: a team of

Figure 16.9

horses, in the film's first daylight sequence, pulling the train through the streets of Baltimore (actually the M-G-M backlot) to avoid engine smoke dirtying laundry lines; a camera pan over to Caleb staring through a frosted train window as he awaits the arrival of a co-conspirator (fig. 16.9).

The studio ultimately inserts a saccharine finale: a view of the U.S. Capitol dome under construction and a dissolve to a prolonged view of the completed dome as "The Battle Hymn of the Republic" plays on the soundtrack, following the belated appearances of passengers Lincoln and trusted protector Allan Pinkerton. This kind of obviousness was not an Anthony Mann trademark and is sufficient evidence that his limited artistic input was detrimental to *The Tall Target*.

SELLING *THE TALL TARGET*

Metro-Goldwyn-Mayer was bereft of exciting ideas for promoting *The Tall Target* in the autumn of 1951. Typical publicity gimmicks encouraged theaters to hire professional or amateur stilt walkers:

> Nail a title "T" at top of each stilt. Sign on his back advertises "The Tall Target" at your theatre. Or, stage "The Tall Target" Stilt Walking Contest at a playground. Prizes to those staying on them the longest.[30]

An equally desperate idea was for cinemas to appeal to audiences eager for free movie prizes by partaking in the "Reach for THE TALL TARGET" in the theater lobby. The studio suggested a theater create "street bally" (ballyhoo, the trade term for flamboyant promotion) by making a giant "T" from wood or compo board for someone to carry. "Should you make it tall and wide, paste a few photo scenes on it in addition to billing and play dates." The promotional ideas became stranger, ranging from offering cash prizes to patrons identifying "an unusually tall man for street identification contest" to approaching anyone over six feet, three inches ("or any unusual size") with free movie tickets. Other ideas included staging basketball tossing contests for children, as well as blindfolding theater patrons and offering free tickets to anyone able to place a bull's eye in the center of a target.[31]

The Tall Target demonstrated potential in certain markets, but M-G-M was too distracted with its major Technicolor musicals *Show Boat* (released in July 1951) and *An American in Paris* (released in October 1951) to invest in its distribution. The Los Angeles premiere at the State and Egyptian cinemas generated a "slow" initial week gross of $22,200 (nearly $200,000 in 2013). That the Mann picture supported the unmemorable Melvin Frank/Norman Panama remake of the Preston Sturges play *Strictly Dishonorable* made these two engagements symbolic. Business was "lusty" at the Roosevelt in the Chicago Loop where *Target* supported the Twentieth Century-Fox western *The Secret of Convict Lake*. In Philadelphia, the Mann picture did "nice" business playing solo at a 4,380-seat theater, and earned a "fine" $21,000 at the Palace in Times Square with live vaudeville despite competition from a Dodgers-Giants baseball game. In spite of these modest successes, M-G-M lost all interest in *The Tall Target* as soon as *An American in Paris* opened the following week at Radio City Music Hall and grossed $158,000 in the first week's engagement.[32]

The Tall Target is Anthony Mann's last black-and-white crime drama. Set as it was in 1861, it symbolically and unwittingly serves as a bridge between his contemporary monochromatic thrillers and period color westerns. In retrospect, we can observe the transformation taking place as Mann employs photographic devices and elements associated with the 1940s and early 1950s *film policier* and *film noir* but within a nineteenth-century framework that will soon be hospitable to the stories of the Wild West. This was not a deliberate move on Mann's part since, as we have seen, this final crime picture was a last-minute studio assignment. *The Tall Target* is also one of the last "small" Mann productions, and when we consider the toll the ensuing epics took on his health and well being in the years ahead, the existence of the film is one to be both cherished and mourned.

True to fashion, Mann did not serve out his "long-term" M-G-M contract. Following *The Tall Target*, Mann and James Stewart made *The Naked Spur* for Metro (released in February 1953) but then abandoned Culver City for Universal-International, Paramount, and Columbia. Mann would not return to M-G-M until his doomed effort to remake *Cimarron*, the results of which were released in 1960. Mann's response to being asked if he regretted leaving U-I after a successful string of pictures could also apply to his 1949–53 phase at Metro:

> No I didn't regret it. I never regret leaving anywhere ... In those days people used to say: "If you've got a contract you're safe." Well, there's no such thing as being safe: particularly in this business. That's the time when you're *un*safe, when you're safe. You think you can lean back, rest, say: "I'm OK, I've got a job." But the next film you do, if it's a flop nobody's going to hire you again anyway. So you gamble on your life every time you make a film, and that's the excitement."[33]

CHAPTER 17

THE LOST *NOIR* OF ANTHONY MANN

Anthony Mann directed another film in 1950, between the James Stewart western *Winchester '73* for Universal-International and his second-unit work in Italy on M-G-M's *Quo Vadis*: the unreleased and lost *Load*. Mann himself never spoke of this short *film noir* drama, which in many respects is the most personal motion picture he ever made. Originally to have been included in the 1952 M-G-M omnibus movie *It's a Big Country: An American Anthology*, Mann's *Load* episode was cut from the feature prior to commercial release.

Figure 17.0. Jean Hersholt in *Load*, the deleted 1950 episode from *It's a Big Country: An American Anthology*, 1952 (Photofest).

THE DUDLEY SCHNABEL STORY

The source material for this missing movie is an unpromising Dudley Schnabel story from *Midland* magazine in May 1931. Middle-aged Anders Anderson (nicknamed "Cold Man Anderson"), an Icelandic load dispatcher for a midwestern public service company, has a son Benny who has previously run afoul of the law due to petty thievery. On the night of a threatened storm, a United States senator is scheduled to address a large meeting in Maychester, and Anders's boss is adamant about the neighborhood not losing power. Anders's wife, Myrtle, telephones in the midst of the weather crisis with the news that Benny was involved in a robbery in which a man was shot. Police searched their home but could not find Benny. What should she do if Benny shows up? Anders has no answer.

As Schnabel writes it, the Andersons are cuddly European immigrant stereotypes, Myrtle straight out of a *Katzenjammer Kids* comic strip ("Oh, my boy, my boy! Now it iss the police, I tell you—").[1] Other characters hardly fare better. When Anders phones the police for information on the robbery, the cop in charge, taking a cue from Edward G. Robinson in an early 1930s Warner Bros. movie, informs the load dispatcher that the robbery victim is now dead. Anders asks how they know Benny was responsible. The policeman responds:

> "Ah, we know, Anderson. We got ways of knowing. I'm telling you, we went to your place, and your wife says he hadn't been home for a week. But we know him and his pal is around there, and we'll get him the minute he shows his mug, see?"[2]

Overwhelmed with grim despair, Anders tries prayer but the words fail to emerge. When the storm strikes full force and trouble calls start coming in to the power station, he focuses only on the emergencies. Maychester loses power and Myrtle calls back with news that Benny has returned and plans to flee by car across the Canadian border. Her tone is flippant:

> "It iss dark now—and he iss going. He will half [sic] to cross Main Street to get to the yards. Keep the lights off—you!"
> Her voice was suddenly big and commanding.
> "He's promised he'd get a boat and go back to grandma's to stay. To Reykjevik! He needs only half an hour of dark now—fifteen minutes, maybe! You hear?"
> Anderson tried to interrupt, but she hurried on.

"The police iss out in cars, they don't watch the yards. Anderson, you got to—you got to gif him the chance—they're all around here, but I kep' him—"

"Well, mama—"

"They would put him in prison, and you can gif him a chance. What good are you up there, Anderson, if you can't—"

Prison? It was murder now, but mama didn't know that. They would put Benny in the electric chair.

"God help you, Anderson, if you turn those lights on now!"[3]

Anders faces dreadful temptation. Maychester was the section he was told to guard from darkness above all else. A crowd of 10,000 has gathered to hear the politico, and darkness could cause panic. Anders's choice is between a code that has been part of his work life for many years and his love for delinquent Benny. In the end, Anders chooses to go against his son. Despite the storm's intensity, darkness comes to Maychester for only three brief seconds. Anders has no difficulty making this decision. When an engineer asks permission to turn on the number three circuit that will illuminate Maychester and thus prevent Benny from escaping, the short story ends with Anders addressing the man: "'Ee-ya,' he said, indistinctly. 'Let 'em—haf it.'"[4]

In 1947, *Americans One and All*, a collection of twenty-three short stories told from twenty-three cultural perspectives, included Schnabel's story among William Saroyan ("The Broken Wheel") and Sinclair Lewis ("Young Man Axelrod") pieces. Metro-Goldwyn-Mayer production executive Dore Schary acquired the rights to this anthology and assigned producer Robert Sisk to develop a feature film. In the end, Sisk and Schary used only two of the twenty-three stories, one of which was "Load." Schary and other screenwriters supplied the remaining seven episodes.[5]

IT'S A BIG COUNTRY: AN AMERICAN ANTHOLOGY

Dore Schary did not cite the multiple-episode feature *It's a Big Country: An American Anthology* in his 1979 autobiography. Nevertheless, this 1951 M-G-M production, inspired by *Americans One and All*, was near and dear to Schary's heart at the time it entered production. Richard Thorpe, John Sturges, Charles Vidor, Don Weis, Clarence Brown, William Wellman, Don Hartman, and Anthony Mann were each assigned to an episode.[6] The picture was intended to make Cold War audiences feel good about the quirky diversity of the United States, but 1952 moviegoers wanted no part of it.

Mann emerged from the disaster professionally unscathed because the studio deleted his episode *Load*. Cinema history is less fortunate.

In July 1950, producer Robert Sisk stated that *It's a Big Country* was to contain eight stories "without pleading anyone's case" and that "we've told it with a very pleasant air of humor in a very modern way. Nothing profound."[7] The structure of the film is as follows: William Powell and James Whitmore open the story in Richard Thorpe's *Interruptions, Interruptions* as passengers on the Hudson River Line where Whitmore bores his intellectual companion by proclaiming himself to love America. In John Sturges's *The Lady and the Census Taker* (photographed by John Alton), kindly Ethel Barrymore implores newspaper editor George Murphy to help her be included in the 1950 census. The third segment is a superficial newsreel montage of prominent U.S. Negroes in the armed forces, show business, sports, and education. The remaining episodes are Charles Vidor's *Rosika the Rose*, with Greek Gene Kelly courting Hungarian Janet Leigh; Don Weis's *Letter from Korea*, with Marjorie Main; William Wellman's *The Minister in Washington*, written by Schary, and featuring Van Johnson as a visiting minister giving short shrift to Lewis Stone's congregation; and Don Hartman's *Four Eyes*, with Frederic March and Nancy Davis (Reagan). These episodes are frivolous at best, embarrassing at worst, as they touch lightly upon ethnic rivalry (the Vidor segment), anti-Semitism (the Weis segment), and the excesses of masculinity (the Hartman segment). Other segments use sentiment (Sturges) and humor (the Brown episode, *Lone Star*, with Gary Cooper) to capture the melting pot of the United States. The soundtrack features "The Stars and Stripes Forever," "God Bless America," "The Rising of the Moon," "Anchors Aweigh," "Columbia, the Gem of the Ocean," "America the Beautiful," and, finally, "My Country, 'Tis of Thee."

Buried somewhere in this ode to Middle American obedience was originally to have been Anthony Mann's "powerhouse tragedy." Despite facing the unenviable task of adapting the Schnabel story into a short film, M-G-M screenwriter Luther Davis managed to deliver an exceptional twenty-two page script that had what Schnabel's short story lacked: three-dimensional characters, genuine trauma and tension, social scrutiny, and a devastating resolution. In addition, by changing some of the locations in the original work, Davis was able to expand the storyline just enough to make it filmic. Regardless of which version of the Davis screenplay was filmed, *Load* would have been a tiny jewel in the crown of Anthony Mann's crime drama cycle. Yet this delicately profound work lacked the "pleasant air of humor" the studio would have expected; the script more than likely shook up anyone at the Metro front office who perused its yellow pages in mid-December 1949.

In retrospect, it is surprising to think that Davis had expected his screenplay to be approved for the pending *It's a Big Country*. But somehow it was, albeit with a few significant revisions. Even in its diluted form, however, the film that Mann directed from the script must have been a beautiful and cinematic work.

In May 1950, Mann was confirmed as director, with Jean Hersholt being courted for the role of Anders Anderson. After considering Marshall Thompson as Benny, the studio chose Robert Sherwood (no relation to the playwright), fresh from the hit Broadway play *Mister Roberts*, to play the son. Ann Harding, a veteran actress known for sophisticated independent female roles back in the early 1930s, was signed to play Hersholt's wife. In June 1950, *Load* was prepared and filmed, although details are sketchy as to who was assisting Mann behind the scenes. With *Side Street* cinematographer Joseph Ruttenberg handling camera and lighting, the visual look of *Load* must have matched the power of the material.[8]

Using several versions of the screenplay (preserved in the University of Southern California's Cinematic Arts Library) written between December 1949 and June 1950, let us now attempt to reconstruct this missing Anthony Mann *film noir* short.

THE LUTHER DAVIS SCREENPLAYS

Luther Davis's initial screenplay draft opens with a cinematic depiction of power station tensions along with views of stormy weather conditions. Anders Anderson is now Nils Anderson, with his ethnicity changed to Swedish. His boss calls Nils on the latter's day off with orders for the load dispatcher to go to the power station to prepare for impending weather problems. Eighteen-year-old Benny Anderson, wounded from a bullet, appears outside the Anderson house from behind shrubs and heads to the kitchen. According to the script:

> *Benny peeks in; sees no one; starts to open door but HEARS a noise in kitchen; cowers back. He is still as much boy as man and his lips tremble with pain and self-pity; he is close to tears. He sees that it's his mother; taps timorously on door.*[9]

The emotional Mrs. Anderson shields Benny from Nils as the latter prepares to leave for work. The screenplay provides a gloomy sense of what a typical walk to work was like for aging Nils Anderson. The man experiences a worsening storm and heavy rainfall as he steps outside the house with his beloved cat. Writer Davis describes the journey:

> Cars passing have their headlights on. Nils pauses to open his coat so that the cat can get inside; steps out. CAMERA PANS WITH HIM as he walks past tenement, a beer joint, and he turns corner onto a thoroughfare of neon-lighted bars, nickelodeon joints. A BLAST of tinny music hits our ears. Nils' expression hardens.

> NILS. The city, is the city my fault, these jump joints, that's what does it, no fresh air, no clean snow winters.[10]

A roving police car makes Nils anxious:

> NILS. You going crazy, Nils? When has policeman's business ever been Anderson business?[11]

Coworker Fisher harasses Nils that night at the power plant:

> FISHER. You ever think, night load dispatcher, what you keep going? Movie theaters, dance halls, gin mills, juke boxes, all the junk?
> NILS. Why you want to say a thing like that?
> FISHER. What life have you had, and for what? This ain't no lighthouse, just a private company making money. When you ever get to see your family?
> NILS. Ja, juke boxes, but hospitals, too, nei?[12]

With this simple exchange, Luther Davis conveys Nils's conflicting emotions about his profession, emotions not present in Schnabel's 1931 story. Mrs. Anderson telephones, and Davis gives her a tone (heard through a filter) of sensible panic rather than sheer bossiness:

> NILS. What's—what happened to Benny?
> MRS. ANDERSON (*o.s., filter*). Nils, they say he's got in some trouble. Done something. Something foolish. They wouldn't say what.
> NILS. Ja.
> MRS. ANDERSON (*o.s., a note of hysteria*). Ja! Ja, what we going to do?
> NILS. I be home midnight, Mama, I—I don't know, Mama.
> MRS. ANDERSON (*o.s.*). I told them Benny hasn't been home all night, we don't know where, they'll come to you. You say that, too.
> NILS. Ja, ja, it's true, isn't it?
> MRS. ANDERSON (*o.s., on filter*). Just remember, you don't know where.[13]

After this phone call, the worsening weather distracts Nils so that he fails to notice the night watchman admitting a policeman and plainclothes detective. Nils blanches when he sees them.

> PLAINCLOTHESMAN. Where's your boy Benny Anderson?

As he gets heavily, wordlessly, to his feet, Nils' eyes fall on the cat; absurdly he moves to stand between them and it.

> NILS. Please—Benny's a good boy—
> PLAINCLOTHESMAN. Where is he?
> NILS. He's eighteen, still in school. What kind of trouble could he be in that's so bad, police bad?
> PLAINCLOTHESMAN. We got the whole Maychester District covered, including your house. He ain't gettin' away.
> NILS. You make it sound like he—please, what's Benny done?[14]

A phone call alerting Nils to the latest updates on weather disturbance repairs interrupts the confrontation. The plainclothesman continues after Nils hangs up:

> PLAINCLOTHESMAN. I'm sorry, Mr. Anderson. He and two other boys, they held up a drug store on Central Avenue.
> NILS. No!
> PLAINCLOTHESMAN. If he's innocent, where is he?
> NILS. What for would Benny hold up a store, I give him money, clothes, no, Mr. Policeman, no!
> PLAINCLOTHESMAN. We got one of the other boys. He talked. The druggist gave a pretty good description. Before he died.

> *Lightning; loud THUNDER; Nils' mouth works and he falls back against desk but we hear no words. Thunder subsides.*

> NILS. You mean, you think our Benny—
> PLAINCLOTHESMAN. He's wanted for murder, Mr. Anderson. He done it, whether you believe it or not, and he's gonna be found. Now where is he?

> *Nils gives a little wordless groan, turns his back; goes to window where he stands looking out, the muscles of his back working as if he were in physical pain. The two cops look at each other.*

COP (*whispering*). He don't know. That mother knows I bet, but he don't know.

Plainclothesman shrugs and looks around at room.

PLAINCLOTHESMAN. Sorta Buck Rogers, ain't it?[15]

Amidst thunder and lightning Nils notices that the cycle meter is on the mark, then he stares out the window at the city at night, lost in reverie:

EXT. LONG SHOT—CITY—FROM BEHIND NILS—NIGHT
We can follow his gaze to the little house in Maychester.

NILS. When we moved here, before Benny was borned, it was country, we kept six chickens. Maychester was a separate town, not even part of the city.

INT. FULL SHOT

The plainclothesman shrugs at the cop; walks towards Nils.

PLAINCLOTHESMAN. I'm sorry, Mr. Anderson, we got a job to do. You know, you got a job yourself, quite a job it looks, now if you'll just—

Nils whirls, interrupting him.

NILS. My job! Twenty-six years, six nights a week, sometimes more, I sat up here and my boy was growing up bad, days I slept, he went to school, and now you think he's—he's murdered—(*he breaks off*) Like Fisher said, just to keep juke boxes running, fancy places lighted! My job!

PLAINCLOTHESMAN (*embarrassed*). Take it easy, Pop—
NILS. I haven't seen Benny!
PLAINCLOTHESMAN. That's all you hadda say. Come on. (*turns away and starts toward door; whispers to cop:*) Acts more like an Eye-tie than a cold Swede, don't he?[16]

After the two cops exit, Anderson "looks up and makes a large, empty gesture toward God" before thunder and weather distract him. Anderson communicates with some engineers after the lights go out in Maychester. He angrily picks up the ringing phone. It is Mrs. Anderson again:

MRS. ANDERSON. Nils—keep them out, half hour.

NILS. (*buzzing on another telephone*) Mama! Mama, right now I got a job—

MRS. ANDERSON. Nils, Benny's here, he can get across to the railroad yards, they're only watching the road. Nils, give our boy half hour!

NILS. (*grabs other telephone*) Hello, Night Load Dispatcher—

THIRD CONTROL ENGINEER (O.S. FILTER). It's point thirty-two, transformer shorted, we won't be able to deliver for an hour . . .

(*Nils hangs up; says into outside phone:*)

NILS. Mama, you gone crazy?

MRS. ANDERSON. Nils, he's started, he's in the alley now, he promises you give him this chance, he'll get a boat, go back to Sweden, back to home. Nils, he's learned his lesson, you're not going to put him in jail!

NILS. Jail! Mama, it's not jail, it's—

MRS. ANDERSON. Nils, you promise me?

NILS. Mama, Mama, I can't!

MRS. ANDERSON. You can't, you sit up there all his life, like God, looking down on everything, so big and strong, every time he does something, it ain't good enough, making him feel ashamed, you owe . . .

Nils crashes the phone down onto its cradle; he holds his head more THUNDER and lightning off, he picks up another telephone, puts it down.

NILS. Like they say, only juke boxes, juke boxes and saloons, what harm if I give my boy another chance, twenty-six years I—[17]

Nils stops himself and picks up the phone to call his Chicago dispatcher, then he looks at his cat: "The electric chair, Kitty, the electric chair—" After the dispatcher says they are ready to "take your load now, Chicago," Nils hangs up. He addresses his cat once more: "An old dog, Kitty. Like I said, too late for new tricks." Nils fills out his report, grabs his Bible and looks up at the darkened city.[18] The Luther Davis script culminates as follows:

INT FULL SHOT

He puts Bible in his pocket. Looks up at dark light bulbs. After a moment the filaments begin to glow; he glances at cycle meter which tremulously begins to move up. Then Nils walks resolutely and unhurriedly toward the windows; breaks them open with an impatient, swimming gesture of his fists, steps through them and falls. CAMERA HOLDS on empty room for a moment; then the lights come up bright, in office and outside in b.g. Cat yawns. HOLD as MUSIC UP.[19]

One can only imagine the reactions of Dore Schary and Robert Sisk when they read this screenplay. Here was an adaptation of cruel honesty. Nils Anderson is no longer the detached and dedicated man barely feeling a sense of guilt in his quest to do the proper thing. He is a man whose personal detachment has alienated his family and prompted him to question his own existence. There is no sentimental resolution here. Nils Anderson reactivating the power in Maychester is not a demonstration of his Old World commitment to moral responsibility. It is not a sign of his incorruptibility. It is not an indication of his need to ensure that even his son abides by society's rules. The reactivation of Maychester's lights is a self-loathing act by a man of broken spirit who no longer believes in the profession for which he served, at the expense of his son, for twenty-six years, six-days-a-week. Suicide is his only escape from shame.

Davis toned down this harrowing message in subsequent drafts, but not by much. While Davis's March 27, 1950, *Load* draft does not end with Nils Anderson's suicide, the tone remains dark. When the plainclothesman tells Nils, "We're just doing our jobs, Mr. Anderson," the Swede's response is shorter and less enraged: "Ja, ja, jobs! We all do our jobs!"[20] This draft focuses on power-station activities as Nils pathetically carries out his duties after learning of Benny's crime. There is thunder and lightning; the lights in town and in the room go off, leaving ignited small stand-by battery-powered bulbs. He plugs in a telephone and communicates with the harbor engineer, barely glancing at the two exiting policemen. Nils hangs up and takes furious notes on his report sheet. A jagged flash of lightning descending on the Maychester part of town illuminates the room, followed by a loud crash of thunder. An alarm bell on the control board rings loudly and warning lights flash on and off. Nils scans the full circle of the darkened city. The cycle meter is at dead zero. The alarm bell continues as he telephones Harbor Control for their damage report. Nils inserts the phone jack into another outlet as an outside telephone rings. Nils reports the harbor load at zero and cuts off the Harbor Control man as the latter indicates their load all the way up. Nils grabs the outside telephone. It is his wife.

The booming voice of the demanding supervisor heard through the resonator creates tension as Mrs. Anderson pleads,

> MRS. ANDERSON (*o.s., filter; whispering, aspirant and hissing*). Nilss—Nilss you keep them out! Keep them lights out![21]

Nils anxiously sets down the phone and speaks into the resonator, saying he will ask Chicago if they can provide load to his power station. The supervisor orders him to stay with it and Nils makes a call from a special telephone on top of his desk. Mrs. Anderson shouts through the suspended telephone, which Nils picks up with hesitation. She tells him Benny is with her and needs only ten minutes to get to the railroad yards. "Ten minutes you leave them out!" cries Mrs. Anderson, "Ten minutes for your boy!"[22]

At this point, Nils Anderson and his wife are brought back into the M-G-M fold when he reminds her,

> Mama—I got no choice. I have to let the load through—You gotta understand. Babies are being born—hospitals, sick people—they gotta have light. It's my job, Mama.
>
> MRS. ANDERSON (*o.s., filter*). Ja, Papa. Ja.[23]

Nils uses an emergency phone to call the Chicago system night load dispatcher for load on the hydroelectric circuit. As the Chicago dispatcher checks, Mrs. Anderson calls again:

> MRS. ANDERSON (*o.s., on filter*). Nilss, Nilss he's out in the alley now, he's going to be crossing the street, they'll shoot him down![24]

Nils informs the Ravenhurst control manager that Chicago will supply load if a distributing point is cleared. There are more thunderclaps as the Chicago dispatcher confirms he can supply Maychester with 25,000 megacycles. The ringing outside phone distracts Nils, but he ignores it. "Nils' expression shows intense pain—almost physical pain," writes Davis. "Then the outside telephone stops ringing." The Chicago dispatcher shouts for a response and Nils, in "a dead voice," confirms that all his lines are grounded without circuit.[25] The cycle meter is at zero. The Chicago dispatcher awaits a response:

> *Nils straightens in his seat; his eyes fixed on the cycle meter.*
>
> NILS. Hello! Hello, point twenty-nine clear! Twenty-nine okay!
>
> CHICAGO LOAD DISPATCHER (*o.s., filter; a lift in his voice*). Twenty-five thousand megacycles through twenty-nine! Here it comes!
>
> A click as he hangs up o.s. [out of shot]. Nils drops the telephone on his desk; holds his head in his hands, defeated. Then he grins weakly at the cat.
>
> NILS. An old dog, Kitty, an old dog.

He strokes the cat's ear. Then he turns to stare at the cycle meter. Pause; the hand of the meter begins to tremble slightly; goes up a tiny measure, trembles; then starts up firmly but slowly. The alarm bell ceases. The filaments of the regular lights in the room begin to glow; hold there several beats, suspended between standby lighting and regular lighting; then we SEE the lights in the city begin to flicker, on and then off, on and then off, cycle hand is at forty.

Very faintly, police siren is HEARD in the distance. Nils winces and closes his eyes. He just sits there, and you hear the siren going. He is just about to cry.[26]

The March 27, 1950, draft ends at that point. Nils Anderson has done his duty as a power-plant dispatcher but emerges a weaker, defeated man. In short, this draft is a compromise from the previous draft, but not a complete surrender. Not content with leaving some ambiguity in the matter regarding Benny Anderson, the revised April 10, 1950, draft adds the sounds of police gunshots as the night dispatcher is on the phone with his suffering wife. By the June 12, 1950, draft, the Anderson family name was changed to Lunderson.[27]

ANTHONY MANN'S *LOAD*

On April 17, 1950, Anthony Mann was approved to direct *Load* and immediately made his presence felt. Mann told a *Los Angeles Times* reporter that he intended to open and close the episode with the camera moving via boom or crane because he felt such shots were motivated. The brief newspaper description confirms the director's visual ingenuity and, sadder still, the incalculable loss of M-G-M not having preserved *Load*:

The camera takes in a panorama of the city lighted by the power company, moves to a skylight and gazes down thoughtfully on the "little man" who controls it, and then continues on down for a close-up of him. It departs the same way.[28]

The shooting scripts of late May to mid-June are slightly different. They open with a panning shot at evening, looking down on Long Beach, which is standing in for a "medium-sized Great Lakes City." The camera pans 180 degrees as the lights go on over this industrial city. Storm clouds (M-G-M matte effects man Warren Newcombe painted them) are visible in the distance. The camera briefly pauses at an electric sign for Great Lakes Cities Light and Power Company, pans down to a lit skylight, and slowly descends.

An optical dissolve gives the impression of the camera moving through the skylight into the building itself. The camera reveals the top floor of the load dispatcher's office, "solidly covered with charts, warning lights, meters for controlling the electric power system of city and environs." Fisher sits at his desk wearing a green eyeshade, supervisor Blount stares through field glasses out the window.[29] The next angle, a long shot of the lake, is from Blount's perspective:

> *A mass of storm cloud, solid down to water's edge, is approaching across lake, we can SEE the line of rain on surface of water; distant thunder SOUND.*[30]

Returning to the office, Blount wants "the Great Dane" brought in to handle the situation despite Fisher insisting he can handle it himself. The storm begins and rain hits the windows. There is sudden darkness in the office and a flash of lightning. Blount switches on lights in the room and more distant thunder is heard. Blount glances at the largest of the wall meters where the permanent marker is at sixty. The meter hand creeps downward and Fisher plugs a telephone into a jack to call the Harbor Generating Plant. A young control engineer responds to Fisher's order to increase the load by two thousand kilowatts. Back at the office, Blount is piqued at Fisher for giving the entire load to the Harbor plant and leaving another below efficiency level. Blount telephones Nils.[31]

In this shooting script, the tenor of the initial scene between Benny and his parents is different. Nils is not yet mentally defeated and speaks to his son in this scene, believing the breaking of a window to have caused the boy's injuries. The naïve Nils gives Benny money to fix the window.[32] Removed from the script and presumably never filmed was the three-page scene of Nils walking to work, with his cat, in the rain.

To the screenplay's benefit, Mann opened up the action to other locations in the climactic section in which Nils is caught between his panicked wife and the voice of the shouting superior. The Chicago load dispatcher and the Ravenhurst control engineer (both filmed at a power plant in Long Beach) are now shown at their posts during the weather crisis. The May/June scripts, written under Mann's influence, also return Mrs. Anderson/Lunderson to the cameras. This time when she phones him back he wearily responds to the call:

> MRS. LUNDERSON (*o.s., on filter*). Nilss, Nilss he's out in the alley now, he's going to be crossing the street, they'll shoot him down! Nils, they shoot him or they hang him! Hang, Nils, hang Benny Lunderson.[33]

With the surrounding chaos distracting him, Nils puts the receiver on the desk to communicate with Ravenhurst about receiving load from Chicago. Soon we see his wife at home in the dark, holding the telephone, saying, "You can give him chance, Nils—what good are you up there, Lunderson, if you can't—" The action cuts back to Nils in his office, oblivious to her cries. The action cuts back to the wife on the phone in the dark: "God help you, Lunderson, if you turn those lights on now. Your boy, I tell you—" Back to Nils at his desk where he sits up staring at the cycle meter to report that point twenty-nine is all right. The Chicago dispatcher is shown announcing the impending arrival of 25,000 megacycles and then an engineer in the engine room plugs in juice as the meter rises.[34]

Mann trimmed the sentiment involving Nils and his cat. He no longer "grins weakly at the cat" but holds his head in his hands and laments, "An old dog, Kitty, an old dog." He neither strokes the cat's ear nor stands up "firmly but slowly" to stare at the meter. This script instead indicates that "Nils stares at it with passionate intensity, a man watching the meter of his son's death."[35] As the lights of the city flicker on and off, Mann substitutes the previous conclusion with a section that must have played magnificently on screen. The action was filmed on a street in Long Beach, California:

EXTERIOR STREET—(LONG BEACH)
CUT to SHOT SHOOTING DOWN on lamp post [sic]. Cops are seen surrounding the house of Nils Lunderson. They are in shadows as the whole street is in darkness. The light from the lamp starts to flicker on. It shines for a moment and then dims out.

INTERIOR HALLWAY—LUNDERSON HOME
CUT to dark, terrified face of Mrs. Lunderson. She is still holding onto phone. The light in the hall starts to dim up. The light blasts Mrs. Lunderson's face with a harsh brilliance. It stays on. Shots are HEARD off stage and Mrs. Lunderson screams into phone:

MRS. LUNDERSON (*screaming*) Nils—Nils—

INTERIOR DISPATCHER'S OFFICE
Mrs. Lunderson's scream is HEARD over the suspended telephone. Nils stares straight ahead, not moving. Long pause. The cat meows loudly, Nils doesn't notice it.

NILS (*looks up emptily, not knowing how to word this prayer*). Lord God, forgive—(*his voice breaks*) Forgive me my—

Nils breaks entirely, buries his head in his hand and sobs.

The CAMERA STARTS TO BOOM AWAY—until Nils Lunderson becomes a tiny figure sitting at a desk sobbing. The CAMERA DISSOLVES THROUGH the skylight onto the city that he just lit up. The lights are blinking and the city once again has light. A siren is HEARD faintly OVER the scene as the CAMERA PANS around the city.[36]

In the end, Anthony Mann was able to restore much of the impact trimmed from previous Luther Davis *Load* screenplays. While the rest of the *It's a Big Country: An American Anthology* directors phoned in their assignments, Mann approached his with the utmost seriousness. Would that M-G-M had shelved the other six original episodes instead of *Load*. This lost reel or two of brilliance is a summation of Anthony Mann the filmmaker who had emerged from Anton Bundsmann, stage and television director.

The narrative of *Load* had to have stricken Mann deeply. The savage irony of an immigrant father abandoning his son, albeit under different circumstances, could not have been lost on Mann when he took on the unusual assignment. These uncomfortable echoes of his own childhood may also account for Mann not mentioning the film in later interviews. Or perhaps he was still disappointed with M-G-M's decision to cut *Load* out of *It's a Big Country*. Nevertheless, a trace of Anthony Mann still remains in opening scenes of the all-star picture as it was released. As narrator Louis Calhern boasts of the enormity and excitement of the United States, aerial views of Manhattan include a high-angle of the Standard Oil Building. The camera pans left towards Wall Street where the New York Stock Exchange is glimpsed far below.

This footage is taken directly from the opening moments of *Side Street*.

POSTSCRIPT

The disappointment of *Load* did not deter Anthony Mann. In September 1950, *Side Street* producer Sam Zimbalist sent Mann to the Cinecittà studios outside Rome where the M-G-M blockbuster *Quo Vadis* was in production. Working for twenty-four nights with assistance from cinematographer William V. Skall (of Alfred Hitchcock's *Rope*), Mann directed the burning of Rome sequence while credited director Mervyn LeRoy supervised the daytime material.[1] Upon return to Hollywood, Mann elaborated on his Italian assignment:

> I shot for four and one-half weeks. We built blocks of streets and squares and bridges and sewers and staircases at the Cinecitta studios. We used 1500 extras a night—got them right off the streets. It was a helluva interesting experience. I won't get any screen credit on the picture. I did it as a favor to the studio.[2]

HOLLYWOOD IN CRISIS

For better or worse, *Quo Vadis* prepared Mann for bigger and bigger productions with massive casts and budgets. With television impacting cinema attendance, the panicked Hollywood studios gradually began shedding lower-tier black-and-white pictures in favor of Technicolor, DeLuxe Color, Metrocolor, and WarnerColor. The square-shaped 1:37 aspect ratio soon gave way to rectangular 1:85, Cinerama, CinemaScope, and VistaVision. Stereophonic sound soon challenged mono sound. By the mid-to-late 1950s, studio epics used 70 mm Todd-AO and Technirama for select roadshow theater engagements. Mann embraced virtually all of these technologies at one point or another as the James Stewart films moved him permanently into "A" level productions after his small scale *The Tall Target*. But Hollywood's theatrical attendance continued to decline. By 1960, weekly cinema admissions in the U.S. stood at 40.4 million.[3]

Television was only part of Hollywood's problems in the 1950s. The 1948 Supreme Court antitrust decree mandated that studios controlling theater circuits divest of those circuits, beginning with Paramount, RKO Radio

Pictures, Twentieth Century-Fox, and Warner Bros. Loew's Incorporated resisted the U.S. government decision until 1959, when it finally agreed to relinquish subsidiary Metro-Goldwyn-Mayer.[4] Without theater networks demanding weekly changeovers of product, studios cut production schedules, focusing more on costlier event pictures and less on the types of low-budget "B" attractions on which Anthony Mann and other directors had learned their crafts. The power was shifting from the studio lots to the talent agencies.

Equally devastating to the industry was the Hollywood blacklist, which returned in full force after the House Committee on Un-American Activities resumed its "anti-communist" tribunals in 1951. Never having joined any radical left-wing political organization, Mann evaded HUAC scrutiny, but many with whom he associated did not. A number of the victims had been Communist Party USA members at one point. In March 1951, *Border Incident* costar Howard da Silva refused to cooperate with HUAC and was blacklisted from pictures for a decade. In April 1951, actors Will Geer (*Winchester '73* and *The Tall Target*) and Victor Kilian (*Reign of Terror/The Black Book* and *The Tall Target*) were blacklisted after refusing to cooperate with HUAC. *Follow Me Quietly* actor Jeff Corey was blacklisted in the fall of 1951. The actor (and later screenwriter) Nedrick Young, who had a bit role in *Border Incident*, was similarly blacklisted after challenging HUAC in 1953. Another casualty was *Tall Target* screenplay contributor Joseph Losey, a left-wing director forced to pursue work in Europe after his 1951 blacklisting. *Two O'Clock Courage* contributing screenwriter Gordon Kahn, author of a 1948 book defending the blacklisted Hollywood Ten, was himself blacklisted after Edward Dmytryk, Budd Schulberg, and others named him in 1951 and 1952. In the worst scenario, Canada Lee, the leftist activist with whom Mann likely interacted during his involvement with the Federal Theatre's *Haiti* in 1938, died in 1952 as a result of HUAC pressures.[5]

There were those on the political periphery who also felt the effects of HUAC. Liberal actress Marsha Hunt from *Raw Deal* became virtually unemployable after participating in Washington, D.C., film industry protests against HUAC during the initial fall 1947 hearings. The radical actor Albert Dekker (who appeared in *The Furies*), although not officially blacklisted, saw his film work decrease after columnist Hedda Hopper red-baited him in the early 1950s. The progressive actor Norman Lloyd, who had acted for Mann in two live NBC television plays in 1939, *Missouri Legend* and *Streets of New York*, as well as in Mann's *Reign of Terror/The Black Book* (1949), had his film career cut short in 1952 until Alfred Hitchcock brought Lloyd back into the fray for the CBS television series *Alfred Hitchcock Presents*.[6]

Mann also directed members of the Hollywood right-wing who benefited from HUAC's presence. Adolphe Menjou of *The Tall Target* and Donald Crisp of *The Man from Laramie* both were members of the anti-communist Motion Picture Alliance for the Preservation of American Ideals, Menjou having, along with *Devil's Doorway* star Robert Taylor, been a key "friendly witness" at the October 1947 HUAC hearings. (*Man of the West* star Gary Cooper had also officially testified on behalf of HUAC's actions in 1947 but shrewdly declined to implicate anyone.) Other Alliance members included Mann stars Barbara Stanwyck (*The Furies*) and George Murphy (*Border Incident*). There were those on the left who bowed under pressure. Larry Parks, the actor originally discussed for *Side Street* and the unproduced Mann/Francis Rosenwald screenplay *Stakeout*, was sacrificed before the committee in March 1951 even after informing on others. Screenwriter Leopold Atlas (*Raw Deal* and Mann's NBC program *See! Hear!*) turned HUAC informer in March 1953 and died the following year of a heart attack. Blacklisted screenwriter Ben Maddow, an uncredited writer on both *The Last Frontier* and *Men in War*, and actor Lee J. Cobb, costar of *Man of the West*, also ended up cooperating with HUAC.[7]

Anthony Mann refrained from publicly commenting on the Hollywood blacklist, unless one accepts the theory that *Reign of Terror/The Black Book* (1949) was intended as a protest statement against the HUAC trials.[8] Nevertheless, his support of blacklisted screenwriter Ben Barzman confirms that he opposed what the federal government and film companies were doing to screen artists. Six cooperative witnesses named Barzman, screenwriter of *The Boy With Green Hair* (1948) and *Give Us This Day* (1949), during 1951–52 HUAC hearings, resulting in the writer being blacklisted. Mann nonetheless hired Barzman as a principal screenwriter for his major 1960s epics, *El Cid* (1961), *The Fall of the Roman Empire* (1964), and *The Heroes of Telemark* (1965).[9]

ANTHONY MANN: THE POST-*NOIR* CAREER

Of the seven consecutive and successful films Mann directed with James Stewart between 1952 and 1955, the most famous were the westerns (*Bend of the River*, *The Naked Spur*, *The Far Country*, and *The Man from Laramie*) which helped to solidify the filmmaker's international reputation in the 1960s and beyond. Mann struggled to obtain directorial independence in Hollywood after ending his alliance with Stewart and began developing and producing his own productions in the late 1950s for United Artists (1957's

Men in War and his final black-and-white production, 1958's *God's Little Acre*). He also directed post-Stewart westerns with Victor Mature (*The Last Frontier*, 1955), Henry Fonda (*The Tin Star*, 1957), and Gary Cooper (*Man of the West*, 1958). Having had a taste of directing casts of thousands in *Quo Vadis*, Mann gravitated towards spectacles, which were the mainstay of the industry in the late 1950s and early 1960s.

On August 21, 1956, Mann and wife Mildred Kenyon divorced after twenty-five years of marriage. One year later Mann, still known legally as Anton Bundsmann, married Spanish actress Sarita Montiel, whom he had directed in the 1956 Mario Lanza opera melodrama *Serenade*. His planned $3 million epic on the life of Spanish painter Goya, with Montiel cast as the Duchess of Alba, failed to materialize.[10] The director continued to pursue massively mounted projects. This led to unhappy experiences directing the *Cimarron* remake at M-G-M (1960), a mission he eventually aborted, and *Spartacus* (1960) at Universal-International, an epic on which Stanley Kubrick replaced him. Mann remained in control of independent producer Samuel Bronston's *El Cid* and *The Fall of the Roman Empire*, as well as his own production of *The Heroes of Telemark*, but the elephantine size of these pictures (and the accompanying celebrity egos) contributed to the decline of his health. The director and Montiel annulled their marriage in 1963 and he quickly married again, this time to Anna Kuzko, a Russian ballerina formerly with Sadler's Wells, who bore him a son, Nicholas, a year before Mann's death.[11]

Anthony Mann died of a heart attack in April 1967 at the age of sixty. He was in the middle of production on *A Dandy in Aspic*, a British Cold War spy thriller for Columbia Pictures. Mann's passing occurred as he was eager to promote himself as an *auteur*. A year prior to his death, a Hollywood trade paper reported that

> Mann ... deplored the fact that the director in this country is overshadowed in significance by the producer.
>
> Mann would like to see directors in America enjoy the supreme status in film production that they do in Europe. He said flatly that "more credit should be given to the director than to the producer in this country."
>
> In noting that the director in Europe is more important than any other single individual in the production of motion pictures, Mann said that directors there are known to the public because, unlike producers, they "are creators."
>
> "In Europe they look for a director's films because they know that he brings something to a picture," Mann stated.[12]

Mann lamented that, unlike Europe, "very little" was being done in the United States to promote a director's personality.[13]

It is unfortunate that the aspects of Anthony Mann's filmography of interest to this book end officially in 1951 with *The Tall Target*. Imagine what might have emerged had the director returned to the crime genre as was his intention in the years leading up to his death. Towards the end of his abbreviated but full life, Mann was in fact showing signs of reactivating his *film noir* origins. A miscarriage of Hollywood justice occurred in the early 1960s when actor Laurence Harvey gained control of *The Ceremony*, an anti-capital punishment project Mann intended to direct. Once again, we find ourselves trying to sort out an Anthony Mann mystery. In an April 1962 *New York Times* interview, Mann expressed eagerness to direct the Ben Barzman screenplay:

> *Ceremony* is an original script by Barzman—I guess you could call it a comparatively contemporary melodrama—dealing with the last few hours in the life of a native of Cyprus, who is condemned to be shot for his efforts to free Cyprus and who learns that his cause and, especially, human beings in general, are worth fighting for. I've discussed it with Laurence Harvey and he appears anxious to do it, but it is unlikely that we will be able to get going on it before early next year.[14]

According to Norma Barzman, Harry Saltzman of the James Bond thrillers was the originally announced producer, but Mann lost the directing assignment because Harvey was having an affair with Joan Cohn, widow of former Columbia Pictures president Harry Cohn, and Mrs. Cohn insisted Harvey direct the project. Harvey did eventually produce, direct, star in, and contribute dialogue to a Ben Barzman screenplay called *The Ceremony*, but that story was not set in Cyprus and not an original script. The black-and-white film Harvey made in 1963 for United Artists, not Columbia, as a U.S.-Spain co-production, was in fact based on a 1951 French Frédéric Grendel novel and set in Tangier where gang leader Sean McKenna (Harvey) is wrongfully arrested for killing a bank guard during a robbery. LeCoq, the French public prosecutor who is eager to set an example, wants a firing squad to execute Sean. Sean's girlfriend Catherine arranges with his brother Dominic to help the accused escape from prison.[15]

Even without the struggles of Cyprus in the background, the heart races at the thought of Mann generating tension and excitement in the prison break sequence where Dominic, having switched clothes with Sean, blows up a powerhouse to create a diversion while Sean walks out dressed in a priest's uniform. Mann would also have made compelling the rivalry between the brothers over their mutual love for Catherine, which results in a very Mann-like fight between the two men. When the police begin to close in, Dominic is still dressed in Sean's prison clothes, and after being seriously burned in a car smashup is taken back to prison by cops presuming him to be Sean. In the end, Dominic is the one executed and Sean ultimately condemns the barbaric act in front of prison authorities.

England's *Monthly Film Bulletin* dismissed the results as "unbelievably pretentious, manifestly infatuated with thoughts of Cinema, Significance, and Orson Welles." The review attacked the picture for being "aesthetically arranged" and awash in dark, moody chiaroscuro photography with an absence of level camera angles. Presumably Mann would have kept such matters in check or at least have incorporated these cinematic methods without drawing attention to their technique.[16]

After making his two Bronston epics, Mann announced plans to film (in color and Panavision) *The Great Train Robbery*, but Peter Yates eventually made that contemporary true-life heist thriller as *Robbery* (UK, 1967). The existentialist J. B. Priestley spy novel *The Shapes of Sleep* was another project Mann announced. In Priestly's 1962 cloak and dagger thriller, an advertising agency hires an investigative reporter to locate a stolen document, the trail leading him to West Germany and British and Communist spies. This project was abandoned in favor of another spy property, *A Dandy in Aspic*, an espionage thriller which (in classic bizarre film industry fashion) starred the actor who had taken *The Ceremony* away from Mann, Laurence Harvey.[17]

Derek Marlowe adapted the film from his novel, and Harvey was cast as a Soviet agent infiltrating British intelligence. The Brits order Harvey to kill the man responsible for liquidating three of their best agents, unaware that it was Harvey who carried out the assassinations. Had Mann not died of a heart attack two weeks before filming was to end, *A Dandy in Aspic* (released in 1968) might have emerged as a less erratic work. With a cast including Mia Farrow and Tom Courtenay, the picture uses European locales to excellent advantage and benefits from the striking color, Panavision compositions of cinematographer Christopher Challis. In the unfolding chain of events, Harvey took control of direction and completed the picture, but there is no telling how the project was affected during the year in postproduction between Mann's death and the film's release. Harvey, for example, allegedly replaced the original score with the final Quincy Jones soundtrack because he felt "the first score was wrong for the picture."[18] Even as deeply flawed as it is, *Aspic* in certain camera angles evokes the most memorable moments from the director's finest black-and-white crime melodramas of the 1942–51 period. *Variety* perceptively confirmed that the contemporary setting and style of the project was something Mann had not pursued in a long while: "*Aspic*, which is Mann's 45th film,[19] also marks a return to the shooting style and atmosphere of his own *T-Men*, shot 20 years ago."[20]

During production on *The Heroes of Telemark*, Jean-Claude Missiaen asked Mann, "In your opinion, did your apprenticeship in police and atmosphere films have happy consequences for the rest of your career?" Mann responded:

> It was a good school, the roughest but the best: the maximum performance with the minimum means. The least shot had to contribute to the significance of the whole, the least gesture typed a character. A bunch of actors, then little known and making their debut, were very useful to me here: Dan Duryea, John Ireland, Raymond Burr, Charles McGraw....[21]

The same observations may be applied to the crime films of Anthony Mann. They were the roughest but the best from a master director achieving the maximum in cinematic impact from minimum means, a cycle of works which have proven over time to be more than useful to aficionados of the *film noir* and *film policier*—and to the Hollywood cinema in the era of artistic giants.

ACKNOWLEDGMENTS

One of the most gratifying aspects in writing this book was discovering the excitement the topic generated among cinephiles and scholars. The mere mention of "Anthony Mann" was enough to brighten faces, lift spirits, and open doors in my quest to uncover information about his mysterious life and times.

No private investigator can function without operatives helping trace leads and solve mysteries. I am indebted to the libraries and archives whose dedicated staffs were supportive of this project from the outset. Barbara Hall of the Academy of Motion Picture Arts & Sciences Margaret Herrick Library made available Production Code Administration reports, Paramount Pictures correspondence and numerous screenplays, cutting continuities, rare script treatments, clippings files, published interviews with *The Tall Target* producer Richard Goldstone, and an electronic database of trade publication data. Edward (Ned) Comstock of the University of Southern California Cinematic Arts Library was lavish in his support by granting access to the M-G-M screenplay collection and Edward Small papers. I am especially grateful to Ned for preserving the original pressbooks for *T-Men* and *Raw Deal*, two delirious examples of pulp fiction publicity writing. I also wish to acknowledge the Performing Arts Special Collections department at the University of California, Los Angeles for making the RKO Studio Records available to researchers; the Wisconsin Center for Film and Theater Research where the Eagle-Lion papers are preserved (a special thanks to cataloger Emil Hoelter); and Rosemary Hanes, Josie Walters-Johnston, and Zoran Sinobad of the Library of Congress for assisting researcher Chuck Willett in locating essential material from the NBC Collection.

This book also could not have existed without the priceless resources of the New York Public Library System, from the newspaper databases and microfilm collections of the Forty-second Street Library to the various holdings at the New York Public Library for the Performing Arts at Lincoln Center. The Lincoln Center library provided many clues pertaining to the 1925–40 stage acting and directing career of Anthony Mann, particularly the Hallie Flanagan papers related to his Federal Theatre plays (a collection in desperate need of restoration). Additional thanks are due the Charles

F. Cummings New Jersey Information Center/The Newark Public Library (James Lewis) for assisting in locating information on the director's formative years in Newark; and the Locust Valley Historical Society/Locust Valley Library (Amy Driscoll) for providing additional data on the Red Barn Theatre.

There were individuals along the way who provided invaluable insight, inspiration, and assistance. It was an honor to speak with the director's daughter, Nina Mann, whose candor and generosity helped shed light on her father's childhood and family life. Karen Krett assisted with genealogical research into Anthony Mann's parents and their work at the Theosophical Society in Point Loma. Screenwriter Stewart Stern provided wonderful anecdotes and information about Mann's Eagle-Lion period, and Norma Barzman graciously shared insights into the director's later career. Researcher Chuck Willett is responsible for helping track the complicated theatrical release patterns and box office performances of fourteen feature films analyzed here. Chuck also did an astounding job at the Library of Congress recovering previously unknown information about Mann's work for NBC Television in 1939–40, including locating original teleplays for several key productions. It is through his tireless efforts that we are now able to comprehend how Anthony Mann learned film direction prior to arriving in Hollywood. Not to be outdone, my Los Angeles researcher Serge Delpierre brilliantly reconstructed the screenplay histories of *He Walked By Night* and *Load* and along with Chuck was helpful in locating publicity and promotional materials on several Mann crime melodramas. Projection and sound engineer Jay Gemski was a vital resource for technical information along the way. Louis Alvarez identified various New York City locations used in *Side Street*, particularly in the climactic car chase sequence. Zbigniew Kozlowski, Dave Kehr, and Jeffrey Marden were essential in gaining access to the early Mann pictures under study here. Nancy Meyer and Patricia Shaheen graciously assisted in the fact-checking process.

Mary Kalamaras, Heather Quinlan, and Ann-Marie McGowan were highly valued business and editorial consultants while Lisa Freda helped keep the project alive and solvent. Former Smithsonian Associates programmer Julia Pelosi; my *Film & Society Series* producer-director Ruth Berdah-Canet; H. Jack Liebermann, and Eric Rock were constant supporters throughout the planning and writing processes. I am likewise indebted to former *Milwaukee Journal* film critic and arts editor Dominique-Paul Noth and to the research services and guidance of Dr. Richard Brigham, Barbara Brigham, Olivier Eyquem, and Michael Walker. Special attention must also be paid Jean-Claude Missiaen, author of the first book ever written on

Anthony Mann, who generously shared his treasured memories of meeting the great director during production on *The Heroes of Telemark*.

Finally, there are those no longer with us who would have appreciated this book: James Auer, another mentor at the old *Milwaukee Journal*, and Robyn Leary Mancini, journalist and media impresario formerly of the American Film Institute in Washington, D.C., who shared my love of the *film noir* universe and its artisans.

ANTHONY MANN CRIME FILMOGRAPHY

A CRIMINAL AT LARGE (1939)

PRODUCTION COMPANY: NBC Television (WSXBS). PRODUCER/DIRECTOR: Anton Bundsmann [Anthony Mann]. TELEPLAY: Edgar Wallace [1932 UK film title, *The Case of the Frightened Lady*]. MUSIC: "Symphony No. 3 in C Major, Op. 52," by Jean Sibelius, "Tamara, Part II," by Mily Balakirev, "Symphonie fantastique No. 1 in C Major," by Hector Berlioz. RUNNING TIME: 60 minutes. PRODUCTION AND AIRDATE: November 17, 1939 (NEW YORK CITY), 8:30–9:30 P.M.

CAST: Charles Gerard (Dr. Leicester Charles Amersham), Derek Fairman (Sgt. John Ferraby/Criminal Investigation Department), Charles Jordan (Sgt. Totty/Criminal Investigation Department), Dennis Hoey (Chief Detective Inspector Tanner/Criminal Investigation Department), Carl Harbord (Lord William Lebanon), Perry Norman (Kelver), Harry M. Cooke (Gilder), Scott Moore (Brooks), Nance O'Neil (Lady Lebanon), Frances Reid (Isla Crane), A. P. Kaye (uncredited).

DR. BROADWAY (1942)

DISTRIBUTOR: Paramount Pictures. DIRECTOR: Anthony Mann. PRODUCER [UNCREDITED]: Sol C. Siegel. ASSOCIATE PRODUCER [UNCREDITED]: Emanuel D. Leshino.[1] FIRST ASSISTANT DIRECTOR: Harve Foster.[2] ADDITIONAL DIRECTION [UNCREDITED]: Hal Pereira. SCREENPLAY: Art Arthur [uncredited: Jay Dratler, Garrett Fort]. ORIGINAL STORY: Borden Chase. DIRECTOR OF PHOTOGRAPHY (BLACK-AND-WHITE): Theodor Sparkuhl. PROCESS PHOTOGRAPHY: Farciot Edouart. MUSICAL DIRECTOR: Irvin Talbot. ORIGINAL MUSIC [UNCREDITED]: Paul Sawtell and Robert Emmett Dolan.[3] ART DIRECTION: Hans Dreier and Earl Hedrick. FILM EDITOR: Arthur [P.] Schmidt. SOUND: Harry Lindgren and Gene Garvin.

CAST: Macdonald Carey (Dr. Timothy Kane), Jean Phillips (Connie Madigan), J. Carrol Naish (Jack Venner), Richard Lane (Det. Sgt. Patrick Doyle), Eduardo [Edward] Ciannelli (Vic Telli), Joan Woodbury (Margie Dove), Arthur Loft (Captain Mahoney), Warren Hymer (Maxie the Goat), Frank Bruno (Marty), Sidney Melton (Louie La Conga), Olin Howlin (The Professor), Gerald Mohr (Red), Abe Dinovitch (Benjamin "Benny" Strevapoulous), Thomas Ross (Magistrate), Charles Wilson (District Attorney McNamara), Spencer Charters (Oscar Titus), Mary Gordon (Broadway "Ma" Carrie),

Jay Novello (Greeny), John Gallaudet (Al), Al Hill (Jerry), Edward Earle (Assistant District Attorney Hayes), William Haade (Dynamo), Phil Arnold (Hershel the Newsboy), John Kelly (Pool Player), Francis Sayles (Clerk), Joe Ploski (Stooge), Don Brodie (Customer), Cyril Ring (Diner), Lou Davis (Weasel-faced Man),[4] Harry Depp (Customer), George Turner (Kid O'Regan), Paul Bradley (Clerk), Lester Dorr (Little Man), Philip Harron (Sinister Man), Walter Soderling (Blind Man "Peep"), Kernan Cripps (Sergeant), John Hamilton (Inspector), George Gray (Western Union Boy), Milt Kibbee (Patient), Cecil Weston (Bit Woman), Eddie Bruce (Cameraman), Billy Wayne (Cabbie), Jack Norton (Drunk), Edward Hearn (Policeman Jim), Lee Prather (Tom the Relief Cop), Howard Mitchell (Spectator), Harry Harvey (Pedestrian), Dick Rush (Policeman), Eddie Fetherston (First Reporter), Jack Egan (Second Reporter).

RUNNING TIME: 67 minutes. USA RELEASE DATES: June 24, 1942 (NEW YORK CITY), August 13, 1942 (LOS ANGELES), August 28, 1942 (CHICAGO), September 3, 1942 (BOSTON).

STRANGERS IN THE NIGHT (1944)

WORKING TITLE: *The House of Terror*
DISTRIBUTOR: Republic Pictures Corp. DIRECTOR: Anthony Mann. A Republic Production. ASSOCIATE PRODUCER: Rudolph E. Abel. ASSISTANT DIRECTOR: Joe Dill. SCREENPLAY: Bryant Ford and Paul Gangelin. ORIGINAL STORY: Philip MacDonald. DIRECTOR OF PHOTOGRAPHY (BLACK-AND-WHITE): Reggie Lanning. FILM EDITOR: Arthur Roberts. ART DIRECTOR: Gano Chittenden. SOUND: Tom Carman. SET DECORATIONS: Perry Murdock. MUSICAL DIRECTOR: Morton Scott. WARDROBE: Adele Palmer.

CAST: William Terry (Marine Sgt. Johnny Meadows), Virginia Grey (Dr. Leslie Ross), Helene Thimig (Mrs. Hilda Blake), Edith Barrett (Ivy Miller), Anne O'Neal (Nurse "Tommy" Thompson), Audley Anderson (Train Conductor),[5] Jimmy Lucas (Waiter),[6] Roy Butler (Cab Driver),[7] Charles Sullivan (Police Driver),[8] Frances Morris (Nurse),[9] George Sherwood (Navy Doctor),[10] Roy Darmour (Sailor),[11] Jack Gardner (Medical Corpsman).[12]

RUNNING TIME: 56 minutes. USA RELEASE DATES: September 27, 1944 (CHICAGO), November 16, 1944 (BROOKLYN), December 12, 1944 (BOSTON), December 31, 1944 (LOS ANGELES AREA).

THE GREAT FLAMARION (1945)

WORKING TITLE: *Dead Pigeon*
DISTRIBUTOR: Republic Pictures Corp. DIRECTOR: Anthony Mann. EXECUTIVE PRODUCER [UNCREDITED]: Howard Sheehan.[13] [ASSOCIATE] PRODUCER: William Wilder. FIRST ASSISTANT DIRECTOR: Raoul Pagel.[14] SCREENPLAY: Anne Wigton, Heinz

Herald, Richard Weil. STORY: Anne Wigton (based on the *Collier's* magazine short story "Big Shot" by Vicki Baum). DIRECTOR OF PHOTOGRAPHY (BLACK-AND-WHITE): James Spencer Brown Jr. FILM EDITOR: John F. Link [Sr.]. PRODUCTION MANAGER: George Moskov. SOUND: Percy Townsend. ART DIRECTOR: F. Paul Sylos. SET DECORATIONS: Glenn P. Thompson. MUSICAL SCORE: Alexander Laszlo. MUSICAL SUPERVISION: David Chudnow. MUSICAL NUMBERS: "Chita," by Faith Watson, "Lights of Old Broadway," by Lester Allen [uncredited song: "Cielito Lindo," by Quirino Mendoza y Cortés].

CAST: Erich von Stroheim (Flamarion), Mary Beth Hughes (Connie Wallace), Dan Duryea (Al Wallace), Stephen Barclay (Eddie Wheeler), Lester Allen (Tony the Clown), Esther Howard (Cleo), Michael Mark (Night Watchman), Joseph Granby (Detective Ramirez), John R. Hamilton (Coroner), Fred Velasco (José the Mexican Dancer), Carmen López (Carmen the Mexican Dancer), Tony Ferrell (Mexican Singer), Kay Deslys (Sally Hampton), Franklyn Farnum (Pop the Stage Manager), Leo Mostovoy (François).

RUNNING TIME: 75 minutes. USA RELEASE DATES: January 13, 1945 (NEW YORK CITY), April 12, 1945 (LOS ANGELES), May 9, 1945 (CHICAGO), May 15, 1945 (BOSTON).

TWO O'CLOCK COURAGE (1945)

(This film is a remake of RKO's 1936 mystery *Two in the Dark*.)

DISTRIBUTOR: RKO Radio Pictures, Inc. DIRECTOR: Anthony Mann. EXECUTIVE PRODUCER: Sid Rogell. PRODUCER: Ben Stoloff. SCREENPLAY: Robert E. Kent. ADDITIONAL DIALOGUE: Gordon Kahn. STORY (BASED ON THE NOVEL BY): Gelett Burgess. DIRECTOR OF PHOTOGRAPHY (BLACK-AND-WHITE): Jack MacKenzie [uncredited retakes: Harry J. Wild]. ART DIRECTORS: Albert S. D'Agostino and L. O. Croxton. MUSIC: Roy Webb. SPECIAL EFFECTS: Vernon L. Walker. SET DECORATIONS: Darrell Silvera and William Stevens. FILM EDITOR: Philip Martin Jr. SOUND: Bailey Fesler. RERECORDING BY: James G. Stewart.[15] ASSISTANT DIRECTOR: Clem Beauchamp. COSTUME DESIGN: Renié.

CAST: Tom Conway (The Man/Theodore "Step" Allison), Ann Rutherford (Patty Mitchell), Richard Lane (Haley), Lester Matthews (Mark Evans), Roland Drew (Steve Maitland), Emory Parnell (Inspector Bill Brenner), Jane [Bettejane] Greer (Helen Carter), Jean Brooks (Barbara Borden), Edmund Glover (O'Brien), Bryant Washburn (Robert Dilling), Philip Morris (McCord), Nancy Marlow (Hat Check Girl), Elaine Riley (Cigarette Girl), Jack Norton (Drunk), Guy Zanett (Headwaiter), Harold de Becker (Judson),[16] Bob Alden (Newsboy), Chester Clute (Mr. Daniels), Elmira Sessions (Mrs. Daniels),[17] Eddie Dunn (Cop), Carl Kent (Dave Rennick), Chris Drake (Assistant Editor), Bob Robinson (Bit Cop), Charles Wilson (Brant), Sarah Edwards (Mrs. Tuttle), Maxine Seamon (Maid).[18]

RUNNING TIME: 66 minutes. USA RELEASE DATES: April 13, 1945 (NEW YORK CITY), May 28, 1945 (LOS ANGELES), June 14, 1945 (BOSTON), July 18, 1945 (CHICAGO).

STRANGE IMPERSONATION (1946)

WORKING TITLES: *You'll Remember Me, A Strange Impersonation*
DISTRIBUTOR: Republic Pictures Corp. DIRECTOR: Anthony Mann. A Republic Production. PRODUCER: William Wilder. SCREENPLAY: Mindret Lord. STORY: Anne Wigton and Lewis Herman. DIRECTOR OF PHOTOGRAPHY (BLACK-AND-WHITE): Robert W. Pittack. FILM EDITOR: John F. Link [Sr.]. ASSISTANT DIRECTOR: George Loper.[19] MUSICAL DIRECTOR: Alexander Laszlo. PRODUCTION MANAGER: Bartlett A. Carré. SOUND: Earl Crain Sr. MAKEUP: Bud Westmore. ART DIRECTOR: Edward C. Jewell.[20] SET DECORATIONS: Sydney Moore.

CAST: Brenda Marshall (Dr. Nora Goodrich), William Gargan (Dr. Stephen Lindstrom), Hillary Brooke (Arline Cole), George Chandler (Jeremiah Wilkins Rinse), Ruth Ford (Jane Karaski), H. B. Warner (Dr. Mansfield), Lyle Talbot (Inspector Malloy), Mary Treen (Nurse), Cay Forrester (Miss Roper), Richard Scott (Detective), Forrest Taylor (Nora's Doctor),[21] Frank O'Connor (Doctor).[22]

RUNNING TIME: 68 minutes. USA RELEASE DATES: March 31, 1946 (POMONA, CALIFORNIA), May 3, 1946 (CHICAGO), May 16, 1946 (BROOKLYN, N.Y.), July 17, 1946 (BOSTON).

DESPERATE (1947)

WORKING TITLE: *Flight*
DISTRIBUTOR: RKO Radio Pictures, Inc. DIRECTOR: Anthony Mann. EXECUTIVE PRODUCER [UNCREDITED]: Sid Rogell. PRODUCER: Michel Kraike. SCREENPLAY: Harry Essex. ADDITIONAL DIALOGUE: Martin Rackin. STORY: Dorothy Atlas and Anthony Mann. DIRECTOR OF PHOTOGRAPHY (BLACK-AND-WHITE): George E. Diskant. ART DIRECTORS: Albert S. D'Agostino and Walter E. Keller. MUSIC: Paul Sawtell. MUSICAL DIRECTOR: C. Bakaleinikoff. SPECIAL EFFECTS: Russell A. Cully. FIREARMS EFFECTS: Jack Lannan. SET DECORATIONS: Darrell Silvera. FILM EDITOR: Marston Fay. SOUND: Earl A. Wolcott and Roy Granville [uncredited]: C. Harris. SECOND UNIT DIRECTOR / ASSISTANT DIRECTOR: Nate Levinson. COSTUME DESIGNER [UNCREDITED]: Adele Balkan.

CAST: Steve Brodie (Steve Randall), Audrey Long (Anne Randall), Raymond Burr (Walt Radak), Douglas Fowley (Pete Lavitch), William Challee (Reynolds), Jason Robards [Sr.] (Det. Lt. Louie Ferrari), Freddie Steele (Shorty Abbott), Lee Frederick (Joe Daly), Paul E. Burns (Uncle Jan), Ilka Grüning (Aunt Klara), Carol Forman (Mrs. Henry Roberts), Cy Kendall (Ace Morgan), Dick Elliott (Sheriff Hat Lewis), Eddie Parks (Bill Frank), Leza Holland and Kay Christopher (Nurses), Erville Alderson

(Simon Pringle), Teddy Infuhr (Richard, the Little Boy), Ralfe Harolde (Walt's Doctor), Elena Warren (Mrs. Oliver), Larry Nunn (Al Radak), Jack Baxley (Dr. Wilson), Hans Herbert (Rev. Alex Sorenson), Bill Wallace and Carl Saxe (Policemen at Warehouse), Ernie Adams, Michael Visaroff and Jay Norris (Villagers), George Anderson (Man on Train), Robert Bray (Policeman with Lt. Ferrari), Robert Clarke (Bus Driver), Charles Flynn (State Trooper), Carl Kent (Detective), Don Kerr (News Vendor on Train), Milt Kibbee (Mac), Art Miles (1st Truck Driver), Glen Knight (2nd Truck Driver), Perc Launders (Manny), Frank O'Connor (Train Conductor), Netta Packer (Woman on Train), Joe Recht (Bellhop), William Bailey and Marshall Ruth (Traveling Salesmen), Grahame Covert (bit man).

RUNNING TIME: 73 minutes. USA RELEASE DATES: June 18, 1947 (SAN FRANCISCO), July 8, 1947 (LOS ANGELES), July 30, 1947 (CHICAGO), October 8, 1947 (NEW YORK CITY).

RAILROADED! (1947)

WORKING TITLE: *Tomorrow You Die*
DISTRIBUTOR: Eagle-Lion Films. PRODUCTION COMPANY: Producers Releasing Corporation. DIRECTOR: Anthony Mann. IN CHARGE OF PRODUCTION: Ben Stoloff. PRODUCER: Charles F. Riesner. SCREENPLAY: John C. Higgins. STORY: Gertrude Walker. DIRECTOR OF PHOTOGRAPHY (BLACK-AND-WHITE): Guy Roe. EDITORIAL SUPERVISION: Alfred DeGaetano. FILM EDITOR: Louis H. Sackin. ART DIRECTOR: Perry Smith. SET DECORATIONS: Armor Marlowe and Robert P. Fox. PHOTOGRAPHIC EFFECTS: George J. Teague. ASSISTANT DIRECTOR: Ridgeway (Reggie) Callow. DIALOGUE DIRECTOR: Stewart Stern. COSTUME DESIGNER: Frances Ehren. MAKEUP: Ern Westmore and Tom Tuttle. HAIRSTYLING: Eunice [King][23] and Evelyn Bennett. SOUND DIRECTOR: Leon Becker. SOUND MIXER: John Carter. MUSIC: Alvin Levin. MUSICAL DIRECTOR: Irving Friedman.

CAST: John Ireland (Duke Martin), Sheila Ryan (Rosie Ryan), Hugh Beaumont (Police Sgt. Mickey Ferguson), Jane Randolph (Clara Calhoun), Ed Kelly (Steve Ryan), Charles D. Brown (Captain MacTaggart), Clancy Cooper (Detective Jim Chubb), Peggy Converse (Marie Weston), Hermine Sterler (Mrs. Ryan), Keefe Brasselle (Cowie Kowalski), Roy Gordon (Jackland Ainsworth), Mack Williams (Doc, Police Criminologist),[24] Gordon B. Clarke (Club Pianist),[25] Ellen Corby (Mrs. Willis),[26] Kenneth Farrell (Burns, Fingerprint Man),[27] Philip Morris (Guard Checking Gate),[28] Herbert Rawlinson (Doctor Attending Cowie),[29] Mack Williams (Police Criminologist 'Doc').[30] The role of "Wilma" is uncredited.

RUNNING TIME: 72 minutes. USA RELEASE DATES: October 28, 1947 (NEW YORK CITY), November 26, 1947 (LOS ANGELES), November 27, 1947 (BOSTON), March 31, 1948 (CHICAGO).

T-MEN (1947)

WORKING TITLE: *T-Man*
DISTRIBUTOR: Eagle-Lion Films. A Reliance Picture. DIRECTOR: Anthony Mann. PRESENTER: Edward Small. IN CHARGE OF PRODUCTION: Bryan Foy. ASSOCIATE PRODUCER: Turner Shelton. PRODUCER: Aubrey Schenck. SCREENPLAY: John C. Higgins [uncredited writers: Robert B. Churchill, Henry Blankfort, George Brickner]. SUGGESTED FROM A STORY BY: Virginia Kellogg. DIRECTOR OF PHOTOGRAPHY (BLACK-AND-WHITE): John Alton. CAMERA OPERATOR: Carl Webster. EDITORIAL SUPERVISION: Alfred DeGaetano. FILM EDITOR: Fred Allen. ART DIRECTOR: Edward C. Jewell. SET DECORATIONS: Armor Marlowe. PHOTOGRAPHIC EFFECTS: George J. Teague. SPECIAL ART EFFECTS: Jack R. Rabin. ASSISTANT DIRECTOR: Howard W. Koch [uncredited: Charles Wasserman]. DIALOGUE DIRECTOR: Stewart Stern. COSTUME DESIGNER: Frances Ehren. MAKEUP: Ern Westmore and Joe Stinton. HAIRSTYLING: Joan St. Oegger and Alma Armstrong. SOUND DIRECTOR: Leon Becker [uncredited: Jack R. Whitney]. SOUND MIXER: Frank McWhorter. MUSIC SCORE: Paul Sawtell. ORCHESTRATIONS: Emil Cadkin. MUSICAL DIRECTOR: Irving Friedman.

CAST: Dennis O'Keefe (Dennis O'Brien), Alfred Ryder (Tony Genaro), Mary Meade (Evangeline), Wallace [Wally] Ford (The Schemer), June Lockhart (Mary Genaro), Charles McGraw (Moxie), Jane Randolph (Diana Simpson), Art Smith (Gregg), Herbert Heyes (Chief Carson), Jack Overman (Brownie Horizantal), John Wengraf (Shiv Triano), Jim Bannon (Agent Lindsay), William Malten (Paul Miller), Gayne Whitman (Narrator), Vivian Austin (Genevieve), James Seay (Hardy, Lab Technician), Lyle Latell (Isgreg), John Newland (Jackson Lee), Victor Cutler (Agent Newbitt/Snapbrim), Tito Vuolo (Pasquale), John Parrish (Harry), Curt Conway (Shorty the Informant), Ricki Van Dusen (Girl on Plane), Irmgard Dawson (Plane Hostess), Robert Williams (Detective Captain), Anton Kosta (Carlo Vantucci), Paul Fierro (Chops), Louis Bacigalupi (Boxcar), Trevor Bardette (Rudy), William Yip (Chinese Merchant), Al Bridge (Agent in Phone Booth), Keefe Brasselle (Cigar Attendant), Leslie [Les] Sketchley, George M. Manning, Paul Hogan (Bits), Jerry Jerome, Bernie Sell, Ralph Brooks, John Ardell (Dice Players), Sandra Gould (Girl at Phone), Cuca Martinez (Dancer in Club), Salvadore Barroga (Filipino Houseboy), Tom McGuire, Mira McKinney (Couple at Car), Frank Ferguson (Secret Service Man), Cecil Weston (Woman Proprietor), Frank Hyer (Ollie), George Carleton (Morgue Attendant).

RUNNING TIME: 92 minutes. USA RELEASE DATES: December 25, 1947 (LOS ANGELES), January 8, 1948 (CHICAGO), January 22, 1948 (NEW YORK CITY), January 22, 1948 (BOSTON).

RAW DEAL (1948)

WORKING TITLE: *Corkscrew Alley*
DISTRIBUTOR: Eagle-Lion Films. A Reliance Picture. DIRECTOR: Anthony Mann. PRESENTER: Edward Small. ASSOCIATE PRODUCER [UNCREDITED]: Aubrey Schenck. PRODUCTION SUPERVISION: James T. Vaughn. SCREENPLAY: Leopold Atlas and John C. Higgins [uncredited: Don Stafford]. SUGGESTED FROM A STORY BY: Arnold B. Armstrong and Audrey Ashley. DIRECTOR OF PHOTOGRAPHY (BLACK-AND-WHITE): John Alton. ADDITIONAL PHOTOGRAPHY: Guy Roe. CAMERA OPERATOR: Lester Shorr. CAMERA ASSISTANTS: Charles Crane, Keith Smith. FILM EDITOR: Alfred DeGaetano. ASSISTANT EDITOR: Fred Allen. ASSISTANT DIRECTOR: Ridgeway [Reggie] Callow. ART DIRECTOR: Edward L. Ilou. SET DECORATIONS: Armor Marlowe and Clarence Steensen. PHOTOGRAPHIC EFFECTS: George J. Teague. SPECIAL ART EFFECTS: Jack R. Rabin. DIALOGUE DIRECTOR: Leslie Urbach. COSTUME SUPERVISION: Frances Ehren. MAKEUP: Ern Westmore and Ted Larsen. SOUND: Leon S. Becker and Earl Sitar. HAIRSTYLING: Joan St. Oegger and Anna Malin. MUSICAL DIRECTOR: Irving Friedman. MUSIC SCORE: Paul Sawtell.

CAST: Dennis O'Keefe (Joseph Emmett Sullivan), Claire Trevor (Pat Cameron),[31] Marsha Hunt (Ann Martin), John Ireland (Fantail), Raymond Burr (Rick Coyle), Curt Conway (Spider), Regis Toomey [as Richard Fraser] (Police Capt. Fields), Whit Bissell (Murderer), Cliff Clark (Gates), Paul Kruger (Guard), James Magill (Cop), John Daheim (Detective), Abe Dinovitch (Mechanic), Carey Loftin (Motor Cop), Gregg Barton (Owner of Car), Richard Irving (Brock), Chili Williams (Marcy), Alex Davidoff (Waiter), Joan Myles, Edna Ryan (Girls at Party), Mike Lally (Man at Party), Lloyd Everett (Ranger), Harry Tyler (Oscar), Ilka Grüning (Fran), David Clarke, Ray Teale (Commanding Officers), Vincent Graeff (Boy), Sam Bernard (Motel Manager), Tom Fadden (Grimshaw), Arnold Stanford (Seaman), Victor Cutler (Officer), Bob Bice (Seaman Simon), Willard Kennedy (Drunk), Frank Hyers (Bit Man).

RUNNING TIME: 78 minutes. USA RELEASE DATES: May 21, 1948 (LOS ANGELES), July 1, 1948 (BOSTON), July 8, 1948 (NEW YORK CITY), August 20, 1948 (CHICAGO).

HE WALKED BY NIGHT (1948)

WORKING TITLES: *29 Clues, The L.A. Investigator, Portrait of a Killer, Los Angeles Police Story*
DISTRIBUTOR: Eagle-Lion Films. A Bryan Foy Production. DIRECTORS: Alfred Werker and [uncredited] Anthony Mann. PRODUCER: Robert T. Kane. SCREENPLAY: John C. Higgins and Crane Wilbur [uncredited: Bert Murray].[32] ADDITIONAL DIALOGUE: Harry Essex. ORIGINAL STORY: Crane Wilbur. DIRECTOR OF PHOTOGRAPHY

(BLACK-AND-WHITE): John Alton. CAMERA OPERATOR: Lester Shorr. PRODUCTION SUPERVISION: James T. Vaughn. TECHNICAL ADVISOR: Sgt. Marty Wynn. ASSISTANT DIRECTOR: Howard W. Koch. FILM EDITOR: Alfred DeGaetano. ART DIRECTOR: Edward [L.] Ilou. SET DECORATIONS: Armo Marlowe and Clarence Steenson. PHOTOGRAPHIC EFFECTS: George J. Teague. SPECIAL ART EFFECTS: Jack R. Rabin. DIALOGUE DIRECTOR: Stewart Stern. COSTUME SUPERVISION: Frances Ehren. MAKEUP: Ern Westmore and Joe Stinton. SOUND: Leon S. Becker and Hugh McDowell. MUSIC: Leonid Raab. MUSICAL DIRECTOR: Irving Friedman.

CAST: Richard Basehart (Roy Morgan), Scott Brady (Marty Brennan), Roy Roberts (Captain Breen), Whit Bissell (Paul Reeves), James Cardwell (Chuck Jones), Jack Webb (Lieutenant Lee), Bob Bice (Detective Steno), Reed Hadley (Narrator), Chief Bradley (Himself), John McGuire (Officer Robert Rawlins), Lyle Latell (Sergeant), Jack Bailey (Pajama Top), Mike Dugan, Garrett Craig (Patrolmen), Bert Moorhouse, Gaylord Pendleton, Robert Williams, Doyle Manor (Detectives), Bernie Suss (Business Suspect), George Chan (Chinese Suspect), George Goodman (Fighter Suspect), Carlotta Monti (Bit Woman), Louise Kane (Mrs. Rawlins), Kay Garrett (Doctor), Florence Stephens (Receptionist), Thomas Browne Henry (Dunning), Harry Harvey (Detective Prouty), Virginia Hunter (Miss Smith), Ruth Robinson (Mrs. Rapport), John Parrish (Vitale), Earl Spainard (Kelly), Alma Beltran (Miss Montalvo), Anthony Jochim (Thompson), Paul Fierro (Mexican Detective), Jane Adams (Nurse Scanlon), John Dehner (Assistant Chief), Bryon Foulger (Avery), Felice Ingersoll (Record Clerk), Wally Vernon (Postman), Dorothy Adams (Housewife), Dick Mason, Donald Kerr (Mailmen), Charles Lang (Policeman), Mary Ware (Dolores), Ann Doran (Woman Dispatcher), Harlan Warde (C. B. Officer), Kenneth Tobey (Detective), Frank Cady (Suspect), Paul Scardon (Father), Charles Meredith (Desk Sergeant), Tim Graham (Uniformed Sergeant), Jim Nolan, Rory Mallinson (Detectives), Bill Mauch, John Perri, Tom Kelly, Rex Downing (Youths), Stan Johnson (Artist), Marty Wynn (Police Sergeant).

RUNNING TIME: 79 minutes. USA RELEASE DATES: November 24, 1948 (LOS ANGELES), January 5, 1949 (BOSTON), January 6, 1949 (CHICAGO), February 5, 1949 (NEW YORK CITY).

FOLLOW ME QUIETLY (1949)

DISTRIBUTOR: RKO Radio Pictures, Inc. DIRECTOR: Richard [O.] Fleischer. PRODUCER: Herman Schlom. SCREENPLAY: Lillie Hayward [uncredited: Martin Rackin]. STORY: Francis Rosenwald and Anthony Mann. DIRECTOR OF PHOTOGRAPHY (BLACK-AND-WHITE): Robert de Grasse. ART DIRECTORS: Albert S. D'Agostino and Walter E. Keller. MUSIC: Leonid Raab. MUSICAL DIRECTOR: C. Bakaleinikoff. ADDITIONAL MUSIC: Paul Sawtell.[33] SET DECORATORS: Darrell Silvera and James Altwies. FIRST ASSISTANT

DIRECTOR: James Casey.[34] FILM EDITOR: Elmo Williams. SOUND: Phil Brigandi and Clem Portman.

CAST: William Lundigan (Lt. Harry Grant), Dorothy Patrick (Ann Gorman), Jeff Corey (Police Sergeant Art Collins), Nestor Paiva (Benny), Charles D. Brown (Police Inspector Mulvaney), Paul Guilfoyle (Overbeck), Edwin Max (Charlie Roy, aka The Judge), Frank Ferguson (J.C. McGill), Marlo Dwyer (Waitress), Archie Twitchell [Michael Branden] (Dixon), Douglas Spencer (Phony Judge), Maurice Cass (Bookstore Proprietor), Wanda Cantlon (Bit Waitress), Howard Mitchell (Don the Bartender), Cy Stevens (Police Lab Technician Kelly), Robert Emmett Keane (Coroner), Paul Bryar (Police Sergeant Bryce), Lee Phelps (1st Detective), Art Dupuis (2nd Detective), Walden Boyle (Interne), Joe Whitehead (Ed), Martin Cichy (Cop), Michael Mark (Apartment Manager), Virginia Farmer (Woman in Bookstore), Nolan Leary (Larson).

RUNNING TIME: 59 minutes. USA RELEASE DATES: July 7, 1949 (NEW YORK CITY), August 11, 1949 (BOSTON), September 4, 1949 (LOS ANGELES), October 6, 1949 (CHICAGO).

BORDER INCIDENT (1949)

WORKING TITLES: *Border Patrol, T-Men on the Border, Wetbacks*

DISTRIBUTOR: Metro-Goldwyn-Mayer. DIRECTOR: Anthony Mann. PRODUCER: Nicholas Nayfack. SCREENPLAY: John C. Higgins. STORY: John C. Higgins and George Zuckerman. DIRECTOR OF PHOTOGRAPHY (BLACK-AND-WHITE): John Alton. ART DIRECTORS: Cedric Gibbons and Hans Peters. FILM EDITOR: Conrad A. Nervig. MUSICAL SUPERVISION: André Previn. RECORDING SUPERVISOR: Douglas Shearer. SET DECORATIONS: Edwin B. Willis. SET DECORATION ASSOCIATE: Ralph S. Hurst. MAKEUP: Jack Dawn.

CAST: Ricardo Montalban (Pablo Rodriguez), George Murphy (Jack Bearnes), Howard da Silva (Owen Parkson), James Mitchell (Juan Garcia), Arnold Moss (Zopilote), Alfonso Bedoya (Cuchillo), Teresa Celli (Maria), Charles McGraw (Jeff Amboy), José Torvay (Pocoloco), John Ridgely (Mr. Neley), Arthur Hunnicutt (Clayton Nordell), Sig Ruman (Hugo Wolfgang Ulrich), Otto Waldis (Fritz), Harry Antrim (John MacReynolds),[35] Martin Garralaga (Colonel Rafael Alvarado),[36] Jack Lambert (Chuck), Lita Baron (Rosita),[37] Gerald Echaverria (The Padre),[38] Fred Graham (Leathercoat with motorcycle),[39] Mitchell Lewis (Older Bracero),[40] Knox Manning (Narrator),[41] Paul Marion (One-Armed Man),[42] William "Bill" Phillips (Jim the Signalman),[43] Lynn Whitney (Bella Amboy),[44] Nedrick Young (Happy).[45]

RUNNING TIME: 95 minutes. USA RELEASE DATES: October 28, 1949 (LOS ANGELES), November 2, 1949 (BOSTON), November 18, 1949 (CHICAGO), November 19, 1949 (NEW YORK CITY).

SIDE STREET (1950)

WORKING TITLE: *Murder Is My Business*
DISTRIBUTOR: Metro-Goldwyn-Mayer. DIRECTOR: Anthony Mann. PRODUCER: Sam Zimbalist. STORY AND SCREENPLAY: Sydney Boehm [uncredited: Helen Deutsch]. DIRECTOR OF PHOTOGRAPHY (BLACK-AND-WHITE): Joseph Ruttenberg. CAMERA OPERATORS: Edward Hyland and Herb Fisher. ART DIRECTORS: Cedric Gibbons and Daniel B. Cathcart. FILM EDITOR: Conrad A. Nervig. MUSICAL SCORE: Lennie Hayton. RECORDING SUPERVISOR: Douglas Shearer. SET DECORATIONS: Edwin B. Willis. SET DECORATIONS ASSOCIATE: Charles de Crof. SPECIAL EFFECTS: A. Arnold Gillespie. HAIR STYLE DESIGN: Sydney Guilaroff. MAKEUP: Jack Dawn. STUNTS: Frank McGrath and Carey Lofton.

CAST: Farley Granger (Joe Norson), Cathy O'Donnell (Ellen Norson), James Craig (Georgie Garsell), Paul Kelly (Capt. Walter Anderson), Edmon Ryan (Victor Backett), Paul Harvey (Emil Lorrison), Jean Hagen (Harriet Sinton), Charles McGraw (Stanley Simon), Ed Max (Nick Drummon), Adele Jurgens (Lucille "Lucky" Colner), Harry Bellaver (Larry Giff), Whit Bissell (Harold Simpsen), John Gallaudet (Gus Heldon), Esther Somers (Mrs. Malby), Harry Antrim (Mr. Malby), George Tyne (Detective Roffman), Kathryn Givney (Miss Carter), King Donovan (Gottschalk), Norman Leavitt (Pete Stanton), Sid Tomack (Louie), Joe Verdi (Vendor), Robert Malcolm (Charlie the Cop), Don Terranova, James Westerfield (Patrolmen), Brett King (Pigeon Man), Peter Thompson (Mickey), John A. Butler (Elevator Man), Herbert Vigran (Photographer), Paul Marion (Dave), William Ruhl (Manny), Ransom Sherman (Superintendent), Ruth Warren (Housekeeper), Eula Guy (Florence), Ed Glover (Fingerprint Expert), William Hansen (Dr. Harry Sternberg), Tom McElhany (Newsboy),[46] Jack Diamond (Bum), George David (Syrian Proprietor), Don Haggerty (Rivers), Mildred Wall (Mrs. Glickburn), Angi O. Poulos (Ahmed), Albert Morin (Ismot Kimal), W. P. McWatters and James O'Neil (Men), Peter De Bear (Tommy Drummon Jr.), Bee Humphries (Mrs. Farnol), Sarah Selby (Nurse Williams), Margaret Brayton (Woman Clerk), Charles McAvoy (Bank Guard), George Lynn (Frank the Technician), John Maxwell (Police Monitor's Voice), Nolan Leary (Doorman), Ralph Riggs (Proprietor at Cleaners), Ben Cooper (Young Man at Cleaners), Marie Crisis (Headwaitress), Lynn Millan (Les Artistes Hatcheck Girl), David Wolfe (Smitty), Ralph Montgomery (Milkman), Minerva Urecal (Landlady), Ollie O'Toole (Voice), Walter Craig, Anthony Dexter (Radio Clerks), Helen Eby-Rock (Mother), Frank Conlon (Night Elevator Operator),[47] John Phillips (Detective), Ellen Loew (Mrs. Rivers), James O'Neill (Priest), Judy Ann Whaley,[48] Mark Rayor,[49] Wilkerson Sherry,[50] Lynn Ashford (Babies in Maternity Ward).[51]

RUNNING TIME: 82 minutes. USA RELEASE DATES: March 23, 1950 (NEW YORK CITY), April 8, 1950 (LOS ANGELES), April 19, 1950 (BOSTON), April 19, 1950 (CHICAGO).

Load (filmed in 1950; unreleased episode from *It's a Big Country: An American Anthology* [1952])
STUDIO: Metro-Goldwyn-Mayer. DIRECTOR: Anthony Mann. PRODUCER: Robert Sisk. SCREENPLAY: Luther Davis. BASED ON A SHORT STORY BY: Dudley Schnabel. DIRECTOR OF PHOTOGRAPHY (BLACK-AND-WHITE): Joseph Ruttenberg. ASSISTANT DIRECTOR: Joel Freeman. MATTE SPECIAL EFFECTS: Warren Newcombe.
CAST: Jean Hersholt (Nils Lunderson), Ann Harding (Mrs. Lunderson), Robert Sherwood (Benny Lunderson).

THE TALL TARGET (1951)

WORKING TITLES: *The Man on the Train, An Instant in the Wind, The Lonely Road*
DISTRIBUTOR: Metro-Goldwyn-Mayer. DIRECTOR: Anthony Mann. PRODUCER: Richard Goldstone. SCREENPLAY: George Worthing Yates and Art Cohn [uncredited: Joseph Losey]. STORY: George Worthing Yates and Geoffrey Homes [Daniel Mainwaring]. DIRECTOR OF PHOTOGRAPHY (BLACK-AND-WHITE): Paul C. Vogel. ASSISTANT CAMERA: Harry Stradling Jr.[52] ART DIRECTORS: Cedric Gibbons and Eddie Imazu. FILM EDITOR: Newell P. Kimlin. RECORDING SUPERVISOR: Douglas Shearer. SET DECORATIONS: Edwin B. Willis and Ralph S. Hurst. SPECIAL EFFECTS: A. Arnold Gillespie and Warren Newcombe. HAIR STYLE DESIGN: Sydney Guilaroff. MAKEUP: William Tuttle. FIRST ASSISTANT DIRECTOR: Jerry Thorpe.[53] ASSISTANT DIRECTOR: Joel Freeman.[54] SCRIPT SUPERVISOR: Leslie H. Martinson.[55]
CAST: Dick Powell (Det. Sgt. John Kennedy), Paula Raymond (Ginny Beaufort), Adolphe Menjou (Caleb Jeffers), Marshall Thompson (Lance Beaufort), Ruby Dee (Rachel), Will Geer (Homer Crowley), Richard Rober (Lt. Coulter), Florence Bates (Mrs. Charlotte Alsop), Victor Kilian (John K. Gannon), Katharine Warren (Mrs. Gibbons), Leif Erickson (Stranger—Wilde), Peter Brocco (Fernandina), Barbara Billingsley (Young Mother), Will Wright (Thomas I. Ogden), Regis Toomey (Inspector Tim Reilly), Jeff Richards (Policeman), Tom Powers (Simon G. Stroud), Leslie Kimmell (Abraham Lincoln), James Harrison (Allan Pinkerton), Dan Foster (Dapper Man), Percy Helton (Beamish), Erville Alderson (Minister),[56] Ken Christy (Detective),[57] Frank Conlon (Clerk),[58] Clancy Cooper (Brakeman),[59] John Damler (Division Manager),[60] Robert Easton (Young Southerner), Budd Fine (Pinkerton Man),[61] Jonathan Hale (Passenger from Carolina),[62] Alvin Hammer (Telegraph Operator),[63] Charles Wagenheim (Telegraph Clerk),[64] Stapleton Kent (New Brunswick Station Manager),[65] Mitchell Lewis (Sleeping Train Passenger),[66] Emmett Lynn (News Vendor),[67] Lou Nova (Zouave Sergeant), Robert Malcolm (Patrolman),[68] Mickey Martin (Messenger),[69] Jeff Richards (Philadelphia Police Officer),[70] Bert Roach (Politician),[71] Frank Sully (Telegram Manager),[72] Dan White (Passenger in Club Car),[73] Wilson Wood (Dispatcher).[74]

RUNNING TIME: 78 minutes. USA RELEASE DATES: August 22, 1951 (LOS ANGELES), September 6, 1951 (CHICAGO), September 27, 1951 (NEW YORK CITY), January 1, 1952 (BOSTON).

NOTES

INTRODUCTION

1. Philip K. Scheuer, "Mann and Stewart Use U.S. as a Set: Director Says Outdoor Scenes Are the Movies' Longest Suit," *Los Angeles Times* (November 15, 1953): IV: 3.

2. Charles Bitsch and Claude Chabrol, "Entretien avec Anthony Mann," *Cahiers du Cinéma* 12, no. 69 (March 1957): 5; Jean-Claude Missiaen, "A Lesson in Cinema: Interview with Anthony Mann," *Cahiers du Cinéma in English* 12 (December 1967): 46.

3. Jean-Claude Missiaen, undated letter to author, June 2012.

4. Christopher Wicking and Barrie Pattison, "Interview with Anthony Mann," *Screen: The Journal of the Society for Education in Film and Television* 10, nos. 4 and 5 (July/October 1969): 33 (hereafter *Screen*).

5. *Variety* reviews: *Born to Kill* (April 16, 1947): 20; *Desperate* (May 14, 1947): 15; *Railroaded!* (October 8, 1947): 8; *Raw Deal* (May 19, 1948): 13; *Border Incident* (August 31, 1949): 8. "Meller" is *Variety* lingo for "melodrama."

6. Others share such enthusiasm for the "*noir*" phase of Mann's filmography: Arlette Mille, "Noir lyrisme: Les films policiers d'Anthony Mann," *Positif* 341–42 (July/August 1989): 49–50; Robert E. Smith provides a detailed study of most of these pictures in his vital essay, "Mann in the Dark: The Film Noirs of Anthony Mann," *Bright Lights* 2, no. 1/5 (*FIAF International Index to Film Periodicals* indicates issue 1; *Bright Lights* website indicates issue 5) (1977): 8–14+. This essay (with frame enlargements) may be viewed at: http://brightlightsfilm.com/76/76mannoirs_smith.php.

7. Alan Branigan, "Stage Director: Bundsmann's Career from East Orange to Maplewood Took 14 Years of Work," *Newark Evening News* (March 16, 1939): 24; Philip K. Scheuer, "Tony Favors Camera Over Film Dialogue," *Los Angeles Times* (June 25, 1950): D3; Ezra Goodman, Long Shots and Closeups, "A Mann to Remember," *(Los Angeles) Daily News* (November 17, 1950): 39; "Biography of Anthony Mann," Warner Bros. Studios, April 26, 1956, 1, Academy of Motion Picture Arts & Sciences, Core Collection, Microfiche.

8. Michael Powell, *A Life in Movies: An Autobiography* (New York: Alfred A. Knopf, 1987), 315.

9. Hedda Hopper, "Colbert Named Star of 'Three Came Home,'" *Los Angeles Times* (March 15, 1949): A6; Thomas F. Brady, "'Rebellion' Ends for Judy Garland," *New York Times* (August 1, 1949): 14; Rudy Behlmer, *Shoot the Rehearsal! Behind the Scenes with Assistant Director Reggie Callow* (Lanham/Toronto/Plymouth, UK: The Scarecrow Press, 2010): 67. Callow reports *Devil's Doorway* having a sixty-four-day schedule; "Paramount Movie to Star John Lund," *New York Times* (October 17, 1949): 18; Edwin Schallert, "McNally Will

Star With [sic] Stewart, Winters; 'Operation Haylift' Set," *Los Angeles Times* (December 24, 1949): 7; *Daily Variety* Production Charts, *Daily Variety* (January 28, 1949), 15; (April 22, 1949): 11; (August 26, 1949): 15; (November 18, 1949): 11; (January 27, 1950): 11.

10. Goodman, ibid. (see n7).

11. Bosley Crowther, "The Screen: New Crime Story," *New York Times* (March 24, 1950): 29; Georges Sadoul, *Dictionary of Film Makers*, trans. Peter Morris (Berkeley and Los Angeles: University of California Press, 1972), 167.

12. Scheuer, "Mann and Stewart Use U.S. as a Set."

13. Missiaen letter (original emphasis).

14. Goodman, ibid.

15. Scheuer, ibid., 3.

16. Anthony Mann, "Empire of Destruction," *Films and Filming* (March 1964). Reprinted in *Hollywood Directors 1941–1976*, ed. Richard Koszarski (Oxford/London/New York: Oxford University Press, 1977), 337–38.

CHAPTER 1

1. Patrick McGilligan, "Philip Yordan: The Chameleon," *Backstory 2: Interviews with Screenwriters of the 1940s and 1950s* (Berkeley/Los Angeles/Oxford: University of California Press, 1991), 356–57.

2. "Peter Ustinov Reminisces," *Spartacus* DVD disc 2 (New York: The Criterion Collection, 2001).

3. Some accounts give Mann's date of birth as 1907. This originated in the annual *Motion Picture Almanac*, which provided a June 30, 1907, birthdate for Mann during the 1940s and up through the 1953–54 edition. From 1955 onward, Mann's year of birth was adjusted to 1906. The November 17, 1947, Eagle-Lion Physician's Report for Mann (in preparation for the *Raw Deal* filming) confirms his birth date as June 30, 1906, as does the 1925 Central High School transcript; USC Cinematic Arts Library, Edward Small Collection, Box 9, *Raw Deal*, Folder 1.

4. Iverson L. Harris interview with Robert Wright [sic], "Reminiscences of Lomaland: Madame Tingley and the Theosophical Institute in San Diego," *San Diego Historical Society Quarterly* 20, no. 3 (Summer 1974). Data for this article was partially obtained from Emmett A. Greenwalt, *The Point Loma Community in California, 1897–1942: A Theosophical Experiment* (Berkeley: University of California Press, 1955).

5. H. P. (Helena) Blavatsky, *The Key to Theosophy Being a Clear Exposition, in the Form of Question and Answer, of the Ethics, Science and Philosophy for the Study of which the Theosophical Society Has Been Founded* (London and New York: The Theosophical Publishing Company, 1889), 19. "Theosophy—The Only Cure for the Unrest of the Age," *Century Path: A Magazine Devoted to the Brotherhood of Humanity, the Promulgation of Theosophy and The Study of Ancient and Modern Ethics, Philosophy, Science, and Art* (hereafter *Century Path* and *New Century Path*) 13, no. 15 (February 13, 1910): 8; Evelyn A. Kirkley, "Starved and Treated Like Convicts: Images of Women in Point Loma Theosophy," *San Diego Historical Society Quarterly* 43, no. 1 (Winter 1997).

6. Harris, ibid.

7. Harris, ibid.

8. Kirkley, ibid. "Outrages at Point Loma. Exposed by an 'Escape' from Tingley. Startling Tales Told in This City. Women and Children Starved and Treated Like Convicts. Thrilling Rescue," *Los Angeles Times* (October 28, 1901): 7.

9. "Reception to the County Superintendents of Schools of State of California; Given by the Teachers and Pupils of the Raja [sic] Yoga Academy and the Children's International Lotus Home, In the Rotunda of the Raja [sic] Yoga Academy, Point Loma, California, November 21, 1906," *New Century Path* 10, no. 5 (December 9, 1906): 14.

10. "Apropos of Child Labor," *Century Path* 10, no. 19 (March 17, 1907): 8; "The Children's Hour: Little Rāja Workers at Lomaland," *Century Path* 13, no. 17 (February 27, 1910): 17.

11. Our Young Folk, *New Century Path* 10, no. 4 (December 2, 1906): 10; "Our Young Folk: The Rāja Yoga Cadets," *Century Path* 10, no. 21 (March 31, 1907): 10; "Our Young Folk: The Highest Class of Boys in the Rāja Yoga Academy, Lomaland," *Century Path* 13, no. 21 (March 27, 1910): 16; "Rāja Yoga Boys and Girls at Drill and Exercises in the Greek Theater," *New Century Path* 10, no. 9 (January 6, 1907): 16; "The Children's Hour: Rāja Yoga Children on the Way to the Greek Theater for Drill," *New Century Path* 13, no. 26 (May 1, 1910): 17.

12. See n9. Source: http://archiver.rootsweb.ancestry.com/th/read/GABIBB/2007-12/1198871769. Prof. Bundsmann's passport applications (available on ancestry.com) from 1902 and 1912 list Macon, Georgia, as his residence. However, an Ellis Island record entry (www.ellisisland.org) gives their residence as San Diego (Karen Krett); Nina Mann, phone interview with author, January 25, 2012.

13. J. H. Fenwick and Jonathan Green-Armytage, "Landscape and Anthony Mann," *Sight and Sound* 34, no. 4 (Autumn 1965): 187.

14. Nina Mann, e-mail to author, March 19, 2012.

15. Nina Mann, ibid.

16. Nina Mann, interview with Leonard Lopate, *The Leonard Lopate Show*, WNYC, July 7, 2008.

17. Nina Mann, phone interview.

18. "Biography of Anthony Mann," Paramount Pictures press release, November 1956, 1, Academy of Motion Picture Arts & Sciences, Core Collection, Microfiche; Anthony Mann, "Empire of Destruction," 336 (see Introduction n16); *Sight and Sound*, ibid.; Nina Mann, phone interview.

19. Nina Mann, phone interview; "Anthony Mann, 60, A Movie Director: Filmmaker Who Favored Westerns Dies in Berlin," *New York Times* (April 30, 1967): 86. The *Times* obituary incorrectly reported the Bundsmann family moving from San Diego to New York City when Emile Anton was ten, and Jeanine Basinger repeats this error in her book, giving the "approximate date" as 1917. Philip Kemp and William Darby repeat Basinger's claim; Jeanine Basinger, *Anthony Mann* (Middletown, CT: Wesleyan University Press, 1979, 2007), xix, 2; Philip Kemp, *World Film Directors, Vol. I: 1890–1945*, John Wakeman, ed. (New York: The H. W. Wilson Company, 1987), 722; William Darby, *Anthony Mann: The Film Career* (Jefferson, NC, and London: McFarland and Company: 2009): 5.

20. *New York Times* obituary; Central High School transcript (author's collection). The *Times* appears to have obtained this information from either a 1950 Paramount press

release in connection with *The Furies* or a 1956 Warner Bros. press release in connection with *Serenade*. Basinger provides a school dropout date of 1923, which is two years too early; "Biography of Anthony Mann," Paramount Pictures, July 1950, 1; Warner Bros. press release (see Introduction n7), Academy of Motion Picture Arts & Sciences, Core Collection; Basinger, ibid.

21. Dore Schary, *Heyday: An Autobiography* (Boston and Toronto: Little, Brown and Company, 1979), 14; Warner Bros. press release. The *Alcestis* legend is repeated in Kemp, 723.

22. Nina Mann, phone interview; Branigan (see Introduction n7).

23. The *Dulcy* performance is mentioned in the following Just For Boys columns of the *Newark Evening News*: (April 24, 1924): 23-X; (May 1, 1924): 20-X; (May 5, 1924): 11-X; (May 6, 1924): 18-X; (May 12, 1924): 8-X; *World Film Directors*, ibid.; Jean-Claude Missiaen, *Anthony Mann* (Paris: Éditions Universitaires, 1964), 5. These books refer to information from the 1956 Warner Bros. press release. The Westinghouse job is also mentioned in the 1950 Paramount press release; Branigan, ibid.

24. Burns Mantle, *The Best Plays of 1924–1925* (New York: Dodd Mead and Co., 1942), 13, 561–62; *The Blue Peter* scrapbook; *Blue Peter* reviews and pictures; program, *The Little Clay Cart*; program, *The Dybbuk* (December 18, 1926): 1; programs, *The Squall*, New York Library for the Performing Arts. Basinger incorrectly cites Mann directing a 1933 Broadway/Theatre Guild production of *The Squall*. The only possible explanation is that she misinterpreted data from the 1967 *Cahiers* biofilmography, which wrongly credited Mann with directing *The Squall* and Theatre Guild with producing it. The biofilmography lists the correct 1933 performance date of *Thunder on the Left* but no year for *The Squall*, so Basinger drew the conclusion that both plays were produced the same year. Basinger, ibid.; "Biofilmography of Anthony Mann," *Cahiers du Cinema (in English)* 12 (December 1967): 52..

25. The "Stephen Lane" myth appears under the heading "Actor-Author" on page two of the Republic Pictures pressbook for *The Great Flamarion* (USC Cinematic Arts Library); Burns Mantle, *The Best Plays of 1928–29* (New York: Dodd Mead and Co., 1929): 507; Nina Mann, phone interview with author; "Theater Colony to Be Guests of Chamber At Dinner in Bristol," *Hartford Courant* (June 26, 1930): 4; Walter Brown, The Observation Post: "Manhattan Repertory at Bristol," *Hartford Courant* (June 26, 1930): 19; "Hartwig was the Force Behind 'Little Theatre,'" *Old News from Southern Maine* website, posted March 9, 2009, http://www.someoldnews.com/?p=270.

26. "Who's Who in Hollywood," *Film Daily* (June 14, 1948): 5; Paramount press release (see n20); Warner Bros. Studios, ibid; Scott Byers, telephone conversation with author, December 2, 2011.

27. Branigan, ibid. The 1950 Paramount press release gives the Bundsmann-Kenyon marriage date as October 17, 1931, and then mentions their children "Anthony Jr." and Nina. The birthdate of the first child is correctly given as April 23, 1938, which would have made Toni nearly one year old at the time the *Newark Evening News* interviewed Bundsmann, not seven months as reported in that same article. Warner Bros. duplicated the "Anthony Jr." mistake in 1956 but went further by misspelling Kenyon's name "Kenyoh." Both press releases describe her as "an executive" with Macy's department store in New York and Philip Kemp repeats this in *World Film Directors, Vol. I: 1890–1945* (ibid). Basinger

likewise repeats the inaccurate press release data on Toni Bundsmann in her book (3); others following Basinger include Kemp (723), Ángel Comas, and William Darby (7). In his biography of Nicholas Ray, Patrick McGilligan states that Ray named his son Anthony after his "older stage-director friend" Anthony Mann, which is impossible considering the latter was still known professionally as Anton Bundsmann when Anthony Ray was born (November 24, 1937); Ángel Comas, *Anthony Mann* (Madrid: T and B Editores, 2004), 23; Patrick McGilligan, *Nicholas Ray: The Glorious Failure of an American Director* (New York: imprint/HarperCollins/itbooks, 2011), 71.

28. Programs, *Streets of New York; Or, Poverty is No Crime, The Bride the Sun Shines On, The Pillars of Society*. New York Library for the Performing Arts; Branigan, ibid.

CHAPTER 2

1. Jeanine Basinger incorrectly cites *Thunder on the Left* as a Theatre Guild production (see Chapter 1 n24); Basinger, xix (see Chapter 1 n19); program, *Thunder on the Left*, New York Library for the Performing Arts. Somehow, "Maxine Elliott's Theatre" was lost in translation in France; Bitsch and Chabrol refer to it as "l'Axine Alley Theatre" in their 1957 *Cahiers* interview and this source influenced Missiaen's 1964 book *Anthony Mann* and Jean Wagner's 1968 Mann essay; Bitsch and Chabrol, 3 (see Introduction n2); Missiaen, 6 (see Chapter 1 n23); Jean Wagner, "Anthony Mann 1906–1967: Pour un portrait," *Anthologie du cinéma, Tome IV* (Paris: L'Avant-Scene-C.I.B., 1968), 383.

2. Christopher Morley, "A Collaboration Without Reproach or Regret: In Which Mr. Morley Tells All About 'Thunder on the Left,'" *New York Times* (November 5, 1933): X3.

3. Marc Eliot, *Jimmy Stewart: A Biography* (New York: Random House, 2006), 63–64; "Red Barn Theatre Sold Out Tonight," *New York Times* (July 23, 1934): 19; "'All Paris Knows' Has Gay Premiere," *New York Times* (July 24, 1934): 20; program, *All Paris Knows*, Red Barn scrapbook, New York Library for the Performing Arts.

4. "Sillman Gets His 'Faces' Back," *Variety* (August 5, 1936): 43; "Who's Boss of 'Faces'? Jones Fires Several Of Cast to Prove It," *Variety* (August 12, 1936): 51; *New Faces of 1936* scrapbook and programs; New York Library for the Performing Arts. Samuel L. Leiter, *The Encyclopedia of the New York Stage, 1930–1940* (New York/Westport, CT/London: Greenwood Press, 1989), 542–43.

5. Burns Mantle, *The Best Plays of 1936–37* (New York: Dodd, Mead and Company, 1937), 495–96.

6. Scrapbook, *The Cherokee Night*. Hallie Flanagan papers, New York Library for the Performing Arts; Leiter, 125–26; Basinger's claim that *The Cherokee Night* was "produced at the Federal Theater in Harlem by the Acting Theater Technical Institute" is incorrect. The Harlem myth previously appeared courtesy of Bitsch and Chabrol, who wrongly cited it as premiere locale for both *The Cherokee Night* and *Big Blow* and reappeared in the 1967 *Cahiers* biofilmography (see Chapter 1 n24); Bitsch and Chabrol, 3 (see Introduction n2); Basinger, ibid. (see Chapter 1 n19).

7. Norma Barzman, phone interview by author, June 9, 2011; "Hollywood is for FDR" advertisement, *Daily Variety* (October 2, 1944): 4–5.

8. "New Plays in Manhattan," *Time* 28, no. 14 (October 5, 1936): 42–43; program/scrapbook, *So Proudly We Hail*, New York Library for the Performing Arts.

9. Burns Mantle, *The Best Plays of 1936-37* (New York: Dodd, Mead and Company, 1937), 7, 409.

10. David O. Selznick, memos dated November 23, 1936, and November 25, 1936, posted at Harry Ransom Center/The University of Texas at Austin web site: http://www.hrc.utexas.edu/exhibitions/web/gwtw/scarlett/; Yolande Gwin, "Mothers of Debutantes Foiled By Seeker for New Movie Types," *Atlanta Constitution* (December 3, 1936): 2.

11. Leonard Lyons, "Leonard Lyons Prowls About Gathering Priceless Nuggets," *Washington Post* (May 2, 1937): T2; *The American Film Institute Catalogue of Motion Pictures Produced in the United States: Feature Films, 1931-1940, Film Entries, A-L* (Berkeley/Los Angeles/Oxford: University of California Press, 1993), 15; Branigan (see Introduction n7).

12. *Screen*: 32 (see Introduction n4).

13. Anton Bundsmann, memo to David O. Selznick, November 6, 1937. The actresses tested were Lenore Ulric (Belle Watling), Katharine Locke (Melanie), Halie Stoddard (Scarlett), Diane Forrest (Scarlett), Eve March (Melanie), Cissie Loftus (Aunt Pittypat), and Josephine Hull (Aunt Pittypat). The author gratefully acknowledges Ángel Comas for citing this memo: Comas, 25 (see Chapter 1 n27). The memo may be viewed online at the Harry Ransom Center/University of Texas website: http://www.hrc.utexas.edu/exhibitions/web/gwtw/scarlett/nysearch.html; Ronald Haver, *David O. Selznick's Hollywood* (New York: Bonanza Books, 1980), 260 (courtesy of Robert Waggoner). Branigan (see Introduction n7).

14. "Gossip of the Rialto," *New York Times* (March 13, 1938): 165. Branigan, Ibid. *Haiti* is also listed among Mann's Broadway credits in a 1948 *Film Daily* profile: "Who's Who in Hollywood," *Film Daily* (June 14, 1948): 5.

15. "A Climactic Scene Of [sic] a Big Battle Gave Him a Fight," *New York Herald Tribune* (March 27, 1938): VI:4.

16. *Big Blow* pressbook, 2; *Big Blow* program, New York Library for the Performing Arts; Leiter, 72.

17. Leiter, ibid.

18. "Equity Opposes More Cuts by WPA: Actors' Group Told of Rumors of Reduction in Theatre Rolls on June 15," *New York Times* (May 27, 1939): 19; "3 WPA Shows Close Amid Hot Protests," *New York Times* (July 1, 1939): 2.

19. Jack Gould, "Maplewood: Theatre 1, Movies 0," *New York Times* (August 14, 1938): 127; News of the Stage, "Maplewood Theatre Change," *New York Times* (January 17, 1939): 28; "'Scandals' Seeks Amos 'n' Andy Act," *New York Times* (April 22, 1939): 14; News of the Stage, "About 'Three Blind Mice,'" *New York Times* (April 15, 1939): 15; "Madge Evans Coming To Maplewood Theatre," *Westfield Leader* (February 16, 1939): 15; "Dorothy Mackaill Coming to Maplewood," *Westfield Leader* (March 2, 1939): 15; "Jane Wyatt in 'Coquette' Coming To Maplewood," *Westfield Leader* (March 9, 1939): 15; "Berle in 'Blessed Event' Next Week at Maplewood," *Westfield Leader* (May 4, 1939): 15; "Jean Muir Coming To Maplewood Theatre," *Westfield Leader* (March 16, 1939): 15; "Maplewood Theatre Reopens Next Monday," *Westfield Leader* (April 6, 1939): 15; "'Torch Bearers' Next At Maplewood Theatre," *Westfield Leader* (April 13, 1939): 15. Back issues of *Westfield Leader* may be viewed at the Westfield Memorial Library website: http://archive.wmlnj.org/.

20. This incorrect theory appears to have originated in the 1967 *Cahiers* "biofilmography" (see Chapter 1 n24), and others, notably Basinger, David Boxwell in *Senses of Cinema*, and Darby, have repeated it; Basinger, ibid. (see Chapter 1 n19); Darby, 7 (see Chapter 1 n19); David Boxwell, "Anthony Mann," *Senses of Cinema* no. 24, Great Directors, January 2003. This essay may be viewed online at: http://sensesofcinema.com/2003/great-directors/mann_anthony/. In 1948, *Film Daily* briefly acknowledged Bundsmann's one-year job as an NBC producer-director; "Who's Who in Hollywood," *Film Daily* (June 14, 1948): 5.

21. Richard Koszarski, *Hollywood on the Hudson: Film and Television in New York from Griffith to Sarnoff* (Piscataway, NJ: Rutgers University Press, 2008), 433, 448.

22. This website lists all W2XBS program schedules from May 1939 through June 1940: http://www.tvobscurities.com.

23. W2XBS Television Production Reports (Library of Congress): *4-H Club with Miss Helen Michael and Miss Marjorie Jensen*, June 20, 1939; *Television Beauty Contest—Interview with Winners: Carryl Smith and Barbara Wall*, June 22, 1939; *Bernice Lambert (International Songs)*, June 21, 1939; *Maxine Gray—Songs*, June 29, 1939; *Betty Allen*, July 1, 1939; *So This is New York* (incorrectly reported as *So This is Broadway*)—George Ross interviewing Eleanor Holm, swimming champion, July 5, 1939; *So This is New York*—George Ross interviewing Hildegarde, July 26, 1939; *J. K. Lee Introducing Professor Wei (Chung Loh)*, July 28, 1939; *Total Eclipse—Howard Reid*, August 18, 1939; *Miss Dixie Tighe of the New York Post* (interviewing Alfred Cheney Johnstone), June 24, 1939; *Ballin and McEvoy*, June 27, 1939; *Facts and Fancies: Alice Maslin with Ray Giles on "How to Sleep*,*"* June 28, 1939; *Facts and Fancies: Alice Maslin with Wray Meltmar—makeup expert*, July 6, 1939; *Facts and Fancies: Alice Maslin Interviewing Helen Sprackling on Setting of Tables*, August 17, 1939; *Facts and Fancies: Alice Maslin interviewing Frank Fogarty, cartoonist*, August 24, 1939; *The Dignified Hitch-Hikers (Joe McKee and Leonard Knighton)*, July 4, 1939; *Adelaide Moffett*, July 7, 1939; *Sergeant Alvin Yorke* [sic], July 25, 1939; *Georgina Dieter*, August 22, 1939; *Dinah Shore*, December 27, 1939; *Tex O'Rourke's Round Up*, January 3, 1940, NBC Detailed Schedule, 1939–Feb. 6, 1947, Box A-917, Weekly Television Schedule (microfilm), Library of Congress (courtesy of Chuck Willett).

24. *Oddities in Hat Wear* script, August 25, 1939, 1–5, NBC-TV Master Books, Box No. TV #5 (microfilm), Library of Congress.

25. *So This is New York—George Ross Interviews Clyde Hagger*, uncredited commercial script, August 16, 1939, 1–2. Original emphasis (ellipses modified from original); *So This is New York—George Ross interviewing Renee Carroll*, August 23, 1939, NBC-TV Master Books, Box No. TV #5 (microfilm), Library of Congress.

26. *Coward Shoes-Fashion Show* script, March 6, 1940, 1, 8, NBC-TV Master Books, Box No. TV #7 (microfilm), Library of Congress.

27. E. B. Ginty, *Missouri Legend: The Story of Jesse James*, teleplay, July 18, 1939, 1, NBC-TV, ibid.; "Maplewood Theatre Change," News of the Stage, *New York Times* (January 17, 1939): 28.

28. Jeff Stafford, "The Man Who Fell Off The Statue of Liberty: An Interview with Norman Lloyd," March 2, 2010. This interview is posted online at: http://moviemorlocks.com/2010/04/03/the-man-who-fell-off-the-statue-of-liberty-an-interview-with-norman-lloyd/#more-20932.htm.

29. Dion Boucicault, *The Streets of New York; Or, Poverty is No Crime* teleplay, August 31, 1939, unnumbered page before prologue, NBC-TV, ibid.

30. Haver, 328; Koszarski, 453–54; Boucicault teleplay, 2 (handwritten camera notes). The existing fragments of *Streets of New York* are in the collection of The Paley Center for Media and portions may be viewed online at: http://www.paleycenter.org/simon-the-dead-sea-scroll-of-tv-history/; Ron Simon, "Introducing Television at the Fair," BIBLION: The Boundless Library (New York Public Library): http://exhibitions.nypl.org/biblion/worldsfair/enter-world-tomorrow-futurama-and-beyond/essay/essay-simon-television.

31. Uncredited *Jane Eyre* teleplay, October 12, 1939. NBC-TV, ibid; Marian de Forest, *Little Women* teleplay, December 23, 1939; Edgar Wallace, *A Criminal at Large* teleplay, November 17, 1939, NBC-TV Master Books, Box No. TV #6 (microfilm), Library of Congress.

32. *A Criminal at Large* teleplay, unpaginated opening scene.

33. Ibid.

34. *A Criminal at Large* teleplay, 65–66.

35. *Pinocchio—Sue Hastings Marionettes*, December 30, 1939; Helen Jerome, *Charlotte Corday* teleplay, February 9, 1940, 73–78, NBC-TV Master Books, Box No. TV #7 (microfilm), Library of Congress.

36. E. P. Conkle, *Prologue to Glory: A Play in Eight Scenes Based on the New Salem Years of Abraham Lincoln*, teleplay, February 23, 1940, 7, NBC-TV ibid; "Theatre Project Faces an Inquiry: Representative Thomas Will Tell House Committee it is 'Communist Hot-Bed,'" *New York Times* (July 27, 1938): 19; "Play Tour by WPA Faces Fight Here: Proposed Shubert Partnership on Lincoln Drama Stirs Producers and Unions," *New York Times* (August 26, 1938): 19; Mark S. Reinhart, *Abraham Lincoln on Screen: Fictional and Documentary Portrayals on Film and Television* (Jefferson, NC, and London: McFarland & Company, 2009), 181.

37. W2XBS television program booking for week of March 25 to March 31, 1940, Library of Congress; Leopold Atlas, *See! Hear! A Visual Digest of the Month, Issue No. 1—March 24, 1940* teleplay, March 27, 1940, opening page 2, script pages 2–3, NBC-TV Master Books, Box No. TV #8 (microfilm), Library of Congress.

38. *See! Hear!*, 33A.

39. Reynold Humphries, *Hollywood's Blacklists: A Political and Cultural History* (Edinburgh: Edinburgh University Press, 2008, 2010), 145.

40. Burns Mantle, *The Best Plays of 1934–35* (New York: Dodd, Mead and Company, 1944), 425–26; Sidney Howard, *Ode to Liberty* teleplay, April 5, 1940, 139, NBC-TV, ibid.

41. "Television to Shut-Down; Station to Be Remodeled," News Notes and Gossip, *New York Times* (July 21, 1940): X10.

42. Bundsmann staged *Off the Record* at the National Theatre in Washington, D.C., on December 2–7, 1940: http://www.nationaltheatre.org/location/timeline.htm. Due in Near Future, *Daily Boston Globe* (December 8, 1940): 57; "'Flying Gerardos' Arrives Dec. 29—Plymouth Gets 'Flight to the West'—'Yohimbe Tree' Sold," News of the Stage, *New York Times* (December 11, 1940): 36.

43. Nina Mann, phone interview with author, January 25, 2012.

44. Obituaries, Deaths, Bundsmann, *New York Times* (January 23, 1941): 21; "Harr Play Opens This Afternoon," *New York Times* (April 18, 1941): 18; Paramount press release, 2 (see Chapter 1 n18).

45. Sandy Sturges, ed., *Preston Sturges by Preston Sturges: His Life in His Words*, (New York/London/Toronto/Sydney/Tokyo/Singapore: Simon and Schuster, 1990), 33–34. Presumably Sturges is referring to the Ponte Vecchio in Florence.

46. *Screen*: 32.

47. *Sullivan's Travels* production correspondence, April 28, 1941: Inter-Office Communication between producer Paul Jones and Preston Sturges lists John H. ("Holly") Morse as assistant director. Daily Production Reports also list Bart Adams, F. Spencer, (Joe) Lefert and (Henry J.) Staudigal in AD capacities; Academy of Motion Picture Arts & Sciences, Special Collections, Paramount Pictures production records, Box 197, f., *Sullivan's Travels*—production.

48. *Screen*: ibid.

CHAPTER 3

1. *Variety* review (May 6, 1942): 8.

2. Jacob H. Karp letter, *Dr. Broadway*, August 20, 1941, Academy of Motion Picture Arts & Sciences, Special Collections, Paramount Pictures production records, Box 56, f.1, *Dr. Broadway*—billing.

3. "Par's 2 New Directors; From Legit and Radio," *Variety* (October 1, 1941): 5.

4. Scheuer, "Tony Favors Camera Over Film Dialogue" (see Introduction n7).

5. Charles Lang later photographed Fritz Lang's *The Big Heat* (1953) and collaborated with Billy Wilder on *Ace in the Hole* (1951), *Sabrina* (1954), and *Some Like It Hot* (1959); Academy of Motion Picture Arts & Sciences, Special Collections, Paramount Pictures production records, Box 56, f.4, *Dr. Broadway*—production.

6. *Screen*: 32–33 (see Introduction n4).

7. *Screen*: 32; Sparkhul's credits for the German Lubitsch films include *Anna Boleyn/Deception* (1920), *Die Puppe/The Doll* (1919), *Madame Dubarry/Passion* (1919), *Meyer aus Berlin* (1919), *Meine frau, die Filmschauspielerin* (1919), and *Ich möchte kein Mann sein!/I Don't Want to Be a Man* (1918).

8. Academy of Motion Picture Arts & Sciences, Special Collections, Paramount Pictures production records, Box 56, f.2, *Dr. Broadway*—budgets, Production Budget. The director is listed as "A. Mann" on reports through November 25, 1941; Special Collections, Paramount Pictures production records, Box 56, f.3, *Dr. Broadway*—costs, Cost Report 10/21/1941 and 11/25/1941; Analysis of Costs of Scenario, Supervision, Direction & Cast, "This detail supports Final Production Cost Issued 7/18/42"; Final Production Cost, Cost to 1–2–43, Date Issued 1–30–43.

9. *Dr. Broadway* production records, Box 56, f.5.

10. *Screen*: 33.

11. Jean-Claude Missiaen, "A Lesson in Cinema: Interview with Anthony Mann," 46 (see Introduction n2); *Reap the Wild Wind* Production File, box 160, f. 6; production reports, box 160, f. 8; schedules, box 161, f. 12; schedules-2nd unit, box 161, f. 12, Paramount Pictures production records, Margaret Herrick Library—Department of Special Collections.

12. *Dr. Broadway*, Box 56, f.5.

13. Ibid.

14. Several original trade reviews of *Dr. Broadway* identify the director as "Anton Mann" despite the film titles clearly identifying him as "Anthony Mann," leading one to ponder whether critics paid more attention to inaccurate publicity materials than opening titles. *Hollywood Reporter, Daily Variety*, and *Monthly Film Bulletin* got Mann's name correct, although weekly *Variety, Harrison's Reports*, and *The Exhibitor* did not; *Variety* (May 6, 1942): 8; *Daily Variety* and *Hollywood Reporter* (May 6, 1942): 3; *Harrison's Reports* (May 9, 1942): 75; *The Exhibitor* (May 20, 1942): 10–11; *Monthly Film Bulletin* 9, no. 102 (June 30, 1942): 70–71.

15. Dialogue and descriptions taken from the motion picture *Dr. Broadway* (Paramount, 1942).

16. "'Dr. Broadway' Augments Program at Paramount," *Los Angeles Times* (August 14, 1942): A10. The review is signed "P.K.S."

17. Special Collections, Paramount Pictures production records, Box 56, f.5.

18. Ibid.

19. Ibid.

20. Luigi Luraschi, letters to Sol Siegel, October 6, 1941 and October 11, 1941, *Dr. Broadway* file, Motion Picture Association of America, Production Code Administration records, Margaret Herrick Library—Department of Special Collections (hereafter PCA).

21. Luigi Luraschi, letter to Sol Siegel, October 21, 1941, PCA.

22. Luigi Luraschi, letters to Sol Siegel, October 14, 1941, and October 24, 1941, PCA.

23. Scheuer, "Tony Favors Camera Over Film Dialogue," ibid.

24. Movie pages, *Los Angeles Times* (August 13, 1942), I:13.

25. The Movie Clock, movie pages, *New York Post* (June 24, 1942): 41; movie pages, *Los Angeles Times* (August 12, 1942): I:17; *Chicago Daily Tribune* (August 28, 1942): 25; *Daily Boston Globe* (September 3, 1942): 21; *Variety* picture grosses: New York (July 8, 1942): 9; Los Angeles (August 26, 1942): 14; Boston (September 16, 1942): 10, (September 23, 1942): 13, and (September 30, 1942): 13; Indianapolis (July 29, 1942): 10; Indianapolis and Seattle (August 5, 1942): 20; Philadelphia and Seattle (August 12, 1942): 10; Seattle (August 19, 1942): 9; Providence (September 2, 1942): 13; San Francisco and St. Louis (September 9, 1942): 8, 10; San Francisco (September 16, 1942): 11; (September 23, 1942): 11 and (September 30, 1942): 13; Buffalo (October 28, 1942): 11; Chicago (September 2, 1942): 15 and (September 9, 1942): 9.

26. Nina Mann, phone interview by author, January 25, 2012.

27. Large Hargrove and Anthony Mann, *To Men As They Need* . . . film treatment, Paul Kohner Agency records, Box 154 f.1447, Academy of Motion Picture Arts & Sciences, Special Collections.

CHAPTER 4

1. Dialogue and descriptions taken from the motion picture *Strangers in the Night* (Republic Pictures, 1944).

2. Joseph I. Breen, letter to Republic Pictures, May 12, 1944, *Strangers in the Night*, Motion Picture Association of America, Production Code Administration records, Margaret Herrick Library—Department of Special Collections.

3. *Screen*: 33 (see Introduction n4).

4. Edwin Schallert, "'Corvettes in Action' Develops; Stack Cast," *Los Angeles Times* (July 25, 1942): 9.

5. *The 1945 Film Daily Year Book of Motion Pictures*, 45–49.

6. *The 1946 Film Daily Year Book of Motion Pictures*, 43; Noah Isenberg, *Edgar G. Ulmer: A Filmmaker at the Margins* (Berkeley: University of California Press, 2014), 177.

7. *The 1943–44 Motion Picture Almanac*, 634; Len D. Martin, *The Republic Pictures Checklist: Features, Serials, Cartoons, Short Subjects and Training Films of Republic Pictures Corporation, 1935–1959* (Jefferson, NC, and London: McFarland and Company, 1998), 1.

8. The correct date of Nina Bundsmann's birth is November 23, *1943*, not 1944, as has been stated elsewhere. She confirmed this to the author in a January 25, 2012, telephone interview. The 1944 date is another piece of misinformation originating from the infamous 1950 Paramount press release, 2 (see Chapter 1 n18); Kemp, 723 (see chap. 1 n19) and Darby, 7 (see Chapter 1 n19) repeat the claim.

9. Edwin Schallert, "'Miserables' Figures Again to Flourish," *Los Angeles Times* (May 12, 1944): 11. This Friday article announced that "Anthony Mann will direct beginning next week." The Friday, May 26, 1944, completion date cited in *Data for Bulletin of Screen Achievement Records* (Margaret Herrick Library) seems to have been established because that is the last date in which the film is listed in the *Daily Variety* Production Chart. No start date is given in *Daily Variety* in the three consecutive weeks the film is listed starting May 12, 1944: 14. The average Republic western in 1944 was 55 minutes. A comparable non-western release matching the length of *Strangers in the Night* was *The Girl Who Dared* (originally 56 minutes). (Additional running times courtesy of Internet Movie Database.) Former M-G-M cameraman Reggie Lanning took his Poverty Row skills to television during the 1950s where he shot fifty-six half-hour episodes for *Alfred Hitchcock Presents*. The Republic Pictures footage estimations are based on budget summaries from early 1950s Republic productions; Todd McCarthy and Charles Flynn, eds., *King of the Bs: Working Within the Hollywood System: An Anthology of Film History and Criticism* (New York: E. P. Dutton and Co., 1975), 26–29.

10. *Daily Variety* (January 24, 1945): 5.

11. François Truffaut, with Helen G. Scott, *Hitchcock* (New York: Touchstone/Simon and Schuster, 1967), 33; Cameron Crowe, *Conversations with Wilder* (New York: Alfred A. Knopf, 1999), 119.

12. Movie pages, Stratford and Sheridan theaters, *Chicago Daily Tribune* (September 27, 1944): 18; movie pages, LaSalle Theatre, *Chicago Daily Tribune* (October 2, 1944): 18; Sumner Theatre advertisement, *New York Amsterdam News* (November 18, 1944): 3B; Brooklyn Regent advertisement, *New York Amsterdam News* (November 25, 1944): 3B; movie pages, Bowdoin and Hamilton theatres, *Daily Boston Globe* (December 12, 1944): 11; movie pages, Park, Hollywood, and Thompson Square theaters, *Daily Boston Globe* (December 17, 1944): D42. The latter two cinemas booked the Sturges-Mann combination.

13. Movie pages, Fillmore theater, *Los Angeles Times* (December 31, 1944), III:2; movie pages, Margo theater, *Los Angeles Times* (January 18, 1945), II:2; movie pages, Orpheum theater, *Los Angeles Times* (January 23, 1945): I:9; *Variety* picture grosses, Los Angeles (January 31, 1945): 14 and (February 7, 1945): 8 (courtesy of Chuck Willett).

CHAPTER 5

1. *Two O'Clock Courage* pressbook, 7, Academy of Motion Picture Arts & Sciences, Core Collection.

2. *Two O'Clock Courage* Script Files, Box 889S, RKO Studio Records, 3, Performing Arts Special Collections, University of California, Los Angeles. Both the July 14, 1944, and August 2, 1944, drafts of *Two O'Clock Courage* open differently: a long shot of a dark deserted street "illumined eerily by a street lamp. Fog throws a dismal haze across the scene." The Man emerges from the fog, his back toward camera.

3. *Exhibitor* (April 18, 1945): 1699. Even as late as 1949, director Nicholas Ray was obligated to employ disorienting comic relief in his RKO crime melodrama *A Woman's Secret*.

4. Robert E. Kent is credited screenwriter on many RKO programmers of the period, including entries in the Dick Tracy, Philo Vance, and The Saint cycles. He later contributed to Max Ophüls's *The Reckless Moment* (1949) and Otto Preminger's *Where the Sidewalk Ends* (1950). Gordon Kahn is credited with cowriting the script for Edgar G. Ulmer's PRC drama *Ruthless* (1948) and authorized *Hollywood on Trial: The Story of the Ten Who Were Indicted* (New York: Boni and Gaer, 1948) before his own blacklisting; *Annual Report of the Committee on Un-American Activities for the Year 1952* (Washington, D.C.: Committee on Un-American Activities, U.S. House of Representatives), December 28, 1952: 48; reprinted in *Film Culture* no. 50–51, Fall and Winter 1970 (hereafter HUAC Report).

5. The origins of RKO can be traced to the 1910s formations of Mutual Film Corp., Pathé Exchange, Inc., W. W. Hodkinson Corp., and Robertson-Cole Company. In 1918, Mutual became Exhibitors Mutual and during the 1920s Robertson-Cole and later Film Booking Offices of America acquired its assets. Joseph P. Kennedy and others took control of FBO in 1927, and in 1928, RCA-Victor and the Keith-Albee-Orpheum theater circuit engaged in a giant merger with FBO and other film interests to form RKO Radio Pictures, Inc. In 1931, RKO acquired Pathé Exchange to briefly create RKO-Pathé. "M-A's New Name," *Variety* (December 6, 1918): 41; *The 1941–42 Motion Picture Almanac* (New York: Quigley Publishing), 712–13; "1931 In Review—The Year's Headlines," *The 1932 Film Daily Year Book of Motion Pictures*, 505.

6. "New President Visits RKO: Schaefer, Successor of Spitz, Arrives From New York Office," *Los Angeles Times* (November 29, 1938): A10.

7. "Charles Koerner Named to Direct All RKO Theatres," *Boston Daily Globe* (May 13, 1941): 12; "Koerner Made Head of RKO Production; Former Boston Man," *Boston Daily Globe* (May 8, 1942): 13. For a sobering account of Koerner's campaign against Welles and his RKO films (including his literal destruction of *The Magnificent Ambersons*), see Clinton Heylin, *Despite the System: Orson Welles versus the Hollywood Studios* (Edinburgh/New York/Melbourne: Canongate Books, 2005), Chapter 4.

8. *Two in the Dark* Production Files, Box 62P; *Two O'Clock Courage* Production Files, Box 145P; *Two in the Dark* Script Files, Boxes 388S and 389S, RKO Studio Records, 3, Performing Arts Special Collections, University of California, Los Angeles.

9. Nicholas Musuraca's 1940–53 RKO credits include *Stranger on the Third Floor, Cat People, The Seventh Victim, The Ghost Ship, The Spiral Staircase, Deadline at Dawn, Bedlam, The Locket, Out of the Past, Blood on the Moon, I Married a Communist/The Woman on Pier 13, Where Danger Lives, Roadblock, Clash by Night*, and *The Hitch-Hiker*. He also photographed Fritz Lang's *The Blue Gardenia* for Warner Bros.; *Two O'Clock Courage* Script Files, Box 389S, RKO Studio Records.

10. Descriptions taken from the motion picture *Two in the Dark* (RKO, 1936).

11. Reviewing the July 14, 1944, estimating script, RKO made clear to producer Ben Stoloff, "You will suggest that Patty is not so readily an accessory to The Man's indicated crimes by having her give him a certain benefit of doubt"; William Gordon, memorandum to Ben Stoloff, July 25, 1944. RKO Studio Records, Production Files Box 145P, Folder B 477.

12. Dialogue and descriptions taken from the motion picture *Two O'Clock Courage* (RKO, 1945).

13. RKO response to Joseph I. Breen July 21, 1944 letter, RKO Studio Records, ibid.

14. Robert E. Kent, *Two O'Clock Courage* screenplay (final draft), August 2, 1944, 87–88, *Two O'Clock Courage* Script Files, Box 389S, RKO Studio Records.

15. The actress Jean Brooks is best remembered for her haunting role in the Val Lewton chiller *The Seventh Victim* (1943).

16. "Ann Rutherford in National Ads," *Two O'Clock Courage* pressbook, 7.

17. "For Classified Ad," ibid.

18. "Sell Them with Headlines," ibid.

19. "Lobby Clock" and "Eye Catching Ballyhoo," ibid.

20. "Mystery Man Hunt," ibid.

21. Movie Clock, movie pages, *New York Post* (April 13, 1945): 13; movie pages, *New York Post* (April 20, 1945): 31 and (April 26, 1945): 26; *Los Angeles Times* (May 28, 1945): II:2; *Boston Daily Globe [morning edition]* (June 14, 1945): 15; *Chicago Daily Tribune* (July 17, 1945): 14; *Variety* picture grosses: New York (April 18, 1945): 18; Los Angeles (May 30, 1945): 20; (June 6, 1945): 20 and (June 13, 1945): 20; Boston (June 20, 1945): 14 and (June 27, 1945): 20; Chicago (July 25, 1945): 17; (August 8, 1945): 11.

CHAPTER 6

1. Vicki Baum, "Big Shot," *Collier's* (September 19, 1936): 7–9, 69–71 (Library of Congress). Coincidentally, Baum had adapted the unproduced Stroheim film treatment *Blind Love* in 1935, which M-G-M rejected; Arthur Lennig, *Stroheim* (Lexington, KY: University Press of Kentucky, 2000), 349.

2. Baum, 9.

3. Jean-Claude Missiaen, "A Lesson in Cinema: Interview with Anthony Mann," 46 (see Introduction n2).

4. Dialogue and descriptions taken from the motion picture *The Great Flamarion* (Republic Pictures, 1945).

5. Lennig, 430–32; Kate Cameron, "Finale's Give-Away Mars Republic Film," *New York Daily News* (January 14, 1945): 71M.

6. Joseph I. Breen, letter to William Wilder, August 31, 1944. This letter followed the initial letter dated August 28, 1944, from Breen, and was followed up by a letter on September 14, 1944; Academy of Motion Picture Arts & Sciences, Special Collections, Motion Picture Association of America, Production Code Administration records (hereafter PCA). For this scene, Breen, following up to an August 31, 1944, meeting between William Wilder, Mann, and two PCA executives, insisted, "There will be no exposure of the Wife's person when the Husband [sic] shoots the shoulder-strap from her gown. Also, she will not raise her skirt too high when displaying her 'shapely legs.'" Breen was concerned with Al's drinking as he was with Connie's sexuality, warning Mann and company against depicting "unnecessary drinking and drunkenness" and not portraying Al as a "rolling" drunk.

7. Joseph I. Breen, letter to William Wilder, Filmdom Productions, Inc., PCA.

8. Archer Winston, "'The Great Flamarion' Ruined by Bad Girl," Movie Talk, *New York Post* (January 15, 1945): 21.

9. Dialogue quoted verbatim from the motion picture *Scarlet Street* (Universal, 1945).

10. The picture was first announced on September 12, 1944, and reported completed on September 30: Edwin Schallert, "Beach Head Battle Will Motivate Screen Play," *Los Angeles Times* (September 12, 1944): A9; *Daily Variety* Production Chart, *Daily Variety* (September 15, 1944): 10; *Data for Bulletin of Screen Achievement Records*, Academy of Motion Picture Arts & Sciences, Core Collection.

11. *Screen*: 34 (see Introduction n4).

12. Ibid.

13. Ibid., 34–35.

14. Breen granted a Production Code Administration seal on November 8, 1944, PCA. Rose Pelswick, "Von Stroheim Stars In Film at Republic," *New York Journal-American* (January 15, 1945): 5; Eileen Creelman, "Erich Von Stroheim in a Tragic Drama of Love and Theatre, 'The Great Flamarion,'" *New York Sun* (January 15, 1945): 19. Special thanks to Edward Comstock of USC for providing these reviews.

15. Movie pages, *New York Post* (January 13, 1945): 11; (April 3, 1945): 19; *Los Angeles Times* (April 12, 1945): A3; New York (January 17, 1945): 16 and (January 24, 1945): 15; Kansas City (April 11, 1945): 9 and (April 18, 1945): 20; Indianapolis (May 2, 1945): 23; Louisville (May 9, 1945): 12; Seattle and Baltimore (April 25, 1945): 16; St. Louis (April 25, 1945): 18; Los Angeles (April 18, 1945): 20 and (April 25, 1945): 18; Buffalo and Boston (May 23, 1945): 16; San Francisco (May 30, 1945): 18.

16. *Screen*: 35.

CHAPTER 7

1. Dialogue and descriptions taken from the motion picture *Strange Impersonation* (Republic Pictures, 1946).

2. Joseph I. Breen, letter to William Wilder, June 25, 1945, *Strange Impersonation* file, Motion Picture Association of America, Production Code Administration records, Margaret Herrick Library—Department of Special Collections (hereafter PCA); John M. Cohen, "In Defense of Lawyers," The Readers Write, *New York Times* (July 14, 1946): 43.

3. Breen, ibid.

4. Fritz Lang's *The Woman in the Window* (1944) influenced the ending of the film, which was already a Hollywood cliché. The *Hollywood Reporter* review opened with, "That cycle which has been sweeping Hollywood of having it all turn out to be a dream has finally struck Republic. But even so, it didn't have to be such a bad dream"; "And Again It All Turns Out A Dream," *Hollywood Reporter* (February 26, 1946): 3.

5. *Sing Your Way Home* Production Files, Box 147P, RKO Studio Records, 3, Performing Arts Special Collections, University of California, Los Angeles. The film entered production as *Follow Your Heart*: Philip K. Scheuer, "Crosby, Fitzgerald Reunited in 'Tavern': Hoagy Carmichael Cast as Singing Taxi Driver in 'Johnny Angel,'" *Los Angeles Times* (November 29, 1944): 10.

6. *Daily Variety* Production Chart, *Daily Variety* (July 13, 1945): 20; Internet Speculative Fiction Database (www.isfdb.org); Steven P. Hill, associate professor, Cinema Studies, University of Illinois at Urbana-Champaign, "Biography for Mindret Lord," Internet Movie Database. Lord's "I Had an Alibi" episode may be heard on the Turner Classic Movies website: http://fan.tcm.com/_Suspense-I-Had-An-Alibi-CBS-01-04-45/audio/911738/66470.html?createPassive=true.

7. A song, "You'll Remember Me," is mentioned in one of the screenplay drafts, but no such song appears in the released version; Joseph I. Breen letter to William Wilder, June 25, 1945, *Strange Impersonation* file, PCA.

8. *Strange Impersonation* file, PCA; *Daily Variety* Production Charts, *Daily Variety* (July 13, 1945): 20 and (August 24, 1945): 9.

9. Movie pages, Fox/Pomona, *Los Angeles Times* (March 31, 1946): III: 3; *New York Post* (May 15, 1946): 46; (May 29, 1946): 17; (June 6, 1946): 37; (June 13, 1946): 37; (June 20, 1946): 41; *Boston Daily Globe* (July 16, 1946): 23; *Variety* picture grosses, Boston (July 24, 1946): 19.

10. *The Bamboo Blonde* Production Files, Box 151P, RKO Studio Records, 3, Performing Arts Special Collections, University of California, Los Angeles. The Motion Picture Association of America estimated 1946 weekly cinema attendance to be 100,000,000. The United States population at the time was 141,388,566; *The 1947 Film Daily Year Book of Motion Pictures*, 55; Historical National Population Estimates: July 1, 1900 to July 1, 1999; Population Estimates Program, Population Division, U.S. Census Bureau: http://www.census.gov/population/estimates/nation/popclockest.txt.

CHAPTER 8

1. A film treatment is written in prose style similar to a short story. Most film treatments consist of descriptions and dialogue but no technical directions. Screenwriters of the old Hollywood studio system used treatments as guides during the screenplay-writing phase. A treatment ranges from dozens to more than 100 pages.

2. Jean-Claude Missiaen, "A Lesson in Cinema: Interview with Anthony Mann," 46 (see Introduction n2).

3. Dorothy Atlas and Anthony Mann, *Flight* treatment, *Desperate* Script Files, Box 1241S, RKO Studio Records, 3, Performing Arts Special Collections, University of California, Los Angeles.

4. Dorothy Atlas and Anthony Mann, *Flight*, 32.

5. Ibid., 18.

6. Ibid., 31.

7. Ibid., 66. Several versions of the famous Mother Goose nursery rhyme exist, among them: "Hey, diddle, diddle/The cat and the fiddle/The cow jumped over the moon/The little dog laughed to see such sport/And the Dish ran away with the Spoon." The treatment refers to the tune by its alternate title, "Hi Diddle Diddle," which was also the title of a 1943 United Artists release.

8. Essex wrote a *Boston Blackie* crime entry for RKO the previous year and went on to contribute to the screenplays of the independent thriller *Dragnet* (1947), *Bodyguard* (1948, with a story co-credited to Robert Altman), *The Killer That Stalked New York* (1950), Phil Karlson's *Kansas City Confidential* (1952), *The Las Vegas Story* (1952), *The 49th Man* (1953), the 3-D *noir I, the Jury* (1953), Jack Webb's *Dragnet* feature (1954), and the television series *The Untouchables* and *77 Sunset Strip*. Rackin's strongest credits are Raoul Walsh's 1951 *film policier*, *The Enforcer* (direction credited to Bretaigne Windust) and John Ford's *The Horse Soldiers* (1959). Ted Tetzlaff's RKO crime drama *A Dangerous Profession* (1949) is one of the weaker films of the genre (Internet Movie Database).

9. Joseph I. Breen, letter to Harold Melniker of RKO, October 17, 1946, Motion Picture Association of America, Production Code Administration records, Margaret Herrick Library—Department of Special Collections (hereafter PCA). The author is grateful to researcher Chuck Willett for his assistance in locating these and other background materials related to the film.

10. "New Teeth in Production Code Kills Any Devices to Cash in On Lurid Sex Sellers; K.O. to the Gangster Cycle," *Variety* (December 10, 1947): 7, 22.

11. Comas, 46 (see Chapter 1 n27). Comas's data on the *Desperate* production schedule and director salary are based on the initial budget. Mann's later claims of a twelve-day schedule and a $1,000 directing fee are incorrect (Missiaen, ibid); "Joan Crawford in Mystery Film," *New York Times* (May 13, 1946): 34; RKO memorandum, February 4, 1947, announcing *Desperate* as the "FINAL TITLE," *Desperate* Production Files, Box 163P, RKO Studio Records.

12. *The Bamboo Blonde* Production Files, Box 151P; *Sing Your Way Home* Production Files, Box 147P, RKO Studio Records. The figures for the other films break down as follows: *Born to Kill* (36 days; 110,000 feet budgeted, 135,760 shot); *The Devil Thumbs a Ride* (29 days; 60,000 feet budgeted, 91,120 shot); *Born to Kill* Production Files, Box 158P; *The Devil Thumbs a Ride* Production Files, Box 159P, RKO Studio Records.

13. Joseph I. Breen, letters to Harold Melniker, October 17, 1946: 1–2; November 18, 1946: 1, PCA; *Desperate* Production Files, Box 163P, RKO Studio Records.

14. *Desperate* Production Files, ibid.

15. Joseph I. Breen, letter to Harold Melniker, October 17, 1946: 1, PCA. By the time the PCA issued its special regulations amendment to the code in late 1947, the tenth statute specifically stated, "There must be no scenes, at any time, showing law-enforcing officers dying at the hands of criminals. This includes private detectives and guards for banks, motor trucks, etc."; *1946-47 Motion Picture Almanac*, 767.

16. Breen ordered this shot deleted to appease the Pennsylvania censors; Breen, Confidential, August 1, 1947, PCA.

17. Dialogue and descriptions taken from the motion picture *Desperate* (RKO, 1947).

18. This line was ordered cut by Breen for the film's release in Ontario, Canada; Breen, Confidential, July 10, 1947 (PCA). The third statute in the December 1947 "Special Regulations on Crime in Motion Pictures" states, "There must be no suggestion, at any time, of excessive brutality"; *Motion Picture Almanac*, ibid.

19. Joseph I. Breen, letter to Harold Melniker, October 17, 1946: 2; Joseph I. Breen, letter to Harold Melniker, November 1, 1946: 1, PCA.

20. Joseph I. Breen, letter to Harold Melniker, November 18, 1946: 1, PCA. In late 1947, Breen gave instructions on approving *Desperate* for Australian censors: "Eliminate all scenes of broken bottle and threat to harm wife"; Joseph I. Breen, Confidential, November 12, 1947, PCA.

21. Joseph I. Breen, letter to Harold Melniker, October 17, 1946: 2 (PCA); Harry Essex, *Flight* screenplay, October 11, 1946, 66-67, Box 1241S, RKO Studio Records. (Breen identifies these pages as 49 and 50.) Symbolically, the "Special Regulations" addendum to the Production Code would state in its twelfth and final statute that "[p]ictures dealing with criminal activities in which minors participate, or to which minors are related, shall not be approved if they incite demoralizing imitation on the part of youth"; *Motion Picture Almanac*, ibid.

22. Joseph I. Breen, letter to Harold Melniker, November 1, 1946: 2, PCA.

23. Ibid., 1.

24. Bernard Eisenschitz, *Nicholas Ray: An American Journey*. Translated by Tom Milne. (London and Boston: Faber and Faber, 1993, 1996), 167-69.

25. "Like Other Steve, Brodie Takes Risk And Survives," *Desperate* exhibitor's pressbook, 2, Academy of Motion Picture Arts & Sciences, Core Collection.

26. Breen, letter to Melniker, October 17, 1946, 3, PCA.

27. Breen, confidential memo, November 12, 1947, Herrick Library.

28. "Ballyhoo Devices," *Desperate* pressbook, 7.

29. "Personal Item," *Desperate* pressbook, 7.

30. "Contest Topic," *Desperate* pressbook, 7.

31. Movie pages, *San Francisco Chronicle* (June 18, 1947): 9; *Los Angeles Times* (July 8, 1947): II:2; *Chicago Daily Tribune* (July 30, 1947): 23); *New York Herald Tribune* (October 8, 1947): 24; (October 15, 1947): 25 and (October 21, 1947): 24; *Variety* picture grosses: San Francisco (June 25, 1947): 13; Los Angeles (July 16, 1947): 8; (July 23, 1947): 16 and (July 30, 1947): 12; Chicago (August 6, 1947): 9 and (August 13, 1947): 9; Louisville (August 20, 1947): 15; Baltimore (September 3, 1947): 11; Providence (September 17, 1947): 11; Omaha and Minneapolis (September 24, 1947): 7, 9.

CHAPTER 9

1. Rob Warden, "Joseph M. Majczek: Perjury Led to Joseph Majczek's Wrongful Conviction for the Murder of a Chicago Policeman in 1933," Center on Wrongful Convictions, Northwestern University School of Law website: http://www.law.north western.edu/wrongfulconvictions/exonerations/il/joseph-m-majczek.html; "J. Majczek; Wrongfully Imprisoned," obituaries, *Chicago Tribune* (June 1, 1983): 2:4.

2. Thomas F. Brady, "Studio to Refilm Scenes in Picture: Eagle-Lion in Agreement With Fox Will Retake Sequences in Completed Melodrama," *New York Times* (August 20, 1947): 24; Jean-Claude Missiaen, "A Lesson in Cinema: Interview with Anthony Mann," 46 (see Introduction n2).

3. Missiaen, ibid.

4. Ted Okuda, *Grand National, Producers Releasing Corporation, and Screen Guild/Lippert: Complete Filmographies with Studio Histories* (Jefferson, NC, and London: McFarland and Company, 1989). *Railroaded!* is not included among the studio releases mentioned (courtesy of James Auer).

5. Steve Jenkins, "Edgar G. Ulmer and PRC: a Detour down Poverty Row," *Monthly Film Bulletin* 49, no. 582 (July 1982), back page; Peter Bogdanovich, "Edgar G. Ulmer," in *King of the Bs*, 387 (see Chapter 4 n9).

6. Stern is referring to the "day-for-night" technique of filtering a camera lens in order to simulate night conditions during the daytime (see Chapter 11).

7. Stewart Stern, phone interview with the author, April 8, 2011.

8. Joseph I. Breen Sr., letter to David Stephenson of Eagle-Lion Films, April 2, 1947, *Railroaded!* file, Motion Picture Association of America. Production Code Administration records, Margaret Herrick Library—Department of Special Collections (hereafter PCA). In 1939, the PCA approved John Brahm's Columbia Pictures crime melodrama *Let Us Live* (also inspired by true events), in which police, district attorney, and State Supreme Court efforts to frame an innocent man (Henry Fonda) are ruthlessly depicted.

9. Joseph I. Breen Sr., letter to David Stephenson, April 17, 1947, PCA.

10. "Studio to Contest Ban on Film," *New York Times* (October 17, 1947):17; Thomas F. Brady, "Metro Buys Option on Schmitt Novel," *New York Times* (November 5, 1947): 36.

11. This dialogue is further misquoted in a *film noir* quotation book which wrongly indicates that Ainsworth is addressing Clara; Charles Pappas, *It's a Bitter Little World: The Smartest Toughest Nastiest Quotes from Film Noir* (Canada: F + W Publications, Inc., 2005), 89.

12. Dialogue and descriptions taken from the motion picture *Railroaded!* (PRC/Eagle-Lion, 1947).

13. Joseph I. Breen Sr., letter to David Stephenson, April 17, 1947, PCA.

14. Joseph I. Breen Sr., letter to David Stephenson, April 2, 1947, PCA.

15. *Screen*: 35 (see Introduction n4). Mann in this interview cited a ten-day production schedule, which is confirmed in the *Daily Variety* Production Charts of April 25, 1947: 11 and May 2, 1947: 15; Thomas F. Brady, ibid.

16. The re-edited picture was screened for the PCA on September 5, 1947. *Railroaded!* file, PCA.

17. "Eagle-Lion Acquires PRC Selling Outlets," *New York Times* (August 18, 1947): 13; Edwin Schallert, "British Launch Hollywood Invasion: Major Production Companies Involved," *Los Angeles Times* (September 8, 1946): C1; "Eagle Lion [sic] Sets Picture Budget," *Los Angeles Times* (June 24, 1946): 7; "PRC, Eagle-Lion Due to Complete Amalgamation No Later Than Sept. 1" and "PRC Has Backlog of Dozen Pictures," *Variety* (August 6, 1947): 7; "PRC Absorption by Eagle-Lion Seen Hypo to E-L Distrib for Independents," *Variety* (August 20, 1947): 7; "Eagle Lion [sic] Switches Top PRC-ers To Own Banner; Other Xchange [sic] Briefs," *Variety* (August 27, 1947): 22.

18. New York release information: Thomas F. Brady, "RKO Will Produce 'The Window' Here: Picture to Be Made at Pathe Studios—Fox Pays $250,000 for 'Call Me Mister' Revue," *New York Times* (October 28, 1947): 28; movie pages, *Los Angeles Times* (November 26, 1947): II:11; *Boston Daily Globe* (November 26, 1947): 18; *Variety* picture grosses: Detroit (October 29, 1947): 12 and (November 12, 1947): 22; Buffalo (November 26, 1947): 8; Los Angeles and Boston (December 3, 1947): 8; (December 10, 1947): 16; Denver (December 17, 1947): 12; Louisville (December 10, 1947): 14; *Body and Soul* grossed $31,700 in its second week at four Los Angeles theaters compared with the combined $19,400 gross of *Railroaded!* at three locations.

CHAPTER 10

1. *Screen*: 35 (see Introduction n4).

2. "Movie of the Week: *T-Men*, Typical 'sleeper' proves a good movie can still be made without a high budget and famous stars," *Life* (February 23, 1948): 135–36, 139; Charles Bitsch and Claude Chabrol, 5 (see Introduction n2). Mann's RKO musical *Sing Your Way Home* (1945) had its central song "I'll Buy That Dream" nominated for an Academy Award. That song was later used as source music in Fritz Lang's *Clash by Night* (RKO, 1952).

3. "'Hollywood May Become Merely Operations Base,'" *T-Men* pressbook, 29, University of Southern California Cinematic Arts Library, Special Collections (hereafter USC). Paramount produced Billy Wilder's *The Lost Weekend* (1945) and Twentieth Century-Fox produced both Henry Hathaway's *The House on 92nd Street* (1945) and Elia Kazan's *Boomerang!* (1947).

4. Will Straw, "Documentary Realism and the Postwar Left," in Frank Krutnik, Steve Neale, Brian Neve, Peter Stanfield, eds., *"Un-American" Hollywood: Politics and Film in the Blacklist Era* (New Brunswick, NJ, and London: Rutgers University Press, 2007), 133.

5. *T-Men* pressbook, 14.

6. Todd McCarthy, introduction, in John Alton, *Painting with Light* (Berkeley/Los Angeles/London: University of California Press, 1995), xviii.

7. *Painting with Light*, xix.

8. *Screen*: ibid.

9. Jean-Claude Missiaen, "A Lesson in Cinema: Interview with Anthony Mann," 46 (see Introduction n2).

10. *Screen*: 38.

11. The House Committee on Un-American Activities began Hollywood investigative hearings on film industry personnel in October 1947, one month after *T-Men* completed production. Composer Paul Sawtell duplicated the essence of his *T-Men* score in *Down Three Dark Streets* (1954).

12. Elmer L. Irey, with William J. Slocum, *The Tax Dodgers: The Inside Story of the T-Men's War with America's Political and Underworld Hoodlums* (New York: Greenberg, 1948), 66–67, 89. For Irey's account of the IATSE affair, see pages 271–88. Those taking issue with the official record of the Hauptmann case include Anthony Scaduto, *Scapegoat: The Lonesome Death of Bruno Richard Hauptmann* (New York: G. P. Putnam's Sons, 1976).

13. Mark Osteen further examines the stylistic differences in his essay, "Face Plates: *T-Men* and the Problem of *Noir* Counterfeiting," *Quarterly Review of Film and Video* 24, no. 2 (Routledge, Spring 2007): 125–42.

14. The author thanks Prof. Reynold Humphries for bringing this to his attention in an e-mail.

15. Dialogue and descriptions taken from the motion picture *T-Men* (Eagle-Lion, 1947).

16. Missiaen, ibid.

17. *Painting with Light*, 54–55.

18. Ibid.

19. Ibid., 62.

20. "Screen's T-Men Must Be Rugged," *T-Men* pressbook, 27.

21. "O'Keefe Gets Frost-Bitten As Thermometer Hits 130°," *T-Men* pressbook, 28.

22. Joseph I. Breen Sr., letter to David Stephenson, July 24, 1947; Joseph I. Breen Jr., letter to Eugene Dougherty of the MPPDA, July 30, 1947; Joseph I. Breen Sr., letter to David Stephenson, August 5, 1947, *T-Men* file, Motion Picture Association of America, Production Code Administration records, Margaret Herrick Library—Department of Special Collections (hereafter PCA).

23. Rudy Behlmer, 65 (see Introduction n9).

24. Ibid.

25. Missiaen, ibid.

26. Curt L. Heymann, "Now It's T-Men: Film Dramatizes Work of Treasury Police Force," *New York Times* (October 26, 1947): 4X.

27. The original Reliance/Eagle-Lion contracts for these screenwriters are dated as follows: John C. Higgins, March 5, 1947; Robert B. Churchill, January 13, 1947; George Brickner, November 7, 1946; Henry Blankfort, October 9, 1946; *T-Men* Production File, Edward Small Collection, Box 10, USC.

28. *T-Men* Production File. The average negative cost for a U.S. feature film in 1947 was $732,449; *The 1948 Film Daily Year Book of Motion Pictures*, 61.

29. *T-Men* Producion File, ibid.

30. "Dennis Is Tired Of [*sic*] Film Realism," *T-Men* pressbook, 25.

31. *T-Men* Production File.

32. "Camera Rule Book Tossed Into Discard For 'T-Men' Movie," *T-Men* pressbook, 29. The *T-Men* actresses clearly wear makeup. Despite publicists authoring many statements or quotations in such materials, Alton was in the process of preparing his famous

cinematography book *Painting with Light* for Macmillan Company: "Coming and Going," *Film Daily* (May 27, 1948): 2.

33. "Looking for a Film Star? Sun Glasses Are No Clue," *T-Men* pressbook, 26.

34. "Glass-Walled Trucks Aid 'T-Men' Filming," *T-Men* press book, 27.

35. *T-Men* pressbook, 22.

36. *T-Men* budget information; Max E. Youngstein, Western Union telegram to Edward Small, November 25, 1947, USC. The *Daily Variety* Production Chart lists a start date of July 8, 1947, but this is not consistent with the Edward Small production records at USC. *Daily Variety* (August 8, 1947): 13.

37. *T-Men* pressbook, 22.

38. *T-Men* pressbook, 11.

39. *T-Men* pressbook, 12.

40. Ibid., 2 (original emphasis). Warner Bros. released William Keighley's *"G"-Men* (1935), Universal-International released Robert Siodmak's *The Killers* (1946) and Jules Dassin's *Brute Force* (1947).

41. Ibid., 13.

42. Ibid., 19.

43. Ibid., 4.

44. Movie pages, *Los Angeles Times* (December 25, 1947): II:10; *Chicago Daily Tribune* (January 8, 1948): 27; *New York Times* (January 21, 1948): 30; *Boston Daily Globe [evening edition]* (January 22, 1948): 10; *Variety* picture grosses: Los Angeles (December 31, 1947): 8 and (January 7, 1948): 60; Los Angeles, Chicago, Philadelphia (January 14, 1948): 14–15, 20; Chicago, Philadelphia (January 21, 1948): 11; Chicago (January 28, 1948): 13; New York (February 4, 1948): 11; (February 11, 1948): 9; (February 18, 1948): 13; (February 25, 1948): 16; San Francisco and Cincinnati (February 11, 1948): 9, 11, 20; San Francisco and Baltimore (February 18, 1948): 12; Pittsburgh, Minneapolis (February 25, 1948), 12–13; Eagle-Lion memo, February 9, 1948: 3 (USC); "Krim Points to EL's Selznick, Wanger, Small, Foy for 'Top Indie' Rating," *Variety* (February 9, 1949): 7.

45. Edward Small, letter to Aubrey Schenck, March 24, 1948, *T-Men* Production File.

CHAPTER 11

1. Arnold B. Armstrong and Audrey Ashley, *Corkscrew Alley* treatment, 41, USC Cinematic Arts Library, Edward Small Collection, Box 9, *Raw Deal*, Folder 1 (hereafter USC *Raw Deal*).

2. Ibid., 2.

3. Ibid., 11.

4. Ibid., 15.

5. Ibid., 16.

6. Thomas F. Brady, "O'Keefe Will Star in New Melodrama: Signs With Eagle-Lion to Take Lead in 'Corkscrew Alley'—Story of a Chain Gang," *New York Times* (September 9, 1947): 28.

7. The Edward Small papers report Don Stafford working on the script during January 2– February 11 and March 25– May 24, 1947; John C. Higgins working from March 25 – May 24, 1947; and Leopold Atlas working from October 9–November 7 and November 10– 15, 1947, USC.

8. *Raw Deal* pressbook, 2; "Dramatic 'Raw Deal' Tells Rugged Story of Love, Vengeance," ibid., 19; University of Southern California Cinematic Arts Library, Special Collections.

9. The establishing shots of the prison were among the stock footage purchased from RKO Radio Pictures and M-G-M for the production; USC Cinematic Arts Library, Edward Small Collection, Box 9, *Raw Deal* Production File.

10. Dialogue and descriptions taken from the motion picture *Raw Deal* (Eagle-Lion, 1948).

11. Joseph I. Breen Sr., letter to Eagle-Lion, December 4, 1947, quoted in Eagle-Lion interoffice memoranda, December 8, 1947, USC *Raw Deal*, Folder 3.

12. Joseph I. Breen Sr., letter to David Stephenson, November 10, 1947, USC.

13. Ibid.

14. Joseph I. Breen Sr., letter to David Stephenson, November 12, 1947, USC.

15. Ibid.

16. Ibid.

17. Ibid.

18. Joseph I. Breen Sr., letter to Eagle-Lion, December 4, 1947, ibid.

19. O'Keefe's salary was $56,250. By comparison, Trevor was paid $25,000, Marsha Hunt $15,625, and Raymond Burr $2,166. USC *Raw Deal*.

20. "Actor O'Keefe and Film Aides Hurt at Studio," *Los Angeles Times* (December 12, 1947): 1. The production files only allude to "1 idle day due to illness of castmember." The article identifies the locale as "Eagle-Lion studios," but actress Marsha Hunt (see below) reported *Raw Deal* filming on the Goldwyn lot.

21. Marsha Hunt, *Raw Deal* screening, Grauman's Chinese Theatre, Los Angeles, April 13, 2012.

22. John Alton, *Painting with Light*, 55 (see Chapter 10 n6).

23. "Hollywood's in a Quandary, 'How Do You Wake Girl?,'" *Raw Deal* pressbook, 22.

24. "Strapless Garment Revealed in Movie," *Raw Deal* pressbook, 22; *Corkscrew Alley* screenplay dated October 14, 1947: 25, 30, 38; Breen Sr., letter to Stephenson, November 12, 1947, USC.

25. *Painting with Light*, 131.

26. Joseph Breen Jr., letter to Joseph I. Breen Sr., November 28, 1947, *Raw Deal* file, Motion Picture Association of America, Production Code Administration records, Margaret Herrick Library—Department of Special Collections.

27. Ibid.

28. Edward Small Collection, USC.

29. "Stars of 'Raw Deal' Wear Glass Undies, But They're Opaque," *Raw Deal* pressbook, 21.

30. Breen Jr. letter, ibid; Scheuer, "Mann and Stewart Use U.S. as a Set" (see Introduction n1).

31. Joseph I. Breen Sr. memo, December 8, 1947; Breen Sr., letter to Stephenson, November 12, 1947; *Raw Deal* screenplay, October 14, 1947, 68–69 and 79–80, USC.

32. Edward Small, letter to William Heineman of Eagle-Lion, March 25, 1948, USC.

33. *Raw Deal* pressbook, 3–4.

34. "One-Day Contest With Prepared Art Sells Both Title and Famous Stars," "Inquiring Reporter Query For Newspaper Quizzer," *Raw Deal* pressbook, 5.

35. "Plant Street Safety Poster," *Raw Deal* pressbook, 6.

36. *Raw Deal* pressbook, 10.

37. Ibid., 8.

38. Ibid.

39. Ibid., 16.

40. Ibid., 14.

41. Movie pages, *Los Angeles Times* (May 19, 1948): 22; *Boston Daily Globe [morning edition]* (July 1, 1948): 24; *New York Times* (July 8, 1948): 19; *Chicago Tribune* (August 20, 1948): II:7; the opening *Raw Deal* Los Angeles gross was $35,800 compared with $53,300 for *T-Men*: *Variety* picture grosses, Los Angeles (May 26, 1948): 13 and 18; and (June 2, 1948): 8; Boston (July 7, 1948): 10; New York (July 21, 1948): 13; and (July 28, 1948): 9; Baltimore (August 4, 1948): 9; Cincinnati/Cleveland (August 18, 1948): 8; Cleveland (August 25, 1948): 12; Chicago (September 1, 1948): 9; "Krim Points to EL's Selznick, Wanger, Small, Foy for 'Top Indie' Rating," *Variety* (February 9, 1949): 7, 22. The Los Angeles *T-Men* figures are adjusted grosses from *Variety* (January 7, 1948): 60 and (January 14, 1948): 14.

42. The HUAC testimony of Leopold Atlas may be viewed at http://archive.org/stream/-investigationofco5unit/investigationofco5unit_djvu.txt; Humphries, 145 (see Chapter 2 n39).

CHAPTER 12

1. This is how the title appears in the opening credits. From an editorial perspective "by" should not be capitalized. Eagle-Lion corrected the error in publicity materials.

2. "Suspect in Highway Patrolman's Killing Shot and Seized in Battle: Man Continues to Fight Police Despite Wounds," *Los Angeles Times* (December 21, 1946): 3.

3. Ibid.

4. "Los Angeles City Briefs: Gun Hunt Futile," *Los Angeles Times* (January 7, 1947): A12.

5. *Los Angeles Times* (see n2).

6. Ibid.

7. "Los Angeles Briefs: Suspect on Mend," *Los Angeles Times* (December 22, 1946): A8; "Officer Slayer Must Die for Crime, Says Judge: Death Sentence of Erwin Walker Held Up Pending Hearing on Motion for New Trial," *Los Angeles Times* (June 12, 1947): 2. The Wikipedia entry for Erwin Walker offers additional details obtained from cited trial transcripts, numerous elements of which appear in the film.

8. Dialogue and descriptions taken from the motion picture *He Walked By Night* (Eagle-Lion, 1948).

9. Philip K. Scheuer, "His Killer Roles Horrify Basehart: Fast-Rising Actor Would Rather Slay 'Em With Comedy Lines," *Los Angeles Times* (February 27, 1949): D1; Ray Kovitz, "Authenticity Themes Dragnet; Star Jack Webb Aims at Adult Entertainment on Police Show," *Los Angeles Times* (August 21, 1952): 26; Maurice Zolotow, "The Names Have Not Been Changed: Just the Facts About the Man who Created 'Dragnet'—Only to Find it's a Monster That Rules his Life," *Washington Post and Times Herald* (October 3, 1954): AW26.

10. Stewart Stern, phone interview by author, April 8, 2011.

11. "Swiss Prize to U.S. Film: 'He Walked by Night' Is Cited as Year's Top Crime Picture," *New York Times* (July 20, 1949): 30.

12. Thomas F. Brady, "Video Problem: Actors Consider Jurisdictional Issues Raised by Television—Studio Notes; Reawakening," *New York Times* (August 7, 1949): X3.

13. Michael Walker, "1063 Anthony Mann," *Film Dope* no. 38 (December 1987): 37. "Biofilmography of Anthony Mann," *Cahiers du Cinéma in English* 12 (December 1967): 54. Both sources credit Mann with directing exterior scenes with Richard Basehart.

14. Michael Walker, e-mail message to author, February 9, 2012; Olivier Eyquem, e-mail message to author, February 12, 2012.

15. Stewart Stern, ibid.

16. Dr. Richard Brigham, e-mail message to author, March 28, 2012.

17. Kevin Brownlow, *The Parade's Gone By...* (Berkeley/Los Angeles/London: University of California Press, 1968): 194; Eisenschitz, 169–73 (see Chapter 8 n24); *Narrow Margin* Production Files, Box 189P, RKO Studio Records, 3, Performing Arts Special Collections, University of California, Los Angeles (courtesy of Serge Delpierre).

18. Richard Fleischer, *Just Tell Me When to Cry: A Memoir* (New York: Carroll & Graf Publishers, 1993): 49.

19. Stewart Stern, ibid.

20. *Men in War* (1957), *God's Little Acre* (1958), *Man of the West* (1958).

21. *El Cid* (1961), *The Fall of the Roman Empire* (1964), *The Heroes of Telemark* (1965).

22. Jean-Claude Missiaen, undated letter to author, June 2012.

23. Ibid. (original emphasis).

24. Philip K. Scheuer, "Crane Wilbur, Star of Silent Films, Carves New Career as Producer," *Los Angeles Times* (November 14, 1948): D1. An early 1948 John C. Higgins screenplay draft (held at the Margaret Herrick Library) is titled *The L.A. Investigator*. Eagle-Lion correspondence and papers include working titles of *Portrait of a Killer* and *Los Angeles Police Story*. Dorothy Moran, letter to Winston Frost, October 11, 1948; production and distribution agreement between Robert T. Kane Productions and Pathe Industries, Inc., March 18, 1948; United Artists Collection, Series 1G—Eagle-Lion Legal (1944–60), Robert T. Kane Productions thru Freedom Productions, Record Group II, Box 18, *He Walked By Night*, Archives Division, The State Historical Society of Wisconsin (courtesy of Dr. Richard and Barbara Brigham), hereafter Eagle-Lion papers.

25. Joseph I. Breen Sr., letter to Joseph Breen Jr., March 23, 1948, *He Walked By Night* file, Motion Picture Association of America, Production Code Administration records, Margaret Herrick Library—Department of Special Collections; "Special Regulations on Crime in Motion Pictures," cit. 6, *1946–47 Motion Picture Almanac*: 767. Regulation 6 specified, "There must be no display, at any time, of machine guns, submachine guns, or

other weapons generally classified as illegal weapons in the hands of gangsters, or other criminals, and there are to be no off-stage sounds of the repercussion of these guns." It is worth noting that although the sounds of Humphrey Bogart's machine gun are heard in Raoul Walsh's *High Sierra* (Warner Bros., 1941), the gun itself is never shown.

26. A May 3 mortgage of Chattels—Pledge and Assignment delivered by Robert T. Kane Productions to Bank of America indicates that the film was now retitled *He Walked By Night*, but trade articles continued to cite the working title for several months; Release of Mortgage from Robert T. Kane Productions to Bank of America, May 3, 1948, Eagle-Lion papers; "Werker Megs 'Clues,'" *The Hollywood Reporter* (March 23, 1948): 1; Edwin Schallert, "Basehart in '29 Clues;' Scott Likely Roxanne," *Los Angeles Times* (April 24, 1948): 9; Thomas F. Brady, "Five Added to Cast of Republic Movie," *New York Times* (April 24, 1948): 11. Both the Los Angeles and New York newspapers report a production start date of "Monday" (April 26) but the *Daily Variety* Production Chart indicates April 19: *Daily Variety* (April 23, 1948): 15; Short Shorts, "Locationing," *Daily Variety* (May 11, 1948): 11.

27. John C. Higgins, *L.A. Investigator*, February 11, 1948, 163, Academy of Motion Picture Arts and Sciences, Core Collection, *He Walked By Night* script (transcription by Serge Delpierre).

28. Ibid., 157.

29. Ibid., 158.

30. Ibid., 161–62.

31. Ibid., 163.

32. Thomas M. Pryor, "Dore Schary Signs Metro Contract," *New York Times* (July 15, 1948): 26; "Adds for '29 Clues,'" *Daily Variety* (July 15, 1948): 3; "E-L Fattening Up '29 Clues' Footage," *Daily Variety* (July 23, 1948): 2 (incorrect date of "July 22, 1948" printed on page); Of Local Origin, *New York Times* (August 12, 1948): 17; "Burr Family Busy," *Daily Variety* (August 16, 1948): 3; reports of a *Reign of Terror* start date of August 23 conflict with the *Daily Variety* Production Chart, which adjusts the date to August 17: *Daily Variety* (August 20, 1948): 15 and (August 27, 1948): 11.

33. PCA files.

34. "You Can Get the Whole Town on the Hunt For He Who Walks by Night Like This," *He Walked By Night* pressbook, 5; Academy of Motion Picture Arts & Sciences, Core Collection, *He Walked By Night*, Cinema Pressbooks From the Original Studio Collections, Part 2, H0110.000, Reel 030. "Link Public Safety Campaign to Film!," *He Walked By Night* pressbook, 5 (original emphasis), ibid.

35. "You Can Bring in the Merchant and Home Protective Services!," *He Walked By Night* pressbook, 6.

36. ". . . and This Stunt on Opening Night," "There's Title Sell in This Suggestion," and "Devices which Fight Night Terrors, Natch!," *He Walked By Night* pressbook, 5–7.

37. "Use police siren!," *He Walked By Night* pressbook, 7.

38. Movie pages, *Los Angeles Times* (November 24, 1948): I:19; "Washington St. Olympia Changes Name to Pilgrim," *Boston Daily Globe* (January 1, 1949): 4; movie pages, *Chicago Daily Tribune* (January 6, 1949): II:7; *New York Post* (February 4, 1949): 37; "'Walk' makes L.A. history!," *He Walked By Night* pressbook, 3; *Variety* picture grosses: Los Angeles/San Francisco (December 8, 1948): 8, 18; San Francisco (December 15, 1948): 9, 18; Chicago/Boston/Philadelphia (January 12, 1949): 13, 16; Boston/Philadelphia/Chicago/Baltimore

(January 19, 1949), 8–9; Philadelphia/Baltimore/Kansas City (January 26, 1949): 8, 18; New York City (February 16, 1949): 11; (February 23, 1949): 15; and (March 2, 1949), 11. Philadelphia, Chicago, Baltimore, New York, and one of the two San Francisco bookings were solo engagements. Direct costs for *He Walked By Night* were $289,492.22 and general overhead costs $73,373.06. J. H. Rothenberg, "Final Negative Cost—'He Walked By Night,'" Eagle-Lion Interoffice Correspondence to legal department, January 14, 1949, Eagle-Lion papers; "Krim Points to EL's Selznick, Wanger, Small, Foy for 'Top Indie' Rating," *Variety* (February 9, 1949): 7, 22.

39. Wikipedia entry on Erwin Walker.

40. *Los Angeles Times* (see n2).

CHAPTER 13

1. Richard Fleischer (see Chapter 12 n18); Francis Rosenwald and Anthony Mann, *Follow Me Quietly*, undated 1947 draft, 1, *Follow Me Quietly* Script Files, Box 1341S, RKO Studio Records, 3, Performing Arts Special Collections, University of California, Los Angeles. The two writers previously collaborated on the treatment *Red Stallion in the Rockies*, which they sold to Eagle-Lion in August 1948, but only Rosenwald is credited in the released film; Dorothy Moran, letter to Winston Frost re: *Red Stallion in the Rockies*, August 24, 1948, Eagle-Lion papers (see Chapter 12 n24).

2. Rosenwald and Mann, 1.

3. Ibid., 2.

4. Dialogue and descriptions taken from the motion picture *Follow Me Quietly* (RKO, 1949); Rosenwald and Mann, 3.

5. Rosenwald and Mann, 4.

6. In the treatment, the dialogue is, "Wouldn't you like to get your hands on this story—?"

7. Rosenwald and Mann, 16.

8. "Garant" in the treatment.

9. "McKee" in the treatment.

10. Rosenwald and Mann, 8–9.

11. Ibid., 13–14.

12. Ibid., 21.

13. "Garant" in the treatment.

14. Rosenwald and Mann, 23–24.

15. Ibid., 40–42; Lillie Hayward, *Follow Me Quietly* blue pages (screenplay), August 9, 1948, 41–43, *Follow Me Quietly* Script Files, Box 1342S, RKO Studio Records.

16. In the treatment, Collins provides the Dummy's voice. In the screenplay and film Grant supplies the voice.

17. Martin Rackin, *Follow Me Quietly* screenplay, February 2, 1948, 74, *Follow Me Quietly* Script Files, Box 1341S, RKO Studio Records.

18. *Follow Me Quietly* Production Files, Box 174P, RKO Studio Records.

19. Darby, 90–91 (see Chapter 1 n19). Darby is in error when he writes, "As the two police officers leave, the camera tracks back into the abandoned room and a figure rises out of the chair, puts the real dummy back there, and goes off into the night." There is no camera track, only a direct cut from the outer office to the inner office.

20. Basinger, 10–11 (see Chapter 1 n19).

21. "Of Local Origin," *New York Times* (August 12, 1948): 17; "Wanger Will View Rough Cut of 'Reign,'" *Daily Variety* (October 20, 1948): 7; A. H. Weiler, "By Way of Report," *New York Times* (October 31, 1948): X5; Michael Walker (see Chapter 12 n13). Walker correctly raises doubts about Mann directing the gas plant sequence.

22. Edwin Schallert, "Gwenn 'Hills' Medico; Douglas Seeks Classic: Don Castle Will Star for Wrather," Drama and Film, *Los Angeles Times* (July 31, 1947): A3; Philip K. Scheuer, "Robert Walker to Play Collegiate Baby Sitter: 'Follow Me Quietly' Slated for Castle," Drama and Film, *Los Angeles Times* (August 23, 1947): A5; Schallert, "'Beauty and the Beast' New on Kanin Schedule: 'Follow Me Quietly' Possible Lamour Subject," Drama and Film, *Los Angeles Times* (September 19, 1947): 11; Schallert, "Mitchum Deal on Fire; Young Stars Promoted," Drama and Film, *Los Angeles Times* (December 24, 1947): 7; Thomas F. Brady, "RKO Buys Mystery as Original Story: Rosenwald and Mann 'Follow Me Quietly' Sold to Studio—Cummings in Comedy," *New York Times* (December 24, 1947): 15. Charles Flynn and Todd McCarthy, "The Economic Imperative: Why Was the B Movie Necessary? (1974)," in *King of the Bs*, 33 (see Chapter 4 n9). Among Hayward's 1932–36 Warner Bros. credits are *Big City Blues*, *They Call It Sin*, *Frisco Jenny*, *Lady Killer*, and *The Walking Dead*.

23. Thomas F. Brady, "Metro Acquires Rights to 'Violet,'" *New York Times* (June 28, 1948): 15; Schallert, "RKO Launching Picture With [sic] Lundigan Starred; Webb to Portray Shade," *Los Angeles Times* (August 13, 1948): 15; "RKO Cutting First Pic To 16 Days," *Daily Variety* (August 17, 1948): 1; *Data for Bulletin of Screen Achievement Records* (November 1, 1948), Academy of Motion Picture Arts & Sciences, Core Collection, *Follow Me Quietly*, Clippings File; *Follow Me Quietly* Production Files, ibid.

24. Rosenwald and Mann, 12.

25. Ibid., 19.

26. *Follow Me Quietly* blue pages (August 16, 1948), 65–66A, RKO Studio Records.

27. Rosenwald and Mann, 27.

28. Ibid., 28.

29. Ibid.

30. Ibid., 29.

31. Ibid., 66–67.

32. "Garant" in the treatment

33. Rosenwald and Mann, 63–64.

34. Ibid., 105.

35. Ibid., 106.

36. Ibid., 107–108.

37. Ibid., 108–109.

38. "Garant" in the treatment

39. Rosenwald and Mann, 110–13.

40. Lillie Hayward screenplay draft, April 23, 1948, 101–14, *Follow Me Quietly* Script Files, Box 1341S, RKO Studio Records.

41. Lillie Hayward screenplay draft, May 27, 1948, 106, RKO Studio Records.

42. *Follow Me Quietly* exhibitors pressbook, Academy of Motion Picture Arts & Sciences, Core Collection.

43. Movie pages, *New York Post* (July 7, 1949): 38; *Los Angeles Times* (September 4, 1949): D2; *Daily Boston Globe [evening edition]* (August 10, 1949): 12; *Chicago Daily Tribune* (October 6, 1949): IV:17; *Variety* picture grosses: New York (July 13, 1949): 9; (July 20, 1949): 11; Boston (August 24, 1949): 13; Los Angeles (September 14, 1949): 12; San Francisco (October 5, 1949): 12 and (October 12, 1949): 11; Chicago and Buffalo (October 12, 1949): 11; Providence, RI (October 19, 1949): 13.

44. Edwin Schallert, "Spike Jones Will Star in 'Really, Mr. Greeley'; McDowall Going Abroad," *Los Angeles Times* (October 24, 1949): B9; Thomas F. Brady, "Zanuck Planning on Film in Israel," *New York Times* (March 22, 1950): 32; *The Doctor's Husband* was the working title for *Emergency Wedding* (1950).

CHAPTER 14

1. *Screen*: 37 (see Introduction n4).

2. *Cynthia* advertisement, *Variety* (June 18, 1947): 23.

3. Dialogue and descriptions taken from the motion picture *Border Incident* (M-G-M, 1949).

4. Ernesto Galarza, *Strangers in Our Fields (Second Edition), Based on a Report Regarding Compliance with the Contractual, Legal and Civil Rights of Mexican Agricultural Contract Labor in the United States, Made Possible Through a Grant-in-Aid from The Fund for the Republic* (Washington, D.C.: Joint United States-Mexico Trade Union Committee, 1956), 5, 10, 18, New York Public Library Microforms (hereafter Galarza report)

5. John Cornell, "Mexican Labor Vital Factor in Southland Agriculture: Consulate Has Special Problem in 'Braceros,'" *Los Angeles Times* (September 27, 1948): A1.

6. "Plane Crash Kills 32 Near Coalinga: Craft Taking Farm Workers to Be Deported," *Los Angeles Times* (January 29, 1948): 1; "Crash Kills 32 on Plane: 28 Deportees En Route to Mexico Dead," *Chicago Daily Tribune* (January 29, 1948): 1; "32 Are Killed In California Plane Crash," *Washington Post* (January 29, 1948): 1.

7. "Esclavos Modernos: En Pleno Siglo de Libertades los Braceros Mexicanos son Objeto de las Mas Inhumanas Explotaciones [Modern Slaves: In Plain Sight of Liberties the Mexican Braceros are Objects of More Inhuman Exploitation]" *El Angelino* (March 4, 1949): 1 (reprinted in Galarza report: 11). Housing, salary, food, and working, conditions information: Galarza report, 22–25, 28, 30–33, 38–39, 40–41, 52–53.

8. George Zuckerman, *Border Patrol* treatment, October 7, 1947, 1–3, USC Cinematic Arts Library, M-G-M Collection, *Border Incident* (hereafter M-G-M/USC).

9. George Zuckerman, *Border Patrol* screenplay, October 27, 1947, M-G-M/USC.

10. Hedda Hopper, Looking at Hollywood (January 14, 1948): 17; "Eagle-Lion Will Do 2nd Pic in Mexico," *Daily Variety* (May 21, 1948): 22; John C. Higgins, *Border Patrol*, incomplete dialogue script, June 16, 1948, M-G-M/USC.

11. Higgins, *Border Patrol*, June 16, 1948, 1.

12. Higgins, *Border Patrol*, September 3, 1948, 175, M-G-M/USC. Accent mark added.

13. Higgins, *Border Incident*, November, 10, 1948, 3–4, M-G-M/USC.

14. Ibid.

15. Higgins, *Border Incident*, November 10, 1948, 4–5. Accent mark added.

16. Higgins, *Border Incident*, October 18, 1948, 121–53, M-G-M/USC.

17. Higgins, *Border Incident*, December 9, 1948, 147, M-G-M/USC.

18. "Burns" in this version of the script, which is an error as the character name at this early stage is "Bryant."

19. Higgins, *Border Incident*, December 18, 1948, 131, M-G-M/USC.

20. Higgins, *Border Incident*, January 11, 1949, 1–2, M-G-M/USC.

21. "Mann Megs 'T-Men,'" *Daily Variety* (September 29, 1948): 2; A. H. Weiler, By Way of Report, *New York Times* (October 31, 1948): X5. Joseph I. Breen Sr., letter to Joseph I Breen Jr., November 5, 1948, *Border Incident* file, Motion Picture Association of America, Production Code Administration records, Margaret Herrick Library—Department of Special Collections (hereafter PCA).

22. "Loew Sees Upswing In Foreign Market," *Hollywood Reporter* (February 10, 1949): 1, 3. It is instructive that M-G-M employees heavily represented the anti-communist Motion Picture Alliance for the Preservation of American Ideals; Humphries, 62 (see Chapter 2 n39); J. Hoberman, *An Army of Phantoms: American Movies and the Making of the Cold War* (New York and London: The New Press: 2011), 13.

23. "Dore Schary Head of RKO Production: Film Industry Veteran of 14 Years Replaces Late Charles Koerner as Studio Chief," *New York Times* (January 2, 1947): 23; Thomas M. Pryor, "Schary Returning to Metro Studios: Likely to be Executive Producer Second to Louis B. Mayer—RKO Leaders in Meeting," *New York Times* (July 14, 1948): 26; Pryor, "Dore Schary Signs Metro Contract: New Vice President in Charge of Production Understood to Have 7-Year Agreement," *New York Times* (July 15, 1948): 26.

24. "Leo Paying E-L 50G For 'Border' Script," *Daily Variety* (November 30, 1948): 1; Hollywood Inside, *Daily Variety* (December 28, 1948): 2; Thomas F. Brady, "Metro is Planning Low-Budget Films: 'Border Incident' to Be Made Next Year, First of Series—Cost Set at $550,000," *New York Times* (December 21, 1948): 33; "500G Films for Metro: Schary to Use 'Border' as Test," *Daily Variety* (December 20, 1948): 1, 8.

25. *Daily Variety*, ibid.

26. *Screen*: 46.

27. Thomas F. Brady, "Eagle-Lion Plans to Reopen Studio," *New York Times* (December 10, 1948): 34.

28. "Montalban Side-Steps 'Mouse Trap'!," *Border Incident* pressbook, 2, Academy of Motion Picture Arts & Sciences, Core Collection.

29. Biographical Director of the United States Congress, George Lloyd Murphy (1902–92): http://bioguide.congress.gov/scripts/biodisplay.pl?index=m001092.

30. *Daily Variety* Production Chart, *Daily Variety* (January 28, 1949): 15; Biofilmography of Anthony Mann, 55 (see Chapter 1 n24). The *Border Incident* filming schedule is listed as thirty-one days.

31. "'Border Incident' Off Again on Location," *Daily Variety* (February 7, 1949): 10; Filmland Briefs, *Los Angeles Times* (February 7, 1949): B5; "Murphy is Good-will Ambassador on 'Border Incident' Location Jaunt," *Border Incident* pressbook, 2; "MGM, With 9 Rolling And [sic] More Ready To Go, Hits 4-Year Peak," *Hollywood Reporter* (March 8, 1949): 1 (incorrect date of "March 7, 1949" printed on first page); "Out Of The Horn's Mouth," *Daily Variety* (March 7, 1949): 14.

32. "Leo Cuts Costs," *Daily Variety* (September 2, 1949): 2.

33. Galarza report: 3.

34. *Screen*: 37.

35. Production Code Administration, letters to M-G-M, December 2, 1949, and July 12, 1950, PCA.

36. Hedda Hopper, Hollywood, *Hartford Courant* (March 7, 1949): 12.

37. Production records do not specify the author or submission date of this end coda; M-G-M/USC.

38. Movie pages, *Los Angeles Times* (October 28, 1949): 21.

39. *Variety* picture grosses: Los Angeles (November 9, 1949): 8; movie pages, *Chicago Tribune* (November 18, 1949), III:14.

40. Movie pages, *Los Angeles* Times (October 28, 1949): 21; *Boston Daily Globe* (November 2, 1949): 26; *Chicago Daily Tribune* (November 18, 1949): III:14; *New York Times* (November 19, 1949): 11 and (November 25, 1949): 27; *Variety* picture grosses: Los Angeles/Philadelphia/Boston/Denver (November 16, 1949): 18, 31; Portland/New York City/Chicago/Pittsburgh (November 23, 1949): 17; Chicago/Denver (November 30, 1949): 11; movie pages, *New York Daily News* (November 19, 1949): 24.

41. *HUAC Report*, 44 (see Chapter 5 n4).

CHAPTER 15

1. "New York's 'Finest' Co-Operate in Filming Gun Battle in Wall Street," *Side Street* pressbook, 3, Academy of Motion Picture Arts & Sciences, Core Collection. Universal-International released Jules Dassin's *The Naked City* in 1948.

2. Jean-Claude Missiaen, "A Lesson in Cinema: Interview with Anthony Mann," 46 (see Introduction n2).

3. Farley Granger with Robert Calhoun, *Include Me Out: My Life from Goldwyn to Broadway* (New York: St. Martin's Press, 2007), 84, 88.

4. Rebecca Prime, "Cloaked in Compromise: Jules Dassin's 'Naked' City," in *"Un-American" Hollywood: Politics and Film in the Blacklist Era*, 150 (see Chapter 10 n4).

5. Dialogue and descriptions taken from the motion picture *Side Street* (M-G-M, 1950).

6. Sydney Boehm, *Murder is My Business* screenplay, November 16, 1948, 1. Producers Releasing Corporation distributing the Michael Shayne mystery *Murder Is My Business* in 1946 may have influenced the eventual title change.

7. Boehm, *Murder is My Business* screenplay, November 15, 1948, 1, USC Cinematic Arts Library, M-G-M Collection, *Side Street* (hereafter M-G-M/USC).

8. Ibid., 1.

9. Ibid.

10. Ibid., 2.

11. Ibid.

12. Ibid.

13. Ibid.

14. Boehm, *Murder is My Business* yellow page revisions, November 16, 1948, 2; November 18, 1948, 9–10, M-G-M/USC.

15. Ibid., November 16, 1948, 2.

16. Ibid.

17. Boehm, *Murder is My Business* yellow page revisions, November 18, 1948, 2, M-G-M/USC. The film narration is, "Three hundred and eighty new citizens are being born today in the City of New York. One hundred and sixty-four couples are being married. One hundred and ninety-two persons will die."

18. Boehm, *Murder is My Business* yellow page revisions, November 15, 1948, 4–5; November 18, 1948, 6, M-G-M/USC.

19. Boehm, November 15, 1948, 3–4.

20. Helen Deutsch, *Murder is My Business* yellow page revisions, July 22, 1949, unpaginated, M-G-M/USC.

21. Helen Deutsch, ibid.

22. W. Kendell Jones, M-G-M script report of *Side Street* by Sydney Boehm, November 10, 1948, USC Cinematic Arts Library, M-G-M Collection, *Side Street*, Material Read November 10, 1948; Report Submitted November 17, 1948.

23. *Daily Variety* Production Chart, *Daily Variety* (April 22, 1949): 11; "MGM Saves 75G by Using One Crew on 4 NY Locationings," *Daily Variety* (July 18, 1949): 5. This article does not mention *Adam's Rib*, but Russell Stewart cited the latter film in "Taxi Acrobatics in Wall Street," *New York Times* (May 8, 1949): X5; "Shoot Added Scenes For 'Side Street,'" *Daily Variety* (June 22, 1949): 2.

24. "MGM Borrows Mann To Direct 'Street,'" *Daily Variety* (March 15, 1949): 1; "Larry Parks Set for Metro's 'Side Street,'" *Daily Variety* (March 10, 1949): 1; Eisenschitz, 102–103 (see Chapter 8 n24); "Jean Hagen Signed After Screen Test Is Flown To Studio," *Side Street* pressbook, 6; "Metro Inks Jean Hagen For 'Side Street' Role," *Daily Variety* (April 27, 1949): 1.

25. "Location New York," Industry, *Newsweek* (April 25, 1949), 92, 94.

26. A. H. Weiler, By Way of Report, "Renoir to Direct Films in India—Metro On the Town—Of Pulitzer Prizes," *New York Times* (April 17, 1949): X5. This article provides a production start date of April 27, 1949. The Data for Bulletin of Screen Achievement Records (held in the Margaret Herrick Library) gives a completion date of June 8, 1949; Academy of Motion Picture Arts & Sciences, Core Collection, *Side Street*, Clippings File. The biofilmography in *Cahiers du Cinéma in English* (see Chapter 1 n24) indicates a production length of 32 days (page 55); "Flies Dirigible To Film Skyscrapers in 'Side Street' Shots," *Side Street* pressbook, 6; Stewart, ibid; in early May 1949 *Daily Variety* reported Granger back in Los Angeles from Manhattan filming; "Chatter," *Daily Variety* (May 9, 1949): 2.

27. "Sidewalk Superintendents a Headache," *Side Street* pressbook, 3.

28. "*Side Street* pressbook, ibid.

29. Stewart, ibid; *Side Street* pressbook, ibid; Hedda Hopper, Hollywood, *Hartford Courant* (April 29, 1949): 11.

30. Hopper, Hollywood, *Hartford Courant* (May 12, 1949): 11.

31. Sydney Boehm, April 14, 1949, 122, M-G-M/USC.

32. Uncredited revised narration, *Side Street*, July 25, 1949, 6, M-G-M/USC. Helen Deutsch was still providing script pages on July 20 and 22, 1949.

33. "Metro Has 9 in Prod'n with Ten Ready to Go," *Daily Variety* (November 16, 1949): 4. Pete Harrison reviewed the finished picture at a late 1949 trade-screening: *Harrison's Reports* (December 24, 1949): 206; Hollywood Inside, *Daily Variety* (January 12, 1950): 2. The other delayed M-G-M releases included John Berry's *film noir Tension*.

34. "Sock-Sell Action Fans!," *Side Street* press book, unpaginated, Academy of Motion Picture Arts & Sciences, Core Collection.

35. Ibid.

36. Ibid.

37. Movie pages, *New York Post* (March 23, 1950): 43; *Los Angeles Times* (April 7, 1950): I:24; *Boston Daily Globe [morning edition]* (April 19, 1950): 24; *Chicago Daily Tribune* (April 19, 1950): III:11; *Variety* picture grosses: New York (April 5, 1950): 11; Los Angeles (April 19, 1950): 12; Washington, D.C. (April 26, 1950): 13; Boston/Chicago/Detroit (May 3, 1950), 8–9; Indianapolis (May 17, 1950): 9.

CHAPTER 16

1. Jean-Claude Missiaen, "A Lesson in Cinema: Interview with Anthony Mann," 46 (see Introduction n2).

2. Dialogue and descriptions taken from the motion picture *The Tall Target* (M-G-M, 1951).

3. Douglas Bell, *Oral History With Richard Goldstone* 3 (Beverly Hills: Academy of Motion Picture Arts and Sciences, 1995), 829–30 (hereafter Goldstone).

4. Missiaen, 50.

5. Hedda Hopper, "Colbert Named Star of 'Three Came Home,'" *Los Angeles Times* (March 15, 1949): A6; "2 Films Planned by New Company: Allen and Dembow Setting Up Firm—Duo of Pictures in Color Already Listed," *New York Times* (November 3, 1949): 38; Philip K. Scheuer, "Miriam Hopkins Takes Ruth Warrick's Role; Petty Girl Versus Lana," *Los Angeles Times* (September 2, 1950): 9; Edwin Schallert, "$6,000,000 'Quo Vadis' Production Completed," Hollywood in Review, *Los Angeles Times* (November 5, 1950): D4.

6. Lona Mosk Packer, Reader Report, George Worthing Yates' *The Lonely Road* (undated), May 2, 1946, 1, USC Cinematic Arts Library, M-G-M Collection, *The Tall Target* (hereafter M-G-M/USC).

7. Lydia Remsten, Reader Report, May 25, 1949, George Worthing Yates's *An Instant in the Wind* (May 18, 1949), M-G-M/USC; Yates and Geoffrey Homes, *The Man on the Train*

treatment, June 6, 1949; Yates and Joseph Losey, *The Man on the Train* working outline, June 9, 1949; Losey supplemental notes, June 21, 1949, M-G-M/USC; Goldstone, 813.

8. Thomas F. Brady, "Metro Acquires 2 New Comedies: Studio Buys 'This Is News,' by Horwin, and 'Darling, I'm Stuck,' by Ruth Flippen," *New York Times* (February 1, 1950): 26; Brady, "Sturges Play Set as First Pinza Film: Metro Buys Rights From U.-I. to 'Strictly Dishonorable' for Opera Star's Vehicle," *New York Times* (February 9, 1950): 44; Edwin Schallert, "Ida Lupino Again Has New Find; U-I Acquires Unique British Play," *Los Angeles Times* (February 13, 1950): A7; Shallert, "Moira Shearer Named Andersen Story Star; Wayne, Gaynor New Duo," *Los Angeles Times* (November 14, 1950): B7; Schallert, "Dick Powell Will Star in 'This Is News;' Schor Productions Launched," *Los Angeles Times* (October 25, 1950): A11; Ezra Goodman, "A Mann to Remember" (see Introduction n7); Hedda Hopper, "Dick Powell Prefers Drama of Lincoln Days," *Los Angeles Times* (December 4, 1950), B12; "Powell To 'Train,'" *Daily Variety* (December 4, 1950): 7; Goldstone 1, 47–48; Goldstone's *The Set-Up* filmed between October 13 and November 11, 1948, with sound dubbing taking place on January 6 and 26, 1949; *The Set-Up* Production Files, Box 174P, RKO Studio Records, 3, Performing Arts Special Collections, University of California, Los Angeles. Goldstone was reported arriving at M-G-M at the beginning of 1949: "Goldstone Handed Film Assigned Rapf," *Daily Variety* (February 9, 1949), 1; "Goldstone Handed 'Man on a Train,'" *Daily Variety* (June 10, 1949): 10.

9. Goldstone, 3, 820; *Screen*: 46 (see Introduction n4).

10. *The Narrow Margin* Production Files, Box 189P, RKO Studio Records, ibid.; Inside Stuff-Pictures, *Variety* (January 19, 1949), 14.

11. Goldstone, 827.

12. Ibid., 3, 819.

13. "Hollywood's Oldest Performer is a Fire-Eater with a Will of Iron!," *The Tall Target* pressbook, unpaginated, Academy of Motion Picture Arts & Sciences, Core Collection; Goldstone 1, 51–52.

14. Ibid. (original emphasis).

15. Ibid., 3, 834.

16. *Daily Variety* Production Chart, *Daily Variety* (February 2, 1951): 9; *MGM News*, January 15, 1951, Academy of Motion Picture Arts & Sciences, Core Collection; Short Shorts/Title Changes, *Daily Variety* (January 26, 1951): 10; *Data for Bulletin of Screen Achievement Records* (August 28, 1951), Academy of Motion Picture Arts & Sciences, Core Collection, *The Tall Target*, Microfiche, Clippings.

17. Robert Easton, phone interview with author, March 11, 2011.

18. Ibid.

19. Goldstone, 3, 832; Frank Miller, "Behind the Camera on Thirty Seconds Over Tokyo," Turner Classic Movies website, 2011.

20. Ibid., 830.

21. Ibid., 833.

22. For examples, see Vincente Minnelli's *I Dood It* (M-G-M, 1943) and George Sidney's *Thousands Cheer* (M-G-M, 1943).

23. Michel Ciment, *Conversations with Losey* (London and New York: Methuen, 1985), 90, 402–3.

24. Ciment, ibid. "Goldstone Handed 'Man on the Train,'" *Daily Variety* (June 10, 1949): 10. The July 19, 1950, Art Cohn treatment suggests Lena Horne or Teresa Celli for the role of Rachel, USC, ibid.; "Ruby Dee Signed For Role in MGM 'Train,'" *Daily Variety* (December 27, 1950): 8.

25. George Worthing Yates and Joseph Losey, *The Man on the Train* working outline, June 9, 1949, 1 (M-G-M/USC).

26. Losey Supplementary Notes, June 21, 1949, 2; Script Pages 1–30 by George W. Yates and Joseph Losey, July 12, 1949; Draft by Losey and Yates, July 20, 1949, and September 20, 1949; Art Cohn, *Man on the Train* screenplay, November 7, 1950, M-G-M/USC; Goldstone, 3, 828.

27. Art Cohn, *Man on the Train* treatment, July 19, 1950, 7–8, M-G-M/USC.

28. Art Cohn, ibid.

29. Short Shorts, "Scribbling," *Daily Variety* (July 27, 1950): 11. Art Cohn was killed in the same plane crash that claimed the life of producer Michael Todd on March 28, 1958; "Showman Mike Todd Killed in Fiery Air Crash: Writer Art Cohn and Two Pilots Die Also With Film Producer," *Los Angeles Times* (March 23, 1958): 1.

30. "Put a Man on Title Stilts," *Tall Target* pressbook, unpaginated.

31. "Make Them Reach for Movie Prizes"; "Street Bally—Man Carries Large 'T'"; "Identify 'The Tall Target' (man)"; "Put the Basketball Through 'The Tall Target'"; "Are You A 'Tall Target'?"; "Place Bull's-Eye in Center of 'The Tall Target'"; *Tall Target* pressbook, unpaginated.

32. Movie pages, *Los Angeles Times* (August 22, 1951): A7; *Chicago Daily Tribune* (September 6, 1951): C7; *New York Times* (September 27, 1951): 37; *Boston Daily Globe* (January 1, 1952): 79; *Variety* picture grosses, Los Angeles (August 29, 1951): 8; (September 5, 1951): 10; Chicago (September 12, 1951): 9; (September 19, 1951): 11; Philadelphia (September 19, 1951): 10; New York (October 3, 1951): 9; (October 10, 1951): 9.

33. *Screen*: 48.

CHAPTER 17

1. Dudley Schnabel, *Load* (typewritten version in treatment format), 1–2, USC Cinematic Arts Library, M-G-M Collection, *It's a Big Country*, "Load" (hereafter M-G-M/USC).

2. Schnabel, 6–8.

3. Schnabel, 18–19.

4. Schnabel, 20.

5. Harry Shaw and Ruth Davis, eds., *Americans One and All* (New York and London: Harper and Brothers, 1947); Edwin Schallert, "Schary Will Launch Big Episode Film; Hugh Marlowe Captures Major Role," *Los Angeles Times* (March 15, 1950): B9; Ezra Goodman article (undated; identified in file as *Daily News, Los Angeles*, March 22, 1950) in Anthony Mann clipping files, Margaret Herrick Library.

6. When the project was first announced in March 1950, the attached directors were, in addition to Vidor and Hartman, Robert Z. Leonard, George Cukor, the team of Norman Panama/Melvin Frank, Gerald Mayer, and Roy Rowland; Schallert, ibid.

7. Philip K. Scheuer, "'Multiple Story' Film New Vogue Following Success of 'Quartet,'" *Los Angeles Times* (July 9, 1950): E4.

8. Schallert, "Martin Gabel, Paget, Bel Geddes in '14 Hours;' Hersholt May Do 'Load,'" *Los Angeles Times* (May 25, 1950): B11; "Marshall Thompson Is Set for Top Role," *MGM News,* April 17, 1950, Academy of Motion Picture Arts & Sciences, Core Collection; Schallert, "Jean Hersholt Teamed With New Stage Find; Whorf Writes Lunt Play," *Los Angeles Times* (June 6, 1950): 19; Schallert, Hollywood in Review, "Two Local Girls 'Arrive' in Films: Jean Hersholt Returns to Hollywood in 'Load,'" *Los Angeles Times* (June 11, 1950), D10; Scheuer, ibid; *Daily Variety* Production Chart, *Daily Variety* (June 23, 1950): 11 and (June 30, 1950): 15.

9. Luther Davis *Load* script, December 12, 1949, 7, M-G-M/USC.

10. Luther Davis *Load* script, December 12, 1949, 9–10.

11. Ibid., 10.

12. Ibid., 12–13.

13. Ibid., 13–14.

14. Ibid., 15.

15. Ibid., 16–17.

16. Ibid., 17. ("Eye-tie" is slang for Italian.)

17. Davis, December 12, 1949 (dated December 14, 1949), 18–20.

18. Ibid., 21–22.

19. Ibid.

20. Davis, March 27, 1950, 15.

21. Ibid., 16.

22. Ibid., 17.

23. Ibid.

24. Ibid., 18.

25. Ibid., 19

26. Ibid., 19–20.

27. Davis, April 10, 1950, 17. Silence and then police sirens follow Mrs. Anderson exclaiming "Nils!"; Davis, April 12, 1950.

28. Scheuer, "Tony Favors Camera Over Film Dialogue" (see Introduction n7).

29. Luther Davis, *Load* screenplays, May 31, 1950 (with June 1, 1950 revisions), June 12, 1950, 1–3, USC Cinematic Arts Library, M-G-M Collection, *It's A Big Country*, "Load" O/K "It's A Big Country" #2.

30. Davis, June 1, 1950, 1–3.

31. Ibid.

32. Davis, June 12, 1950, 6–8.

33. Ibid., 16.

34. Ibid., 16–18.

35. Ibid., 19.

36. Ibid., 19–20.

POSTSCRIPT

1. Philip K. Scheuer, "Miriam Hopkins Takes Ruth Warrick's Role; Petty Girl Versus Lana," *Los Angeles Times* (September 2, 1950): 9; Biofilmography of Anthony Mann (see Chapter 1 n24): 56; Ezra Goodman, "A Mann To Remember" (see Introduction n7).

2. Goodman, ibid.

3. *The 1966 Film Daily Year Book of Motion Pictures*, 103.

4. Chester B. Bahn, "The Industry's Year: Corporate and Executive," in *The 1960 Film Daily Year Book of Motion Pictures*, 69.

5. The dates these Mann associates appeared before HUAC were as follows: Larry Parks and Howard da Silva, March 21, 1951; Will Geer, April 11, 1951; Victor Kilian, April 13, 1951; Jeff Corey, September 21, 1951; Nedrick Young, April 8, 1953. Leo Townsend named Joseph Losey on September 18, 1951. Writer Richard Collins was the first to name Gordon Kahn before HUAC, on April 12, 1951; *Film Culture* 50–51: 1 and *HUAC report*, 40, 44–45, 48–49 (see Chapter 5 n4); Humphries, 145 (see Chapter 2 n39); Kahn (see Chapter 5 n4).

6. Humphries, 150. The 2007 documentary *Who Is Norman Lloyd?* addresses this aspect of the actor's career.

7. Ibid., 145; Comas (see Chapter 1 n27), 155–56; Patrick McGilligan and Paul Buhle, *Tender Comrades: A Backstory of the Hollywood Blacklist* (New York: St. Martin's Griffin, 1997), 52; McGilligan, *Backstory 2: Interviews with Screenwriters of the 1940s and 1950s* (see Chapter 1 n1), 157–60.

8. Hoberman, 102–104 (see Chapter 14 n22). Hoberman states that the film was still known in March 1949 by its working title *The Bastille* and that producer Walter Wanger was inspired to change the title to *Reign of Terror* after reading about "Communist-influenced culture critics" using "an intellectual reign of terror" to pressure artists into supporting the Cultural and Scientific Conference on World Peace (held March 25–27, 1949, at the Waldorf-Astoria Hotel in Manhattan). In truth, *Reign of Terror* was announced under that title more than a month prior to its August 17, 1948, production start; Thomas F. Brady, "U-I to Make Film of 'Night Watch': Buckner's Novel on Palestine Purchased by the Studio—Author Will Produce," *New York Times* (July 6, 1948): 20.

9. HUAC report, 42; Norma Barzman, *The Red and the Blacklist: The Intimate Memoir of a Hollywood Expatriate* (New York: Thunder's Mouth Press/Nation Books: 2003), chapters 24–27. Those identifying Barzman to HUAC were Leo Townsend (September 18, 1951), Martin Berkeley (September 19, 1951), Charles Daggett (January 21, 1952), Stanley Roberts (May 20, 1952), Roy Huggins (September 29, 1952), and George Glass (January 21, 1952).

10. "Director, Actress Plan 2nd Wedding," *Los Angeles Times* (August 30, 1957): B1; Edwin Schallert, "Sarita Montiel Vies With Ava for Alba Role; Rennie, L'Amour in Deal," *Los Angeles Times* (August 15, 1957): B9; "Goya's Life Story Planned as Film: Anthony Mann Will Direct Picture in Spain—Hughes Associate Lists 3 Movies," *New York Times* (August 15, 1957): 18.

11. "Anthony Mann, 60, A Movie Director: Filmmaker Who Favored Westerns Dies in Berlin," *New York Times* (April 30, 1967): 86; "Film Producer Anthony Mann Dies in Berlin," *Los Angeles Times* (April 30, 1967): F4; Norma Barzman confirms Mann and Kuzko

were romantically involved at the time *The Ceremony* was being discussed as his next project: Barzman, 306.

12. Louis Pelegrine, "Director Is the Top Banana, Says Mann," *Film Daily* (March 8, 1966): 1, 4.

13. Ibid.

14. A. H. Weiler, By Way of Report: "Directors List a Variety of Independent Films," *New York Times* (April 22, 1962): X7.

15. Barzman, ibid; *Monthly Film Bulletin* 31, no. 364 (May 1964): 67–68. In a June 9, 2011, phone interview, Norma Barzman discussed Mann's interest in her husband's screenplay and how embarrassed she was with Harvey's film.

16. Ibid.

17. Pelegrine, ibid. "'Bond-Size' Films Back to Reality, Mann Prophesies," *Variety* (April 19, 1967): 5; "'Great Train Robbery' Anthony Mann's Next," *Hollywood Reporter* (October 14, 1965): 2.

18. "Harvey Will Direct Final 'Aspic' Scenes," *Los Angeles Times* (May 4, 1967): E15; Anne Sinai, *Reach for the Top: The Turbulent Life of Laurence Harvey* (Lanham, Maryland, and Oxford: The Scarecrow Press, 2003), 320. This book is a questionable source considering how Mann is described as being "in his mid-sixties" at the time of his death (319).

19. *A Dandy in Aspic* was actually Mann's fortieth film as director.

20. *Variety*, ibid.

21. Missiaen: 46 (see Introduction n2).

FILMOGRAPHY

1. Internet Movie Database.
2. Ibid.
3. Ibid.
4. *Call Bureau Cast Sheets* (Margaret Herrick Library).
5. Internet Movie Database.
6. Ibid.
7. Ibid.
8. Ibid.
9. Ibid.
10. Ibid.
11. Ibid.
12. Ibid.
13. Ibid.
14. Data for Bulletin of Screen Achievement Records (November 18, 1944) (Margaret Herrick Library).
15. This is how the name appears in the film's opening credits. Internet Movie Database lists technician as "James A. Stewart."
16. Call Bureau Cast Sheets spelling.

17. Call Bureau Cast Sheets spelling. IMDB lists actress as "Almira Sessions."
18. Call Bureau Cast Sheets spelling.
19. Internet Movie Database.
20. Ibid.
21. Ibid.
22. Ibid.
23. Ibid.
24. Ibid.
25. Ibid.
26. Ibid.
27. Ibid.
28. Ibid.
29. Ibid.
30. Ibid.
31. The character's name is "Pat Regan" in the end credits and in *Call Bureau Cast Sheets*, but she is referred to as "Pat Cameron" in the film.
32. *Daily News Los Angeles* (December 9, 1948), Academy of Motion Picture Arts & Sciences, Core Collection, *He Walked By Night*, Clippings.
33. Internet Movie Database.
34. *Data for Bulletin of Screen Achievement Records* (November 1, 1948)
35. Internet Movie Database.
36. Ibid.
37. Ibid.
38. Ibid.
39. Ibid.
40. Ibid.
41. Ibid.
42. Ibid.
43. Ibid.
44. Ibid.
45. Ibid.
46. Spelling from *Call Bureau Cast Sheets* (1949).
47. *Call Bureau Cast Sheets* (1949).
48. Hedda Hopper, Looking at Hollywood, *Chicago Daily Tribune* (May 31, 1949): A4.
49. Ibid.
50. Ibid.
51. Ibid.
52. Internet Movie Database.
53. *Data for Bulletin of Screen Achievement Records* (August 28, 1951).
54. Internet Movie Database.
55. Ibid.
56. Ibid.
57. Ibid.
58. Ibid.

58. Ibid.
59. Ibid.
60. Ibid.
61. Ibid.
62. Ibid.
63. Ibid.
64. Ibid.
65. Ibid.
66. Ibid.
67. Ibid.
68. Ibid.
69. Ibid.
70. Ibid.
71. Ibid.
72. Ibid.
73. Ibid.
74. Ibid.

ARCHIVAL SOURCES

ACADEMY OF MOTION PICTURE ARTS AND SCIENCES MARGARET HERRICK LIBRARY, BEVERLY HILLS

Data for Bulletin of Screen Achievement Records
Motion Picture Association of America, Production Code Administration records
Paramount Pictures production records
Turner and Shelton papers
Files on: Anthony Mann and his films, exhibitor press books, *To Men as They Need . . .* film treatment, *He Walked By Night* and *Desperate* screenplays
Daily Variety, Film Daily

CHARLES F. CUMMINGS NEW JERSEY INFORMATION CENTER/THE NEWARK PUBLIC LIBRARY SYSTEM, NEWARK, NEW YORK

Newark Evening News

FORTY-SECOND STREET LIBRARY/NEW YORK PUBLIC LIBRARY SYSTEM, NEW YORK

ProQuest newspaper database (*New York Times, Los Angeles Times, Boston Daily Globe, Chicago Daily Tribune, Atlanta Constitution*)
Variety, New York Times, New York Post, New York Herald Tribune, New York Journal-American, San Francisco Chronicle, Time, Newsweek (microfilm)
Ernesto Galarza bracero report (microfiche)
Manhattan city and telephone directories (microfilm)

LIBRARY OF CONGRESS, WASHINGTON, D.C.

NBC-TV schedules and teleplays (1939–40)
Newspaper microfilm collection
Collier's magazine

LOCUST VALLEY HISTORICAL SOCIETY/LOCUST VALLEY LIBRARY, LOCUST VALLEY, NEW YORK

Red Barn Theatre programs

NEW YORK PUBLIC LIBRARY FOR THE PERFORMING ARTS, NEW YORK

Hallie Flanagan papers
Programs and scrapbooks for Anton Bundsmann plays
Anthologie du cinéma, Burns Mantle's *The Best Plays* editions, *Cahiers du Cinéma*, Collection of Newspaper Clippings of Moving Picture Criticism, *Daily Variety*, *Film Dope*, *Film Literature Index (1973–2004)*, *Hollywood Reporter*, *Positif*, *Quarterly Review of Film and Video*, *Screen: The Journal of the Society for Education in Film and Television*, *Sight and Sound*, *Variety*

PERFORMING ARTS SPECIAL COLLECTIONS, UNIVERSITY OF CALIFORNIA, LOS ANGELES

RKO Studio Records
Flight and *Follow Me Quietly* film treatments
Two O'Clock Courage, Desperate, Follow Me Quietly screenplays
Production files for *Two O'Clock Courage, Desparate, Fllow Me Quietly, The Set-Up, The Narrow Margin, The Devil Thumbs a Ride,* and *Born to Kill*

CINEMATIC ARTS LIBRARY, SPECIAL COLLECTIONS, UNIVERSITY OF SOUTHERN CALIFORNIA, LOS ANGELES

Edward Small Collection
T-Men and *Raw Deal* screenplays
M-G-M Collection (*Border Incident, Side Street, The Tall Target, Load* screenplays)

WESTFIELD MEMORIAL LIBRARY, WESTFIELD, NEW JERSEY

Westfield Leader

WISCONSIN CENTER FOR FILM AND THEATER RESEARCH, MADISON

Eagle-Lion papers

BIBLIOGRAPHY

Alton, John. *Painting with Light.* Reprint. Berkeley/Los Angeles/London: University of California Press, 1995.

The American Film Institute Catalogue of Motion Pictures Produced in the United States: Feature Films, 1931–1940, Film Entries, A-L. Berkeley/Los Angeles/Oxford: University of California Press, 1993.

Armstrong, Arnold B., and Audrey Ashley. *Corkscrew Alley.* Film treatment, 1946.

Atlas, Dorothy, and Anthony Mann. *Flight.* Film treatment, 1946.

Atlas, Leopold. *Corkscrew Alley.* Various 1947 screenplay drafts. Eagle-Lion Films, RKO Radio Pictures.

Atlas, Leopold. *See! Hear! A Visual Digest of the Month, Issue No. 1—March 24, 1940.* NBC teleplay, 1940.

Baer, D. Richard, ed. *Harrison's Reports Film Review Index 1919–1962, Volume 15.* Hollywood, CA: Hollywood Film Archive, 1995.

Barzman, Norma. *The Red and the Blacklist: The Intimate Memoir of a Hollywood Expatriate.* New York: Thunder's Mouth Press/Nation Books, 2003.

Basinger, Jeanine. *Anthony Mann.* Middletown, CT: Wesleyan University Press, 1979, 2007.

Baum, Vicki. "Big Shot." *Collier's,* September 19, 1936.

Behlmer, Rudy. *Shoot the Rehearsal! Behind the Scenes with Assistant Director Reggie Callow.* Lanham/Toronto/Plymouth, UK: The Scarecrow Press, 2010.

Bell, Douglas. *Oral History With Richard Goldstone.* Beverly Hills: Academy of Motion Picture Arts and Sciences, 1995.

Blavatsky, H. P. *The Key to Theosophy Being a Clear Exposition, in the Form of Question and Answer, of the Ethics, Science and Philosophy for the Study of which the Theosophical Society Has Been Founded.* London and New York: The Theosophical Publishing Company, 1889.

Boehm, Sydney. *Murder is My Business.* Various screenplay drafts. M-G-M, 1948, 1949.

Boucicault, Dion. *The Streets of New York; Or, Poverty is No Crime.* NBC teleplay adaptation, 1939.

Brownlow, Kevin. *The Parade's Gone By. . . .* Berkeley/Los Angeles/London: University of California Press, 1968.

Ciment, Michel. *Conversations with Losey.* London and New York: Methuen, 1985.

Cohn, Art. *Man on the Train.* M-G-M treatment, 1950.

Comas, Ángel. *Anthony Mann.* Madrid: T & B Editores, 2004.

Conkle, E. P. *Prologue to Glory.* NBC teleplay, 1940.

Crowe, Cameron. *Conversations with Wilder.* New York: Alfred A. Knopf, 1999.

Darby, William. *Anthony Mann: The Film Career.* Jefferson, NC, and London: McFarland & Company, 2009.

Davis, Luther. *Load*. Various screenplay drafts. M-G-M, 1949, 1950.
Eisenschitz, Bernard. *Nicholas Ray: An American Journey*. Translated by Tom Milne. London/Boston: Faber and Faber, 1993, 1996.
Eliot, Marc. *Jimmy Stewart: A Biography*. New York: Random House, 2006.
The 1932 Film Daily Year Book of Motion Pictures
The 1945 Film Daily Year Book of Motion Pictures
The 1946 Film Daily Year Book of Motion Pictures
The 1947 Film Daily Year Book of Motion Pictures
The 1960 Film Daily Year Book of Motion Pictures
The 1966 Film Daily Year Book of Motion Pictures
Fleischer, Richard. *Just Tell Me When to Cry: A Memoir*. New York: Carroll & Graf Publishers, 1993.
Galarza, Ernesto. *Strangers in Our Fields (Second Edition), Based on a Report Regarding Compliance with the Contractual, Legal and Civil Rights of Mexican Agricultural Contract Labor in the United States, Made Possible Through a Grant-in-Aid from The Fund for the Republic*. Washington, D.C.: Joint United States-Mexico Trade Union Committee, 1956.
Ginty, E. B. *Missouri Legend*. NBC teleplay, 1939.
Granger, Farley, with Robert Calhoun. *Include Me Out: My Life from Goldwyn to Broadway*. New York: St. Martin's Press, 2007.
Greenwalt, Emmett A. *The Point Loma Community in California, 1897–1942: A Theoretical Experiment*. Berkeley: University of California Press, 1955.
Hargrove, Large, and Anthony Mann. *To Men As They Need. . . .* Film treatment, 1942.
Haver, Ronald. *David O. Selznick's Hollywood*. New York: Bonanza Books, 1980.
Heylin, Clinton. *Despite the System: Orson Welles Versus the Hollywood Studios*. Edinburgh/New York/Melbourne: Canongate Books, 2005.
Higgins, John C. *Border Incident*. M-G-M screenplay drafts, 1949.
———. *Border Patrol*. M-G-M screenplay drafts, 1948, 1949.
Higgins, John C. *The L.A. Investigator*. Eagle-Lion Films screenplay, 1948.
Hoberman, J. *An Army of Phantoms: American Movies and the Making of the Cold War*. New York and London: The New Press, 2011.
Howard, Sidney. *Ode to Liberty*. NBC teleplay, 1940.
Humphries, Reynold. *Hollywood's Blacklists: A Political and Cultural History*. Edinburgh: Edinburgh University Press, 2008, 2010.
Irey, Elmer L., and William J. Slocum. *The Tax Dodgers: The Inside Story of the T-Men's War with America's Political and Underworld Hoodlums*. New York: Greenberg, 1948.
Jerome, Helen. *Charlotte Corday*. NBC teleplay, 1940.
Koszarski, Richard, ed. *Hollywood Directors 1941–1976*. Oxford/London/New York: Oxford University Press, 1977.
———. *Hollywood on the Hudson: Film and Television in New York from Griffith to Sarnoff*. New Brunswick, NJ: Rutgers University Press, 2008.
Krutnik, Frank, Steve Neale, Brian Neve, and Peter Stanfield, eds. *"Un-American" Hollywood: Politics and Film in the Blacklist Era*. New Brunswick, NJ, and London: Rutgers University Press, 2007.

Leiter, Samuel L. *The Encyclopedia of the New York Stage, 1930–1940*. New York/Westport, CT/London: Greenwood Press, 1989.
Lennig, Arthur. *Stroheim*. Lexington, KY: University Press of Kentucky, 2000.
Mantle, Burns. *The Best Plays of 1924–1925*. New York: Dodd Mead and Co., 1942.
———. *The Best Plays of 1928–29*. New York: Dodd Mead and Co., 1929.
———. *The Best Plays of 1933–34*. New York: Dodd, Mead and Company, 1934.
———. *The Best Plays of 1934–35*. New York: Dodd, Mead and Company, 1944.
———. *The Best Plays of 1936–37*. New York: Dodd, Mead and Company, 1937.
———. *The Best Plays of 1938–39*. New York: Dodd, Mead and Company, 1939.
Martin, Len D. *The Republic Pictures Checklist: Features, Serials, Cartoons, Short Subjects and Training Films of Republic Pictures Corporation, 1935–1959*. Jefferson, NC, and London: McFarland & Company, 1998.
McCarthy, Todd, and Charles Flynn, eds. *King of the Bs: Working Within the Hollywood System: An Anthology of Film History and Criticism*. New York: E. P. Dutton and Co., 1975.
McGilligan, Patrick. *Backstory 2: Interviews with Screenwriters of the 1940s and 1950s*. Berkeley/Los Angeles/Oxford: University of California Press, 1991.
———. *Nicholas Ray: The Glorious Failure of an American Director*. New York: imprint/ HarperCollins/itbooks, 2011.
———, and Paul Buhle. *Tender Comrades: A Backstory of the Hollywood Blacklist*. New York: St. Martin's Griffin, 1997.
Missiaen, Jean-Claude. *Anthony Mann*. Paris: Éditions Universitaires, 1964.
The 1941–42 Motion Picture Almanac. New York: Quigley Publishing.
The 1943–44 Motion Picture Almanac. New York: Quigley Publishing.
The 1953–54 Motion Picture Almanac. New York: Quigley Publishing.
Okuda, Ted. *Grand National, Producers Releasing Corporation, and Screen Guild/Lippert: Complete Filmographies with Studio Histories*. Jefferson, NC, and London: McFarland & Company, 1989.
Pappas, Charles. *It's a Bitter Little World: The Smartest Toughest Nastiest Quotes from Film Noir*. Canada: F + W Publications, Inc., 2005.
Powell, Michael. *A Life in Movies: An Autobiography*. New York: Alfred A. Knopf, 1987.
Reinhart, Mark S. *Abraham Lincoln on Screen: Fictional and Documentary Portrayals on Film and Television*. Jefferson, NC, and London: McFarland and Company, 2009.
Robson, Eddie. *Film Noir*. London: Virgin Books, 2005.
Rosenwald, Francis, and Anthony Mann. *Follow Me Quietly*. Film treatment, 1947.
Sadoul, Georges. *Dictionary of Film Makers*. Translated by Peter Morris. Berkeley and Los Angeles: University of California Press, 1972.
Scaduto, Anthony. *Scapegoat: The Lonesome Death of Bruno Richard Hauptmann*. New York: G. P. Putnam's Sons, 1976.
Schary, Dore. *Heyday: An Autobiography*. Boston and Toronto: Little, Brown and Company, 1979.
Schnabel, Dudley. "Load." *The Midland Magazine*, May 1931.
Shaw, Harry, and Ruth Davis, eds. *Americans One and All*. New York and London: Harper and Brothers, 1947.

Sinai, Anne. *Reach for the Top: The Turbulent Life of Laurence Harvey*. Lanham, Maryland, and Oxford: The Scarecrow Press, 2003.

Sturges, Preston. *Preston Sturges by Preston Sturges: His Life in His Words*. Edited by Sandy Sturges. New York/London/Toronto/Sydney/Tokyo/Singapore: Simon and Schuster, 1990.

Tingley, Katherine, ed. *Century Path: A Magazine Devoted to the Brotherhood of Humanity, the Promulgation of Theosophy and The Study of Ancient and Modern Ethics, Philosophy, Science, and Art*. 1906–1910 issues, Google Books.

Truffaut, François, with Helen G. Scott. *Hitchcock*. New York: Touchstone/Simon and Schuster, 1967.

Wakeman, John, ed. *World Film Directors, Vol I: 1890–1945*. New York: The H. W. Wilson Company, 1987.

Wallace, Edgar. *A Criminal at Large*. NBC teleplay, 1939.

Yates, George Worthing, and Joseph Losey. *The Man on the Train*. M-G-M working outline, 1949.

Zuckerman, George. *Border Patrol*. M-G-M film treatment and screenplay, 1947.

Internet Broadway Database: www.ibdb.com
Internet Movie Database: www.imdb.com
Internet Speculative Fiction Database: www.isfdb.org
http://archive.wmlnj.org/TheWestfieldLeader/1939/
Wikipedia.com

INDEX

Page numbers in **bold** indicate an illustration.

Abbott, Bud, 59
Abel, Walter, 52, 54
Academy Awards, 101
Adam's Rib (1949), 204, 293n23
Adam-12 (TV), 139
Adventures of Tom Sawyer, The (1938 film), 22–23
Alcestis (play), 15, **16**
Alfred Hitchcock Presents, 242, 273n9
All Paris Knows (1934 staging), 19
Allen, Lester, 62
Allied Artists, 134, 162
Altman, Robert, 278n8
Alton, John, 204, 215; and *Border Incident*, 171–72, 181, 183–84, 186, 190; on cinematography, 108–9, 126; and *Devil's Doorway*, 190; and *He Walked By Night*, 140, 143, 144, 146–47, 149, 151; and Mann, 104, 204, 215; other films photographed by, 46, 50, 103, 229; and *Raw Deal*, 120, 122, 125, 126–27, 130–31; and *T-Men*, 101, 103–4, **103**, 106–7, 108–9, 113–14, 282–83n32
American in Paris, An (1951), 224
American Tobacco Company, 47
Americans One and All, 228
Anderson, Eddie, 59
Anti-trust decrees, 241–42
Antrim, Harry, 174
Are Husbands Necessary? (1942), 42
Armstrong, Arnold B., 117
Ashley, Audrey, 117
Assigned to Danger (1948), 134
Astaire, Fred, 42, 197

Atlantic City (1944), 50
Atlas, Dorothy, 75, 78, 79
Atlas, Leopold: blacklisting of, 134, 243; *Raw Deal* screenplay of, 119, 122, 128, 284n7; *See! Hear!* teleplay, 29–30
Atwill, Lionel, 16
August, Jan, 116

Bachelor and the Bobby-Soxer, The (1947), 88
Ball, Lucille, 189
Bamboo Blonde, The (1946), 47, 75, 80, 84
Bari, Lynn, 142
Barkleys of Broadway, The (1949), 197
Barrett, Edith, **44**, 45
Barrymore, Ethel, 229
Bart, Jean, 16
Barzman, Ben, 21, 243, 245, 298n9, 299n15
Barzman, Norma, 21, 245, 298n11, 299n15
Basehart, Richard, 118, **135**, 138, 142, 151, 152, 286n13
Basinger, Jeanine, 161, 265n19, 266n24, 266–67n27, 267n1, 267n6, 269n20
Bates, Florence, 221
Baum, Vicki, 61, 275n1
Beaumont, Hugh, **89**, 95, 96
Bedoya, Alfonso, 184
Behind Locked Doors (1948), 96–97
Behlmer, Rudy, 111–12
Bellaver, Harry, 202
Bend of the River (1952), 36, 243
Bennett, Joan, 66
Berkeley, Martin, 298n9
Berle, Milton, 24

Bernhardt, Curtis, 204
Between Midnight and Dawn (1950), 84
Big Blow (1938 play), 24, 221
Big Bluff, The (1955), 73
Big Heat, The (1953), 129, 193
Big Shot (1936 short story), 61
Bissell, Whit, 130, 142, 143
Bitsch, Charles, 267n1, 267n6
Black, Jean Ferguson, 19
Black Book, The (1949), 28, 140, 151, 161, 171, 184, 216, 242, 243, 287n32, 298n8
Black Dragons (1942), 68
Black Hand (1950), 209, 215
Black Tuesday (1954), 193
Blankfort, Henry, 112–13, 282n27
Blavatsky, Helena, 10
Blind Love (1935 film treatment), 275n1
Blood on the Moon (1948), 162
Blue Angel, The (1930), 60
Blue Peter, The (1925 play), 16
Bluebeard (1944), 92
Body and Soul (1947), 99, 281n18
Boehm, Sydney, 192–96, 198, 202, 207–8
Boetticher, Budd, 96
Bogart, Humphrey, 287n25
Bogdanovich, Peter, 92
Bond, Ward, 54
Boomerang! (1947), 102, 281n3
Border Incident (1949), 242; censorship, 186, 188; production, 6, 182–83, 214, 292n30; publicity and distribution, 189; screenplay, 172, 174, 176–79, 292n37
Border Patrol. See *Border Incident*
Born to Kill (1947), 81, 278n12
Borzage, Frank, 46
Boston Strangler, The (1968), 155
Boucicault, Dion, 17, 26
Box office statistics, 75, 241, 277n10
Boxwell, David, 269n20
Boy With Green Hair, The (1948), 214, 243
Bracero program, 174–76
Brady, Scott, 138, **141**, 142
Brahm, John, 280n8

Brando, Marlon, 181
Brasselle, Keefe, 91
Breen, Joseph, Jr.: and *Border Incident*, 179; and *He Walked By Night*, 148; and *Railroaded!*, 94; and *Raw Deal*, 128
Breen, Joseph I., Sr.: and *Border Incident*, 179, 186; and *Desperate*, 79–80, 81–83, 85, 279n16, 279n18, 279n20; and *Dr. Broadway*, 41–42; and *The Great Flamarion*, 65, 68, 276n6, 276n14; and *He Walked By Night*, 148, 151; and *Railroaded!*, 93–95, 96, 97, 98; and *Raw Deal*, 121, 122–24, 127, 128, 130; and *Strange Impersonation*, 71–72, 73; and *Strangers in the Night*, 46; and *T-Men*, 110; and *Two O'Clock Courage*, 56
Brewster's Millions (1945), 68
Bribe, The (1949), 204
Brickner, George, 113, 282n27
Bride the Sun Shines On, The (1931 play), 17
Bridge of San Luis Rey, The (1944 film), 50
Brigham, Richard, 141
Bright Honor (1936 play), 22
Bring on the Girls (1945), 69
Brion, Patrick, 140
Broadway (1942), 42
Brodie, Steve, **76**, 77, 84, 200
Bronston, Samuel, 244
Brooks, Jean, 275n15
Brown, Charles D., **89**, 95
Brown, Clarence, 228–29
Brown, Katharine (Kay), 22
Brute Force (1947), 87, 115, 283n40
Bundsman, Emile Anton. See Bundsmann, Anton
Bundsmann, Anton: childhood, 10–15, **16**, 265n19–20; confusion about birth date of, 264n3; early acting work, 15–17; early job experiences, 15, 266n23; and Federal Theatre Project, 20, 23–24; Lomaland experiences, 13–15; Maplewood Theatre directing, 24; marriages, 16–17, 266n27;

name change, 36; NBC television work, 24–30; Paramount hiring, 31; politics of, 21, 31; on quitting acting, 17; Red Barn Theatre directing, 19; and Selznick International Pictures, 22–23, 45; stage directing work, 19–24, 27, 30, 266n24, 267n1; and Preston Sturges, 32–33. *See also* Mann, Anthony

Stage and television direction of:
All Paris Knows, 19; *Big Blow*, 24; *Charlotte Corday*, 28; *The Cherokee Night*, 20–21; *Coward Shoes-Fashion Show*, 26; *A Criminal at Large*, 27–28; *Dulcy*, 15–16; *Haiti*, 23; *Jane Eyre*, 27; *Little Women*, 27; *Missouri Legend*, 26; *New Faces of 1936*, 20, 72; *Oddities in Hatwear*, 25; *Ode to Liberty*, 30; *Our Town*, 24; *Pinocchio*, 28; *Prologue to Glory*, 28–29; *See! Hear! . . .*, 29–30; *So Proudly We Hail*, 21–22; *So This Is New York*, 25; *The Streets of New York . . .*, 26–27; *Thunder on the Left*, 19; *We Die Exquisitely*, 19

Bundsmann, Emil Theodore (father), 12–13, 15, 265n12
Bundsmann, Nina (daughter). See Mann, Nina
Bundsmann, Toni (daughter), 17, 266n27
Burgess, Gelett, 52
Burr, Raymond, 77, **81**, 117, 119, 125, 247, 284n19

Cahiers du cinéma, 143, 266n24, 267n1, 267n6
Calhern, Louis, 240
Call Northside 777 (1948), 90, 97, 99, 100
Callow, Reggie, 263n9
Cameron, Rod, 37
Canon City (1948), 141, 148
Capone, Al, 105, 112
Cardwell, James, 138
Carey, Macdonald, **34**, 35, 37, 38, 39
Carlito's Way (1993), 181

Case of the Frightened Lady, The (1931 play). See *Criminal at Large, A*
Castle, Don, 162
Catholic Legion of Decency, 41
Cavalcanti, Alberto, 87
Celli, Teresa, 184, 296n24
Century Path magazine, 12
Ceremony, The (1963 film), 245, 246, 298–99n11, 299n15
CFI (Consolidated Film Industries), 47
Chabrol, Claude, 267n1, 267n6
Challee, William, 82
Challis, Christopher, 246
Champagne for Caesar (1950), 209
Chandler, George, 71
Chaplin Studios, 67
Charlotte Corday (1940 TV), 28
Chase, Borden, 36, 43
Chatterton, Ruth, 24
Cherokee Night, The (1936 play), 20–21, **21**, 221
Chicago Times, 89
Chienne, La (1931), 37, 60
Children of Divorce (1927), 142
Christians, Mady, 30
Churchill, Robert B., 113, 282n27
Ciannelli, Eduardo (Edward), 36, 39
Cimarron (1931), 53
Cimarron (1960), 38, 53, 224, 244
Ciment, Michel, 219
Cinecittà, 241
Cinémathèque Français, 140
City That Never Sleeps (1953), 168
Civil War (1861–65), 219
Clark, Maurice, 23
Clash by Night (1952), 281n2
Cobb, Lee J., 243
Coca, Imogene, 20
Cohn, Art, 220, 222, 296n24, 296n29
Cohn, Harry, 47, 245
Cohn, Joan, 245
Collier's Magazine, 61
Collins, Richard, 298n5

Columbia Pictures, 23, 47, 50, 84, 142, 169, 189, 198, 224, 244, 245, 280n8
Comas, Ángel, 267n27, 268n13, 278n11
Communist Party USA, 103, 242
Communist Political Association, 30
Compulsion (1959 film), 73
Conkle, E. P., 29
Connelly, Marc, 15
Conrad, William, 106
Consolidated Film Industries (CFI), 47
Conspirators, The (1944), 50
Constant Nymph, The (1943), 71
Converse, Peggy, **89**, 90
Conway, Tom, 51, **51**, 54, 57
Cooper, Clancy, 29, **89**, 94
Cooper, Gary, 243, 244
Corey, Jeff, 156, 242, 298n5
Corey, Wendell, 14
Corkscrew Alley (treatment), 117–18, 122. See also *Raw Deal*
Costello, Lou, 59
Cotton, Will, 17
Coulouris, George, 27
Courtenay, Tom, 246
Coward, Nöel, 94
Coward Shoes-Fashion Show (1940 TV), 26
Craig, James, 199
Criminal at Large, A (1939 TV), 27–28
Crimson Kimono, The (1959), 105
Crisp, Donald, 243
Cromwell, John, 84
Cromwell, Richard, 22
Cronenberg, David, 110
Crosby, Bing, 42
Crossfire (1947), 162, 180
Crowe, Cameron, 49
Crowther, Bosley, 7
Cruze, James, 65
Cry Terror! (1958), 168
Cukor, George, 204, 297n6
Cultural and Scientific Conference on World Peace (1949), 298n8
Cummings, Robert, 99
Cynthia (1947), 171

da Silva, Howard, 186, 190, 242, 298n5
Daggett, Charles, 298n9
Daily Variety, 49, 73, 181, 272n14, 273n9, 280n15, 283n36, 287n26, 287n32, 293n26. See also *Variety*
Daily Worker, The, 103
Dandy in Aspic, A (1968 film), 209, 244, 246–47, 299n19
Darby, William, 161, 265n19, 267n27, 269n20, 289n19
Dassin, Jules, 193, 283n40, 292n1
Davies, Marion, 20
Davis, Bette, 73
Davis, Jefferson, 212
Davis, Luther, 229, 230–35, 240
Davis, Nancy, 229
De Palma, Brian, 181
Deadly Is the Female (*Gun Crazy*) (1949), 77
Dee, Ruby, **210**, 218, 219, 220, 221–22
Dekker, Albert, 242
DeMille, Cecil B., 38
Desperate (1947), 77, 128; censorship, 79–80, 81, 82, 83, 85, 279n16, 279n18, 279n20; production, 80–82, 84–85, 92, 112, 180, 278n11; publicity and distribution, 87–88, 99; screenplay, 79–80, 139, 160, 162, 193, 200–201; screenplay treatment, 75, 78–79, 278n7
Detour (1945), 47, 92
Deutsch, Helen, 198, 294n32
Devil Thumbs a Ride, The (1947), 81, 278n12
Devil's Doorway (1950), 6, 21, 171, 190, 243
Dick Tracy film series, 274n4
Dietrich, Marlene, 99
Dillinger (1945), 83–84
Dionne Quintuplets, 20
Diskant, George E., 84
Disney, Walt, 58, 141
Dmytryk, Edward, 155, 242
Docks of New York (1945), 68
Doctor and the Girl, The (1949), 204
Donahoe, Jack, 136–37

Donen, Stanley, 204
Double Indemnity (1944), 63
Dougherty, Eugene, 123
Douglas, Gordon, 84
Down Three Dark Streets (1954), 282n11
Down to Earth (1947), 88
Dr. Broadway (1942): Borden Chase stories, 36, 43; censorship, 41–42; production, 33, 37–41; publicity and distribution, 42–43; reviews of, 40, 272n14
Dragnet (TV series), 138
Dreier, Hans, 37
Dreyer, Carl Theodore, 23
Druten, John Van, 19
Du Bois, William (W. E. B.), 23
Duke Ellington Orchestra, 50
Dulcy (1924 play), 15–16
Duncan, Isadora, 32
Dupree, Minnie, 22
Duran, Michel, 30
Duryea, Dan, 62, 247
Dybbuk, The (1926–27 staging), 16

Eagle-Lion Films, 99, 134, 189; and *Border Incident*, 176, 177, 179, 181; and *He Walked By Night*, 135, 138, 139, 140, 142, 148, 151–52, 285n1, 286n24; history of, 99; and *Railroaded!*, 90, 92, 94, 97–98; and *Raw Deal*, 118, 119, 122, 123–24, 128, 131, 132–33, 264n3; and *Red Stallion in the Rockies*, 288n1; and *Reign of Terror/The Black Book*, 28, 161; and *Repeat Performance*, 141; and *Side Street*, 204; and *T-Men*, 100, 103, 104, 113, 114–16
Earl Carroll Vanities (1945), 68
East Side, West Side (1949), 204
Eastern Promises (2007), 110
Easton, Robert, 217
Easy Living (1949), 169
Edge of the City (1957), 202
Edouart, Farciot, 37
Edwards, Sarah, 56

El Cid (1961), 9, 243, 244
Elliott, Dick, 77
Emergency Wedding (1950), 169, 290n44
Emery, Catherine, 19
Enchanted Cottage, The (1945), 58
Endfield, Cyril, 97
Erickson, Leif, 211
Essex, Harry, 79, 139, 278n8
Ethiopia (play), 20
Exhibitor, The, 272n14
Eyquem, Olivier, 140

Falcon, The, film series (RKO), 57
Fall of the Roman Empire, The (1964), 243, 244
Far Country, The (1955), 36, 243
Farmer, Frances, 24
Farrow, John, 142–43
Farrow, Mia, 246
Federal Theatre Project, 20, 23–24, 242
Feist, Felix A., 81
Ferguson, Frank, 157
Figueroa, Gabriel, 184
Film Dope, 140, 143
Fisher, Herb, 206
Five Graves to Cairo (1943), 62
Flanagan, Hallie, 20
Fleischer, Richard, 73, 142–43, 155, 159, 162, 189, 193, 216
Flight. See *Desperate*
Flynn, Errol, 50
Follow Me Quietly (1949), 242; film treatment, 155, 156–60, 162–68, 192, 202, 288n6, 288n16; original ending of, 166–68, 192; production, 161, 162; publicity and distribution, 168–69; screenplay, 79, 160, 163, 168
Fonda, Henry, 32, 244, 280n8
Foolish Wives (1922), 62
Ford, John, 8, 24, 278n8
Ford, Ruth, 71
Ford, Wallace, 55, 102, 109, 112
Forrest, Diane, 268n13
Forrest, Helen, 87

Fowley, Douglas, 83
Fox Film Corp., 141
Foy, Brian, 148
Frank, Melvin, 224, 297n6
Fregonese, Hugo, 193
French Connection, The (1971), 166
Friedkin, William, 166
Frightened Lady, The (1932), 27
Fuller, Samuel, 105, 198
Furies, The (1950), 7, 14, 43, 214, 242, 243, 266n20

Gable, Clark, 217
Galarza, Ernesto, 175, 183
Garfield, John, 99
Garralaga, Martin, 174
Garrett, Betty, 169
Geer, Will, 218, 242, 298n5
Gerard, Charles, 27
Ginty, E. B., 26
Gish, Dorothy, 17
Give Us This Day (1949), 243
Glass, George, 298n9
G-Men (1935), 115, 283n40
God's Little Acre (1958), 9, 244
Golden Earrings (1947), 99
Goldstone, Nat C. *See* Nat C. Goldstone Agency
Goldstone, Richard, 211, 214–18, 220, 295n8
Goldwyn, Samuel, 24, 53, 180, 204
Gone With the Wind (1939 film), 9, 22–23, 30, 217
Goodman, Ezra, 8
Gordon, Roy, 91
Gordon, Waxey, 105
Grahame, Gloria, 129
Grahame, Margot, 52, 54
Grand Hotel (1932), 61
Grande Illusion, La (1937), 62
Granger, Farley, 81, **191**, 192, 199, 204
Grant, Cary, 88
Great Flamarion, The (1945), 63–67, 70, 103; censorship, 65, 276n6; distribution, 68–69; Mann on, 62; production, 54, 67–68, 72, 103, 276n10; reviews of, 66, 68; screenplay, 73
Great Gabbo, The (1929), 65
Great Train Robbery, The (1965), 246
Greed (1924), 62
Green, Doe Doe, 24
Greer, Jane (Bettejane), 56
Grendel, Frédéric, 245
Grey, Virginia, 45
Gun Crazy (1949), 77, 169
Guthrie, Woody, 175

Hagen, Jean, 199, 204
Hail the Conquering Hero (1944), 50
Hairy Ape, The (1944 film), 50
Haiti (1938 play), 23, 29, 221, 242
Hale, Alan, Sr., 55
Hall, Bing, 125
Haller, Ernest, 147
Harding, Ann, 230
Hargrove, Large, 43
Harrison, Joan, 129
Harrison, Pete, 294n33
Harrison's Reports, 272n14
Hartman, Don, 228–29, 297n6
Hartwig, Walter, 16–17
Harvey, Laurence, 245, 246, 299n15, 299n18
Harvey, Paul, 198
Hathaway, Henry, 37, 90, 193, 281n2
Hauptmann, Bruno, 105, 282n12
Having Wonderful Crime (1945), 68
Hawks, Howard, 25
Haymes, Dick, 87
Hayward, Lillie, 162, 163, 168
Hayward, Susan, 99
Hayworth, Rita, 88
He Walked By Night (1948): censorship, 94, 148; and Mann, 98, 143–47, 286n13; production, 138, 146–47, 148, 151, 202, 286n13, 287n26, 288n38; publicity and distribution, 151–52, 288n38; questions of authorship, 139–42, 151; screenplay, 79, 148–51; and title discrepancy, 285n1; and William Erwin

Walker case, 136–37; and Alfred Werker, 98, 139, 141–42
Hearst, William Randolph, 20
Hello, Sister! (1933), 141
Henry Busse Orchestra, 100
Heroes of Telemark, The (1965), 140, 243, 244, 247
Hersholt, Jean, **226**, 230
Heston, Charlton, 181
Hidden, Frances, 25
Hidden Valley Outlaws (1944), 50
Higgins, John C.: and *Border Incident*, 170, 177, 178, 179, 190; early career of, 93; and *He Walked By Night*, 148–51; and *Railroaded!*, 90, 92, 93, 94, 99; and *Raw Deal*, 119, 128, 284n7; and *T-Men*, 112–13, 181, 282n27
High Sierra (1941), 287n25
His Kind of Woman (1951), 142
Hitchcock, Alfred, 8, 23, 35, 45, 49, 53, 73, 76, 204, 209, 211, 241, 242, 273
Hoberman, J., 298n8
Hoey, Dennis, 28
Hoffman, Bernard, 129
Holden, William, 71, 189
Holiday Inn (1942), 42
Hollywood Reporter, The, 272n14, 277n4
Holmes, Phillips, 24
Homes, Geoffrey. *See* Mainwaring, Daniel
Hoover, J. Edgar, 29
Hopper, Hedda, 242
Horne, Lena, 219, 296n24
Horse Eats Hat (play), 20
Hotel Berlin (1945), 68
House by the River (1950), 46
House Committee on Un-American Activities (HUAC), 21, 29, 134, 181, 189–90, 242–43, 282n11, 285n42, 298n5, 298n9
House of Rothschild (1934), 141
House of Terror, The. See *Strangers in the Night*
House on 92nd Street, The (1945), 102, 115, 281n2

Howard, Sidney, 30
Howard, Trevor, 87
HUAC. *See* House Committee on Un-American Activities
Huggins, Roy, 298n9
Hughes, Howard, 88, 155, 162, 168, 181, 216
Hughes, Mary Beth, **60**, 63, 68
Hull, Josephine, 268n13
Humphries, Reynold, 282n14
Hunnicutt, Arthur, 185
Hunt, Marsha, 119, 125–26, **125**, 127, 132, 242, 284n20
Hurricane, The (1937), 24
Huston, John, 184
Hutton, Betty, 42
Hyland, Edward, 206

I Am a Fugitive from a Chain Gang (1932), 171
I Dood It (1943), 295n22
I Had an Alibi (*Suspense* radio episode), 72
IATSE. *See* International Alliance of Theatrical Stage Employees and Moving Picture Machine Operators
Ibsen, Henrik, 17
Imazu, Eddie, 217, 218
Immigration and Naturalization Service, 172, 179
In a Lonely Place (1950), 78
Ince, Thomas, 180
Indian Agent (1948), 152
Informer, The (1929 film), 37
Infuhr, Teddy, 83
Ingram, Rex, 23
Intermezzo (1939 film), 23
International Alliance of Theatrical Stage Employees and Moving Picture Machine Operators (IATSE), 105, 282n12
Invasion of the Body Snatchers (1956), 215
Ireland, John, 90, 123, 125, 128, 247
Irey, Elmer Lincoln, 105, 112, 172, 177, 282n12
It Can't Happen Here (play), 20

It's a Big Country: An American Anthology (1952), 214, 226, 228–30, 240

Jagger, Dean, 26
Jane Eyre (1939 TV), 27, 28
Jergens, Adele, 204
Jerome, Helen, 28
Jigsaw (1949), 189
Johnny Eager (1941), 189
Johnny Richards Orchestra, 59
Johnson, Van, 229
Jones, Alan, 68
Jones, Jennifer (Phyllis Isley Walker), 27
Jones, Quincy, 246
Just Off Broadway (1942), 42

Kahn, Gordon, 53, 242, 274n4, 298n5
Kane, Robert, 141
Karlson, Phil, 215, 278n8
Katzell, William, 177
Kaufman, George S., 15
Kazan, Elia, 20, 181, 281n2
Keaton, Buster, 118
Keighley, William, 283n40
Kellogg, Virginia, 113
Kelly, Ed, **89**, 91
Kelly, Gene, 204, 209, 229
Kelly, Paul, 193
Kelly, Thomas, 22
Kelly, William D., 204
Kemp, Philip, 265n19, 266n21, 266–67n27, 273n8
Kendall, Cy, 77
Kennedy, Joseph P., 53, 274n5
Kent, Robert E., 53, 274n4
Kenyon, Mildred (first wife), 16–17, 31, 43, 244, 266n27
Kidnapped (1938), 141
Kilian, Victor, 213, 218, 242, 298n5
Killers, The (1946 film), 106, 115
Kipling, Rudyard, 60
Koch, Howard W., 93
Koerner, Charles, 53, 274n7
Kosta, Anton, 107

Koszarski, Richard, 27
Krasker, Robert, 147
Krim, Arthur B., 116, 181
Kubrick, Stanley, 244
Kuzko, Anna, 244, 298n11

L.A. Investigator, The. See *He Walked By Night*
Ladd, Alan, 37
Lady Eve, The (1941), 32
Lady Without Passport, A (1950), 215
Lake, Veronica, 37, 69
Lamour, Dorothy, 162
Landru, Henri Désiré, 163
Lane, Richard, 39, 55
Lang, Charles, 37, 271n5
Lang, Fritz, 36, 37, 46, 60, 66, 76, 129, 155, 193, 271n5, 275n9, 277n4, 281n2
Langner, Lawrence, 17
Lannan, Jack, 84
Lanning, Reggie, 48, 273n9
Lanza, Mario, 244
Last Frontier, The (1955), 243, 244
Lawless, The (1950), 215
Lee, Canada, 23, 242
Lee, Rowland V., 50
Leigh, Janet, 229
Leonard, Robert Z., 171, 297n6
Leopold-Lobe case, 72–73
LeRoy, Mervyn, 171, 204, 241
Leslie, Joan, 141
Let Us Live (1939), 280n8
Lewis, Joseph H., 169, 193
Lewis, Mitchell, 185
Lewis, Sinclair, 228
Lewton, Val, 53, 275n15
Liberté Provisoire (play). See *Ode to Liberty*
Life Magazine, 101
Lincoln, Abraham, 211, 212, 220, 223
Lincoln and the Baltimore Plot, 1861, 214
Lindbergh, Charles, 105
Little Clay Cart, The (1926 play), 16
Little Women (1939 TV), 27
Lloyd, Frank, 142

Lloyd, Norman, 26–27, 242, 298n6
Load (1950), 226, 229, 241; production, 214, 230, 237, 238–39; screenplay, 229–40, 297n27; short story of, 227–28, 231
Locke, Katharine, 268n13
Locket, The (1946), 162
Loeb, Richard, 72
Loew, Marcus, 180
Loew's Incorporated, 180, 242
Lofton, Carey, 206
Loftus, Cissie, 268n13
Lomaland (School for the Revival of the Lost Mysteries of Antiquity), 10–15, 11. *See also* Rāja Yoga Academy
Long, Audrey, 77, 87
Lord, Mindret, 20, 71, 72–73
Los Angeles Times: and bracero program, 175–76; exposé of Lomaland, 12; reports on William Erwin Walker, 137; review of *Dr. Broadway*, 40
Losey, Joseph, 155, 214, 215, 219–20, 242, 298n5
Lost Moment, The (1947), 99
Lost Weekend, The (1945), 102, 281n2
Louis Prima Orchestra, 88
Lubitsch, Ernst, 30, 36, 37, 218, 271n7
Lugosi, Bela, 68
Lumet, Sidney, 20
Lundigan, William, **154**, 156, 162
Lundy, William, 89

M (1931 and 1951), 155
Macao (1952), 142
Macbeth (1936 Harlem staging), 20
Machine Gun Walker. *See* Walker, William Erwin
Mackaill, Dorothy, 24
Macy's, 17
Mad Wednesday (1950), 74
Maddow, Ben, 243
Madonna's Secret, The (1946), 46
Magnificent Ambersons, The (1942), 274n7
Main, Marjorie, 229
Mainwaring, Daniel, 214–15

Majczek, Joseph, 89–90
Majczek, Tillie, 90
Malten, William, 109
Man from Laramie, The (1955), 243
Man of the West (1958), 243, 244
Man on the Train. *See Tall Target, The*
Mandel, Louis, 169
Mann, Anthony, **16**, 35, 43, 61, 90, 100, 117, **125**, 142, 149, 153, 191, **215**, 219, 224, 229, 242, 243–47, 276n6, 281n2, 288n1; and John Alton, 101, 103–4, 106–7, 109, 113, 116, 122, 126, 131, 140, 143, 144, 146, 147, 151, 171, 181, 183, 186, 190; and *The Bamboo Blonde*, 47; birth of, 10, 264n3; on *Border Incident*, 170, 179, 181, 186; and *The Ceremony*, 245, 299n15; childhood of, 14; children of, 17, 244, 273n8; on cinematography, 8, 36–37, 104; death of, 15, 244, 246, 299n18; and *Desperate*, 77, 78, 80, 278n11; on directing, 244; on *Dr. Broadway*, 37, 38; and Eagle-Lion Films, 134, 135, 142, 179; on his early films, 3–4; on editing, 7; on film violence, 7; and *Follow Me Quietly*, 155, 156–59, 161–64, 166, 169, 192, 289n21; on *The Great Flamarion*, 62, 63, 67; and John C. Higgins, 90, 92, 94, 99, 112, 113, 170, 181, 190; and Hollywood blacklist, 242–43, 298n5; and *Load*, 230, 237; marriages of, 16–17, 244, 298n11; and M-G-M, 170–71, 181, 183, 190, 191, 214, 224–25, 226, 241, 244; myths about, 9–10, 15, 16, 17, 24, 266n25, 267n27, 269n20, 273n8, 299n18; name changes of, 15, 17, 31, 36, 38, 113, 244, 271n8; 1949–50 production schedule of, 6–7; and Dennis O'Keefe, 109–10, 113, 114; and Paramount Pictures, 31, 36–38, 42, 46; politics of, 21, 216, 243; and Producers Releasing Corp., 92–93, 97; on *Quo Vadis*, 241; and on *Railroaded!*, 90, 91–92; on *Raw Deal*,

129; recurring themes in films of, 21, 35, 73, 95, 263n6; religious views of, 13, 43; and Republic Pictures, 46, 48, 59, 61–62, 70, 72, 75, 92; RKO Radio Pictures, 53–54, 59, 72, 75, 78, 80, 112, 281n2; screen credit confusion of, 272n14; and David O. Selznick, 22–23, 45; on *Side Street*, 192, 199; on stage vs. screen direction, 36–37; and James Stewart, 19, 36, 224, 241, 243; and *Strange Impersonation*, 71, 72; on *Strategic Air Command*, 104; on Erich von Stroheim, 62, 67, 69; and Preston Sturges, 33, 69, 273n12; on *The Tall Target*, 211; on *T-Men*, 101, 102, 107, 112; and Universal Pictures/Universal-International, 7, 9, 42, 47, 48, 52, 214, 224, 226, 244; unproduced film projects of, 43, 169, 179, 214, 244–46. *See also* Bundsmann, Anton

Film direction of: *The Bamboo Blonde*, 75; *Border Incident*, 171–73, 179, 182–88; *Cimarron*, 38, 53, 224, 244; *A Dandy in Aspic*, 244, 246–47, 299n19; *Desperate*, 75, 79, 80, 81–86, 110, 112, 180; *Devil's Doorway*, 171; *Dr. Broadway*, 36, 37–41; *The Great Flamarion*, 62–68, 72, 73; *He Walked By Night*, 8, 98, 135, 139–42, 143–47, 149, 151, 286n13; *Load*, 226, 228–29, 230, 237–40; *Quo Vadis*, 214, 226, 241; *Railroaded!*, 74, 88, 90–91, 95–99, 113, 286n15; *Raw Deal*, 122, 123, 124–32, **125**, 148; *Reign of Terror/The Black Book*, 28, 140, 151, 161, 179; *Side Street*, 77, 79, 193, 194, 196–208, 240; *Sing Your Way Home*, 72; *Strange Impersonation*, 73–75; *Strangers in the Night*, 49–50, 273n9; *Strategic Air Command*, 104; *The Tall Target*, 55, 212–13, 214–19, 221, 222–23; *T-Men*, 8, 88, 104–14; *Two O'Clock Courage*, 54–57; *Winchester '73*, 7, 226

Mann, Nina: birth of, 17, 48, 273n8; on father's political views, 21; on father's religious views, 13; on father's theater work, 16; on home life, 43; on Lomaland, 13–15
Maplewood Theatre, 24, 27
March, Eve, 268n13
March, Fredric, 229
Marcinkiewicz, Theodore, 90
Marlowe, Derek, 246
Marshall, Brenda, 45, 70–71, *70*
Maté, Rudolph, 23
Mature, Victor, 244
Matuschka, Szilveszter, 163
Mayer, Gerald, 297n6
Mayer, Louis B., 171, 180
McCarthy, Todd, 103
McCrea, Joel, 32
McGilligan, Patrick, 267n27
McGrath, Frank, 206
McGraw, Charles, **101**, 106, 172, 186, 197, 247
Meade, Mary, 109
Melniker, Harold, 79–80
Men in War (1957), 9, 243
Menjou, Adolphe, 211, 212, 243
Menschen im Hotel (1929 novel), 61
Menzies, William Cameron, 142, 216
Merry Widow, The (1925 film), 62
Metro-Goldwyn-Mayer (M-G-M), 15, 16, 47, 61, 75, 93, 168, 169, 209, 242, 273n9, 275n1, 284n9, 294n33, 295n8, 295n22; and *Border Incident*, 6, 170, 177, 179, 181–83, 188, 189; and *Cimarron*, 38, 53, 224, 244; and *Devil's Doorway*, 6, 171, 190, 215; history of, 179–80; ideologies of, 171, 180, 291n22; and *Load*, 226, 228–29, 235, 237, 240; and *Quo Vadis*, 214, 226, 241; and *Side Street*, 191, 193, 197, 200, 202, 204, 205, 207, 208–9; and *The Tall Target*, 214–19, 220, 222, 223–24
Milland, Ray, 42

Mille, Arlette, 263n6
Miller, Watson B., 179
Mills Brothers, 116
Minnelli, Vincente, 295n22
Miss Grant Takes Richmond (1949), 189
Missiaen, Jean-Claude, 4, 8, 62, 140, 142, 147, 247, 267n1
Missouri Legend (1939 TV), 26, 218, 242
Mister Roberts (play), 230
Mitchell, James, 176, 183
Monogram Pictures, 162
Montalban, Ricardo, 171, 174, 181–82, 183
Monthly Film Bulletin, 246, 272n14
Montiel, Sarita, 244
Moonlight in Havana (1942), 42, 47, 52
Moonrise (1948), 46
Morley, Christopher, 19
Moss, Arnold, 173, 184
Motion Picture Alliance for the Preservation of American Ideals, 243, 291n22
Motion Picture Association of America (MPAA), 277n10
Motion Picture Production Code of Ethics, crime regulation changes in, 80, 279n15, 279n18, 279n21, 286–87n25
MPAA. *See* Motion Picture Association of America
Muir, Jean, 24
Murder, My Sweet (1944), 162
Murder Is My Business. *See Side Street*
Murder Is My Business (1946), 292n6
Murnau, F. W., 60
Murphy, George, 68, 174, 182, 190, 229, 243
Musuraca, Nicholas, 54, 275n9
My Best Gal (1944), 48

Naish, J. Carrol, 35, 39
Naked City, The (1948 film), 192, 193, 292n11
Naked Spur, The (1953), 224, 243
Narrow Margin, The (1952), 142, 216
Nat C. Goldstone Agency, 78
Natwick, Mildred, 26
Naughty Nineties, The (1945), 59

Nayfack, Nicholas, 182, 188, 214
NBC Television. *See* W2XBS
Negulesco, Jean, 50
Neighborhood Playhouse, 16
Nervig, Conrad A., 186
New Century Path magazine, 12
New Faces of 1936, 20, 72
New York Repertory Company, 17
New York Times: and *The Ceremony*, 245; and *He Walked By Night*, 139; Mann interviews by, 179; Mann obituary errors, 15, 265n19, 265–66n20; and *Strange Impersonation*, 72
Newcombe, Warren, 237
Ninotchka (1939), 30, 218
Nobody's Darling (1943), 48
Nocturne (1946), 129
North, Theron, 75
Nova, Lou, 217

O'Brien, Edmond, 93
O'Brien, Margaret, 189
Oddities in Hat Wear (1939 TV), 25
Ode to Liberty (1940 TV), 30
Odlum, Floyd, 162
O'Donnell, Cathy, 193, 200–201, 204
O'Keefe, Dennis, 47, 68, **101**, 102, 109–10, 112, 113, 114, 115, 116, **117**, 119, **121**, 124, 125, 127, 131, 132, 139, 284n19
On the Town (1949), 204
O'Neil, Nance, 27
O'Neill, Eugene, 50
Ophüls, Max, 274n4
Orchestras. *See individual names*
Osteen, Mark, 282n13
Our Town (play), 24
Out of the Blue (1947), 99
Out of the Past (1947), 56, 215
Overman, Jack, **101**, 108

Pacino, Al, 181
Painting with Light (book), 103, 126, 282–83n32

Panama, Norman, 224, 297n6
Paramount Pictures, 7, 9, 22, 24, 31, 46, 47, 48, 50, 69, 99, 214, 224, 241, 281n3; and "B" division, 36, 42; and *Dr. Broadway*, 36–43, 271n8; history of, 31–32; publicity, 17, 265–66n20, 266n23, 266n27, 273n8
Parks, Larry, 88, 169, 204, 243, 298n5
Parnell, Emory, 55
Parsons, Louella, 20
Passion of Joan of Arc, The (1928), 23
Pat Novak for Hire (radio series), 138
Pathe Laboratories, 92
Patrick, Dorothy, 156
PCA. *See* Production Code Administration
Peeping Tom (1960), 155
Pereira, Hal, 39
Phenix City Story, The (1955), 215
Phillips, Jean, **34**, 35, 37, 38, 39
Philo Vance film series, 274n4
Pillars of Society, The (1932 play), 17
Pinkerton, Allan, 214, 223
Pinocchio (1939 TV), 28
Pittack, Robert W., 73, 74
Plane Wreck at Los Gatos (Deportee) (poem), 175
Postman Always Rings Twice, The (1946), 72
Poverty Row: economics of, 47; and Mann, 47, 92–93
Powell, Bob, 133
Powell, Dick, 55, 210, **210**, 212, 214, **215**
Powell, Michael, 6, 155
Powell, William, 229
Powers, Tom, 210
Pratt, Theodore, 24
PRC. *See* Producers Releasing Corporation
Preminger, Otto, 36, 274n4
Previn, André, 183
Price, Vincent, 142
Priestley, J. B., 246
Private Lives (play), 94, 280n11
Producers Releasing Corporation (PRC): and Eagle-Lion Films, 99; film released by, 292n6; history of, 92, 99; and *Railroaded!*, 92, 94, 97, 99, 280n4; studio facilities of, 93; and *T-Men*, 112; and Edgar G. Ulmer, 47, 92, 97
Production Code. *See* Motion Picture Production Code of Ethics
Production Code Administration (PCA), 41, 65, 68, 71, 73, 75, 79–80, 93, 122, 127, 148, 151, 186, 276n6, 276n14, 280n8, 280n16; and *Border Incident*, 179, 186; and *Desperate*, 79–80, 83; and *Dr. Broadway*, 41; and *The Great Flamarion*, 65, 68, 276n6, 276n14; and *He Walked By Night*, 148, 151; and *Railroaded!*, 93, 280n16; and *Raw Deal*, 122–23, 127; and *Strange Impersonation*, 71, 73, 75; and *Two O'Clock Courage*, 56
Prologue to Glory (1940 TV), 28–29
Provincetown Playhouse, 20
Public Enemy, The (1931), 118

Quo Vadis (1951 film), 214, 226, 241

Racket, The (1951), 84
Rackin, Martin, 79, 160, 161, 168, 278n8
Raft, George, 129
Railroaded! (1947), 29, 74, 113, 118, 123, 204, 280n4; censorship, 93–95, 148, 280n16; distribution, 99–100, 281n18; Mann on, 90, 91–92; production, 88, 97–98, 113, 131, 204, 280n15; screenplay, 90, 93–95, 98–99, 190, 280n11
Rāja Yoga Academy, 11–12. *See also* Lomaland
Randolph, Jane, **89**, 90, 113
Rank, J. Arthur, 99
Ratoff, Gregory, 23
Raw Deal (1948), 68, 104, 242, 243; censorship, 94, 121–24, 128; Mann on, 129; production, 97, 113, 124–29, 131, 139, 140, 148, 284n9, 284n20; publicity and distribution, 116, 119, 128, 132–34;

screenplay, 29, 119–22, 128, 131, 134. See also *Corkscrew Alley*
Ray, Nicholas, 77, 84, 142, 200, 204, 208, 267n27, 274n3
Ray, Tony, 267n27
Raymond, Paula, **210**, 212
Reagan, Nancy Davis, 229
Reagan, Ronald, 99, 182
Reap the Wild Wind (1942), 38
Rebecca (1940), 23, 45–46
Rebel Without a Cause (1955), 138
Reckless Moment, The (1949), 274n4
Red Barn Theater, 19, 21
Red Stallion in the Rockies (1949), 288n1
Reed, Carol, 145, 147
Reformer and the Redhead, The (1950), 209
Reid, Frances, 28–29
Reign of Terror (1949), 28, 140, 151, 161, 171, 184, 216, 242, 243, 287n32, 298n8
Reinhardt, Max, 48
Reluctant Dragon, The (1941), 141
Renoir, Jean, 37, 60, 62
Renovant, George, 33
Repeat Performance (1947), 141–42
Republic Pictures: and *The Great Flamarion*, 61–62, 68, 72; history of, 47; and *Strange Impersonation*, 70, 72–73, 75; and *Strangers in the Night*, 46–48, 50; thematic styles of, 46
Revolt of the Beavers, The (play), 20
Rhodes, Betty Jane, 37
Riesner, Charles F., 118
Riggs, Glenn, 25
Riggs, Lynn, 20
Ritt, Martin, 202
RKO Radio Pictures, 22, 28, 47, 52, 68, 129, 142, 152, 160, 241–42, 274n3–4, 274n7, 274n9, 278n8, 284n9; and *The Bamboo Blonde*, 47, 75, 80; and *Desperate*, 75, 78, 79–85, 87–88, 92, 112, 180; and *Follow Me Quietly*, 155, 160, 161–62, 168; history of, 53, 274n5; and Howard Hughes, 88, 155, 162, 168, 181, 216; and *The Narrow Margin*, 216; and Dore Schary, 15, 16, 180–81, 214; and *The Set-Up*, 216, 220, 295n8; and *Sing Your Way Home*, 72, 80, 277n5, 281n1; and *They Live by Night*, 200, 204, 208; and *Two O'Clock Courage*, 53–55, 56–59, 67, 275n11
Robards, Jason, Sr., 84
Robbery (1967), 246
Roberts, Roy, **141**, 148
Roberts, Stanley, 298n9
Robinson, Edward G., 66
Rockefeller family, 53
Roe, Guy, 96–97, 131
Rogell, Sid, 162
Rogers, Ginger, 197
Rogue Cop (1954), 193
Romano, Amelia, 24
Rombeau, Earle, 136, 153
Roosevelt, Franklin Delano, 20, 21, 58
Roosevelt, Loren, 136
Root, George Frederick, 212
Rope (1948), 73, 204, 241
Roseanna McCoy (1949), 169
Rosenwald, Francis, 155, 156, 157, 158, 159, 161–62, 163, 164, 169, 243, 288n1
Ross, George, 25
Rossellini, Roberto, 220
Rossen, Robert, 99
Rowland, Roy, 189, 193, 297n6
Ruban, José, 28
Rutherford, Ann, 45, **51**, 52, 54, 57
Ruthless (1948), 274n4
Ruttenberg, Joseph, 203, 204, 205–6, 215, 230
Ryan, Sheila, 91
Ryder, Alfred, **101**, 102, 112

S. Bergerman Agency, 162
Saboteur (1942), 76
Sadoul, Georges, 7
Saint, The, film series, 274n4
Saltzman, Harry, 245
Sammy Kaye Band, 42
Sandburg, Carl, 219

Saroyan, William, 228
Savoir, Alfred, 19
Sawtell, Paul, 110, 131, 282n11
Scaduto, Anthony, 282n12
Scarface (1983), 181
Scarlet Street (1945), 60, 66–67
Scene of the Crime (1949), 189
Schaefer, George, 53
Schary, Dore, 15, **15**, 180–81, 214, 220, 228, 229, 235
Schenck, Aubrey, 105, 116, 123, 179
Schenck, Joe, 105
Schenck, Nicholas, 180
Scheuer, Philip K., 40
Schlom, Herman, 162
Schnabel, Dudley, 227, 229, 231
School for the Revival of the Lost Mysteries of Antiquity. *See* Lomaland
Schulberg, Budd, 242
Screen Actors Guild, 182
Sea Hawk, The (1940), 71
Seamon, Maxine, 55
Secret Garden, The (1949), 189
Secret of Convict Lake, The (1951), 224
See! Hear! . . . (1940 TV), 29–30, 243
Selznick, David O., 9, 22–23, 53, 214
Selznick International Pictures, 22–23
Semi-documentaries, 102, 192, 196
Serenade (1956), 15, 244, 266n20
Sergeant York (1941), 25
Set-Up, The (1949), 216, 220, 295n8
Seven Thieves (1960), 193
Seventh Victim, The (1943), 275n15
Shadow of a Doubt (1943), 35
Shapes of Sleep, The, 246
Sherwood, Robert, 230
Shield for Murder (1954), 93
Shock (1946), 141–42
Shockproof (1949), 198
Shorr, Lester, 125
Show Boat (1951 film), 224
Side Street (1950), 81, 241, 243; location filming, 81, 155, 166, 196–99, 201–7,

240; Mann on, 191–92; production, 6, 183, 204–7, 214, 230, 241, 293n26; publicity and distribution, 208–9; reviews of, 7; screenplay, 77, 79, 192–96, 293n17
Sidney, George, 295n22
Siegel, Don, 215
Siegel, Sol C., 38
Sillman, Leonard, 20
Sin of Harold Diddlebock, The (1947), 74
Sing Your Way Home (1945), 72, 80, 277n5, 281n2
Siodmak, Robert, 106, 283n40
Sirk, Douglas, 198
Sisk, Robert, 228, 229, 235
Skall, William V., 241
Skelton, Red, 209
Slave Girl (1947), 87
Small, Edward, 68, 112, 114, 116, 118, 119, 131
Smith, Kent, 162
Smith, Robert E., 263n6
Sniper, The (1952), 155
So Proudly We Hail (1936 play), 21–22
So This Is New York (1939 TV), 25
Something in the Wind (1947), 87
Song of My Heart (1947), 134
Sound of Fury, The (1950), 97
Sparkuhl, Theodor, 37, 271n7
Spartacus (1960), 9, 244
Squall, The (1927 staging), 16, 266n24
Stafford, Don, 119, 284n7
Stage Fright (1950), 209
Stagers, The, 16
Stakeout (1949 treatment), 169, 243
Stanwyck, Barbara, 7, 14, 32, 243
Steamboat Bill, Jr. (1928), 118
Steele, Freddie, **81**
Stephenson, David, 122
Sterler, Hermine, 97
Stern, Stewart, 92–93, 138, 140, 142, 146–47, 280n6
Sternberg, Josef von, 60, 142
Stewart, James, 19, 36, 93, 104, 224, 226, 243
Stoloff, Ben, 53, 54, 275n11

Stone, Lewis, 229
Strange Impersonation (1946), 45, 70; censorship, 71–72; distribution, 72, 75; production, 73; reviews of, 277n4; screenplay, 20, 71–73, 277n7
Strangers in the Night (1944 film), 45, 62; censorship, 46; distribution, 50, 75, 134, 273n12; production, 48, 273n9; public reaction to, 49, 50; and Republic Pictures, 46; running time of, 45, 48, 273n9; screenplay, 45
Strangers on a Train (1951), 204
Strategic Air Command (1955), 104
Streets of New York; Or, Poverty Is No Crime, The, 242; 1931 staging, 17; 1939 NBC-TV play, 26–27, **26**
Strictly Dishonorable (1951 film), 224
Stroheim, Erich von, **60**, 61–65, 66–68, 69, 103, 141, 275n1
Stromboli (1950), 220
Sturges, John, 228–29
Sturges, Preston, 32–33, 43, 50, 69, 73, 224
Sue Hastings Marionettes, 28
Sullivan's Travels (1941), 32–33, 271n47
Sunrise: A Song of Two Humans (1927), 60
Suspense (radio series), 72
Suspicion (1941), 45

Taking of Pelham One Two Three, The (1974), 168
Talbot, Irvin, 38
Talbot, Lyle, 75
Tall Target, The (1951), 55, 210–13, 241, 242, 243, 245; Mann on, 211; production, 214–19; publicity and distribution, 223–24; screenplay, 214, 219–22
Taylor, Elizabeth, 171
Taylor, Robert, 243
TCM Classic Film Festival (2012), 125
Temple, Shirley, 88, 99
10 Rillington Place (1971), 155
Terry, William, 45, 48, 49
Tetzlaff, Ted, 278n8
Thalberg, Irving, 180

That Hagen Girl (1947), 99
Theosophy and Theosophical movement, 10
They Live by Night (1949), 77, 84, 200, 204, 208
They Live in Fear (1944), 50
They Made Me a Fugitive (1947), 87
Thiele, Wilhelm, 46
Thimig, Helene, **44**, 45, 48–50
Third Man, The (1949), 145, 147
Thirty Seconds Over Tokyo (1944), 217
39 Steps, The (1935), 76
This Gun for Hire (1942), 37
This Is News, 214
Thomas, J. Parnell, 29
Thompson, Marshall, **210**, 212, 230
Thorpe, Richard, 228–29
Thousands Cheer (1943), 295n22
Three Caballeros, The (1944), 58
Thunder on the Left (1933 play), 19, 266n24
Tierney, Lawrence, 80, 83, **84**, 142
Time magazine, 22
Tin Star, The (1957), 21, 244
Tingley, Katherine Augusta Westcott, 10–12
T-Men (1947), 68, 88, 118, 119, 131, 132, 133, 134, 137, 139, 161, 170, 172, 173, 177, 178, 179, 180, 181, 190, 202, 218, 247; and *Border Incident*, 179; censorship, 110; Mann on, 101, 102, 104, 107–8, 109; production, 98, 99, 112–14, 139, 202, 282n11, 282n27, 282n32, 283n36; publicity and distribution, 113, 114–16, 139; and semi-documentary style, 102, 181; visual look of, 104–12, 282n13
T-Men on the Border. See *Border Incident*
To Men As They Need . . . (1942 film treatment), 43
Todd, Michael, 296n29
Tommy Dorsey Orchestra, 42
Tomorrow You Die. See *Railroaded!*
Toomey, Regis, 210
Touch of Evil (1958), 181

Tourneur, Jacques, 93, 215
Townsend, Leo, 298n5, 298n9
Traitor, The (1949 play), 204
Trapped (1949), 189
Treasure of the Sierra Madre, The (1948), 184
Trevor, Claire, 119, **121**, 284n19
Truffaut, François, 49
Try and Get Me! (1950), 97
Twelve Against the Underworld, 179
20th Century-Fox, 42, 47, 90, 97, 99, 141, 181, 242, 281n2
29 Clues. See *He Walked By Night*
Twist, John Stuart, 19
Two in the Dark (1936), 52, 54
Two O'Clock Courage (1945), 45, 51–53, 56, 57; censorship, 56, 275n11; publicity and distribution, 57–59; production, 54, 56, 67; reviews of, 53; screenplay, 53, 55, 242, 274n2

UCLA Special Collections, 161
Ulmer, Edgar G., 47, 92, 97, 274n4
Ulric, Lenore, 268n13
Uncertain Glory (1944), 50
Undercover Man, The (1949), 193
United Artists, 47, 50, 168, 189, 209, 243, 245
Universal-International, 7, 9, 87, 99, 193, 214, 224–25, 226, 244, 283n40, 292n1. See also Universal Pictures
Universal Pictures, 42, 47, 52, 59. See also Universal-International
U.S. Department of the Treasury, 105, 112
U.S. Immigration Service, 172, 179
USC Cinematic Arts Library, 230
Ustinov, Peter, 9–10

Variety newspaper, 36, 49, 171, 247; box office reports, 42, 59, 87, 99, 169, 189; on *A Dandy in Aspic*, 247; on *Dr. Broadway*, 35, 272n14; terms for crime films, 4–5, 263n5. See also *Daily Variety*

Vidor, Charles, 228, 229, 297n6
Viertel, Joseph M., 21
Violent Saturday (1955), 193
Virgin Queen, The (1955), 73
Viva Zapata! (1952), 181
Vogel, Paul C., 215, **215**, 217, 218

Wagner, Jean, 267n1
Walk East on Beacon! (1952), 142
Walker, Gertrude, 93
Walker, Michael, 140, 289n21
Walker, Phyllis Isley (Jennifer Jones), 27
Walker, William Erwin, 136–37, 145, 148, 153
Walking Down Broadway (1932–33), 141
Wallace, Edgar, 27
Wallis, Hal, 7
Walsh, Raoul, 50, 278n8, 287n25
Wanger, Walter, 298n8
Warner Bros. Pictures, 15, 16, 17, 47, 50, 68, 77, 99, 118, 162, 171, 242, 266n20, 266n23, 266n27, 283n40, 287n25, 289n23
Watts, William E., 162
Waxelbaum, Bertha (mother), 12–15, 30
We Die Exquisitely (1934 play), 19
Webb, Jack, 138–39, 278n8
Wedding March, The (1928), 62
Weis, Don, 228–29
Welles, Orson, 20, 53, 181, 274n7
Wellman, William A., 118, 228–29
Wengraf, John, **101**
Werker, Alfred, 98, 139, 140–42, 148, 151
Where the Sidewalk Ends (1950), 274n4
Whitman, Gayne, 104
Whitmore, James, 229
Whitney, Jack R., 102
Wigton, Anne, 73
Wilbur, Crane, 148
Wilde, Elizabeth, 20
Wilde, Oscar, 94
Wilder, Billy, 49, 62, 63, 271n5, 281n2
Wilder, Thornton, 24, 50
Wilder, William, 63, 73, 276n6
Willett, Chuck, 125, 278n9

William, Warren, 16
Williams, Chili, 128–29
Williams, Elmo, 160
Williams, Esther, 182
Winchester '73 (1950), 7, 36, 214, 226, 242
Windust, Bretaigne, 278n8
Winston, Archer, 66
Wisconsin Center for Film and Theater Research, 140
Wise, Robert, 81, 162, 216
Withers, Jane, 48
Woman in the Window, The (1944), 277n4
Woman's Secret, A (1949), 274n3
Woodbury, Joan, 38–39
Works Progress Administration (WPA), 20
Wrather, Jack, 162
Wright, Teresa, 24
Wright, William, 37
W2XBS: Bundsmann television work for, 25–30; early history, 24–25
Wyatt, Jane, 24
Wynn, Marty, 136–37, 138
Wynn, Nan, 59

Xavier Cugat Orchestra, 209

Yates, George Worthing, 214, 219
Yates, Herbert J., 47, 70
Yates, Peter, 246
Yellow Cab Man (1950), 209
Yordan, Philip, 9
York, Alvin (Sgt.), 25
You Only Live Once (1937), 77
You'll Remember Me. See *Strange Impersonation*
Young, Nedrick, 242, 298n5
Young Don't Cry, The (1957), 142
Young in Heart, The (1938), 22–23
Youngman, Henny, 134
Youngstein, Max E., 114–15

Zehner, Harry, 123
Ziegfeld Follies (1946 film), 72, 75
Zimbalist, Sam, 202, 204, 241
Zinnemann, Fred, 93
Zuckerman, George, 176–77

www.ingramcontent.com/pod-product-compliance
Lightning Source LLC
Chambersburg PA
CBHW030607230426
43661CB00053B/1874